£ 1-80

UNITY
1942–1944

GENERAL DE GAULLE

WAR MEMOIRS

UNITY

1942-1944

Translated from the French by Richard Howard

WEIDENFELD AND NICOLSON
20 NEW BOND STREET LONDON W I

PRINTED IN GREAT BRITAIN
BY THE SHENVAL PRESS
LONDON, HERTFORD AND HARLOW
SET IN 10 POINT BASKERVILLE
R.6397

Contents

I. INTERLUDE

DURING THE THIRD spring of the war came the climax in our fortunes. The die was cast; the scales began to tip the other way. The
huge resources of the United States were transformed into means of
battle; Russia had made a recovery, as we were to see at Stalingrad;
the British managed to re-establish themselves in Egypt; Fighting
France was growing stronger, both at home and overseas; the resistance of the oppressed peoples, in particular the Poles, the Yugoslavs
and the Greeks, assumed military significance. While the German
war effort had touched its limit, while Italy grew demoralized and
the Hungarians, Rumanians, Bulgarians and Finns lost their last
illusions, while Spain and Turkey reaffirmed their neutrality, while
the Japanese advance in the Pacific had been checked and the defence
of China reinforced, everything was persuading the Allies to strike
rather than to endure. An operation of major scope was under way
in the west.

I saw this enterprise take shape. Alone among my well-buttressed
associates, a poor man among the rich, I was comforted by hope but
racked with anxiety too, for France would be at the centre of this
undertaking, whatever happened. At stake was not only expulsion
of the enemy from her territory, but also her future as a nation and a
state. Should she remain prostrate until the war's end, her faith in
herself would be destroyed, and with that faith her independence as
well. From the 'silence of the sea' she would pass into a permanent
coma, from a slavery imposed by her enemies she would decline to a
subordination enforced by her allies. On the other hand, nothing
was lost if she returned to the ranks with her unity restored. Once
again the future could be safeguarded on condition that France, at
the end of the drama, was a belligerent reunited by a commitment
to a single central authority.

But to which? Certainly not to Vichy; that regime personified, to the French as to the world, the acceptance of disaster. Whatever the circumstances that might account for the mistakes of Vichy's princes, they were so great that the demon of despair now compelled them to persist in them. Of course, one or other of those men might repent and play a notable part, but who would see anything more than a recognition of expediency in such belated repentance? Had a great military leader summoned the army to honourable battle, he could probably have rallied around him the professionals who were secretly hoping for nothing better. But such initiative would have no effect on people whose allegiances were already determined. Furthermore, it was inconceivable that in France's agony the faith and hope of the masses would re-embrace the political system which the disaster had recently swept away. The people most representative of the French were firmly decided on this point. Some joined Vichy, many came over to de Gaulle, some had not yet declared themselves, but not one dreamed of taking the helm of the former ship of state.

But the Communist Party was there. Since Hitler had invaded Russia, it had made itself the champion of war. Committed to a resistance in which no losses were spared, invoking the nation's misery and the people's woes in order to merge in a single rebellion the national insurrection and the social revolution, it coveted for it-self the halo of public welfare. Provided with an organization which no scruple embarrassed and no divergence restrained, a past master at setting up its cells in other organisms and in speaking every tongue, the Communist Party wished to seem the element capable of assuring order of a kind on the day when anarchy would be unleashed upon the state. Indeed, did it not offer despised France the active support of Russia, the greatest European power? Thus the Communist Party counted on Vichy's collapse to clear the way for the establishment of its dictatorship in France. Yet this calculation was mistaken if the state could be differently reconstituted, if the place of supremacy in the French way of thinking were taken by a national government, if its leader, in the light of victory, were suddenly to appear in Paris.

Such was my task! To reinstate France as a belligerent, to prevent her subversion, to restore a destiny that depended on herself alone. Yesterday it was enough to throw a handful of Frenchmen into action on the fields of battle and to take a stand in the face of events. To-morrow everything would depend on the question of which central power the nation hailed and obeyed. In this critical time, it was no longer for me a question of sending a few troops into battle, rousing the allegiance of an occasional strip of territory or singing to France the ballad of her greatness. It was the entire French people, as they stood, whom I would have to rally round me. Against the enemy, despite the Allies, regardless of terrible dissensions, I would have to centre round myself the unity of lacerated France.

It is understandable how eagerly I wanted to penetrate the mystery in which meanwhile Americans and British alike wrapped their plans. As a matter of fact, the decision was up to the United States, since the principal effort henceforth devolved upon her. In Washington the President, the Secretaries, the great leaders sensed that they had become the directors of the coalition. In England the advance guard of the American Army, Air Force and Navy could be seen establishing themselves in British bases and camps. The streets, the shops, the cinemas, the London pubs were filled with good-natured, bad-mannered Yankee soldiers. The Commander-in-Chief, General Eisenhower, and General Clark, Admiral Stark and General Spaatz, respectively in command of the American land, naval and air forces in Europe, were deploying the brand-new apparatus of their general staffs in the midst of the traditional machinery of the War Office, the Admiralty, the Royal Air Force. The British, whatever their self-control, did not conceal their gloom at no longer being masters in their own country and at finding themselves dispossessed of the leading role they had played—and so magnificently!—for the last two years.

It was not without concern that I watched them being taken in tow by the newcomers. Certainly one could gather from public opinion as well as official circles that many people were finding this kind of subjection hard to tolerate. This was particularly true of the Foreign Office. But the supplying of lend-lease overwhelmingly re-pressed all independent impulses. Mr Churchill himself, whether by craft or by conviction, affected to be no more than 'Roosevelt's lieutenant'. Should France be unable to play her traditional leading role on the Continent, this obliteration of England, who had been hitherto so directly involved with that leadership despite her island position, was a distinctly evil omen of the way in which the affairs of Europe were ultimately to be settled.

For the moment, the Americans were hesitating over their strategy. Two different conceptions attracted Roosevelt and his advisers.

From time to time, yielding to the impetus of the national war machine which a magnificent effort of armament and organization had brought to its peak, Washington toyed with the idea of a swift invasion. The Russians, suffering agony and death in the grip of the German armies, loudly demanded the opening of the 'second front'. Their insistence impressed the British, who were privately worried about an eventual *volte-face* on the part of Moscow. However secretive the American leaders were about their plans, we were not unaware of the fact that they were preparing an operation that towards the end of the year would establish at least a bridgehead in France.

But even while toying with audacity, America heeded the counsels of prudence. The plan of a landing in North Africa was also considered, postponing until later the great shocks of a war on European soil. At the moment of engaging their country's armed might on the other side of the Atlantic, the American leaders were actually a prey to many misgivings. This was the first time in history that the Americans had had to take the lead in operations of a major scope. Even during the First World War they had not appeared in force on the field of battle until the last engagements, and even then it was as a contributory factor and, so to speak, in the capacity of a subordinate. Since 1939, however, the United States had felt obliged to become a first-rate military power. But though the American Navy, already the world's strongest, easily absorbed as many ships and planes as could be turned out, the land and air armies, still embryonic yesterday, required time to adapt themselves to such colossal dimensions. Hence, while many divisions were mass-produced in camps at General Marshall's instigation, the anxious question in the barely finished Pentagon was what would be the effect against the Wehrmacht of so many hastily organized units, summarily instructed officers, and general staffs newly formed from top to bottom. On the eve of battle, America's inclination was to commit herself by stages and instalments.

This was all the more so since the British were little disposed to hasten matters on their side. Having had to renounce the leadership, they felt that a victory which would no longer be essentially their own need not cost them too dearly. Postponing the major battles would mean there would be time to increase the American armies and to husband the British forces. Moreover, observing the mounting stockpile of American armaments, London calculated that the mater-

ial superiority the Allies already possessed would become considerable by 1943 and overwhelming by 1944. Besides, what good would
it do to precipitate danger and perhaps run the risk of another
Dunkirk, when every passing day contributed to the enemy's exhaustion on the Russian front? The bombing of German cities by the
Royal Air Force and the flying squadrons of the United States was
beginning to do severe damage to the Reich's industry, whereas the
Luftwaffe now attacked England only rarely. The deployment of
American convoys and escorts had decided the question of transporting supplies. It must be added that England's strategy, in line
with her usual policy, was directed chiefly toward the Mediterranean,
where she was defending positions acquired in Egypt, in the Arab
countries, in Cyprus, in Malta, in Gibraltar—and she had every intention of obtaining still others in Libya, in Syria, in Greece and in
Yugoslavia. It was therefore toward this theatre that the British were
attempting to orient the Anglo-American offensive.

According to whether Washington favoured landing in France or
seizing Morocco, Algeria and Tunisia, its intentions and attitude
toward Fighting France were completely different. In the first case
the co-operation of the French resistance movement would be needed
at once. Of course everyone knew, though there was some pretence
of doubting the fact, what action General de Gaulle would be in a
position to take. A place would therefore have to be found for him.
The second hypothesis, however, would involve a return to the plan
the State Department had followed since 1940: securing North
Africa by obtaining the co-operation of local authorities and excluding de Gaulle from the operation altogether. We were, in fact, to
see our American allies practise each of these policies towards us
alternately.

Towards the end of May 1942, they tended towards reconciliation.
On May 21st John Winant, their splendid ambassador in London,
consulted me formally as to the prospects a cross-Channel offensive
would offer, the direct role we could play in it, and the relations
which would consequently be established between the French
National Committee and the Allied governments. On June 1st the
ambassador requested a second interview. This time Mr Eden was
present; in fact, the British insisted on taking part in our conversations. On June 29th Mr Eden discussed the question of recognition

with me alone, submitting—like a good broker—a formula proposed
by Washington. The next day, accompanied by Pleven, I had still
another conversation with Winant. During this time Churchill, who
was in Washington discussing questions of strategy, was urging the
President to adopt towards me some appearance of compromise.

All this ended on July 9th, in a memorandum addressed to me by
the State Department after I had approved its terms. The document,
which, according to its preamble, General de Gaulle had 'read with
pleasure', declared that the Government of the United States and
the French National Committee were already practising a close
co-operation in certain zones and that in order to make this co-
operation still more effective, Admiral Stark was appointed as
Washington's representative, so that concerted plans might be made
with the National Committee on all questions dealing with the conduct of the war. The United States recognized General de Gaulle's
contribution and the efforts of the National Committee to keep alive
the traditional spirit of France and its institutions, and that our
common goals would be more easily achieved by America's lending
total military aid and every possible support to the National Committee, symbol of French resistance against the Axis powers.

Four days later the British in their turn enlarged the basis of their
relations with us by public proclamation, agreeing that the Free
French movement would be known henceforth by the name of
'Fighting France'; that Fighting France consisted of all French
nationals, wherever they might be, and the French territories which
joined forces to co-operate with the allied nations in the war against
their common enemies; and that in the United Kingdom, the French
National Committee represented the interests of those nationals and
those territories. If the words had any meaning, this declaration
implied, at the very least, a guarantee on England's part that she
would not prevent me from exercising my authority over the parts
of France and her Empire which returned to the fight.

Other signs, other actions indicated that, among the Allies, intentions had become more favourable to us. On July 14th, as I was reviewing the French troops in London, I noticed the presence of
General Eisenhower and Admiral Stark. That same day Mr Eden,
broadcasting greetings to the French people on the occasion of their
national holiday, declared, 'I speak to you not as to friends but as to
allies . . . Thanks to General de Gaulle's decision, France has never

been absent from the fields of battle . . . England has hopefully and admiringly watched the French people's resistance grow . . . In our eyes, the re-establishment of France in its greatness and independence is not only a promise but a necessity as well, for it would otherwise be futile to attempt the reconstruction of Europe.'

On July 23rd General Marshall and Admiral King, both in London again, asked to meet me. I saw them, along with Arnold, Eisenhower and Stark. During our meeting I informed the American leaders of our position relative to the opening of the second front, of the co-operation which France could provide from within the nation as well as without, and finally of the conditions to which the Allies must subscribe in order for the co-operation among us to be satisfactory.

Naturally I was in favour of a direct offensive in Europe, to be launched from England. No other operation would bring matters to a head. Moreover, the best solution for France was the one that would shorten the trials of the invasion and hasten national unification—that is, battle waged on the soil of metropolitan France. Doubtless Vichy would continue to co-operate with the Germans; but would thereby lose whatever credit it still had. The invader would probably occupy the free zone, but in that case, all misunderstandings dispelled, the African army and perhaps the fleet would return to battle, while in France herself many would come over to the side of the resistance. It would become possible to reunite in a single authority the various French commands, thereby preventing subversion within the nation and assuring a worthy representation of France abroad.

It was still essential to keep the Allies from being thrown back into the sea. In my exchange of opinions with Churchill, Eden, Winant, Marshall, *et al*, I estimated the forces necessary to the invasion. I said and wrote:

> The Germans have in France, according to the information provided by our intelligence networks, twenty-five, twenty-six or twenty-seven divisions, depending on the time of reckoning. They could obtain some fifteen more from Germany. Therefore it is some forty divisions that the Allies must face at the outset. Considering the inexperience of a large portion of the Anglo-American troops and the advantage to the enemy of a prior

organization of the terrain, the Allies must start out with at least
fifty divisions at their disposal, of which six or seven will be
armoured. Furthermore, there must be a crushing superiority
of Allied air power. If the offensive takes place during the coming autumn, the Germans, who will then be heavily engaged in
Russia, will be unable to remove their troops from the eastern
front without great difficulty. Besides, the combined action of
the Allied air power and the French resistance on enemy communications, following the Green Plan established by Fighting
France, will seriously hamper the transport of German reserves
and supplies on French territory.

I pointed out to the Allied leaders that the Free French would be
in a position to engage, in the first wave, one division from the Middle
East, one mixed brigade from French Equatorial Africa, detachments of commandos and parachutists, four Air Force groups and all
the warships and cargo vessels at our disposal. At the beginning of
July, I had given the necessary instructions so that these various elements were ready to move when it was required. I anticipated, moreover, that once a bridgehead had been established in France, our
forces there would be replenished from the resources of the liberated
territory. I considered it likely that eight divisions and fifteen Air
Force groups which might be constituted in North and West Africa,
as well as many of our ships temporarily immobilized at Toulon,
Alexandria, Bizerta, Casablanca, Dakar and Fort-de-France, could
and would, after several weeks' reconditioning, take part in a second
landing, this one to be effected on our Mediterranean coast and in
Italy. Finally, as the Allies made headway on French soil, a third
echelon of French forces, having as its core the elements of the underground army, would be set up. On July 21st I had addressed to Mr
Churchill and to General Marshall and communicated to Moscow a
note concerning the military co-operation which France was capable
of providing in the successive phases of the war, and specifying what
armaments and equipment I would request from the Allies.

Nevertheless it soon appeared that the Anglo-American forces
would not risk a landing in France in 1942. They would therefore
aim for North Africa, preventing us from joining in. We realized
from many particular incidents that the Americans did not want the
Free French to concern themselves with Morocco, Algeria and

Tunisia. Although we had been able to maintain our intelligence systems there until the spring of 1941, we had been cut off subsequently from all direct communication with these territories; our emissaries never reached their destinations and messages addressed to us never arrived, especially those from Colonels Breuillac in Tunisia and Luizet in Algeria, from Colonel Lelong and Funk-Brentano in Morocco. Washington's intervention was evident. But by making use of roundabout methods, we were nevertheless kept informed as to the efforts the United States was making, both in Vichy and on the spot, to obtain co-operation on its own behalf.

We knew that Mr Robert Murphy, American consul general in Algiers, was the source of the 'special' activities conducted in France by the embassy, the consulates and the American secret services. Mr Murphy, skilful and determined, long familiar with the smart world and apparently rather inclined to believe that France consisted of the people he dined with in town, was organizing an underground movement in North Africa to help the Allied landing. He was also trying to produce a 'palace revolution' in Vichy itself. It was with this in view that Mr Murphy had first supported General de la Laurentie who, upon his return from Paris, professed to take the resistance into his own hands in order to put pressure on Marshal Pétain and gain access to the government. 'And de Gaulle?' he was asked. 'All right, we'll grant him an amnesty!' Murphy had also urged certain officers in Weygand's entourage to persuade the latter to make a pronunciamento which might enable him to take Laval's place. Finally, since La Laurentie rallied no one and Weygand refused to rebel against Pétain, Mr Murphy made contact with General Giraud, who had escaped from captivity, was burning to return to the fight, and seemed to him capable of rousing the African army as soon as he presented himself before it.

As for me, I had attempted to consolidate my contacts with General Giraud. Since May 1942, when I referred to him during a press conference, I had spoken of him in the most favourable terms. In June and July, several of my correspondents had seen him on a number of occasions in order to express our hopes that we should ultimately join forces. This great leader of whom I thought so highly had not been able, in 1940, to win success at the head of the Seventh Army. Later, unexpectedly named to the command of the Ninth Army, which was in full retreat, he had been overpowered and seized by the enemy before he could act. But it was quite likely that if he were enabled to act in other circumstances, he would be able to avenge his misfortunes. And now his remarkable escape from a German fortress was offering the opportunity. His going over to the resistance, in my opinion, would be an event of the greatest importance. Considering it essential that North Africa should re-enter the war, I felt that Giraud could play a major part in that conversion, and I was ready to help him do so to the limit of my powers, provided that he acted without equivocation so far as Vichy or any foreign power was concerned; after which it was to be expected that in the battle of liberation, he should assume command of the reunited French Army. Such, from my point of view, were the perspectives that opened before him. I hoped that he would respond to them in one way or another and that he would secretly express some tribute to those who for two years had kept our flag flying before the enemy. No such thing happened. My advances to General Giraud met with nothing but silence. But since he was as prolific elsewhere as he was reserved with me, I lost no time in discovering his state of mind.

For him the problem was a purely military one. Once an important French force reappeared on the field of battle, all other questions could be relegated to an accessory status. The moral and political aspects of our country's drama seemed secondary matters to him. He believed that the very fact of being in command of the most numerous forces immediately guaranteed him power. He did not doubt that his rank and his prestige would ensure him the obedience of all the mobilized and mobilizable elements and the deferential co-operation of the Allied general staffs. From the moment he found himself at the head of the army, and therefore of the nation, Giraud would deal with the Marshal as with an extremely venerable old man whom he would liberate if he must, but who would be entitled only to a pedestal. As for General de Gaulle, he could do nothing but submit himself to the orders of his superior. Thus national unity would be re-established simply because it would be identified with the military hierarchy.

General Giraud's train of thought was a constant source of concern to me. Apart from the fact that it sprang from a somewhat over-simplified notion of the respective domains of military and political activity, that it obviously proceeded from an illusion as to the natural authority with which he invested his own person, I saw in it the probable source of national divisions and foreign interventions. The majority of the French resistance would certainly not accept a central authority founded solely on a professional general's success and, on the other hand, Pétain would not fail to condemn him. Finally, with an unsupported government like Giraud's at their mercy, the Allies would be tempted to take every advantage to France's detriment.

Certainly General Giraud was convinced that he was in a position to bring one capital advantage to the coalition. The reports that reached me in London indicated that he had a plan of his own devising. According to Giraud, the bridgehead was already in existence—in the so-called free zone. It was simply a matter of the Anglo-American forces landing there on a specified day; he himself would go so far as to ensure protection for their landing, thanks to the armistice army, of which he would take command and which would reinforce the resistance contingents. But to my way of thinking, this project had no chance of success. If it was likely at best that scattered units of the 'free' zone might follow Giraud despite the injunctions and curses the Marshal would pour upon them, it was more than doubtful, in view of the inadequacy of their armaments, that these dispersed fragments would be in a position to resist the Wehrmacht's onslaught and the Luftwaffe's raids. Furthermore, the Allies would not adopt a plan which involved the greatest possible risk for themselves. The success of the landing and the subsequent operations implied, in fact, the engagement of a very considerable air force and fleet, and consequently the utilization of airfields and ports that were both numerous and near at hand. Yet if the Allies set foot in the south of France without being assured of North Africa beforehand, they would have only Gibraltar and Malta as bases, both of them terribly confined, without resources, and vulnerable. And what, finally, in this hypothesis, would be the attitude of the fleet at Toulon? At the outset the latter would only obey Pétain and Darlan; if, on their orders, the fleet should oppose the Allies, Giraud's plan would become more problematical still.

By the end of July I foresaw what would happen. Although their intentions were carefully concealed from us, it seemed extremely likely to me that the Americans would limit their year's effort to seizing North Africa, that the British would willingly comply with this plan and the Allies would employ General Giraud in its accomplishment. They would exclude me from the operation altogether, so that these first steps to our liberation, auspicious though they were from many points of view, would confront us as Frenchmen with inner torments that would raise fresh obstacles to national unity.

Under these conditions I decided I must play the French hand exclusively, since the rest were also playing for themselves and only themselves. I decided that, above all, the unity of Fighting France must be strengthened so that she should appear on every occasion as a solid breakwater to the tide of general consent. I deliberately adopted the tough, rigid attitude such concentration required. To encourage it meanwhile, I decided to visit the Levant and Free French Africa and to review our troops serving in the Middle East and Chad. The Allies, who in May were flatly opposed to this action and had dissuaded me from it because of the imminent opening of the second front, did not attempt to prevent my trip this time; so I assumed they were preparing operations in which I was not to be included. On the other hand, while tightening the inner links of that fragment of empire and fraction of army which still remained to us, I meant to hasten the unification of the resistance in France. Since André Philip had just arrived from France, I appointed him, on July 27th, National Commissioner of the Interior, to support with all the equipment, personnel and propaganda at our disposal, the mission entrusted to Jean Moulin.[1] I also appointed Jacques Soustelle Commissioner of Information, and invited to London Frenay, D'Astier and Jean-Pierre Lévy, respectively heads of *Combat*, *Libération* and *Franc-Tireur*, in order to bring them to decisive common action. To hasten the fusion of the para-military elements, I selected General Delestraint to command the secret army of the future. Finally, intending to give greater weight to our organization, I asked certain men of quality to join us, men like Viénot, Massigli, General d'Astier de La Vigerie, General Cochet. It was Passy's job to establish liaison and to regulate the communications between France and England in such a way that I could determine each man's role on my return from Africa and the Near East.

I left on August 5th, having first seen Mr Churchill and Mr Eden, whose somewhat embarrassed remarks confirmed my feeling that they were going to be party to an enterprise incompatible with the agreement which had bound us since June 1940. Mr Averell Harri-

[1] Unifying the resistance in metropolitan France.—TR.

man, whom Roosevelt was sending to Moscow as ambassador, was in the plane taking me to Cairo; this ordinarily frank and fluent diplomat seemed on this occasion to be nursing some weighty secret. As we passed through Gibraltar I saw the tremendous projects being completed there and noticed the sibylline behaviour of the governor, General MacFarlane, so expansive on other occasions. All these symptoms confirmed my view that a major operation would soon be under way without us in the Mediterranean. I reached Cairo on August 7th.

Here the atmosphere was as heavy as the heat. The recent reverses suffered by the Eighth Army still weighed on everyone's minds. Although Rommel had halted his advance six weeks before, he was at El Alamein, from which point the next attack could carry his armoured units to Alexandria. At the Ministry of State, at the embassy, at the British general headquarters, the enigmatic attitude of King Farouk and of many Egyptian leaders was being anxiously scrutinized, for they seemed ready to adapt themselves to an ultimate Axis victory. It is true that Nahas Pasha, a former adversary of the British lately reconciled with them to both parties' advantage, had been appointed by the King to head the government on the warm recommendation of the British ambassador, Sir Miles Lampson, who had arrived at the palace for an audience escorted by a squadron of tanks. The year before, Nahas Pasha had said to me, 'You and I have one characteristic in common. In our countries we have a majority, but no power.' Now he had the power too, but where would his majority be if the Italo-German forces reached the capital?

As for the British military men, I found General Auchinleck as calm and direct as ever and Air Marshal Tedder in full possession of himself and his skill. But many beneath them seemed bitter and anxious, expecting great changes in the high command, harassed by the criticisms of Parliament and the London press, exasperated by the disagreeable conduct and comments of the Egyptians, who, for instance, pointedly cheered only the Free French troops in the streets or the cinemas and, when I arrived in Cairo, spread the rumour that General de Gaulle would assume command in the Middle East. On the other hand of course, leaders and general staffs alike were receiving the splendid troops, aviation squadrons and high-quality equipment which the British Government unstintingly poured into Egypt in preparation for the forthcoming engagement.

If the British appeared divided between hope and depression, our men were in a state of euphoria. Bir Hakeim had consecrated them in their own eyes. I went to see them. On August 8th and 11th, Larminat presented me to the troops. During a magnificent review of the First Light Division, I bestowed the Cross of the Liberation on General Koenig and several others, including Colonel Amilakvari. I also inspected the Second Light Division, commanded by Cazaud, and the unit under Rémy, all well-equipped and eager for battle. I visited our airmen and parachutists in turn. Together they constituted a force tempered by the ordeals of battle which I was certain nothing could alienate from my command. The sight of the battalions, the batteries, the armoured units, the services, completely motorized, mingling in their ranks good soldiers of every race, led by officers who in advance had sacrificed everything to glory and to victory, marching past in dazzling formation beneath the blistering August sun, filled me with confidence and pride. A contact was established between us, a spiritual accord that released a mutual current of joy, making the very sand beneath our feet resilient to our stride. But when the last of our troops had passed, I felt this exaltation fade, and my thoughts reverted to the other French soldiers, sailors and airmen who because of senseless orders were fated to fight against the 'Gaullists' and the Allies.

At our delegation in Cairo I made contact with the important French colony in Egypt. Here Baron de Benoist worthily represented France. Thanks to him, and also to Baron de Vaux, René Filliol and Georges Gorse, who seconded him, our cultural, religious and economic interests found effective support, until the Egyptian Government recognized the French National Committee. The Egyptian press and radio received every possible assistance from our delegate, and most of the French in Egypt considered themselves morally pledged to him. At the same time M. de Benoist, whom we supported strongly and unceasingly from London, managed to maintain the French character of the Suez Canal services, although the British Admiralty would gladly have taken them over. It was in fact the French who operated the canal for the whole duration of the war—an important and meritorious contribution to the Allied war effort, since the communications of the fleets and the armies in the East, as well as the supplies bound for Syria, the Lebanon, Palestine and Transjordan, passed through Port Said, while the Germans were continually bombing the convoys and the locks. Consequently I went to Ismailia to see the canal staff and to visit the tiny room from which De Lesseps had directed the execution of this glorious work, so vital now to the war in progress.

At the same time that I was giving the Free French there the encouragement they deserved, I approached our allies on the questions that were dividing us. Mr Churchill was in Cairo; we lunched together on August 7th.

'I am here,' he told me, 'to reorganize the command. At the same time, I shall look into our disagreements over Syria. Then I shall go to Moscow. All of which means that my trip is of very great importance and of considerable concern to me.'

'It is certainly true,' I replied, 'that these are three serious questions. The first is entirely your affair. As for the second, which involves me, and the third, concerning Stalin—whom you will doubtless inform that the second front will not be opened this year—I can understand your fears. But you will easily overcome them if your conscience is clear.'

'My conscience,' Mr Churchill growled, 'is a good girl. I can always come to terms with her.'

Indeed, I was to discover that England continued to deal with the Syrian question without any scruples at all. On August 8th I saw Mr Casey, who, although Australian, was Minister of State in the London government and in charge of co-ordinating British policy in the Middle East. He spoke to me immediately about the elections in the Levant States, which he considered an urgent matter.

I felt I must make things clear to this sympathetic interlocutor. 'The French National Committee,' I told him, 'has decided that there will be no elections this year in Syria or in the Lebanon, because the mandatory power does not intend to have the people vote while Rommel is at the gates of Alexandria. Are there to be elections in Egypt, Iraq or Transjordan?'

Then, taking the offensive, I listed objections to the policies that England was pursuing in violation of her agreements with us. It was Casey's turn to hear me draw the conclusions I had often expressed before. 'Of course,' I told him, 'you are now much stronger in this part of the world than we are. Because of our weakness and because of the successive crises in Madagascar, in North Africa, and ultimately in metropolitan France that will be added to those we are

now grappling with, you are in a position to force us to leave the
Levant altogether. But you will achieve this objective only by
arousing the xenophobia of the Arabs and by abusing your power
in relation to your allies. The results will be that your position
in the Middle East grows more unstable every day, and the French
people will have an ineffaceable grievance against you.'

Annoyed, Mr Casey protested his good intentions, alluding at the
same time to the 'higher responsibilities that weighed upon Great
Britain in this zone'. However, at that meeting and on August 11th
when I saw him next, he did not revert to the elections.

Marshal Smuts, Prime Minister of the Union of South Africa, was
also in Cairo, and we had a long discussion. This man, eminent and
engaging but with something odd about him, this hero of Trans-
vaal independence who had become the leader of one of His
Majesty's dominions, this Boer dressed up as a British general, was a
worthy contender against all the problems of this war. Although his
capital, Pretoria, was as out of the way as it could possibly be,
although his country, where black and white lived together and
quite apart, was gripped by extreme racial tensions, although he
himself was fighting a powerful opposition, Smuts wielded a genuine
influence over the London leaders. He owed this privilege not only
to the fact that in English eyes he embodied the success of their con-
quest, but still more to the friendship of Churchill, whom he had
held captive for several months during the Boer War and who in
turn had seized the occasion to captivate Smuts for good.

Prime Minister Smuts expressed his esteem for Fighting France
clearly. 'If you, de Gaulle,' he told me, 'had not rallied Equatorial
Africa, I should never have been able to hold South Africa together.
Once the spirit of capitulation had triumphed at Brazzaville, the
Belgian Congo would have succumbed in its turn, and from then on
those elements in my country which oppose our military alliance
with England would certainly have taken the upper hand and con-
trived a collaboration with the Axis powers. German hegemony
would have been established from Algeria to the Cape. Had you
done nothing but what you did in Chad and on the Congo, you
would have rendered a great service to our common cause. It is
essential for us all that your authority should now extend throughout
the French Empire and, I hope, soon to France herself.'

I thanked Marshal Smuts for this friendly appreciation but indicated that not all our allies seemed to share it. As evidence I told him first of the British action in Syria and the Lebanon, then of what was happening in Madagascar, and finally of the forthcoming Anglo-American action in North Africa, where the invading forces would attempt to set up an authority that was not mine.

Smuts agreed that I had reason to fear for the cause of Free France. 'But,' he declared, 'these annoyances can only be incidental. The Americans always make mistakes at the start. As soon as they discover their error, they will draw the obvious conclusions. As for the English, two different points of view influence the conduct of their affairs: that of routine, supported by offices, committees and general staffs, and that of long-range views, embodied from time to time by a statesman—Churchill to-day—and supported by the feeling of the people as a whole. But believe me, the second is favourable to you, and in the long run it is always the second that prevails.'

When we turned our attention to the practical problems posed by the situation in Madagascar, Smuts told me that the British were still pursuing the chimera of an *entente* with a governor loyal to Vichy, and that once they were disabused of this illusion they would resume the operations halted after the taking of Diégo-Suarez. He added that they would try to establish an administration functioning under their direct authority on the island, and that they would ultimately hand it over to the French National Committee, a solution which Smuts himself had been recommending from the start. He led me to understand that, so far as I was concerned, British consent that the Cross of Lorraine be raised over Madagascar was regarded as a valuable trump card by London, with which it would be compensated whatever annoyance Allied policy might elsewhere inflict upon Fighting France. To conclude, Marshal Smuts promised me that the Union of South Africa would countenance no dispossession of France in Madagascar, but on the contrary would urge London to allow General de Gaulle to establish his authority there. I must add that in Pretoria the acts which followed this assurance in no way contradicted it.

On August 12th I left for Beirut. I wanted to spend a month in Syria and the Lebanon, to take men and affairs in hand once again, to cement relations with governments and influential circles alike, to reawaken popular feeling and demonstrate the predominance of France in both fact and spirit. In this connection, the country's welcome furnished as striking a demonstration as possible. When I entered Beirut, accompanied by M. Alfred Naccache, President of the Lebanese Republic, I was greeted by an extraordinary wave of public feeling. The same thing happened in El Bika, in southern Lebanon, particularly at Saida, and among the Maronite mountain people who had come *en masse* to Bekerbe to surround their patriarch, whom I was visiting. Accompanied by General Catroux, I crossed the Hauran, now peaceful and loyal to our cause; and reached Jebel Druz, a volcanic territory in every respect. At Suweida, after the review of the Druz squadrons, I received authorities and notables at the Maison de France and then, at the Seraglio, the eager and picturesque crowd of delegates from every canton. There, amidst a storm of acclamations, the speakers assured me of the devotion of a population by whom, in the past, the French had been less well treated.

With Sheik El Tageddine, President of the Syrian Republic, beside me, I made my entrance into Damascus, which vibrated with an enthusiasm it rarely showed. The official reception by the head of the state and by the government, the visits I was paid by the *corps constitué*, the delegates of various religions, the representatives of every minority and every activity, enabled me to realize how much, since the preceding year, the young republic had consolidated itself in its stately capital. I then went to Palmyra, where the homage of the Bedouin tribes awaited me, and passed on to the ancient yet new territory of the Euphrates. At Deir-ez-Zor, as elsewhere, the political, administrative and economic situation compared well with what I had found there on the morrow of the pathetic battles of 1941. Aleppo, the great northern city where the ethnic, religious and commercial currents that cross Asia Minor have been mingling for centuries, surrounded me with enthusiastic demonstrations. Then the Territory of the Alawis was lavish in my honour with tokens of its traditional friendship for France. But it was in the cities of Homs and Hama, generally regarded as citadels of Islamic and Syrian hostility, that the fervour of the reception, of which former President Hachem Bey el Atassi graciously set the example, seemed most spectacular. On the way back, Tripoli and Batrun gave evidence of moving loyalty.

Nevertheless, beneath the waves of popular acclaim I saw the responsibilities which were incumbent upon the French mandate.

Unquestionably France was still carrying the burden of that mandate over territories which did not belong to her and which treaties forbade her to arrogate to herself. On the other hand, it was apparent that the Syrian and Lebanese *élite*, whatever their differences, were unanimous in their desire to set up in their own countries an independence to which France had always promised to lead them and to which I myself was solemnly pledged. Conviction in this matter was so strong in both countries that it would have been absurd to oppose it. Beyond doubt the economic, diplomatic and cultural interests in the Levant that had fallen to France's share for many generations must be preserved, but that seemed possible to reconcile with the states' independence.

Nevertheless we did not intend to abolish the principle of our authority in Damascus and Beirut at once. Had we done so, the British would merely have taken our place, invoking strategic needs. Furthermore, I did not feel I had the right to tear up our mandate. Apart from the fact that here as elsewhere I was accountable to the nation, the international responsibility assumed by the French mandate could not, without being abdicated, be surrendered except by agreement with the mandators, and present circumstances kept such an agreement from being reached. That was why, while transferring to the Damascus and Beirut governments the powers of which we could reasonably strip ourselves during a state of war, while deciding to restore a normal basis to the local authorities by means of elections as soon as Rommel had been repulsed, while committing ourselves to the accomplishment of the international acts that would make the independent régimes juridically valid as soon as possible, I was not willing to renounce French authority in Syria and the Lebanon for the moment. Whatever impatience this delay might arouse among professional politicians, we were certain of making the necessary changes without serious obstacles if England did not intervene and spoil our chances.

But she did spoil them altogether. M. Naccache was subjected to attacks by Spears, who openly excited his adversaries and went so far as to threaten the President because some of his ministers were not satisfactory to the British or because he did not take it upon himself to proceed with immediate elections in the Lebanon. Then again, under pressure from the British, who threatened to cut off all communication with other countries, Catroux had agreed to introduce

them into the Franco-Syrian-Lebanese wheat board. They availed
themselves of this to obstruct the board's operation and to provoke
opposition from the Damascus Government. Overriding our right of
option, they had assumed responsibility for the construction and
ownership of the Haifa-Tripoli railway. When, near Tripoli, at the
terminus of the Iraq Petroleum Pipeline, the French authority put
into operation a refinery that enabled them to furnish the Levant
with petrol deducted from France's petrol allocation, the British
tried in every way possible to close down our establishment so that
we and the Levant States would be completely dependent on them
for this vital raw material. Finally, arguing from the financial agreement which I had made with them on March 19th, 1941, and by
virtue of which their treasury furnished us with a part of our public
funds in the form of advances, they claimed jurisdiction over the use
made of those funds in Syria and the Lebanon and, by extension,
over the budgets of the Damascus and Beirut Governments. In every
domain, every day, everywhere, there was interference from our
allies, multiplied by an army of uniformed agents.

I was determined to oppose this suffocation, and, if it happened
that we had to give way to it, to make sure that these abuses were
publicly exposed. Having verified the state of affairs on the spot, I
began my campaign by addressing a formal protest to Mr Churchill
on August 14th:

> Since the beginning of my stay in the Levant States under
> French mandate [I wrote to him], I have regretfully remarked
> that the agreements concluded between the British Government
> and the French National Committee concerning Syria and the
> Lebanon are being undermined . . . The constant interventions
> of the representatives of the British Government . . . are not
> compatible with the political disinterestedness of Great Britain
> in the Lebanon and Syria or with respect for the position of
> France, or with the mandatory regime . . . Furthermore, these
> interventions and the reactions they produce are encouraging
> the people of the whole Arab world to believe that serious diver-
> gences are compromising the understanding between Great
> Britain and Fighting France, though they are allies . . . I find
> myself compelled to ask you to re-establish in these countries
> the application of our agreements . . .

The Prime Minister received my message while he was in Moscow. He replied on August 23rd from Cairo *en route* to London. The British, he wrote, were in no way seeking to destroy France's position in the Levant; they thoroughly agreed that in the political realm the initiative must remain in the hands of the French authorities and that the mandate, from a technical point of view, could not be surrendered at this time. But although he made his bow to our agreements, Mr Churchill, as usual, overrode them by invoking the unilateral claims on which Great Britain prided herself. Syria and the Lebanon, he said, comprised part of a vital theatre of operations, the events occurring in that zone affected British military interests directly or indirectly and London was eager that its guarantee of the Catroux proclamation declaring the independence of the Levant States be put into effect. Repeating what he had said in his speech of September 9th, 1941, in the House of Commons, he added that the position of the Free French in Syria could not be the same as that heretofore enjoyed by Vichy. Mr Churchill concluded, in an intentionally banal and lenitive fashion, by saying that he fully realized the importance of a close collaboration between our respective representatives in the Levant. 'Our supreme objective is the defeat of the enemy . . .'

I was expecting this disguised refusal to change their policies despite my protest, but I had decided to force them out of the equivocations by which they were attempting to conceal their hand. Furthermore, in consideration of the probable results, I concluded that it was wise to adopt a general attitude that would exclude all compromise. I immediately wired to Mr Churchill:

> It is impossible for me to accept your idea that the political interference of the British representatives in the Levant is compatible with the commitments made by the British Government in respect to the position of France and her mandate . . . Furthermore, the kind of Franco-British rivalry created in Syria-Lebanon by the interference and the pressure of your representatives is harmful to the war effort of the allied nations . . . I urge you to reconsider this pressing and essential matter at once.

By using such language I was relying less on the present, which offered me few means of continuing the argument, than on the future, when France perhaps would have the wherewithal to resume it, provided that those who spoke in her name steadfastly refused to give way. This was important as other abuses of the same kind were now seen in Madagascar, would appear tomorrow in North Africa, and threatened to spring up one day in Paris itself. We would resist those that loomed in the future only if we opposed those that were upon us now. Besides there was no reason why we should let ourselves be despoiled in silence. I therefore considered it necessary to advise America and Russia of what was happening. Even if their governments, duly informed, did nothing to induce the British to change their ways, at least the dispute would obtain world-wide attention.

On August 16th, I had received a visit from the United States consul general, the excellent Mr Gwynn, who had just heard the news and was considerably disturbed by it. I did nothing to reassure him. On August 24th I invited him to see me and gave him a note for his government. This document set forth what was involved in the situation and what results it might have. The next day Mr Gwynn returned. He told me of the text of a cable sent by Mr Cordell Hull to Mr John Winant, American ambassador in London, stressing the seriousness of this situation and instructing him to question the British closely on the matter. This was precisely what I had hoped for. The Secretary of State told his ambassador that Spears seemed at the very least to have thought of his task in a wider sense than was customary for a foreign diplomatic representative. The United States Government, he said, could not remain indifferent to a controversy which might affect the common war effort.

Mr Hull also instructed Mr Gwynn 'to thank General de Gaulle for having informed him so completely', but, since he needed to conclude with a little venom, he urged him to make clear to me with equal frankness the serious importance that the United States, as a nation engaged in the common struggle, attached to the pledges made to Syria and the Lebanon, which must be scrupulously respected.

Meanwhile Dejean in London had revealed our disagreement to M. Bogomolov and had forewarned our Moscow delegation. On September 11th the Soviet ambassador came to tell him that his government was 'disposed to assist us within its means'.

I felt all the less inclined to compromise now that I had definite knowledge of the decisions taken by the Anglo-American leaders in regard to North Africa. Not, of course, that the Allies had told anything of their plans; on the contrary, everyone concerned with these preparations continued to observe absolute secrecy. But if this conspiracy of silence seemed ungracious to us, it was also futile. For information flowed in from America, from England and from France. A kind of rumour slipped across the face of the world, while in the Middle East everything in sight indicated that there would soon be an African campaign under way. Passing through Cairo, Mr Churchill had appointed General Alexander Commander-in-Chief, and had put Montgomery at the head of the Eighth Army. Many reinforcements, especially of armoured units, continued to arrive from Great Britain. Tedder, the Air Force chief, received many planes. Everything heralded major operations that were not aimed at Europe.

On August 27th I was in a position to announce to our London delegation:

> The United States has now decided to land troops in French North Africa. The operation will be launched in conjunction with a forthcoming British offensive in Egypt . . . The Americans have arranged for local co-operation by making use of the good will of our partisans and giving the impression that they are acting in agreement with us . . . Should the occasion arise, Marshal Pétain will certainly give orders to fight against the Allies in North Africa . . . The Germans will make the affair a pretext to rush in . . . The Americans thought at first that they would be able to open a second front in France this year. That is why, having need of us, they took the position indicated by their memorandum of July 9th. Now their plans have changed . . .

From then on everything was clear. The Allies' strategy was apparent, determined by events. As for their political behaviour, it had as its basis a kind of consecrated egoism. Therefore I was less than ever inclined to put faith in the ideological formulas they employed to conceal it. How could I take seriously the scruples paraded by Washington, scruples which affected to keep General de Gaulle at a distance under pretext of leaving the French free to choose their eventual government and which at the same time maintained official relations with the Vichy dictatorship and was preparing to deal with whoever would open the gates of North Africa to the American troops? How could I believe in the sincerity of declarations from

London which, in order to justify British intervention in the Levantine States where France had a mandate, invoked the Arab right to independence, when at the same moment the British were imprisoning Gandhi and Nehru in India, were severely punishing the followers of Rashid Ali in Iraq, and were dictating to King Farouk in Egypt the choice of his own government? No, the same today as yesterday, the interests of France were the only end to pursue.

Mr Casey, meanwhile, thought that he should show his hand. But however good his intentions, he did so in a way that did not make matters easier. On August 29th he proposed that we have a 'frank discussion' to establish more satisfactory relations in the interests of both countries, for, he wrote, these relations, in Syria and the Lebanon, had reached a critical point. Unfortunately the British Minister of State felt obliged to stipulate that we meet in Cairo and to add that failing this meeting he would be obliged to submit the situation as he saw it to the Prime Minister.

The terms of his message forced me to reply that I had been ready to discuss these serious matters with him, but at Beirut, 'since during the two visits I had the pleasure of making to you in Cairo we were unable to reach an agreement'.

Then Mr Churchill entered the lists again. On August 31st he telegraphed me from London that he too considered the situation a serious one, that according to his way of thinking it was essential for him to talk it over with me with as little delay as possible. He urged me to hasten my return to London and to let him know on what date he could expect me. I could only thank the British Prime Minister 'for the invitation you were so kind as to extend' and tell him that I would certainly undertake such a trip as soon as possible, but that the situation did not permit me to leave the Levant. I repeated that in any case, 'I was ready even to-day to meet Mr Casey at Beirut'. Finally, on September 7th, carrying the tension to its peak, I sent Ambassador Helleu, who had just reached me from Teheran, to Casey with a memorandum setting out our grievances.

At the same time that I was stirring up this controversy, I applied myself to clarifying the mandate's internal affairs. It was a matter of convincing the two local governments to play their role firmly, particularly in the realms of finance and provisioning, where matters were making scarcely any progress. Further, it was essential to clarify our intentions with reference to the elections. Alfred Naccache and Sheik

Tageddine came to see me on September 2nd and 4th respectively.
I received them with great ceremony. Both lavished upon me assurances of their good will. As a matter of fact, they felt encouraged in
their own tasks by the solidity of the French authority and no longer
hesitated to entertain measures capable of balancing the budgets, of
operating the wheat board or of limiting speculation. In agreement
with them and with General Catroux, I kept to the decision made by
the National Committee not to proceed with election plans until the
following summer. But the elections would take place then, unless
strategic necessity forced their postponement.

During the time I spent in Beirut I made numerous contacts,
according to the custom of the Middle East, where it is deemed both
reckless and unbecoming to make judgments and take measures
without having sampled opinion and paid respects. At the Résidence
des Pins, where I was installed, I received many visitors; a number
assured me of their desire to see the state fully acquit itself of its
obligations in their country, but each appointed himself the apostle
of one or another of the special interests that since the dawn of
history have prevented such situations from becoming a reality. All
confirmed me in my conviction that Syria and the Lebanon, upon
their accession to independence, had everything to gain and nothing
to lose from the presence of France.

The advantages which our presence ensured to both countries
were incontestable and, what is more, uncontested. Whether in the
matter of public services, public works, construction, universal education, or law and order, the thousands of professional, intellectual and
domestic relations established by our people with the Syrians and the
Lebanese were responsible for interest and feeling on both sides. In
the many offices, ship and building yards, schools, societies and hos-
pitals I visited, everyone agreed that they must be maintained whatever régime was set up to deal with future political relations between
Paris, Damascus and Beirut.

Naturally I also tried to give the strongest possible encouragement
to the military organization. The majority of the elements of the
French Army, properly speaking, were then in Egypt. We had only a
few detachments left in the Levant. The extreme scantiness of French
strength proved again that the authority of France had other foundations than that of force alone. It was therefore incumbent on the
'special' troops—that is, the Syrian and Lebanese forces—to guaran-

tee the immediate security of the two states. Yet this security was likely to be questioned at any moment. By the end of the summer of 1942, the Wehrmacht was actually penetrating into the heart of the Caucasus, while the Italo-German desert army threatened the Nile delta. If the enemy should win a victory in either of these theatres, Asia Minor would be laid open. That is why we did not spare our efforts to increase the value of the local forces of the Levant.

Thus embryonic armies were formed; Syria furnished nine infantry battalions, one cavalry regiment, three groups of partially motorized squadrons; the Lebanon provided three rifle battalions; while two artillery groups, one tank battalion and some engineering, transport and transmission units remained common to both countries. From the École Militaire at Homs a splendid class graduated each year. Several French officers co-operated in the formation of the special troops, but it was apparent that among the troops valuable new officers were developing, whether Syrian like Colonels Znaim and Shishakli, or Lebanese like Colonels Shehab and Naufal. The supplies recovered at Dentz enabled us to provide these troops with creditable armament and equipment, the maintenance of which was assured by the well-stocked artillery depot at Beirut.

I myself had the honour of inspecting the French, Syrian and Lebanese units remaining on guard in the Levant under the command of General Humblot, Commander Kolb-Bernard and Lieutenant-Colonel Gence for the land, sea and air forces respectively. Twenty-five thousand dedicated men protected the two states from enemy attack; these sufficed, with the local police forces, to preserve order in a land that for thousands of years had comprised irreconcilable groups, a land one-third the size of France, having about 1,500 miles of frontier and bordering on Iraq, Transjordan and Palestine, where chronic agitation prevailed. The fact that the part of the Levant under French mandate was so calm and was held by such reliable troops considerably assisted the strategy of the Allies at this period of the war, removing from their armies fighting in Egypt, Libya and Ethiopia all serious concernas to their rear, confirmnig the Turks in their refusal to permit the Germans passage through their country, and deflecting the entire Arab world, disturbed by the events of the war, from hostile action.

Nevertheless, active though my stay was, the fundamental problems remained unsolved. I had been able to change the atmosphere and put the helm hard over, permitting us to gain time. How could I do more when I had brought no reinforcements of men or money? A policy is worth as much as its means. In the Middle East more than anywhere else, affairs would be settled by the appearance of fresh forces and not by arguments.

A distinguished visitor came from America to confirm this point for me. This was Wendell Wilkie, whom the Republican Party had opposed to Roosevelt in the Presidential election of 1940. Now the President, anxious to show that war made unity sacred, authorized his recent adversary to travel round the world and learn the facts from its leaders on the spot. Wendell Wilkie had asked to pass through the Levant on his way to see Stalin and Chiang Kai-shek. He arrived on September 10th and stayed twenty-four hours as my guest.

At his request I explained the circumstances of the French position in the Levant. But Wendell Wilkie, who had never before been to the Middle East, apparently had already made up his mind on every issue. When he returned to Washington he affected to be convinced, in the summary manner of American public opinion, that the friction in Beirut was merely an episode in the rivalry between two equally detestable colonial systems. Referring to me, he employed the standard malevolent banter in the book that appeared in his name upon his return. Because we had conferred together in the High Commissioner's office, which M. de Martel had recently provided with a suite of Empire furniture, Wilkie represented me as aping the Napoleonic style; because I was wearing the standard officer's summer uniform of white linen, he saw an ostentatious parody of Louis XIV; and because one of my men spoke of 'General de Gaulle's mission', Mr Wilkie hinted that I took myself for Joan of Arc. In this matter, Roosevelt's rival was also his imitator.

The very day I was conferring with the President's envoy a new item concerning France appeared on the bulletin of current events. At dawn on September 10th, the British had again taken action in Madagascar. Realizing after five months of negotiations that they could obtain no valid guarantee from Governor-General Annet, that Vichy might let the Japanese take over the island at any moment, and that the Laval ministry had given orders to let the latter do as they liked in that event, our allies had decided to occupy Madagascar for themselves.

B

Once more they were going into action without the co-operation of the Free French forces. But at least, and by contrast with what had happened at the time of the attack on Diégo-Suarez, they informed us before they acted. On September 7th Mr Eden, expressing to Pleven and Dejean his government's irritation at my attitude on the Levant, let them know beforehand that a forthcoming event in Madagascar would require their agreement. On September 9th, requesting the presence of our two national commissioners, he informed them that British troops would land at Majunga the next day, that his government had every intention of recognizing the authority of the French National Committee over Madagascar as soon as the military campaign was over, and that he was eager to open negotiations with me for an agreement on this matter as soon as possible. On September 10th, London announced that British forces had established a bridgehead at Majunga and that 'a friendly administration, eager to collaborate wholeheartedly with the United Nations and to contribute to the liberation of France, would be established on the island'. On the 11th Mr Strang declared to Maurice Dejean: 'The British Government intends the French National Committee to be the "friendly administration" mentioned in the communiqué. It depends on you alone to see that this is the case. As for us, we are convinced that we can reach an understanding.'

I decided to return to London, although I knew I would find the atmosphere disagreeable. It was plain that it would be to my advantage in some ways to establish residence in a territory under French sovereignty when the American operation in North Africa got under way, and the settlement of the Madagascar affair would certainly not be reached without delays and without suffering, but the stakes were such that I could not hesitate. I therefore addressed a message of good will to Mr Eden, telling him that I had received reports from Pleven and Dejean, and that my intention was to accept his and the Prime Minister's friendly invitation soon. Eden immediately replied that he would be happy to discuss with me our relations in the Levant and the future civil administration of Madagascar, in accordance with what had been envisaged in his conversation of September 9th with Pleven and Dejean.

Before reaching England I decided to spend about ten days in Free French Africa. There, as in the Middle East, I intended to reaffirm the cohesion of Fighting France on the eve of events that threatened to shake it, and to determine the mission of our military forces in the forthcoming operation in North Africa. For the first time I was able to reach the Congo from Syria without having recourse to British planes. The fact is that under the direction of Colonel de Marmier, seconded by Colonel Vachet, several French airlines were beginning to operate again, from Aleppo and Deir-ez-Zor to Damascus and Beirut, from Damascus to Brazzaville, and between Fort-Lamy, Bangui, Brazzaville, Pointe-Noire and Douala, thanks partly to several private planes salvaged in the Levant, but above all to eight Lockheeds obtained from the United States in exchange for our authorization to use the base at Pointe-Noire, and to the Air France personnel, long marooned in Argentina and Brazil, that had now rejoined us.

On September 13th, I made the flight of nearly 2,000 miles nonstop from Damascus to Fort-Lamy; it was possible to travel between the Taurus and the Atlantic without landing anywhere that was not Free French territory.

Leclerc was waiting for me at Fort-Lamy. Expecting the resumption of the Libyan offensive, he was completing the conditioning of his desert forces. Once again I was to see the motorized columns, squadrons formed of combat and transport vehicles, armed and equipped for the wide open spaces, manned by crews eager for distant adventures, ready, under the orders of Ingold, Delange, Massu and Dio, to leave the ports of Faya, Zouar and Fada for ever in order to navigate and fight on the ocean of stones and sand. I visited the small motorized corps which was preparing to leave from the shores of Lake Chad and seize Zinder. At Douala, Libreville, Pointe-Noire, Bangui and Brazzaville I made contact with the various sections of the two brigades, one headed for Antananarvo, another for Cotonu, Abidjan or Dakar as the opportunity arose. Colonel Carretier commanded the better part of the air groups we had left below the equator. Commander Charrier, with four small ships, a few planes and some guard posts, was keeping the long coast of the Cameroons, the Gaboon and the lower Congo under surveillance. The artillery, the commissariat and the health service worked wonders to furnish everyone with the necessary supplies despite distance and climate. Each man looked forward impatiently to the operations that would soon be under way between the Atlantic and

the Nile and which even the enemy, as the bombing of Fort-Lamy
indicated, seemed to be expecting.

On September 22nd I entrusted Leclerc with his mission in the
form of a 'personal and secret instruction'. He was to seize the oases
of Fezzan, to organize the administration of the region in the name
of France, then debouch to capture Tripoli, making sure of Gat and
Gadàmes on the way. The operation was to begin as soon as the
British Eighth Army had retaken Cyrenaica and penetrated into
Tripolitania. Leclerc would be subordinate to Alexander and Montgomery only after the junction of their forces. Then he would participate, under their strategic command, in the eventual battle for
Tunisia. On the other hand, in case the Vichy leaders were opposed
to the landing and, aided by the Germans, gave battle to the Allies,
we were to seize from them the French territories within our grasp.
Moreover, our missions of Ponton in the Gold Coast and Adam in
Nigeria provided us with valuable information as to the Ivory Coast
—Upper Volta, Togo, Dahomey and Niger. My instructions therefore stipulated that Leclerc was to take his troops, should the occasion
arise, into French West Africa, starting at Niger. Finally, he must
prepare the Madagascar-bound units to serve as a nucleus for future
military regrouping. This was a great deal to do at one time, but we
had no misgivings. The Free French in Africa constituted a working
force that no ordeal could daunt.

As for the native Africans, their loyalty left nothing to be desired.
Whether it was the sovereigns and traditional chieftains, like the sul-
tans of Wadai, Kanem, Fort-Lamy, the influential Orahola at Fort
Archambault, Ahmed Bey at Maho, who had recently been forced
out of the Fezzan by the Italians, Chief Mamadou M'baiki at
Bangui, the Queen of the Batekes in the Congo, the King of the Vili
at Pointe-Noire, Prince Felix of Gaboon, High Chief Paraiso at
Douala, the King of the Abrons, who escaped from the Ivory Coast
with his men to rejoin General de Gaulle, or the officials attached to
the administration, to the Army, to commerce, to public education,
or the mass of men themselves, farmers, soldiers, workers, servants—
all made the cause of Fighting France their own and willingly
assumed a large part of its sacrifices. But at the same time, a thrill
of hope and liberation made these Africans tremble. The drama
shaking the world to its foundations, the almost miraculous crusade
the 'Gaullists' had undertaken on their own continent, the spectacle

of the efforts that the war had aroused and that were changing the conditions of their existence led thousands of black men in cabins and camps, savannas and forests, in the deserts and along the great rivers of their continent, men hitherto oppressed by ages of servitude, to raise their heads and question their destiny.

Governor-General Eboué concentrated his energies on controlling this profoundly inspired movement; as a convinced humanist he regarded such a tendency as salutary, since it aimed at raising the people above what they had been, but as a great administrator he felt that the French authority should turn it to account as well. He did not shrink at all before the material, moral and political transformation that was soon to penetrate the 'impenetrable' continent, but he hoped that this revolution would bear the stamp of Africa herself and that the changes made in the life, the customs and the laws of her people, far from abolishing the ancestral rules, would instead be carried out so as to respect traditional institutions and forms. It was thus, according to Eboué, that Africa's progress, France's power and glory, and interracial co-operation would best be served. He oriented in this direction the administration of which he was the head and, in consequence, provided it with instructions as to the leadership of territories and societies, the working conditions of the natives, the police, the dispensation of justice, and the collection of taxes. At Brazzaville I congratulated him on his achievements; his views corresponded to my own, and in this domain as in others the unity of Fighting France seemed solidly cemented.

September 25th! Suddenly, on my arrival in London, everything changed. How distant were the loyal territories, the eager troops, the enthusiastic crowds which yesterday surrounded me with the assurance of their devotion. Here, once again, was what is known as power, stripped of the contacts and the recognition that occasionally manage to sweeten it. Here were nothing but hard problems, harsh negotiations, painful choices among men and disadvantages. Again I would have to bear our burden in the heart of a country that was of course friendly, but alien, where everyone pursued a goal and spoke a language not our own, and where everything made me feel that our prize was out of all proportion to our poor means of achieving it.

The resumption of contact with the British Government was inevitably something of a shock. On September 28th, accompanied by

Pleven, I called at Number 10 Downing Street, where Churchill and
Eden were expecting us. It was to be expected that the British
ministers should express their irritation over affairs in the Levant;
we were quite ready to express our own to them, after which one
might hope that the conversation would take a more practical turn;
In particular perhaps, the settlement of the Madagascar question
might have been sketched out. But on this occasion, because of the
Prime Minister's behaviour, the bitterness of the discussion did not
subside.

Mr Churchill began, it is true, by thanking me for having come to
London in response to his invitation. I received this compliment with
the humour with which it was intended. Then the Prime Minister
proceeded to the usual airing of our respective grievances in the
Middle East. The British Government, he said, insisted that elections be held this very year in Syria and in the Lebanon. I replied
that this would not be the case so he concluded our exchange on this
subject by declaring that no agreement was possible with me in the
realm of Franco-British collaboration in the Levant. 'We are taking
note of that,' he said, to which I made no objection.

Then he broached the subject of Madagascar. But this was only
to declare: 'In consideration of the state of affairs at Damascus and
Beirut, we are not at all eager to open a new theatre of operations
with you at Antananarivo. I do not see why we should install a
Gaullist command there.'

I reacted strongly to this declaration, which seemed to me to com-
prise both the negation of England's commitment and a piece of
bargaining at our expense. Pleven, too, did not conceal his feeling
on this matter.

Mr Churchill then attacked me in a bitter and highly emotional
tone. When I pointed out that the establishment of a British-con-
trolled administration in Madagascar would constitute an interference with the rights of France, he exclaimed furiously: 'You claim
to be France! You are not France! I do not recognize you as France!'
Then, still as vehemently: 'France! Where is France now? Of course
I don't deny that General de Gaulle and his followers are an important and honourable part of the French people, but certainly
another authority besides his could be found which would also have
its value.'

I interrupted him. 'If, in your eyes, I am not the representative of France, why and with what right are you dealing with me concerning her worldwide interests?' Mr Churchill did not reply.

Mr Eden then intervened and brought the discussion back to the subject of the Levant. He repeated the justifications the British claimed to have for interfering with our affairs there. Then, losing his temper in his turn, he complained bitterly of my behaviour. Mr Churchill outdid him, shouting that in my Anglophobia a desire for prestige and personal aggrandisement through the use of the French people was dictating my behaviour. These imputations by the British ministers seemed inspired by their eagerness to create grievances that would somehow justify the fact that Fighting France was to be kept out of French North Africa. I told them as much without softening my terms. By the time the discussion had reached this point it was futile to continue it. We agreed on this and separated.

The weeks that followed were extremely tense. We were surrounded by ill will. The British went so far as to cut off delivery, for eleven days, of telegrams addressed from London by the National Committee to the French authorities in Africa, the Levant and the Pacific. The Foreign Office, concentrating on Maurice Dejean the full force of all its departments and brandishing before his eyes the spectre of a complete breakdown of relations—the last straw for a diplomat—upset him sufficiently for him to start wondering what concessions we could make to re-establish good relations. Concessions? I would not hear of them! Dejean therefore handed in his resignation, with great dignity, and several weeks later became our representative to the governments in exile in Great Britain. Pleven, handing over the Ministry of Finance to Diethelm, took over the Foreign Affairs post during the interim, while waiting for the arrival of Massigli, whom I had invited to come from France.

Nevertheless, as usual the tempest soon subsided. The London telegraph offices again agreed to dispatch our wires. On October 23rd Mr Churchill sent Mr Morton, his chief private secretary, to congratulate me on the exploit of the French submarine *Juno*, which had just sunk two large enemy ships off the coast of Norway, to express the thanks of the British Government for the important and costly contribution our troops had made the day before in the Allied offensive at El Alamein and, finally, to inform me of the good will Mr Churchill himself had never ceased to feel towards me. On October 30th Marshal Smuts, in London again, asked to see me and declared that the British had decided to recognize the authority of Fighting France at Antananarivo. He added that this would also be the case sooner or later in North Africa. Some days before, the Foreign Office had in fact resolved to open negotiations with us in order to reach an agreement about Madagascar.

The first proposal was that once our administration was installed the British command should exercise a controlling influence over it, and that in addition the English should have at their disposal all bases, lines of communication and transmission facilities existing on the island. We rejected these claims. As we saw it, French authority on Madagascar must be sovereign in the political and administrative realms. As for the island's eventual defence, we proposed that the strategic command, in case of operations against the common enemy, be entrusted to a British general officer for as long as the British were our numerical superiors there. If the balance of forces were to change, a French officer would assume command. Then again, it would be up to the French authority to lend our allies, according to their needs, the use of our installations and of our public services. I had already appointed General Legentilhomme High Commissioner for the Indian Ocean with maximum civil and military powers. At the same time Pierre de Saint-Mart, Governor of Ubangi-Chari, was appointed Governor-General of Madagascar. Both left to assume command as soon as operations on the island were completed and the conclusion of our own negotiations with the British allowed them to exercise their functions effectively.

The British Government soon came to an agreement with us on the essential points involved. In Madagascar itself, as Vichy's power waned, the British discovered among both the French and the natives the nearly universal desire to join the cause of General de Gaulle. If the London cabinet still postponed the solution, it was obviously with the intention of offering it to us as an appeasement when, as expected, the Allied landings at Algiers and Casablanca provoked discords in our relations. Thus when on November 6th, the day after the Madagascar armistice had been concluded, Mr Eden, all sugar and honey, proposed that we issue a joint communique from the British Government and the French National Committee, announcing General Legentilhomme's immediate departure, I realized that events in North Africa were coming to a head.

Others who suspected as much were eager to give us proof of their preference for our cause. On August 6th, when I was flying to the Middle East, President Beneš had solemnly declared to Maurice Dejean, as the latter reported to me, that he 'considered the National Committee under the direction of General de Gaulle as the real government of France'. He had requested the Commissioner of Foreign Affairs to ask me on his behalf if we did not consider that the moment had come to repudiate, in the name of France, the Munich agreements and the amputations which had resulted from them in the case of Czechoslovakia. I had answered affirmatively. On my return I saw Beneš and we easily reached an agreement, which resulted on September 29th in an exchange of letters between myself and Monsignor Shramek, President of the Czechoslovak Council. In my letter I declared:

> The French National Committee . . . rejecting the Munich agreements, proclaims that it considers those agreements as null and void . . . and that it commits itself to do all in its power in order that the Czechoslovak Republic, within its pre-1938 frontiers, may obtain every guarantee concerning its military and economic security, its territorial integrity and its political unity.

In Monsignor Shramek's reply the Czech Government committed itself, on its part, to every effort in order that France might be restored to 'its strength, its independence and the integrity of its metropolitan and overseas territories'. The next day, speaking on the radio, I made public these reciprocal promises and emphasized their moral and political significance.

From Moscow came signs that were equally encouraging. The Soviet Government, aware of what the British intended to do in North Africa, remarking the United States' attitude toward Fighting France and discerning in Litvinov's reports from Washington Roosevelt's intention of becoming the arbiter among the French minorities, was seriously concerned by this American tendency toward hegemony. On behalf of his government M. Bogomolov led me to understand that Russia, engaged in a struggle to the death against the invader, was unable at the present time to intervene directly, but that she nevertheless disapproved of the Anglo-American policy and would know how to oppose it should the circumstances warrant her intervention. On September 28th, in a widely publicized communi-

qué, Moscow announced that the Soviet Union recognized in
Fighting France 'all French citizens and territories . . . which, by
every means in their power, are contributing to the liberation of
France, wherever they may be', and in the National Committee 'the
executive body of Fighting France, alone qualified to organize the
participation of French citizens and territories in the war'. In
Russian eyes, there could be neither a third force nor a third power
between Vichy and Fighting France.

It must be said that if America, the new star of world history,
believed herself in a position to direct the French nation, the European states, after centuries of experience, had no such illusion. Now
France had made her own choice. The information that reached us
every day showed that the resistance was expanding all the time,
which was the same as saying that all those who took part in it were
morally pledged to General de Gaulle and that any government
established without him would be rejected by the people immediately
after the liberation.

Moreover, the way in which the Germans and their collaborators
were behaving in metropolitan France was helping this development.
On June 22nd Laval declared, to the general indignation, 'I hope for
a German victory'. In July a 'legion' of young Frenchmen was sent
to fight in Russia under German orders and in German uniforms.
In August the Marshal issued a law putting an end to the 'activity'
of both Chambers, which had previously gone through the motions
of survival. Immediately the parliamentarians began to curse the
regime they themselves had set up. A public letter of protest was
addressed to the Marshal by M. Jeanneney, President of the Senate,
and M. Herriot, President of the Chamber of Deputies. The latter,
having returned his Legion of Honour cross to indicate his disapproval of the award of decorations to the 'volunteers' fighting the
Russians, was arrested shortly afterwards, while Messrs Paul Reynaud, Daladier, Blum, Mandel, General Gamelin and others remained in the prisons into which Vichy had thrown them on the
day of its accession to power, without their having been condemned
by law or even formally indicted. During the summer the persecution of the Jews grew worse, conducted by a special 'commissariat' in
collaboration with the invader. In September, because the Reich
required an increasing number of French workmen and because
volunteers were no longer enough to meet its quota, an obligatory

workers' levy was instituted. The total sum of the occupation expenses reached two hundred billion francs at the beginning of this month, double what it had been for September the preceding year. Finally, German reprisals redoubled in violence and severity. During these same four weeks a thousand men were shot, one hundred and sixteen on Mont Valérien, and more than six thousand went to prison or to concentration camps.

Upon my return from the Levant and Africa, I found unimpeachable witnesses waiting for me in London—Frénay, the head of *Combat*, and D'Astier, the head of *Libération*—who gave me their reports on action in the unoccupied zone. Their accounts emphasized the enthusiasm of the organization and the pressure from the rank and file towards unity, but also the extreme individualism of the leaders, which resulted in great rivalry amongst them. Nevertheless, when they discovered the obstacles which our allies set in our path and which were scarcely suspected in France, and particularly when they learned what was to happen in Algeria and Morocco, these responsible men could estimate how vital was unity in metropolitan France.

I instructed them to hasten the formation, around Jean Moulin, of the National Council for the Resistance, which would include the representatives of every movement, syndicate and party. I also urged them to unite their combat groups into the secret army which was to be set up. These groups would then depend in each region on a single authority, the military delegate whom I would appoint. For the occupied zone, I instructed Rémy to take the same directives to our movements there, the Civil and Military Organization, Men of the Liberation, Men of the Resistance, Liberation North, the Voice of the North, and even the Communist-led Francs-Tireurs and Partisans organization, which asked to be affiliated to us.

Of course we let Washington and London know what we had heard from France. Frénay and d'Astier saw the British ministers and services as well as the American diplomats and intelligence. André Philip left for Washington, armed with documentary proof and instructions, to give Roosevelt a letter from General de Gaulle explaining the realities of the French situation. Mendès-France, having escaped from metropolitan France, carried out a mission to the United States to inform those who were not aware of what was happening in France of the circumstances there. Félix Gouin, who

had arrived in August and who represented the Socialists, informed
the workers' parties that the former French left was now ranged
beneath the Cross of Lorraine. Shortly after, Brossolette, returning
from the occupied zone, brought with him Charles Vallin, one of the
bright hopes of the former right and of the Croix de Feu League.
Vallin, hitherto a disciple of the Vichy regime, now renounced his
errors; this ardent patriot, an apostle of tradition, joined my cause
with all his heart. He publicly detailed his reasons for doing so, then
left to take command of a combat company. General d'Astier de la
Vigerie and General Cochet, both important Air Force chiefs,
joined us in their turn. The Communists did not lag behind; from
France they prepared to send us Fernand Grenier; while in Moscow
André Marty came several times to inform our delegate Garreau
that he considered himself at my disposal. Finally, men as diversely
oriented as Mandel, Jouhaux and Léon Blum, then imprisoned by
Vichy, as well as Jeanneney, Louis Marin, Jacquinot, Dautry and
Louis Gillet, sent me their advice as well as assurances of their
support.

Thus whatever the immense difficulties of action in France, despite
danger and loss, despite rivalry among leaders and the separate
enterprises of certain groups employed by foreign powers, the cohesion of the resistance continually grew and became ever more pronounced. Because I had been able to give it the inspiration and
direction which saved it from anarchy, I found in it at the crucial
moment a valuable instrument in the struggle against the enemy
and, in relation to the Allies, an essential prop for my policy of
independence and unity.

We were now in the early days of November 1942. At any moment
America would begin her western crusade and direct her ships,
troops and air squadrons towards Africa. Since October 18th the
British, aided by French forces, had been striving to drive the
Germans and the Italians out of Libya in order to join the United
States army in Tunisia later on, with perhaps a French army as
well. On the eastern front, along the Volga and far into the Caucasus,
the enemy was being exhausted by Russian might.

What an opportunity was still open to France! How clear and
simple everything might be now for her unhappy sons were it not
for the inner demons that strove to divide them and the evil genius
that inspired foreign powers to make use of their dissensions. It was

not without anxiety that I waited for the curtain to go up on the next act of the drama. But I felt sure of my people. I believed they were sure of me. I knew to whom France was looking. Let the play go on!

II. TRAGEDY

ALL DAY LONG on November 7th the American and British stations kept repeating, 'Robert arriving! Robert arriving!' Hearing this, I had no doubt that 'Robert'—Murphy's first name—was the agreed term designating the American forces going to the French in North Africa whose co-operation had been secured. This meant that the landing had begun. The next morning's news confirmed the fact.

At noon I went to Downing Street at Mr Churchill's invitation. Mr Eden was also there. During the conversation the Prime Minister lavished upon me every sign of his friendship but could not conceal the fact that he felt some little embarrassment. He told me that though the British fleet and air force were playing an essential role in the operation now under way, British troops were serving in a purely accessory capacity. For the moment, Great Britain had had to leave all the responsibilities in the hands of the United States; Eisenhower was in command. The Americans were now demanding that the Free French be left out.

'We have been obliged to go along with them in this,' Mr Churchill declared. 'Rest assured, however, that we are not revoking any of our agreements with you. Ever since June 1940, we have promised you our support. Despite whatever incidents have occurred, we intend to keep that promise. Besides, as the North African engagement increases in scope, the British must come on the scene; we shall then have our word to say. And that word will be on your behalf.' And Mr Churchill, showing signs of emotion, added, 'You have been with us during the worst moments of the war. We shall not abandon you now that the horizon shows signs of brightening.'

The British ministers then informed me that the Americans were in the process of landing at several points in Morocco, as well as at Oran and Algiers. The operation was being carried out with considerable difficulty, especially at Casablanca, where French forces were putting up a vigorous resistance. General Giraud had been taken on to a British submarine off the Côte d'Azur and brought to Gibraltar. The Americans were counting on him to take command of the French troops in North Africa and to reverse the situation. But already his success seemed dubious.

'Did you know,' Churchill asked me, 'that Darlan is in Algiers?'

To these explanations I replied in substance: 'The fact that the Americans have landed in Africa, where both English and Free French forces have been struggling for over two years, is in tiself a highly satisfactory development. I can see in it, for France, the possibility of recovering an army and perhaps a fleet which would join the struggle for her liberation. General Giraud is a great soldier. My hopes accompany him in his endeavour. It is too bad that the Allies have prevented him from coming to an agreement with me, for I would have been able to procure other help for him besides hopes. But sooner or later we shall see eye to eye, and all the more readily if the Allies keep out of our way. As for the operation now in progress, I am not surprised that it is a difficult one. In both Algeria and Morocco there are military elements that opposed us in Syria last year and which you permitted to go free despite my warnings. Furthermore, the Americans wanted to play off Vichy against de Gaulle in North Africa. I have never doubted that, should the occasion arise, they would have to pay for such an attitude. Now they are paying for it, and of course we French must pay for it as well. All the same, given the feelings in our soldiers' hearts, I believe that the battle will not be long. But however short it is, the Germans will rush in.'

I then expressed to Churchill and Eden my astonishment at discovering that the Allied plan did not first of all aim at Bizerta, for the Germans and the Italians were obviously going to land there in Tunisia. If it were not for American reluctance to risk a direct landing and if I had been consulted, we could have brought in the Koenig Division. The British ministers admitted this, while repeating that the operation was under American control. 'I cannot understand,' I told them, 'how you British can stand aside so completely in an operation that is of primary concern to Europe.'

Mr Churchill asked me what I felt about future relations between Fighting France and the North African authorities. I replied that,

so far as I was concerned, achieving unity was all that mattered.
This implied that relations should be established as soon as possible,
and also that the Vichy régime and its supporters be expelled from
Algiers, since the resistance movement as a whole would not tolerate
their staying in power. If, for example, Darlan were to control North
Africa, agreement would not be possible. 'Whatever the case,' I said
in conclusion, 'nothing matters more today than to reach a cease-fire.
We shall see afterwards about the other things.'

That evening in a broadcast 'to the leaders, soldiers, sailors, airmen, officials and French *colons* of North Africa', I urged them:
'Rise up and help our allies, join them without reservations. Don't
worry about names or formulas—rise up! This is the great moment.
This is the hour of common sense and of courage. Frenchmen of
North Africa, let us re-enter the lists from one end of the Mediterranean to the other, and thanks to France the war will be won.'

Actually the information arriving at Carlton Gardens indicated
that the Americans were still fighting against heavy resistance everywhere. Their advance intelligence had certainly functioned effectively. General Mast, in command of the Algiers division, and
General Monsabert, in command of the Blida sub-division, as well as
Colonels Jousse, Baril, Chrétien, Commander Barjot and others had
been able to make things easier for them for a few hours, while at
Casablanca General Béthouart vainly tried to do the same. Groups
of 'Gaullists', acting under the orders of Paufilet, Vanhecke, Achiary,
Esquerre, Aboulker, Calvet, Pillafort and Dreyfus, the last two of
whom were to be killed in the operation, had temporarily managed
to take possession of certain administrative buildings in Algiers and
even to hold Admiral Darlan overnight in forced captivity in the
villa of Les Oliviers. Some prominent men, such as Rigault,
Lemaigre-Dubreuil and De Saint-Hardouin, who had negotiated
with the Americans, were playing their expected role as to local
information and liaison work; and Giraud's proclamation—which
made no mention whatever of Fighting France—had been widely
publicized by radio and American leaflets, while loyal officers and
resistance elements of every kind organized a command post for him
at Dar Mahidine. Nevertheless, it was clear on the whole that the
plan prepared by Leahy, Murphy and Clark to allow the Allies to
land without firing a shot, and the messages sent by Roosevelt to
Pétain, Noguès and Estéva, had not had the desired effect.

On November 9th the situation was not at all promising. The Vichy authorities had everywhere retained or resumed the upper hand. The Marshal had given formal orders to fight off the 'assailant'. At Gibraltar, General Giraud, realizing that the Allies were not at all interested in putting themselves under his command, had not yet left for North Africa, where his proclamation had had no effect at all. At Algiers, Darlan had just ordered the garrison to cease fire, but he allowed the 'defence plan' to be carried out everywhere else and continued to defer to Pétain and Laval. At Oran, a full-fledged battle was under way. But the fighting was especially bitter in Morocco where Casablanca, Port Lyautey and Fedala were the scenes of particularly fierce battles. And lastly Admiral Platon had reached Tunis, sent by Vichy to instruct Admiral Estéva, the Resident-General, and Admiral Derrien, the port admiral at Bizerta, to let the Germans land. In fact the latter, during the course of the day, landed their parachute troops near El Alaouina without firing a shot.

That evening there were long faces in Allied headquarters in London. Many wondered if the operation would turn into a prolonged struggle between the French troops and Eisenhower's forces, with the subsequent irruption, throughout the region, of enemy forces to which Spanish troops would be joined willy-nilly.

But on the spot good sense carried the day. General Juin, who had been commander-in-chief until Darlan's arrival and second in command since the latter had been in North Africa, realized how absurd it was to join battle with the Allies and what disastrous consequences the Italo-German break through would involve. He knew that this was the real feeling of his subordinates and urged Darlan to order a general cease-fire, to which the latter agreed on November 10th. Juin then made contact with Giraud, who had finally reached Dar Mahidine. Receiving him at Les Oliviers, Darlan informed Giraud that he was prepared to resign his own position to him. He ordered General Barré, in command of the troops in Tunisia, to group his forces near Medjez-el-Bab and to be in a position to open fire on the Germans. On the morning of November 11th, hostilities between the French and the Allies came to a general halt.

It was a costly operation. On the French side, three thousand men had been killed or wounded. The following ships were sunk or damaged beyond repair: the cruiser *Primauguet*, the destroyers *Albatros*, *Epervier* and *Milan*, seven torpedo boats, ten submarines, a considerable number of smaller craft—dispatch boats, patrol and escort vessels—and several cargo ships. In addition, the battleship *Jean-Bart* was heavily damaged and two submarines had made for Toulon, where they were soon to be scuttled. Lastly, out of the hundred and sixty-eight planes based on Morocco and Algeria, a hundred and thirty-five were destroyed on the ground or in combat. On the Allied side, losses reached three thousand killed, wounded or missing. The Royal Navy lost the destroyers *Broke* and *Malcolm*, the escort vessels *Walney* and *Hartland*, and several transport ships. In the American fleet, the battleship *Massachusetts*, the cruisers *Wichita* and *Brooklyn* and the destroyers *Murphy* and *Ludlow* were seriously damaged, one hundred smaller craft used in the landing were destroyed offshore or on the beaches, and seventy plane were shot down.

While these senseless battles were dying out, I took care to establish contact with French North Africa. As early as the afternoon of November 9th I asked Admiral Stark to meet me. He arrived with tears in his eyes, profoundly moved, he said, by my radio appeal to the French on the preceding day, but also deeply upset by the Franco-American struggle, which he had not believed possible. 'Eisenhower is also surprised and grieved to hear of it,' he added.

'I should like to send a mission to Algiers,' I told him. 'I am asking the United States Government to arrange for this mission to reach its destination.'

Stark promised that this would be done. The next day I wrote to Churchill, asking him to intervene on my behalf with Roosevelt, and alerted Pleven, Billotte, d'Astier and Frénay to leave at a moment's notice.

On November 11th a great rally which the 'French of Great Britain' had long been awaiting took place. Never had the Albert Hall been so packed. Obviously the thought of North Africa stirred the crowd and seeing and hearing this, I sensed that beneath the surge of enthusiasm minds were torn between joy and anxiety. While it was clear that union was the goal, it was equally to be feared that de Gaulle and Fighting France might be forced into some unworthy compromise. When, from the top of one of the balconies, a retired general who had taken refuge in England raised his voice to adjure me to subordinate myself to Giraud, the poor man was immediately dragged from his seat by outraged groups of people and expelled from the hall, pursued by the shouts of the crowd.

In my speech, I reaffirmed our goal amidst the events happening now and those looming on the horizon. I did so quite moderately, in order to keep the door open for men of good will everywhere, but also distinctly enough to make clear that what was said would indeed be done. I began by drawing attention to a new phase of the war, in which, after so many reversals, the balance of forces was at last inclining toward liberty. I stated that, as always, France was at the heart of the drama. Then in an appeal for unity I cried, 'France! a single nation, a single territory, a single law!' Then I proceeded to explain how our people, dispersed by the disaster, had rallied to the resistance, and that Fighting France and only Fighting France was guiding this national movement and providing its leaders.

'The cement of French unity,' I said, 'is the blood of the Frenchmen who have never recognized the armistice, of those who since Rethondes have died all the same for France. We are the core of our unity, we are the France that fights. To the nation cast into a dungeon, we have offered since the first day of her captivity the means of combat, the light of day, and that is why the nation now gives Fighting France her authority. And so our hope is to reunite all our peoples and all our territories. We shall suffer no one to come and divide our country's war effort by any of those so-called parallel enterprises, whose fate will soon be assured by the secret but powerful expression of the national will. Thus it is in the name of France that the French National Committee speaks when it calls for the help of all to wrest our country from the enemy and from Vichy, to re-establish French liberties, and to ensure that the laws of the Republic are observed.' I ended by crying, 'A united battle for a united country!'

The audience clearly understood that in this difficult situation I was ready to join with whoever deserved our alliance, but that I would abandon none of my fundamental commitments, and a tremendous ovation showed the approval of this throng of Frenchmen. Afterwards I was to discover that the effect of my words on the Allies was quite different. Their leaders and spokesmen, sighing and nodding their heads, censured our intransigence.

They were less squeamish than we were. Of course the Americans, with whom the British aligned themselves, had been astonished and annoyed by Giraud's failure, but since Eisenhower had found no other way of quelling French opposition than to come to an agreement with Darlan, then it was with the latter that America would open negotiations. On November 10th General Clark, hearing of the cease-fire which the Admiral had just declared, announced in the tones of a conqueror who holds the vanquished at his mercy that, under these conditions, 'all civil and military authorities will be maintained in their present functions'. On November 13th Nogués, Chatel and Bergeret met Darlan. It was understood among them that the Admiral would become High Commissioner for North Africa, and Boisson would soon put himself under his command. Giraud, isolated from Vichyists and 'Gaullists' alike, had done so immediately, with the result that he was named Commander-in-Chief of the troops. On November 15th Darlan announced these measures and proclaimed that they had been taken 'in the name of Marshal Pétain'.

As the grounds for these measures were rather suspect, an appearance of legality had to be found. It was declared that Nogués, having been delegated powers by the Marshal during Darlan's temporary confinement, had transmitted them to the Admiral, who was now, therefore, reinvested with that authority. But this casuistry did not long suffice, even to the most unscrupulous. In fact Pétain himself, after hysterical sessions during which, according to our intelligence, Weygand and Auphan urged him to approve the North African cease-fire and Laval demanded that he condemn it, took the latter course. By means of both radio and the press, he made public his great indignation at his proconsuls' 'felony'. He declared that 'Darlan had betrayed his mission'; he published a letter Giraud had written to him on May 4th, promising on his honour as a soldier never to do anything that would contradict his or Laval's policies; he let it be known that he himself would take command of the French armies and repeated his order to oppose the Anglo-American forces and leave the way open to the Axis armies. On December 1st Admiral Platon, the minister sent by the Marshal 'to co-ordinate the military affairs of the three branches', broadcasting to the African troops declared, 'It is in France that, after so many ordeals, the Marshal and his government will reconstitute the national army . . . France will reconquer Africa. Then you will see the traitors flee in foreign baggage trains.'

Hence another subterfuge to 'legitimize' Darlan's authority had to be found. It was alleged that a telegram had been sent by a subordinate, of which neither the text nor the signer's name was ever published but of which the mere mention permitted the tribe of augurs to insinuate to the gallery that Pétain secretly gave his approval to the Admiral. Finally, the supreme argument of those whom Vichy called 'the perjurers' would be that, because of the occupation of the southern zone of France, the Marshal was henceforth at the mercy of the Germans and could no longer give valid orders, and that consequently authority belonged to those upon whom he had conferred it when he was free.

It required no more than this for President Roosevelt to overcome, as regards Darlan, the democratic and legalistic scruples which, for over two years, he had opposed to General de Gaulle. On Roosevelt's orders Clark recognized the 'High Commissioner' and entered into negotiations that led, on November 22nd, to an agreement by virtue of which Darlan governed and commanded, provided that he gave satisfaction to his Anglo-American conquerors. True, the President issued a statement declaring that the political arrangements made by Eisenhower and Darlan were only 'a temporary expedient'. But on the 23rd, when he received André Philip and Tixier and grew annoyed at their protests, he shouted at them, 'Of course I'm dealing with Darlan, since Darlan's giving me Algiers! Tomorrow I'd deal with Laval, if Laval were to offer me Paris!' He added, however, 'I should very much like to see General de Gaulle to discuss these matters, and I want you to tell him how desirable his visit to Washington would be.' Finally, on December 7th, Darlan, having obtained the Allies' consent, decreed himself head of the French state in North Africa and Commander-in-Chief of land, naval and air forces, with the assistance of an 'Imperial Council' consisting of Noguès, Giraud, Chatel, Boisson and Bergeret.

While in Algiers, Casablanca and Dakar the officials made an about-face to keep their positions, in France itself the enemy reaction was unleashed, the German forces flowed into the 'free' zone, and Vichy forbade any opposition to them. The 'armistice army' was to lay down its arms pending demobilization. General de Lattre, labouring under an illusion, tried valiantly to apply the defence plan and occupy a position in the Montagne Noire with the troops around Montpellier. He was immediately repudiated, forsaken by all and imprisoned. It was at this time that he made contact with Fighting France, which was later to help his escape and send him to London where he was to join me for good. General Weygand, who had attempted to take cover at Guéret, was arrested by the Gestapo and deported to Germany. Thus, without Vichy's firing or allowing a single shot to be fired, was dissipated the lying pretence of independence which this régime had claimed to justify its capitulation and to deceive so many well-intentioned Frenchmen. Of the traces of its sovereignty there remained only the fleet at Toulon. It was not to be there for long.

This fleet—of which the permanently unattached portions were commanded by Admiral de Laborde, and the rest, more or less disarmed—was assigned directly to Admiral Marquis, the port admiral. Remaining under Pétain's orders, they refused to sail for Africa despite Darlan's urging, and saw the Germans appear within striking distance of the harbour. The 'neutrality' agreement Vichy had made with the enemy helped to keep our sailors from effecting some last-minute revolt. It was a stage on the road to annihilation. For my part, I was all the more convinced of this since, having recently written in secret to Admiral de Laborde to attempt to enlighten him as to the course both honour and duty commanded, I knew that he had given vent to a series of outrageous remarks about me and had threatened my emissary, Colonel Fourcault, though he kept my letter. On November 26th, the Germans rushed on Toulon to seize our ships.

Since they had previously occupied the hilltops dominating the arsenal, installed trench mortars in the harbour's immediate proximity and sown the roadstead with mines, the French fleet was at their mercy. And the Marshal, his ministers, the port admiral and the fleet Commander-in-Chief, paralysed by the consequences of their own surrender, found nothing to order these powerful warships to do save to send themselves to the bottom. Three battleships, *Dunkerque*, *Strasbourg*, *Provence*, eight cruisers, *Colbert*, *Dupleix*, *Foch*, *Algérie*, *Jeande-Vienne*, *La Galissonnière*, *Marseillaise*, *Mogador*, seventeen destroyers, sixteen torpedo boats, sixteen submarines, seven dispatch vessels, three patrol boats, some sixty transport ships, tankers, mine sweepers and tugs thus committed, on orders, the most pitiful and sterile suicide imaginable. One destroyer, one torpedo boat and five tankers were not scuttled in time and were seized by the Germans. Only five submarines, on the initiative of their valiant commanders, went over to the 'dissidents' and attempted to leave the harbour. *Casabianca*, under Lherminier, *Glorieux*, under Meynier, and *Marsouin*, under Mine, succeeded in reaching Algiers. *Iris*, under Degé, was forced by lack of fuel to take refuge in a Spanish port. *Vénus*, under Crescent, foundered in the roadstead. As for myself, submerged in seas of anger and disappointment, I was reduced to watching what had been one of France's major hopes sink out of sight, to hailing by radio the few courageous episodes that accompanied the disaster, and to receiving by telephone the British Prime Minister's nobly expressed but secretly complacent condolences.

Meanwhile, however, the turn events had taken generally strengthened the cohesion of the French who were already pledged to de Gaulle and inclined favourably toward him many of those who had not yet been won over. The last surrenders on the part of Vichy and the total occupation of metropolitan France, in fact, produced final evidence that the country's only salvation lay in resistance. Further, the arrival of Darlan in North Africa with the support of the Americans provoked general indignation. Never before had I encountered among our people, on any subject whatever, such unanimity as there was on that score.

Of course some people—as was our case—who saw their allies deal with their adversaries felt frustrated and offended, and in their disapproval there was also the revolt of idealism. For example, it was with rage that we heard the American radio commentators, rebroadcast by the BBC, twang out the motto of the Free France radio, '*Honneur et patrie*', to introduce their reports of Admiral Darlan's words, deeds and empty gestures. Finally, noting the reactions of the people who, in the depths of their suffering, condemned both the régime of defeat and that of collaboration, we were certain that if de Gaulle were to stand aside or worse still compromise, it would be the Communist ideology which would win the allegiance of the disgusted masses. The National Committee was convinced of this. Our comrades, wherever they were, no longer doubted the fact. For this reason, as for many others, I counted on the support of an undivided coalition when I informed the Washington and London governments that there was not the slightest chance of an agreement between Fighting France and the North African 'High Commissioner'.

On November 12th I requested that Admiral Stark inform his government of this decision on my behalf. In Washington, Philip and Tixier employed identical terms in conversations with Sumner Welles on the 13th and Cordell Hull on the 14th. On the 20th, Colonel de Chevigné repeated our message to McCloy. On the 23rd, Philip and Tixier very strongly confirmed their views to Roosevelt. On November 16th I had been to see Churchill and Eden, who had invited me to participate in a discussion as soon as Darlan's proclamation that he was retaining power in the Marshal's name and with the agreement of the Allies, had reached London. It must be said that this news had caused profound discontent in many circles in England and even in the heart of the British cabinet, and that the echoes of a shocked public opinion were noticeable in London. The atmosphere that day was therefore more strained than ever and the Prime Minister, without going so far as to repudiate Roosevelt, insisted on indicating some reservation as to the policy the President was pursuing.

He declared to me at once that he understood and shared my sentiments, but that what was most important was to drive the Germans and the Italians out of Africa. He guaranteed that the measures Eisenhower had taken at Algiers were essentially provisional and let me read the telegrams he and Roosevelt had exchanged on this subject.

'England gave her consent to this move,' he declared, 'only on condition that it be merely an expedient.'

'I am taking note of the British position,' I told the British ministers. 'My own is quite different. You invoke strategic reasons, but it is a strategic error to place oneself in a situation contradictory to the moral character of this war. We are no longer in the eighteenth century when Frederick the Great paid the courtiers of Vienna in order to be able to take Silesia, nor in the Italian Renaissance when one hired the myrmidons of Milan or the mercenaries of Florence. In any case we do not put them at the head of a liberated people afterwards. Today we make war with our own blood and souls and the suffering of nations.' I then showed Churchill and Eden telegrams from France that revealed the stupefaction of public opinion. 'Think,' I told them, 'of the risks you may be running. If France one day discovers that because of the British and the Americans her liberation consists of Darlan, you can perhaps win the war from a military point of view but you will lose it morally, and ultimately there will be only one victor: Stalin.'

We then spoke of a communiqué the French National Committee was circulating to make known that it had nothing in common with the Allied commitments in Algiers. In order to obtain wide publicity, we had to have the BBC antennae at our disposal. I asked the Prime Minister not to oppose us in this matter, although the London radio, as far as the North African question was concerned, was subject to American approval.

'Of course,' Churchill said. 'Moreover, I shall telegraph Roosevelt that General de Gaulle must have the means to make his position public.'

As we were about to separate, Eden, moved to the points of tears, took me aside to tell me how deeply disturbed he was personally. I replied that, knowing him, I was not at all surprised, for 'speaking man to man, we must agree that this is a dirty business'. His attitude confirmed me in my feeling that Churchill's readiness to follow the American policy was distasteful to Eden and no doubt to part of the British cabinet.

After lunch in Downing Street, during which all of Mrs Churchill's grace and charm was hard put to to enliven conversation among the preoccupied guests, the Prime Minister and I resumed our discussion privately. 'For you,' Churchill declared, 'if the present is painful, the prospect is magnificent. At present Giraud is politically liquidated. In any event Darlan would be impossible. You will remain the only choice.' And the Prime Minister added, 'Don't confront the Americans head on. Be patient! They will come to you, for there is no other alternative.'

'Perhaps,' I said. 'But how much crockery will be broken in the meantime! And I fail to understand your own position. You have been fighting this war since the first day. In a manner of speaking you personally *are* this war. Your army is advancing in Libya. There would be no Americans in Africa if, on your side, you were not in the process of defeating Rommel. Up to this very moment, not a single one of Roosevelt's soldiers has met a single one of Hitler's soldiers, while for three years your men have been fighting in every latitude of the globe. Besides, in this African campaign it is Europe that is at stake, and England belongs to Europe. Yet you let America take charge of the conflict, though it is up to you to control it, at

least ethically. Do so! All of European public opinion will follow
you.'

This sally struck Churchill; I watched him waver. We parted
after having agreed that we must not permit the present crisis to
crack Franco-British solidarity, which was more than ever in accord
with the natural order of things when the United States intervened
in the affairs of the Old World.

That evening the London radio announced, as I had requested,
that 'General de Gaulle and the National Committee took no share
and assumed no responsibility in the negotiations in progress in
Algiers', and that 'if these negotiations were to lead to arrangements
preserving the Vichy regime in North Africa, they would obviously
be unacceptable to Fighting France'. Our communiqué concluded:
'The union of all the overseas territories in the battle for liberation is
possible only under conditions in accord with the will and the dignity
of the French people.'

But the good impulse of the British could not resist American
pressure for long. Three days later the British cabinet refused us permission to use the BBC facilities to broadcast a declaration made in
support of our own by the organizations of the French resistance.
This was contained in a note from France addressed to the Allied
governments and signed by representatives of the three movements
of the southern zone, *Combat, Libération* and *Francs-Tireurs*; of the
French workers' movement, including the CGT and the Christian
syndicates; and of the four political parties, the Socialist Action
Committee, the Republican Federation, the Popular Democrats
and the Radicals. The note stated:

> General de Gaulle is the uncontested leader of the resistance
> movement, which now more than ever before unites the entire
> country behind him . . . In no case will we agree to consider
> the about-face of those responsible for our political and military
> betrayal an excuse for their past crimes . . . We urgently request
> that the destiny of liberated French North Africa be put into
> General de Gaulle's hands as soon as possible.

The censors from Washington had vetoed the publication of this
document.

On November 21st I myself met their opposition. In an address
to the French nation which had already been recorded by the BBC,

I asked 'whether the national liberation is to be dishonoured' and of course replied, 'No!' A few minutes before broadcasting time, Mr Charles Peake came to tell me that under the terms of the agreements made between the Allies and for military reasons, the London radio could not proceed with broadcasts about North Africa without the consent of the United States, that this consent had been requested for my address but that the reply required a postponement, for which the British Government profoundly apologized. It was therefore the broadcasting facilities of Fighting France at Brazzaville, Douala and Beirut, free of all foreign interference, that carried my message and that of the resistance.

On November 24th, during one of our discussions, Mr Churchill felt that he must mention, though he did so with considerable embarrassment, the BBC's delay in broadcasting my address. 'Since the problems you were dealing with concerned the lives of American and British soldiers,' he told me. 'I thought it politic to telegraph President Roosevelt for his approval. He has not yet given it.'

'I did not know,' I answered, 'that on British territory the radio was not at my disposal.' But Churchill's behaviour made me realize that it was not at his either.

Among many such upsets, I attempted to remain steadfast and unwavering—as much by will and reason as by temperament, for the system established at Algiers seemed to me too artificial to resist the battering ram of events for long, whatever external support it might receive. The men who were in control obviously found themselves in a false position to every section of public opinion. Opposed as they were to de Gaulle, repudiated by Pétain, alarming the procrastinators, they were supported by no popular current, strengthened by no mystique, and their successive attitudes, it was only too obvious, were derived from mere speculation. Why then concede anything to an oligarchy that has neither future nor hope? Even less when, at the very moment it came to power in Algiers, careful preparations were swelling our own strength. Immediately after the American landings in Morocco and Algeria, Fighting France extended its authority to all the French possessions in the Indian Ocean.

Of these, it was Réunion that first came over to our side. Isolated in the South Seas, away from the convoy route that doubled the Cape, poor in resources and inhabited by an extremely varied but ardently pro-French population, the island did not enter directly into the Allied plans. But it was exposed to a combined German-Japanese raid, especially now that the enemy was cut off from possible access to Madagascar. We were quite aware that the majority of Réunion's inhabitants wanted their country to take part in the war effort and I had long been looking for an opportunity to unite the island with Fighting France. The British, however, while preparing their Madagascar campaign and the Americans, who were getting ready to invade Africa, put off my intervention in order not to alert Vichy and the enemy. Therefore it was not until November 11th that I decided to effect the coalition with Réunion.

For several months the destroyer *Léopard*, under Commander Richard-Evenou, had been taking part in escort and patrol action off South Africa with just this intention. I gave orders that it make for Réunion and do what was necessary there, taking along Administrator-in-Chief Capagorry, whom I named governor in advance. On November 28th the ship reached St Denis. At the sight of the Cross of Lorraine, the people rushed to the harbour *en masse* to welcome our sailors, while many officials and military men showed their sympathy. Only the Galets peninsula battery gave signs of hostility. The *Léopard* answered by a broadside of cannon shots and landed a detachment which, with the co-operation of Director of Public Works Decugis and a zealous local group, made short work of the incident. Unfortunately Decugis was killed, as well as several spectators. Since Governor Aubert had retired to his residence in the mountains, Commander Richard-Evenou made contact with him there. It was agreed 'for reasons of public safety' that all resistance should cease and that Governor Capagorry assume responsibility for the island. Amidst the liveliest enthusiasm, General de Gaulle's representative assumed his new functions.

The same thing happened a month later in Madagascar. Since Governor-General Annet's surrender to the British, in fact, the huge island's destiny was theoretically determined, but practically everything remained in suspense. True, on November 11th, at Mr Eden's reiterated request, I had agreed to the publication of a joint communiqué announcing that the French National Committee and the British Government were holding conferences on the subject of Madagascar and that the National Committee had appointed General Legentilhomme High Commissioner. But I did not intend to take control of Madagascar into my own hands if those hands were not free. It was essential, therefore, that the British agree to stand aside in political and administrative matters.

Yet it was on just these points that negotiations lagged and their conclusion was delayed by the behaviour of the British colonials. After trying to bring the Vichy administration under their influence by using the British military command as a go-between, these colonials had tried to seize authority for themselves and had appointed Lord Rennell to direct their affairs, taking advantage of the co-operation of well-intentioned French officials. Lord Rennell and his group now abandoned their attempt and admitted that it was necessary for Fighting France to take control. But they would have preferred to retain at the very least a controlling influence, which of course we did not want. The agreement that was finally signed on December 14th by Mr Eden and myself, guaranteed all that was necessary. That evening, in a broadcast, I announced the happy event, declaring, 'By this act our great and beautiful colony will . . . be able to play an important military and economic role in the war effort', and emphasizing 'the complete loyalty which our splendid and traditional ally England' had manifested once again.

The agreement specified that the arrangements had as goal 'the re-establishment of the exercise of French sovereignty in Madagascar and its dependencies', the Comorro Islands, Crozet, Kerguelen, St Paul and Amsterdam; that the High Commissioner assumed all the powers delegated to the governor-general by French law, as well as the powers of command over the French forces and that the defence of Madagascar, its dependencies and Réunion would be ensured jointly. The High Commissioner was to proceed with the reorganization of the French forces as soon as possible. Until he could have the necessary means at his disposal, a British general would be in charge of the defence of the territory. At Diégo-Suarez a British naval officer would be in command.

Once this agreement was signed, General Legentilhomme left for Antananarivo, where he was to join a mixed detachment sent by Free French Africa. Legentilhomme, seconded by Governor-General de Saint-Mart and by the military commander, Colonel Bureau, was to put in motion the administration, the economy and the public services, re-establish trade and foreign exchange, and reorganize the troops. At the same time he was to do everything in his power to restore morale. Thus, several weeks after his arrival, half of his officers, two-thirds of his non-commissioned officers and all of the soldiers from the units that had just been fighting against the Allies on Vichy's orders, had resumed service under the authority of Fighting France. The remainder, transferred to England, would return to North Africa as soon as unity could be effected there.

In sending General Legentilhomme to Antananarivo, I had the satisfaction of being able to order him to pass through Djibouti, which Fighting France had taken on December 28th. This was, of course, a result of the recent events in Madagascar, for since the beginning of the British intervention there the Vichy authorities of the Somaliland coast had been unable to get necessary supplies from the huge island, but it was also due to the efforts made for two years by our mission to East Africa. Palewski and Chancel in turn, by maintaining every possible contact with the colony and spreading our propaganda there, actively representing our cause to the Negus at Addis Ababa and to the British command at Nairobi, had brought about this change of allegiance. Colonel Appert and his detachment, too, who were posted in direct contact with the garrison there, had urged it to join us and, setting the example of a leader and a corps of the highest quality, had gradually influenced the outlook of a great many of the men. Despite everything, however, our forces had had to enter the colony.

Indeed General Dupont, governor of Djibouti (where he had replaced Noailhetas), did not decide to transfer allegiance, though his feelings inclined him to do so and though I had written urging it. Realizing this, part of the garrison led by Lieutenant-Colonel Raynal, had crossed the frontier and joined Colonel Appert's detachment at the beginning of November. Other groups let it be known that they would be willing to do the same. Thereupon the Washington Government, in order to keep the colony from going over to de Gaulle, had sent its consul from Aden to Djibouti. But the latter could find no solution that agreed with American policy— that is, the exclusion of both Vichy and de Gaulle. On the other hand, his intervention had resulted in irritating the 'Gaullists' and had forced them to act. On December 26th, Fighting French troops under the orders of Appert and Raynal and with British agreement entered French Somaliland and reached the outskirts of the city without a shot being fired. The question was decided. On December 28th General Dupont signed an agreement with Chancel, my delegate, and General Fowkes, the representative of the British Government, transferring the colony to the French National Committee. Chancel immediately took control. On December 30th Bayardelle, appointed governor of Djibouti, took up his position there.

The recovery of Somaliland was of considerable importance. All the French territories in the Indian Ocean had thereby re-entered the war, providing the Western powers with strategic positions that covered Africa and the East in the event of a new threat from Japan. The city of Djibouti again became the transit port at the entrance to the Red Sea and the outlet for Ethiopia. Besides these facts, Fighting France found in the three hundred officers, the eight thousand men and the supplies equipping the base of operations a precious reinforcement for our troops in Libya and for those which we were preparing to regroup in Madagascar. Finally, at a political level, it was significant that during the very weeks when the Algiers system was breaking down, the National Committee should have succeeded in restoring to unity and to the war effort such distant and sought after territories.

But the supreme fact that in Africa both parts of the French Army were henceforth fighting the same enemy was to encourage them to unite. No quibbling could conceal from the officers and soldiers taking up positions along Tunisia's 'dorsal' coast that they were now doing precisely the same thing as their comrades engaged in Libya and Fezzan. The 'government' that yesterday had condemned the latter was today repudiating the former under the same pretext, that all were 'adding to the country's woes'. In France the resistance movement, linked with the men who had not ceased fighting, was also about to join forces with those who were turning their scanty arms against the invader in Tunisia. The French people who put their hopes in de Gaulle and his followers included all French soldiers fighting the same battle in those hopes. I was therefore sure that the desire for unity would swell each day from Rabat to Gabès. Thus although I could still not control the troops of French North Africa, I followed their operations with the same eager attention I accorded the others.

After several confused days of which the enemy took advantage to gain a foothold in the Regency, the Tunisian troops under Barré's

orders were regrouped. One section went towards Beja and Medjez-
el-Bab, the other towards Tebessa, to block the roads to Algeria.
Then the Constantine Division, under General Welwert, reached
Tebessa in its turn, making with Barré's units a sector of army corps
under General Koeltz, while, farther south, General Delay entered
the campaign with his Sahara troops. On November 16th Juin took
command of this 'army detachment' which, on the 19th, opened fire
on the Germans at Medjez-el-Bab and, on the 22nd, reoccupied
Gafsa and Sbeitla. By the end of November, something like a front
line extending from northern to southern Tunisia, weak in parts but
held by determined men, assured a primary cover to the emplacements of Allied battle corps.

The month of December saw both camps reinforced, for the
Germans and the Italians, under General Nehring's orders, received
troops and equipment carried from one shore of the Straits of Sicily
to the other or else brought from Tripolitania along the Gabès road.
The British First Army under General Anderson sent its advance
guard corps into line along the coastal region west of Tunis and
Bizerta, while General Giraud completed Juin's forces, first with the
Algiers Division under Deligne and then with a division from
Morocco under Nathenet. The Americans added, on the one hand,
an armoured division to support the British and on the other parachute troops and tanks to relieve the French.

All in all General Eisenhower, two months after landing, still had
not been able to contact the enemy with anything more than a small
number of Anglo-American units. He was delayed in his deployment by the fear of seeing the Spanish take the offensive in Morocco,
the desire not to engage his inexperienced troops hastily, and lastly
by the difficulties he was having to find bases for his planes, to
transport his supplies and organize his communications in territory
as extensive as French North Africa, while at sea enemy ships and
planes were ceaselessly attacking his convoys. The first months of
1943 were indeed to see the greatest tonnage losses of the whole
war. During this critical period the fate of the campaign as a whole
rested essentially on the effort of the French troops—a role the more
praiseworthy for them because they played it with obsolete armaments and virtually no planes, armoured units, heavy artillery, anti-
aircraft guns, anti-tank weapons and trucks. All their equipment
had been returned to the armistice commissions or else destroyed

during the fighting against the Americans. There remained only a few pieces kept in the units or camouflaged in up country shelters.

Meanwhile Bizerta had been the theatre of a final surrender. Admiral Derrien, on orders brought from Vichy by Platon, had allowed the German troops to infiltrate freely into the area. On December 7th Nehring ordered the wretched man to disarm the garrison and hand over ships, harbour, arsenal and defences, which he did at once. An important base of operations thus passed into the hands of the enemy, who also seized one destroyer, three torpedo boats, two dispatch boats and nine submarines handed over intact in the roadstead or in the harbour basin. This deplorable episode marked the end of a shameful series. From now on, with the exception of the 'African Phalanx' which fought against the Allies side by side with the enemy, Vichy no longer controlled any of our arms in Africa. The few that remained were in the hands of soldiers who would know how to wield them in the service of France, some in Tunisia, the rest in Libya.

Indeed, it was with the co-operation of the Larminat Group that the British opened their offensive against Rommel. In the brilliantly handled break-through effected on October 23rd by Montgomery near El Alamein, the First Light Division under Koenig had been placed on the southern wing of the front along the steep slopes of Himeimat. Fighting over difficult terrain and on a very wide front against a solidly entrenched enemy, this division suffered serious losses, in particular that of brave Amilakvari, killed at the head of the Legion. Several days later the Second Light Division, under Colonel Alessandri's command, and the armoured column of Colonels Rémy and Kersauson played an active part in the start of the pursuit undertaken by the Eighth Army. I had previously approved the use which was being made of our forces, but now the Anglo-American landing in Morocco and Algeria and the opening of the Tunisian front convinced me that it would be a mistake to let the Larminat Group exhaust itself at the present time. It seemed wiser to enable it to take part in full force in the later phase of operations, the one that would see the juncture of the Allied armies from east and west, the reunion on French territory of our troops under the Cross of Lorraine with those of North Africa and the destruction of the enemy on the shores of *mare nostrum*.

I therefore ratified the decision of the British command which, on

C

November 10th, had retired the Free French from the front in order
to place them in reserve in the Tobruk region. Shortly afterwards I
accepted Larminat's proposal to form a line division by combining
both light divisions. We were soon able to give this magnificent unit
the striking power of three brigades—Brosset, Alessandri and Lelong
—and to equip it completely with artillery, thanks to the stores of
various arms recovered at Djibouti. Thus the Free French First
Division was drawn up. Larminat and his troops, controlling their
impatience, waited for the moment to re-enter the line, decisively this
time, in the great Battle of Africa which had lasted for two years
and in which our troops had never ceased to take part.

During this period we took the long awaited opportunity to conquer the Fezzan and to bring to the fighting on the Mediterranean
coast a French corps that had crossed the Sahara from Chad. For
the execution of this project, my goal from the day when Eboué and
Marchand joined us at Fort-Lamy, Leclerc had been preparing
since 1940 by a series of *tours de force*: the formation of desert columns,
the establishment of supply lines, the taking of Cufra and the
advance of reconnaissance units into the heart of the Italian positions. The moment had come to risk all to gain all. On November 14th, confirming my instructions of the preceding September
22nd, I ordered General Leclerc to open the offensive having 'the
French occupation of the Fezzan as the first objective, with possible
reconnoitring either towards Tripoli or Gabès in conjunction with
the Allied operations in Tripolitania'. I added, 'For this offensive,
you will be under my sole command. But you must act in agreement
with General Alexander, British Commander-in-Chief for the Middle
East, so that from the moment you reach the Fezzan you can receive
an increasingly extensive air support . . . At the latest, I count on
your launching the drive by the time the Allies have reached the
Gulf of Sidra.' As a matter of fact, at the time of the Anglo-American
landing in Algeria and Morocco, I had thought of effecting a break-
through of our troops in southern Libya to coincide with their entry
into the Niger and had given orders to push the column prepared
for this mission as far as Zinder. But the conclusion of the struggle
between the French and the Allies inclined me to suspend this
secondary operation; only the main one would now take place.

The opening moves were particularly arduous and included the
launching of columns from the Chad bases, the long approach of

about 1,500 miles to contact the enemy's fortified bases and the
transport to the site of fuel, munitions, supplies and equipment
reserves on which the attack proper would depend. Since by the end
of November Montgomery's offensive was proceeding well and the
Allied front in Tunisia was on the way to being established, I gave
Leclerc orders to go ahead on November 28th, specifying that he
was to launch his attack after December 2nd on his own initiative,
taking into consideration General Alexander's suggestions. But
despite the eagerness to cross swords with the enemy which inspired
Leclerc and his troops, their offensive did not begin until December
12th because of a halt in the Eighth Army advance level with El
Agheila.

Meanwhile we had had to parry the British intention to extend
their authority over the Fezzan once we had conquered it. General
Alexander had written to Leclerc on November 28th informing him
that he was sending officers to administer the occupied territory.
The British Commander-in-Chief made plain that these officers 'are
delegated to accompany the forces under your command. They will
be responsible for the territories occupied by you until the definitive
co-ordination of all Tripolitania under British military authority
can be established.' Alexander further informed Leclerc that London's economic policy prohibited the use of francs as currency in the
Fezzan. On December 1st Mr Charles Peake, upon whom, either in
spite of or because of his merit, fell the frequent burden of thankless
tasks, presented me with Mr Eden's note, under no delusion as to
its reception, to the same effect. I replied to Mr Peake with as
friendly a refusal as possible and telegraphed to General Leclerc:
'The Fezzan must be France's share in the battle of Africa. It is the
geographical link between southern Tunisia and Chad. You must
utterly decline all forms of British interference in this region, whether
political, administrative, monetary, etc.'

On December 22nd the preliminaries were finished and the attack
began. In two weeks of bitter fighting the Ingold and Delange commands, making respectively toward Oum-el-Araneb and Gatrún and
supported by the 'Bretagne' air group, seized enemy positions after
having knocked out their mobile columns. Dio, Massu, Geoffroy,
Sarazac, D'Abzac and others covered themselves with glory and
spoils. On January 12th the taking of Sebha opened the road to
Tripoli. On the 13th the Murzuq base fell into our troops' hands.

We had taken approximately a thousand prisoners, including forty officers, twenty big guns, a number of armoured vehicles and hundreds of mortars, machine-guns and automatic arms. While Leclerc's troops were preparing to drive northward, Colonel Delange assumed the functions of military commander of Fezzan.

Thus by sheer audacity and ingenuity, this succulent fruit of the desert was plucked at last. On January 13th, 1943, I announced our success to the nation. 'Perhaps,' I said in my broadcast, 'the effort of these splendid soldiers is some consolation for the misery of France. Yes—the long, hard ordeals of a rigorous preparation beneath the equatorial sun, the mortal fatigue of the columns launched across deserts of sand and stone, the exhausting flights of the air squadrons, the bloody engagements against enemy bases with their highly trained troops and planes, all the fine, strong men who bore the brunt of this battle, from their young and glorious general to the most obscure soldier among them, have made it a humble gift fervently offered to the pain and the pride of France.'

But if on a military level the outlook seemed to be brightening, politically it was darker than ever. At Carlton Gardens we were kept well informed, for among the military men, officials and journalists who came and went between Africa and England, many made it their duty to bring us messages and information. Furthermore, certain Algerian and Moroccan 'Gaullists', profiting by the general confusion, managed to join us.

We knew, therefore, that the fact of Darlan's continued command was causing virulent local criticism. The Vichyists were shaken by the Marshal's formal repudiation, the 'Gaullists' had rebelled against the 'temporary expedient' and the prominent men who had negotiated with Murphy for Giraud's abortive accession found their hopes frustrated. Among the last, several military men and officials received severe punishment, General Béthouart, Colonel Magnan and Controller Gromand, arrested in Morocco on Noguès's orders, narrowly escaped the firing squad; with great difficulty Eisenhower had them transferred to Gibraltar. General Mast and Colonel Baril had to seek refuge in the Levant. In the Navy, the Air Force and the Army there was indignation at seeing Darlan profit by his *volte-face* while the wrecks of ships and planes and the bodies of soldiers, for whose loss he was responsible, were still being counted. Lastly, the fact that the Toulon fleet had sunk itself rather than obey him made many feel that Darlan's presence as leader could henceforth offer nothing but disadvantages.

This state of affairs increased my eagerness to make contact with Algiers. The mission for which I had originally asked leave of Roosevelt and Churchill to send to Africa had not, of course, been allowed to go, Washington and London invoking a thousand pretexts to prevent it. At the beginning of December I addressed myself to General Eisenhower, asking him to receive in Algiers General d'Astier de la Vigerie, whom I appointed to liaise with the French leaders there. On this occasion as on several others afterwards, I discovered a sympathy on the American commander-in-chief's part which the political pressures of his country refused me. He acceded to my request. It is true that Eisenhower, struck by the resistance he had encountered during the landing, distressed by the cabals too many Frenchmen made before him and disturbed by the unrest he perceived among the people, was haunted by the fear of seeing this agitation turn into a general disorder which would compromise the security of his communications in the middle of the battle of Tunisia. Therefore my intention of finding common ground in North Africa with those worthy of consideration seemed to him to correspond to the common interest of the Allies.

General d'Astier reached Algiers on December 20th. What he saw and heard there gave him the impression of a bitter conflict, smothered for better or worse by the police machinery with which the authorities had surrounded themselves, but straining against its restrictions.

He found General Giraud annoyed at not having been able to persuade the Army to follow him at the moment of landing, embittered by the Americans' refusal of his request that the Allied command be entrusted to him and humiliated by depending for employment on Darlan's pleasure. His discontent made him open to our suggestions. When my envoy invited him to come to an agreement with Fighting France, notably in connection with the co-ordination of military operations and the recruiting of troops, Giraud indicated his willingness to co-operate.

The Comte de Paris, arriving from Morocco, informed General d'Astier how serious and harmful to the interests of France the situation seemed to him. Nothing, he declared, was more necessary, more urgent, than to dismiss the Admiral and then to unite all

Frenchmen of good will. He was himself in Algiers to gather his followers together to use them in the best interests of unity, and to offer himself for any arbitration that might be asked of him. The prince showed himself to be as disinterested as possible in what, should the occasion arise, was most to his own advantage.

As for Monsieur Lemaigre-Dubreuil, he did not conceal the fact that he, like his friends, was embittered by not being appointed to the command posts which, he claimed, his political capacities and the services he had rendered to the Americans deserved. Under the aegis of General Giraud, who was to have become Head of the State following Monsieur Lemaigre-Dubreuil, he declared himself ready to assume the presidency of the Council in a coalition government and to entrust to General de Gaulle the portfolio of National Defence.

D'Astier next was informed that the local political circles, long silent and resigned, were being reawakened by the tornado. On November 24th Saurin, Froger and Deyron, presidents respectively of the general councils of Oran, Algiers and Constantine, joined by an Algerian deputy, Monsieur Sarda, had written to Darlan:

> By placing yourself under the authority of the Marshal, whom you nevertheless recognize as not free to act, and by assuming the functions of a delegate of his government in North Africa, you are fulfilling none of the conditions that would confer upon you the powers of a legal and independent government.

Among the Americans, finally, my representative noted that even while collaborating with Admiral Darlan, Eisenhower and his General Staff affirmed that the High Commission must be only a transitional phase and stressed their desire to enter into direct relations with General de Gaulle.

As for the crowd of those who for various motives had joined the resistance under Vichy, General d'Astier pointed out that they were secretly a prey to the most violent disturbance. Some of them had given assistance to the Allied intervention and now found themselves persecuted as much as ever. The general's brother Henri, who occupied an important post in the High Commission, Professor Capitant, leader of the Combat movement in North Africa, and many other informed visitors described the atmosphere of conspiracy in which these resistance elements were steeped as one which at any moment might precipitate some bloody incident.

Greatly influenced by all these reports and with the encouragement of Mr Murphy, General d'Astier agreed to an interview with
Darlan. He had expected that their meeting would be a private one,
but found the Admiral surrounded by an Aereopagus where, among
others, were General Giraud and General Bergeret. Every man
looked gloomy, strained, full of suspicion and complaints. Darlan,
visibly exhausted but eager, probably, to encourage his entourage,
felt that he must strike an attitude in front of my envoy. He declared
that he had matters well in hand and that the necessity of forcing
the French to unite was foremost in his mind. In order to bring this
about he had agreed to amnesty those who had helped the Allies
since the armistice, and to make public his intention to retire as soon
as the war was over, but that in the meantime he represented the
only possible rallying point. This pretence of assurance contrasted
too cruelly with the realities of the situation, the nervousness the
Admiral himself betrayed and with the atmosphere that surrounded
him, for anyone to be deceived by it.

D'Astier said as much to Darlan, giving him an account of public
opinion in France, where he had just been. Then the Admiral,
carried away, reproached him for coming to Algiers and stirring up
trouble.

'Is that your opinion,' d'Astier asked Giraud, 'when I ask for your
reply to General de Gaulle's proposal to co-ordinate the operation of
your troops with that of the forces of Fighting France?'

Giraud having remarked that he was ready to settle the question,
Darlan interrupted dryly, 'No, General. This is my affair.'

There followed a profound silence. To end this painful scene
General d'Astier told the Admiral quite bluntly that it was his
presence which was the chief obstacle to unity, and that he could do
nothing better than to stand aside at once.

After this meeting, the Americans informed d'Astier that Darlan
insisted on leaving Algiers and that they had agreed. D'Astier returned to London on December 24th. From his sojourn at Algiers he
was convinced that Darlan, feeling the ground give way beneath
him, would shortly abandon his position.

On the afternoon of the same day, leaving a Christmas-tree light-
ing ceremony for our sailors, I learned of Admiral Darlan's death.
The man who had killed him, Fernand Bonnier de la Chapelle, saw
himself the instrument of the aggravated passions that had heated

public opinion to the boiling point, but behind such emotions, perhaps, there moved a policy liquidating a 'temporary expedient' after
having made use of him. This young man, almost a child, was overwhelmed by the idea of so many unpleasant events, and thought his
action would be a service to his tortured country. He hoped to
remove from the road to French reconciliation an obstacle shameful
in his eyes. He believed, moreover, as he again and again said up to
the moment of his execution, that an intervention would be made
on his behalf by some outside source so high and powerful that the
North African authorities could not refuse to obey it. Of course no
individual has the right to kill, save on the field of battle, and
Darlan's behaviour, as a governor and as a leader, was answerable
to national justice, certainly not to that of a group or of an individual.
Yet how could we fail to recognize and understand what inspired
this young man's rage? That is why the brutal and summary way
the investigation was conducted in Algiers, the abbreviated trial
before a military tribunal convened at night in private session, the
immediate and secret execution of Fernand Bonnier de la Chapelle,
the orders given to the censors that not even his name should be
known—all pointed to the suspicion that someone wanted to conceal
at any price the origin of his decision, and constituted a kind of
defiance of the circumstances which, without justifying the drama,
explained and to a certain degree excused it.

Nevertheless, the tragic manner of Darlan's disappearance from
the scene could not fail to be condemned by many, though the very
fact that he was forced from the stage seemed in accord with the
harsh logic of events. For history, in its great moments, tolerates in
positions of authority only men capable of directing their own
course. As matters were by then, Darlan could neither help nor
hinder and could no longer affect the position whatever he did.
Everyone—the Admiral first of all—realized that for him the page
had been turned.

He had missed his chance. In 1940 the Navy was indeed in a
position to play a leading national role, whereas for centuries the
continental destiny of France had maintained it as a secondary
power. Amid the military collapse of metropolitan France, it remained almost fortuitously intact. At that moment the oceans, the
distances and the speed that were its elements became all-important.
It had at its disposal the Empire, also untouched. The Allies, threat-

ened by sea, would not have haggled for its co-operation. Combining its force with theirs, it could obstruct and hamper the enemy,
cover and command Africa, transport there the requirements of the
liberating army, and, one day, return the latter to our own shores.
But for such a task it would have required a leader, not merely
intrepid, but inspired with a national passion to serve France irres-
pective of what might happen to the fleet. This Darlan did not possess.

His ambitions, his efforts had been dedicated to the Navy, but to
the Navy alone. Because he lacked an ideal which his country, during
almost the whole of his professional life, could not inspire, it was this
great force which had exclusively absorbed his interest, his inclination and his skill. He had been able, in peacetime, to persuade the
authorities by his ardour and expertise to build a well-equipped
navy, but it was a fief that existed through him and on his account
alone.

When France was defeated, what seemed of prime importance to
Darlan was that the Navy should not be defeated. When the surrender was concluded, for him to accept it, it was enough to believe
that the Navy would remain beyond the reach of the disaster. When
the conflict became world-wide, it was more than ever imperative
that the Navy should be preserved to fight again. It was in the fleet's
name that Darlan wanted to become chief of the Vichy Government; it was in hopes of assuring it a field of action and a *raison d'être*
that despite the subjection exacted by the enemy he repeatedly gave
orders to fight the 'Gaullists' and the Allies. It was because he
wanted to continue what he felt to be an essentially naval dispute
that he persisted in collaboration with the German invader against
England. In his ultimate decision to call off the battle waged by his
orders on the shores of Africa against the Anglo-American forces,
what carried most weight in his soul? Was it a belated passion to
overcome his country's invader, or rather the hope of recovering the
scattered fragments of the fleet by changing camps? But when at
Toulon, at Fort-de-France and at Alexandria the sailors refused to
listen to him, and at Casablanca, Oran and Bizerta the ships were
nothing more than wrecks, Admiral Darlan knew that even if France
won the war, he himself had lost his own battle.

France, without a great navy, could not remain France. But this
Navy had to be her own. It is the governing powers who must form
it, inspire it and employ it as an instrument of the national interest.

Unfortunately this was just what the régime, which for so many, many years had floated upon the nation's surface without directing its vital forces, did not know how to do. In my eyes, the outrage at Algiers illuminated in its turn the principal cause of our miseries. Like other notorious misfortunes that had rained down upon France, Admiral Darlan's faults, the sad fate of our fleet and the fathomless wound inflicted upon the pride of our sailors were the consequences of years of disease within the state.

III. COMEDY

DARLAN'S DISAPPEARANCE from the scene had great bearing on French unity. I would have to turn it to my advantage. On December 25th I telegraphed General Giraud that the outrage in Algiers was 'a symbol and a warning', and that now more than ever it was necessary to establish a national authority. Then I wrote:

> I propose, General, that we meet as soon as possible on French territory, either in Algeria or in Chad. We will study ways to enable us to concentrate under a provisional central power all the forces of both metropolitan France and her overseas territories, which are capable of joining the struggle for the liberation and the welfare of France.

I was in a hurry to send this message because I wanted to emphasize the fact that we had no right to delay once there was a possibility of agreement and I addressed it to General Giraud because I believed he would be Darlan's successor. The way was now clear for the Americans to establish at Algiers the very man they had chosen at the outset and whose accession the Admiral's presence had delayed. As for the necessary formalities, they depended only on the 'Imperial Council', that is, on Noguès, Boisson, Chatel and Bergeret, all apparently ready to do Eisenhower's and Murphy's bidding. On December 26th, in fact, General Giraud was invested with the powers and the rather astonishing title of 'Civil and Military Commander-in-Chief'. If he accepted my proposition, if we could meet unhampered by the intrigues and foreign influences that surrounded us, if we offered an example of co-operation to those who wanted to drive the enemy from our country, then the foundation of a wartime government capable of asserting itself might be laid at once and long months of disorganization be avoided. But, apart from the grudges and pretensions of certain Frenchmen who happened to be on the spot, the Allied desire to keep the authority in North Africa under their control and to prevent France from reappearing as a sovereign power before the end of the war was to delay the triumph of national common sense.

The reply General Giraud sent me on December 29th was dilatory in the extreme. After agreeing on the need for French unity he resorted, in order to postpone it, to the same motive I had invoked to hasten it. He wrote that as a result 'of the disturbance the recent assassination has caused in both civil and military circles in North Africa . . . the atmosphere is at present unfavourable to a meeting between us'. As regards the military situation, however, he offered as his own, though not without modifying it, the suggestion I had originally made to him through General d'Astier to organize a reciprocal liaison: 'I think that, so far as you are concerned, it would be better to send me a qualified representative to help co-ordinate the French forces engaged in the struggle against the common enemy.'

Obviously I could not put up with this evasive attitude. No sooner had I received General Giraud's answer than I telegraphed my reply, on January 1st. In this second message I expressed satisfaction 'that a first exchange of views has taken place between us', but I declared that 'the unification of the Empire as a whole and of all French forces in contact with the resistance must not be postponed . . . My conviction,' I wrote, 'is that only a provisional central power, based on national unity in the war effort, can ensure the leadership of the French forces, the complete maintenance of French sovereignty and the fair representation of France abroad.' I then renewed my offer of a meeting and added: 'I am quite aware of the complexity of the situation in Algiers. But we can meet without hindrance either in Fort-Lamy, in Brazzaville or in Beirut, if you prefer it. I confidently await your reply.'

Even as I was drafting these appeals for unity, I strongly doubted whether the telegrams could have the right result. It was too much to hope that secret documents, minutely examined in Algiers under the surveillance of Anglo-American agents, would suffice to raise the great wind capable of sweeping away controversies and oppositions. I therefore wanted to speak directly to French public opinion, hoping as a last resort that its pressure would be irresistible. On January 2nd I made a public statement, calling upon the nation as my witness.

It so happened that a serious incident which had occurred in Algiers two days before reinforced my arguments. Giraud had arrested several dozen people, all of whom had aided the Americans during the landing and of whom several held positions in the police or the administration. The 'Civil and Military Commander-in-Chief' explained to the Allied newspapermen who flocked to his press conference that he was heading off a conspiracy aiming at new murders, particularly, he said, 'that of Mr Robert Murphy'. It seemed, in fact, that certain disillusioned people who had hitherto been connected with the activities of the American diplomat now wanted to settle accounts. I therefore had a splendid opportunity to emphasize in my statement the confusion reigning in French North Africa. I accounted for it chiefly by the exclusion of Fighting France and detailed the consequences: 'A difficult situation . . . for military operations; the fact that France is now deprived, at a crucial moment, of the trump card which the unity of her vast Empire would constitute . . . the stupefaction of the French people, overwhelmed in its misery . . .' I indicated the remedy: 'the establishment . . . of an extensive provisional central power, having for its foundation national unity, for its inspiration the spirit of combat and of liberation, and for its laws the laws of the Republic'. I also formally made known my offer to meet Giraud and my conviction that 'France's situation and that of the war in general' permitted no delay.

This declaration and the comment it aroused touched Washington on a sensitive point. It was disagreeable for the American Government to have the distance separating its doctrines from its practices so publicly measured. As soon as it was known that I was proposing an agreement with Giraud and that he was delaying its acceptance, everyone realized that his attitude was a direct reflection of Murphy's suggestions. How, therefore, could one avoid the conclusion that the Americans, while preaching unity, were doing everything they could to oppose it?

As a matter of fact, President Roosevelt, under cover of proclamations to the contrary, intended that French affairs should fall within his own sphere of influence, that the leading strings of our divisions should end up in his hands and that the public powers eventually emerging from this disorder should derive their authority from him. That is why he had backed both de Gaulle and Pétain at the start, then launched Giraud when a rupture with the Marshal was inevitable, then lowered the barrier in front of Darlan as soon as Giraud's failure was apparent, and finally put Giraud back after the Admiral's assassination. Now the President found it convenient to keep Fighting France and the system at Algiers separate, until the moment when he could himself impose on both parties the solution of his choice, which, furthermore, would certainly not be the formation of a true French Government.

I was not unaware of Roosevelt's intentions and I was therefore not surprised to learn that my declaration had been taken in bad part by Washington. On January 4th Under-Secretary of State Sumner Welles, receiving our delegate Tixier, informed him that his government disapproved of my invitations to Giraud and the publicity they had received, because in them I had given priority to political problems. When Tixier asked why this was troublesome, the American diplomat alleged once again the exigencies of the military situation, as if the agreement proposed by de Gaulle threatened Eisenhower's communications in North Africa!

I had had certain proof that the President had decided to intervene on the spot when, the day after Darlan's death, the Americans requested me to postpone my forthcoming trip to Washington. Yet Roosevelt himself, after the landing of his troops in Africa, had had me asked to visit him. Apparently everything had been arranged for this visit: I was to leave on December 27th, reaching Accra by plane and board there an American cruiser that would take me to the United States. Admiral Stark preceded me, having left London on December 20th to clear the routes. General Catroux, appointed to accompany me, reached Accra from Beirut on the 24th. But that day Darlan was assassinated, and at the same time the President's new policy of intervention became clear. I immediately recognized the switch, for on the 26th Mr Churchill, obviously acting on Mr Roosevelt's behalf, asked me whether, in view of the circumstances, I did not think it advisable to postpone my departure. The next day the American Government sent me a note to the same effect.

I was therefore convinced of the reasons why Giraud asked for a delay. His answer to my second message, which reached me on January 6th, completed my enlightenment. He agreed with me in principle as to a meeting in Algiers and no longer spoke of the un-favourable atmosphere created by Darlan's death. But invoking 'previous commitments', he said he could see no possibility of a

meeting before the end of January. I then replied, this time somewhat bluntly:

> I regret that your previous engagements should force you to
> postpone until the end of January the meeting I suggested to
> you on December 25th. I must tell you frankly that the National
> Committee and I have an altogether different sense of the
> urgency which the unification of the Empire and the combina-
> tion of its efforts with those of the national resistance demand.

But while I was expecting a reaction from Mr Roosevelt, it was
Mr Churchill who suddenly made a move. On January 17th Mr
Eden sent me a telegram which the Prime Minister had addressed
to me from Morocco. Mr Churchill asked me to join him there,
writing that he might be able to arrange a meeting between Giraud
and me in conditions of complete privacy and under the most
favourable auspices.

My reaction was unfavourable. Doubtless Mr Eden meant me to
understand that Mr Roosevelt was also in Morocco, where the Allied
leaders were holding a conference in order to determine their joint
plans. But why, then, had Churchill neglected to tell me so? Why
did he not assign any other goal to the invitation than a meeting
with Giraud? Why was this invitation sent to me in his name alone?
If I must go to the Anfa conference to enter a race wearing the
British colours while the Americans backed their own entry against
me, the resulting comedy would be indecent, not to say dangerous.
My reply to Churchill was negative. It was dispatched to him
at the same time as a message I addressed to Giraud: 'Remember
that I am still prepared to meet you on French territory, as one
Frenchman with another, when and where you choose.'

Two days later Eden sent me another telegram from Churchill
who, pained by my refusal—all the more so since he had had to
endure it under American eyes—urged me to reconsider the question. If I did not do so, he declared, public opinion would be very
severe towards me, and he himself would do nothing more to aid
Fighting France *vis-à-vis* the United States as long as I remained at
the head of the 'movement'. But this time he declared he was
authorized to inform me that the invitation to the conference had
been addressed to me by the President of the United States as well
as by himself, that questions concerning North Africa would be those

primarily under discussion, and that the President, like himself, would be happy if I would join in the talks on these subjects.

Without paying much attention to the threats in this message—which, after many like experiences, no longer affected me very strongly—I decided that the circumstances of the war and France's immediate situation did not allow me to refuse to meet the President of the United States and His Britannic Majesty's Prime Minister. It was in such terms that I finally drafted my acceptance, calling attention to the fact that the questions which were to be discussed were the result of an enterprise in which Fighting France was not taking part and which, it seemed, had 'led to a situation scarcely satisfactory for the Allies and . . . not at all so for France'.

Before dispatching my reply, I formally convoked the National Committee, which after an exhaustive study of the question agreed that I should go to Anfa, if only to see Roosevelt there in person. We purposely took some time over our deliberations, and afterwards I made no particular haste to begin my trip with my designated colleagues: Catroux, d'Argenlieu, Palewski (now chief of my personal staff) and Hettier de Boislambert (who had recently arrived from France after escaping from the Gannat prison, where Vichy had incarcerated him because of his role in the Dakar affair). At the last moment, bad weather conditions delayed our departure still further. We did not arrive at Fedala until January 22nd.

We were received in great secrecy by the American General Wilbur, whom I had previously known at the École Supérieure de Guerre and who greeted me on behalf of President Roosevelt, by Mr Codrington, who brought me Mr Churchill's compliments, and by Colonel de Linarès, sent by General Giraud to invite us to lunch. No troops presented arms, although American sentries cleared a wide space around us. Some American cars drove up next to the plane. I stepped into the first one. Wilbur, before getting in with me, dipped a rag in the mud and smeared all the windows. These precautions were taken in order to conceal the presence of General de Gaulle and his colleagues in Morocco.

At Anfa the Allies had requisitioned a group of villas, all of whose inhabitants had been billeted elsewhere; even the houses surrounding those we were to occupy had been emptied. A barbed-wire fence encircled the conference area. American sentries were posted both inside and outside this circle, and no one was allowed to enter or to leave. American soldiers were assigned to household tasks in every-one's lodgings. In short, it was captivity. I had no objection to the Anglo-American leaders imposing it on themselves, but the fact that they were applying it to me, and on territory under French sove-reignty, seemed a flagrant insult.

My first words to General Giraud were therefore something less than cordial. 'What is this?' I said to him. 'I ask you for an interview four times over and we have to meet in a barbed-wire encampment among foreign powers? Don't you realize how distasteful this is from a purely national point of view?'

Giraud, embarrassed, replied that he had not been free to act otherwise. I had in fact suspected as much, given the position in which he had put himself with the Americans.

Nevertheless, the meal was a cordial one. We discussed experiences we had shared, and at my request our host recounted his extra-ordinary escape from Koenigstein. But once we had left the table, General Giraud spoke of other matters. He insisted over and over again that he gave his attention solely to military matters and that he did not wish to concern himself with political questions. He said that he never listened to anyone who tried to interest him in a theory or a programme, and that he never read a newspaper or turned on the radio. Whether it was as a result of his convictions or in con-sequence of prior commitments, he declared himself on the side of the 'proconsuls'—Noguès 'indispensable to Morocco', Boisson 'who was able to defend his colony against every foreign attack, even that of Germany', Peyrouton, recently arrived to replace Chatel in the Algerian Government-General, and 'a man with a fist', and Bergeret, 'the one strategic mind of the lot'. He did not conceal the fact that apart from his determination—unquestionably resolute—to join battle with the Germans, he had nothing against the Vichy regime. He indicated, lastly, that the elementary, popular and revolutionary character of the resistance in France was incomprehensible if not reprehensible to him. After this first conversation, I left Giraud's villa for my own.

Later in the afternoon, keeping to my quarters with calculated reserve, I received a visit from Mr Macmillan, the British Secretary of State assigned to Algiers to co-ordinate British affairs in the western Mediterranean. Macmillan told me that, in co-operation with Murphy, he was doing his best to find a formula for unity

acceptable to both Giraud and myself which Roosevelt and Churchill could propose to us. Here indeed was the expected intervention.
I explained to Macmillan that a Giraud-de Gaulle *entente* could be
realized only between Frenchmen. However, at the British minister's
urgent request, I went to Churchill's quarters.

As soon as I met the Prime Minister, I told him in no uncertain
terms that I would never have come had I known I was to be surrounded, on French territory, by American bayonets.

'This is an occupied country!' he cried.

Both of us having relieved our feelings somewhat, we began to
discuss fundamental questions. The Prime Minister informed me
that he and the President had agreed on a solution to the problem
of the French Empire. General Giraud and General de Gaulle
would be established as joint presidents of a governing committee
on which they and all the other members would enjoy equal status
in every respect. But Giraud would exercise supreme military command, since the United States, having to equip the reunified French
Army, did not intend to deal with anyone else. 'Undoubtedly,' Mr
Churchill remarked, 'my friend General Georges could make your
group complete in the capacity of a third president.' As for Noguès,
Boisson, Peyrouton and Bergeret, they would retain their positions
and sit on the committee. 'The Americans have now accepted them
and want them to be trusted.'

I replied to Mr Churchill that this solution might appear adequate
at the quite respectable level of an American sergeant, but that I
did not dream he himself could take it seriously. As for me, I was
obliged to consider the remnants of French sovereignty. I had, as he
well knew, the highest consideration for him and for Roosevelt, but
could not recognize in any way their authority to deal with questions of sovereignty within the French Empire. The Allies had,
without me and against me, instituted the system now operating in
Algiers. Apparently finding it only half satisfactory, they were now
planning to submerge Fighting France in it too. But Fighting France
would not play their game; if it must disappear it preferred to do so
honourably.

Mr Churchill did not seem to grasp the ethical aspect of the problem. 'Look here,' he said. 'Consider my own government. When I
formed it recently, appointed as I was because I had fought so long
against the spirit of Munich, I included in it all our most notorious

Munich partisans. Well, they followed along so well that today you can't tell them from the rest.'

'To speak in that way,' I replied, 'you must have lost sight of what has happened to France. For my part, I am not a politician trying to make up a cabinet and find a majority in Parliament.'

The Prime Minister urged me nevertheless to reconsider the project he had just explained to me. 'Tonight,' he added, 'you will confer with the President of the United States, and you will see that we are both firmly resolved on this matter.'

He accompanied me as far as the garden gate, where a British sentry presented arms. 'Please observe,' he remarked, 'that if there are American sentries here, there are also British soldiers side by side who are co-operating with them.'

A little later, Mr Roosevelt sent someone to arrange our meeting, to which I went late that evening. We spent an hour together sitting on the same couch, in a large room of the villa where he was quartered. Although my host pretended to be alone with me, I noticed shadows at the rear of the balcony and saw curtains moving in the corners. I learned later that Mr Harry Hopkins and several secretaries were listening secretly and that armed police were guarding the President. Because of these shadowy presences, the atmosphere of our first discussion was a strange one. That evening, as on every occasion when I saw him afterwards, Roosevelt showed himself eager to reach a meeting of minds, using charm rather than reason to convince me, but committed once and for all to the decisions he had made.

Franklin Roosevelt was governed by the loftiest ambitions. His intelligence, his knowledge and his audacity gave him the ability, the powerful state, whose leader he was, afforded him the means and the war offered him the occasion to realize them. If the great nation he directed had long been inclined to isolate itself from distant enterprises and to mistrust a Europe ceaselessly torn by wars and revolutions, a kind of messianic impulse now swelled the American spirit and oriented it towards vast undertakings. The United States, delighting in her resources, feeling that she no longer had within herself sufficient scope for her energies and wishing to help those who were in misery or bondage anywhere, yielded in her turn to that taste for intervention which concealed the instinct for domination. It was precisely this tendency that President Roosevelt espoused. He had

therefore done everything to engage his country in the world conflict. He was now fulfilling his destiny, impelled as he was by a secret
premonition of death.

But from the moment America entered the war, Roosevelt meant
the peace to be an American peace, convinced that he must be the
one to dictate its structure, that the states which had been overrun
should be subject to his judgment and that France in particular
should recognize him as her saviour and arbiter. The fact that France
was reviving in the heat of battle, not as fragmentary and thereby
pliant resistance, but as a sovereign and independent nation,
thwarted his intentions. He had no sympathy with me politically—
especially since he was criticized unendingly by public opinion in
his own country. It was America that conferred his power upon him,
but she could also deprive him of that power. During the course of
the war Roosevelt twice had to submit to elections, and during the
intervals was harassed by the press, the radio and every sort of special
interest. Tireless at charming others, but hampered deep within
himself by the painful disease against which he struggled so valiantly,
Roosevelt was sensitive to partisan reproaches and gibes. Yet it was
precisely his policy in regard to General de Gaulle that aroused the
fiercest controversies in America. It must be added that like any star
performer he was touchy as to the roles that fell to other actors. In
short, beneath his patrician mask of courtesy, Roosevelt looked at
me without goodwill.

That evening we set to in earnest, but by mutual agreement we
maintained a certain vagueness on the question of France. He
sketched lightly the same figure that Churchill had outlined so
heavily and gently allowed me to understand that such a solution
would be adopted in the end because he himself had decided upon it.
I pointed out as delicately that the national will had already made
its choice and that, sooner or later, the authority established in the
Empire and ultimately in metropolitan France would be the one
France chose for herself. Nevertheless we took care not to meet head
on, realizing that the clash would lead to nothing and that for the
sake of the future we each had much to gain by getting along together.

The following day I received General Giraud. We spoke together
alone quite openly. 'What do you mean to do?' I asked him.

He explained his plan which was, on the whole, that of Roosevelt
and Churchill. There would be three of us at the top: he first of all,

myself second and General Georges, whom the British would send for from France, third. So that we might enjoy equal status, I was to be named General of the Army! But Giraud would keep the military control entirely for himself, he would be Commander-in-Chief of the French forces, including those of Free France and the armed elements of the resistance, and in this capacity he would be subordinate only to Eisenhower. The 'proconsuls' would remain at their posts, only Bergeret might be discarded. An 'Imperial Council', including Noguès, Boisson and Peyrouton, to whom Catroux and perhaps Eboué might be added, as well as several 'secretaries', would co-ordinate the administration of the Empire, but without exercising any political action.

I regarded Giraud's proposal as unacceptable. 'What you suggest,' I told him, 'boils down to your having the real power under Roosevelt's protection while establishing beside you a more or less impressive collection of supernumeraries. Actually it is the Consulate at the mercy of foreign powers. But Bonaparte as First Consul, during the war and afterwards, enjoyed the virtually unanimous approval of the people. What kind of plebiscite are you planning? If you hold one, will it be in your favour? Besides Bonaparte came forward as a leader who had showered France with great victories and conquered vast provinces. I hope with all my heart that you will do as much, but at the moment what are your triumphs? I should add that the First Consul excelled in the business of legislation and administration. Are you really skilled in such matters? Furthermore, you cannot fail to know that in France public opinion will from now on condemn Vichy, yet it is primarily from Darlan and then from Noguès, Boisson, Chatel and Bergeret that you derive your powers. It is in the Marshal's name that you have assumed them. Everyone knows of your letter to Pétain in which you gave your word that you would never act against his policies. Do you think that under these conditions you can gain even an elementary support from the French people, without which a government is either an illusion or indeed the target of a revolution? Lastly, how will you safeguard French interests when the artificiality of your power makes you dependent on the Anglo-American authorities?'

General Giraud declared once more that these were political matters and he had no desire to concern himself with such things. For him the question was simply to re-create the French Army and he had full confidence in our American allies. 'I have just signed an agreement with President Roosevelt,' he said, 'wherein the United States is committed to equip as many units as I can draw up. I expect to have a dozen divisions at my disposal within six months. Will you have even half as many in the same time? And who will give you weapons for them?'

'The question is not one of a rivalry between us in fighting strength,' I replied. 'The troops now in North Africa belong to France, they are not yours. You will soon find this out for yourself if we fail to reach an agreement. The problem is one of French unity within the Empire and within metropolitan France and calls for the institution of a central authority that answers these needs. Once this is done, the various forces will be united and employed with no difficulty. It so happens that Fighting France symbolizes resistance to the enemy, the upholding of the Republic and the revival of the nation, and thus it is to Fighting France that popular feeling naturally turns when the illusion that was Vichy is on the point of dissolution. However, many people esteem you highly as a military leader and I consider you in this way as a French asset I should be extremely unwilling to lose. The common-sense solution therefore would be the following: de Gaulle should form at Algiers a wartime government which at the right moment will become that of the Republic, while Giraud receives from this government the command of the army of liberation. If necessary, should a transition seem mandatory, we should represent the central authority together. But from the start this central authority must condemn Vichy and proclaim that the armistice was always null and void. It must identify itself with the Republic and, in the eyes of the world, with the independence of France.'

General Giraud held to his point of view, but realizing that he was stubborn rather than actually convinced, I continued to hope that the pressure of events would ultimately lead him to change his mind. Meanwhile problems of national interest required concerted solutions. This was the case as regards military action, finances, exchange, currency, the fate of Tunisia and of Indo China, the allegiance of the Antilles and French Guiana and of the Alexandria fleet. We therefore agreed to establish a reciprocal liaison. I announced my intention to send a mission to North Africa with General Catroux at its head; to this Giraud immediately agreed, after which he and his staff lunched at our table. Catroux, d'Argenlieu, Palewski and Boislambert, as well as Linarès, Beaufré and Poniatowski, informed by their contacts, learned without surprise though not without disappointment that no agreement had been reached. The luncheon was a gloomy one.

Mr Robert Murphy later paid me a visit. He seemed convinced that everything would turn out according to the plans he had drawn up. When I expressed my doubts and asked him what he thought the public reaction would be in Morocco and Algeria when it was learned that no agreement had been reached at Anfa, he answered that many would be satisfied and even relieved. 'North Africa,' he added, 'is not ten per cent Gaullist.' He confirmed the fact that President Roosevelt and Mr Churchill had just signed an agreement with General Giraud providing for certain deliveries of weapons and supplies to North Africa—which I approved unreservedly—but, on the other hand, according the 'Civil and Military Commander-in-Chief' a recognition that, until now, had been neither formulated by the United States nor accepted by Great Britain. The agreement specified:

> In the interests of the French people, and in order to safeguard the past, present and future of France, the President of the United States and the Prime Minister of Great Britain recognize that the French Commander-in-Chief, whose headquarters are at Algiers, has the right and the duty to act as director of the French military, economic and financial interests which are or will be associated with the liberation movement now established in North Africa and in French West Africa. They pledge themselves to aid him in this task by every means in their power.

Thus America and England, appointing themselves arbiters of the interests of France, were dealing with General Giraud only, and he, under pretext of not playing politics, accepted their authority. I learned that Mr Churchill had of his own accord, while talking with Giraud the day before, written on a corner of the table that the pound sterling would be worth two hundred and fifty French francs in North Africa. According to the agreements we had made with London, it was worth only one hundred and seventy-six francs. I also learned that President Roosevelt had entertained the Sultan of

Morocco at dinner and had spoken to him in terms unsuitable to the ruler of a French protectorate, without Giraud finding anything in this to criticize.

In the evening came Mr Harold Macmillan with a tirade of concern about the future of Fighting France. Lastly, General Wilbur informed me that the conference would be over within twenty-four hours and delivered messages which the French officers on duty in Casablanca had asked him to transmit to me. I asked him to inform his superiors how strange it seemed to me that during the height of the Battle of North Africa, in which the French Army—including Free French forces—was participating in strength, none of the Allied military authorities assembled for the Anfa conference had considered it pertinent to say the least word to me either about plans or operations.

Early the next day Macmillan and Murphy sent me a communiqué drawn up during the night by Roosevelt and Churchill which the latter asked Generals de Gaulle and Giraud to authorize and make public. Giraud had already agreed to do so. According to this Anglo-American text, which was now to become French, the two generals would proclaim themselves in agreement 'with the principles of the Allied Nations' and announce their intention of forming a joint committee to administer the French Empire during the war. Certainly the formula was too vague to commit us to much, but it had the triple disadvantage of being dictated by the Allies, of implying that I renounced whatever was not merely the administration of the Empire, and lastly of giving the impression that an agreement had been reached when in reality no such thing had happened. After finding out the opinion—unanimously negative —of all four of my colleagues, I informed the messengers that enlargement of French national authority could not be the result of the intervention of a foreign power, no matter how high and how friendly. Nevertheless, I agreed to see the President and the Prime Minister before the conference was concluded the next afternoon.

My meeting with Mr Churchill was characterized by great bitterness on his side. Of all our encounters during the war, this was the most ungracious. The Prime Minister showered me with bitter reproaches in which I could see nothing but an alibi for his own embarrassment. He declared that on his return to London he would publicly accuse me of having obstructed the agreement, would rouse public opinion in his country against me personally and would appeal to the people of France. I confined myself to replying that my friendship for him and my attachment to our alliance with Britain caused me to deplore such an attitude on his part. In order to satisfy America at any cost, he was espousing a cause unacceptable to France, disquieting to Europe and regrettable for England.

I then went to see Roosevelt. My reception at his hands was a skilful one—that is, kind and sorrowful. The President expressed his disappointment that French support should remain uncertain and that he had not been able to prevail upon me to accept even the text of a communiqué. 'In human affairs,' he said, 'the public must be offered a drama. The news of your meeting with General Giraud in the midst of a conference in which both Churchill and I were taking part, if this news were to be accompanied by a joint declaration by the French leaders—even if it concerned only a theoretical agreement—would produce the dramatic effect we need.'

'Let me handle it,' I replied. 'There will be a communiqué, even though it cannot be yours.'

Thereupon I presented my colleagues to the President and he introduced me to his. Then Mr Churchill, General Giraud and their suites came in, followed by a crowd of military leaders and Allied officials. While they were all gathering round the President, Churchill loudly reiterated his diatribe against me with the evident intention of flattering Roosevelt's disappointed vanity. The latter affected to pay no attention, adopting instead the kindest manner in order to make me a last request on which he had set his heart.

'Will you at least agree,' he said, 'to being photographed beside me and the British Prime Minister, along with General Giraud?'

'Of course,' I answered, 'for I have the highest regard for this great soldier.'

'Will you go so far as to shake General Giraud's hand before the camera?' the President cried.

My answer, in English, was, 'I shall do that for you.'

Then Mr Roosevelt, delighted, had himself carried into the garden where four chairs had been prepared beforehand, with innumerable cameras trained on them and several rows of reporters lined up with their pencils poised. The four actors put on their smiles. The gestures agreed upon were made. Everything went off perfectly! America would be satisfied, on such evidence, that the French question had found its *deus ex machina* in the person of the President.

Before leaving Anfa, I drafted a short communiqué which I submitted to Giraud, naturally without letting the Allies get wind of it. It began, 'We have seen each other. We have spoken together', and, going on to affirm our faith in the victory of France and in the triumph of human liberties, announced the establishment of a permanent liaison between us. Giraud signed. On his request I substituted 'human liberties' for the expression 'democratic principles' which I had written originally.

The weeks that followed were painful. I had thought that after Anfa I would go to Libya, where our troops were fighting. But the Allies opposed this intention. Alleging technical difficulties, they permitted us no other means of leaving the Anfa enclosure than a British plane flying directly to London. We returned on January 26th. During a press conference on February 9th, I made clear that what had actually happened at Anfa bore little resemblance to what the Anglo-American sources had publicized. I emphasized strongly the real motives of the American officials and opinion-mongers who reproached Fighting France for 'playing politics' and thereby hoped to keep France from having any of her own. Subsequently, when once more I voiced my intention of going to the Middle East, the British Government informed me on March 3rd, this time in writing, that it was refusing me the means to do so.

The contest of ill-will in which London and Washington were engaged found its widespread echo in the press and on the radio. With a few noble exceptions, the newspapers and commentators in America and even in Great Britain seemed to entertain no doubt that French unity must be centred around Giraud. Almost everything that one could find to read or to hear spread the severest possible judgments about me. 'Deplorable pride', said some, or else 'frustrated ambition'. Many were of the opinion that I was a candidate for dictatorship and that my entourage, riddled with fascists and felons, was encouraging me to establish an absolute personal power in France after the liberation. General Giraud, on the other hand, was a soldier with no political pretensions or, for that matter, intentions, and the bulwark of democracy. The French must rely on Roosevelt and Churchill to prevent me from enslaving them.

Of course those among the French emigrants who had not joined me and who because of that depended on foreign powers, espoused and inspired this point of view. In America the newspaper

Pour la Victoire, in England the daily *France*, the *Agence Française Indépendante*, the magazine *La France Libre* and even the majority of the staff of 'Les Français Parlent aux Français' at the BBC openly declared themselves for Giraud. On the other hand, the 'Gaullist' organs of expression, such as Henry Torrès' *La Voix de la France* in New York, François Quillici's *La Marseillaise* in London, the voice of Maurice Schumann on the British radio and the chief station of Fighting France at Brazzaville, hailed our decision.

One must admit that if the Allies pelted us with abuse, in French Africa the evidences of approval kept multiplying. The Combat movement in which the 'Gaullists' gathered was swelled with new members; René Capitant came to London to report this to me. Those of Leclerc's units that made contact with the Sahara troops near Gadàmes received an enthusiastic welcome and numerous requests to be allowed to join them. In Niger, in Dahomey, in Togo, in Guinea, in the Ivory Coast, in Upper Volta, our envoys now found the friendliest reception. But it was among the sailors that the popular choice made itself most felt. Many of the crews from warships and merchant vessels who reached American or British ports from Morocco, West Africa or Algeria took advantage of the opportunity to sign up at the recruiting offices of Fighting France. Thus the *Richelieu*, sailing from Dakar to New York to be reconditioned, saw three hundred sailors abandon her in order to serve on ships of the Free French Navy. The destroyer *Fantasque*, the tanker *Wyoming*, the cargo ship *Lot*, also docking in America, were emptied in the same manner. In the Scottish port of Greenock the crews of the transport vessels *Eridan*, *Ville d'Oran*, *Champollion*, *Groix*, *Meonia* and *Jamaïque* rallied to General de Gaulle and forced their vessels to fly the Cross of Lorraine.

Such incidents as these exasperated Washington—all the more since there were many indications that once the Italo-German army still separating Giraud's troops from Leclerc's and Larminat's men in Tunisia was cut down, an irresistible current would sweep many military units of North Africa into the Free French forces. Therefore the Americans, feeling that the end of the North African campaign would provoke a 'Gaullist' tidal wave, made a great effort to bring us to some compromise.

They did so with a heavy hand. In the United States some of the sailors who had left their ships to join Fighting France were arrested and imprisoned. Our delegate, Adrien Tixier, and Admiral Gayral, chief of our naval mission, were assailed by comminatory proceedings from the State Department and the Navy. In Great Britain, while the English were content to regret the matter, the Americans threatened the French crews from Africa who asked to join me. The ship *Jamaïque*, docked at Greenock, was actually occupied by a detachment of American Marines. At Carlton Gardens, Admiral Stark, distressed at having to oppose a cause to which his mind and his heart were both attached, but bound by his instructions, made importunate complaints to d'Auboyneau, our Naval Commissioner, to Diethelm, whose responsibilities included the merchant marine, and occasionally to me. The United States press and radio publicized official and semi-official declarations accusing General de Gaulle of sabotaging the war effort by preventing French ships from carrying out their missions.

I had, indeed, given orders that the volunteers should be incorporated, considering their choice a desirable one so long as the Algiers organization functioned without us. I believed that it was in accord with the interest of the service to use these men where they preferred to be, rather than to press them into a framework where they would exist in a state of secret revolt and I thought, too, that their demonstration would enlighten worldwide public opinion. I invited Algiers, through Admiral Fénard, the chief of its naval mission in America, to man the emptied warships with its own men in place of those who were changing command. As a matter of fact, there was no shortage of men in North Africa, since many ships had been scuttled during the Allied landing. As for merchant vessels, I intended to order them to return, under the Cross of Lorraine, to their Algerian or Moroccan bases, provided that their adherence to the Free French was accepted as fact. Receiving Admiral Stark on March 11th, I notified him of these arrangements, which in fact had already been carried out.

The United States, incidentally, offered us honey along with its vinegar. On February 22nd Sumner Welles wrote to Tixier that Roosevelt hoped once again to receive me in Washington. Again I replied that I was ready to leave, and again the invitation was not forthcoming. This project, vanishing as soon as it appeared, seemed to play a sort of fantastic sea-serpent role in White House policy.

But the uproar abroad did not deter us from seeking to learn the opinions of the French nation. There had not been the shadow of a doubt on this point since the day when the enemy, occupying the whole of the country, completely enslaved Vichy. On November 17th Laval, so that he could operate freely, forced Péta n to give him, on his return from the Fuehrer's headquarters, the right to promulgate all laws and decrees over his own signature alone. During the course of the winter the persecution of the Jews redoubled, despite public indignation. The protests of bishops—such as Monsignor Saliège in Toulouse and Cardinal Gerlier in Lyon—and the condemnation of Pastor Boegner, president of the French Protestant Federation, went unheard. On January 30th, 1943, the militia was created, and was put into active service hunting down patriots. Darnand, already a member of the German police, was its secretary-general. On February 16th the compulsory labour service was instituted to provide the 'government' with means of furnishing the enemy the unlimited manpower he required. On April 29th Hitler, receiving Laval again, drew up supplementary collaboration measures with him. If part of the population, either from distress or pity, condoned the Marshal, the mind of every Frenchman—with the exception of a few fanatics—condemned the policies pursued in his name. The nation's leading school of thought was now the resistance, and the resistance was identified with Fighting France.

Hence comings and goings between metropolitan France and London went on increasing. The offices in Carlton Gardens, the house in Duke Street where the BCRA[1] was working, and various private houses in the city and suburbs witnessed the secret visits of those whom planes, vedette boats and trawlers had fetched from France and those who were beginning to be taken back there. During the first four months of 1943, while the African crisis was reaching its peak, our 'air and naval operations service' transported in one direction or the other hundreds of emissaries and delegates. Our central office was expanded by many well-known people, among them René Massigli, whom I appointed National Commissioner of Foreign Affairs on February 5th; General of the Army Beynet, who was to direct our military mission in Washington; General de Lavalade, soon appointed commander of the troops in the Levant; General Vautrin, who was sent to Libya as chief of staff of the

[1] *Bureau Central de Renseignements et d'Action*—Central Intelligence and Operations Office—TR.

Larminat Group and who was to be killed in action at this post;
Jules Moch, who immediately took up his service in the Navy;
Fernand Grenier, who was brought over by Rémy at the Communists' request and who, under Soustelle, worked on propaganda
showing every trace of the most rigorous 'Gaullism'; Pierre Viénot,
an intelligent, sensitive idealist whom I planned to make the French
ambassador to England when the National Committee was established in Algiers, and who was to die at his post; André Maroselli,
placed in charge of our prisoner-of-war relief organization which
managed to send more than a million packages every month;
Georges Buisson and Marcel Poimbœuf, delegated respectively by
the CGT and the Christian Workers group and forming, with Albert
Guigui, who had preceded them, and Henri Hauck, my colleague
from the early days, an active trades union representation. The well-
known Members of Parliament, Gouin, Queuille, Farjon, Hymans
and, shortly after, Jacquinot, Auriol, Le Troquer and Louis Marin,
as soon as they arrived, hastened to declare on the radio and in the
press, and to repeat to the Allied politicians, diplomats and journalists, what elsewhere Jeanneney, Herriot, Blum, Mandel, Paul-
Boncour and others were affirming—namely, that no government
except General de Gaulle's would be conceivable after the liberation.

In France itself the resistance, in proportion as its activities and its
sufferings increased, cemented its unity. Moreover, the occupation
of the so-called 'free' zone effaced certain differences and encouraged
concentration. At the end of 1942 I had been able to make the
acquaintance of the leaders of several movements. Now I saw others,
who came between one full moon and the next, emerging suddenly
from the haze of feverishness, guile and anguish in which they concealed their weapons, their raids, their printing presses, their letter
boxes, and returning just as suddenly. Among those of note who
crossed over during this period were Cavaillès, a philosopher whose
nature inclined him towards prudence but whose hatred of oppression impelled him to the greatest feats of audacity, until he suffered
torture and death for France; Daniel Mayer, the methodical artisan
of the Socialist Action movement; the modest and intrepid Jean-
Pierre Lévy, and Saillant, a splendid trade unionist sent by Léon
Jouhaux. Several, such as Pineau and Sermoy-Simon, were visiting
us for the second time. During the same period, our own delegates
went everywhere in France: Rémy, a magnificent practical organi-

zer, animating and directing underground activity as if it were a
huge, calculated sport, operated chiefly in Paris and in the west;
Bingen focused his activity on the Midi; Manuel inspected our local
intelligence networks and communications. In January Brossolette,
and a month later Passy-Dewavrin, reached France. A young British
officer, Yeo Thomas, accompanied the chief of the BCRA on our
invitation in order to furnish the London cabinet with direct information. Passy and Brossolette, acting together, were to make contact with the various organizations, to persuade those of the north
to set up a genuine co-ordination among themselves as an example
to those of the south, and to prepare the union of both by means of
a common council and a single military system.

In February Jean Moulin, my delegate in metropolitan France,
arrived, and General Delestraint, commander of the secret army. I
met the former again, impressive now in conviction and authority
alike, conscious that his days were numbered but determined to
accomplish his task of unification before their end. I instructed the
latter, who found himself invested with a mission for which, in many
respects, his career had not prepared him, but which he undertook
with the steadfastness of a soldier who is surprised by nothing in the
line of duty.

I directed Moulin, who had prepared the way for some time, to
form the National Council of Resistance without further delay. It
was to include representatives of all the movements in both zones, of
all the political parties and of the two trade union movements. The
orders I gave him regulated this arrangement, defined the council's
role and specified the nature of the relations linking it to the National
Committee. Jean Moulin himself was to head the new body. I
appointed him a member of the French National Committee and
awarded him the Cross of the Liberation during a most moving
ceremony in my house at Hampstead. Delestraint, during his stay,
was able to work usefully with the Allied leaders, in particular with
General Brooke, General Ismay and Admiral Stark, who recognized
him as one of their peers. Thus the operations of the secret army
during the landing in France would be linked as closely as possible
to the plans of the Allied command. The instructions which General
Delestraint received from me established his authority as that of an
inspector-general before the great battle began, and ultimately as
that of an army commander when it was necessary to co-ordinate

operations within the nation with those from without. But a few months after his return to France this man of honour was arrested by the enemy, deported and, at the end, hypocritically struck down at the gates of a concentration camp, offering his country the life which he had long since dedicated to it. Moulin and Delestraint left on March 24th for battle and for death.

All these signs of the progress French unity was making at home were to help that of the Empire. The National Committee immediately took the initiative in the negotiations with Algiers. Eight days after our return from Anfa, General Catroux returned to North Africa, where he saw many people. Having made it clear that our goal was mutual understanding and that the undesirables whose elimination we sought could be counted on the fingers of both hands, he then returned temporarily to Beirut, while Marchal, Charbonnières, Pechkoff, Pélabon and others installed our liaison mission at Algiers. Shortly afterwards, General Bouscat arrived in London as General Giraud's delegate to me. The exchanges of outlook were beginning.

On February 23rd the National Committee drew up the terms of a memorandum addressed to the 'Civil and Military Commander-in-Chief' specifying the conditions indispensable to unity. These conditions were to regard the 1940 armistices as having always been null and void, to admit the political and moral impossibility of retaining certain men in the positions of command they now occupied and to re-establish republican law in North Africa. Once these principles were accepted by the Giraud organization, a central power having all the prerogatives of a government must be formed, in order that France would have at its disposal in the war a single responsible authority and a single representation. Further, a consultative assembly of the resistance must be created to furnish as wide an expression as possible of the public opinion of the 'suffering and militant' nation. Thus we formulated our position once again. The memorandum was sent to Giraud on February 26th and published on March 12th.

It was henceforth impossible for the Algiers system to adopt a different attitude publicly. For, independently of the happenings in France, in Africa things were going our way at an accelerated rhythm. Among most people the fundamental feeling prevailed that de Gaulle had won, since Vichy had lost. In influential circles the artificial character of the 'Civil and Military Commander-in-Chief's' powers and his dependence on the Americans inspired a growing uneasiness. Furthermore, under the pressure of the Anglo-American missions, themselves scrutinized by the journalists and legislators of their own countries, political censure of our action and attitude was falling off. The scales fell from many eyes. The news from France, the statements made by those whom the occupation of the former 'free zone' or the desire to fight, now brought to North Africa, the battle raging in Tunisia—all gave the final lie to the anti-Gaullist nonsense which the authorities had professed for so long.

Some of the men around General Giraud had enough political sense to try to channel this current. M. Jean Monnet was the instigator of this development. In February he had left Washington for Algiers in order to give Giraud the benefit of his economic and administrative abilities and his American connections. The National Committee's memorandum made him realize that he must rapidly transform the features of the 'Civil and Military High Command'. On this point M. Monnet soon found himself in harmony with the adroitness of Mr Murphy and the shrewdness of Mr Macmillan. The month of March was therefore filled with democratic manifestations from Giraud.

On the 4th a new statute of the *Légion des Combattants* was decreed in Algiers. On the 5th Giraud declared on the radio 'France has no racial prejudices'. On the 8th he confiscated the *Journal Officiel d'Afrique du Nord* of the day before, which, like the numbers preceding it, promulgated Marshal Pétain's decrees picked up by radio. On the 14th, during an assembly of Alsatians and Lorrainers, Giraud read out a speech condemning Vichy and paying homage to the Republic. On the 15th he wrote to General Catroux, 'I insisted on explaining yesterday the principles guiding my conduct. There remains therefore no equivocation between us . . . I am ready to receive General de Gaulle in order to give a concrete form to this union. I ask you to invite him.' On March 18th Giraud signed a series of ordinances abolishing Vichy legislation in many areas.

The following day we heard Churchill and Cordell Hull, who had not seemed to notice the French National Committee's memorandum when it appeared, declare that their respective governments gave their complete support to the principles General Giraud had enunciated. On the 19th General Noguès and on the 21st Governor-

D

General Boisson made public their full agreement with 'the republican actions and words of the Civil and Military Commander-in-
Chief'. Then General Bergeret, M. Rigault and M. Lemaigre-
Dubreuil resigned from their posts. As these actions occurred, most
American and English newspapers and commentators raised a
chorus of eulogies and urged Fighting France to join with Giraud,
to whom, they declared, the 'Gaullists' could no longer raise any
valid objection.

Meanwhile taking advantage of Giraud's speech of March 14th
and of the message he had asked Catroux to send me, the National
Committee announced that 'the declarations made in Algiers show,
in many respects, a great progress towards the doctrine of Fighting
France, as it has been upheld since June 1940 and again expressed
by the memorandum of February 23rd'. I myself let General Giraud
know that I had received his message with pleasure and that I expected to be able to go to North Africa in the near future. I announced this news on the radio, invoking national union in such a
way and in such a tone that those listening knew that French unity
had not changed its champion, nor the latter his principles. I telegraphed General Eisenhower that I would be pleased to see him
upon my arrival in Algiers, to which he replied that he would be
delighted. I requested that when the time came the British Government should put a plane at my disposal. But I also declared quite
openly that I was adhering strictly to my well-known position and
that before leaving I would wait until the National Committee had
received a satisfactory reply from Algiers to the February 23rd
memorandum. It was then that the supreme effort to cut us down
was launched.

Mr Macmillan opened fire. On March 17th in Algiers he summoned Guy de Charbonnières, in the absence of General Catroux.
'Now that the Civil and Military Commander-in-Chief has publicly allied himself with the principles Fighting France insists on,' he
said, 'there is nothing to prevent the union from being constituted
around General Giraud.' When Charbonnières showed he had
several reservations, the British Secretary of State gave vent to a
violent outburst of irritation. 'If General de Gaulle refuses the hand
held out to him today,' he exclaimed, 'be assured that America and
Great Britain will abandon him altogether, and then he will be
nothing.' Although Mr Macmillan showed more moderation later in

the discussion, his behaviour could not be considered as anything but a first assault.

The next was conducted by Archbishop Spellman of New York. He arrived from Algiers and asked to see me on a special mission from the President of the United States. I met the archbishop-ambassador on March 23rd. This eminently devout prelate approached the problems of this world with an evident concern to serve the cause of God alone. But even the greatest piety could not keep *les affaires* from being *les affaires*. Therefore it was with particular urgency that the Archbishop of New York gave me counsel out of his wisdom.

'Liberty, equality, charity'—this, according to him, was the motto that most suitably should inspire my conduct. 'Liberty' meant that I should refrain from stipulating conditions for Fighting France's union with General Giraud, 'equality' that I must join the triumvirate mentioned to me at Anfa, 'charity' that pardon was called for in the case of the men in office in Algiers, Rabat and Dakar. 'Think,' Monsignor Spellman reminded me, 'what a misfortune it would be for you if someone were to refuse you the benefit of a formula you have refused others! Can you see yourself condemned to remain in England and officially kept out of action while France is liberated without you?'

I replied to the archbishop that in that case there would be no such thing as the liberation of France, since victory would consist in the imposition upon my country of an authority chosen by the Anglo-American powers in place of the one that had ruled it by favour of the Germans. One could be sure beforehand that the French people would then turn to a third liberator with whom the Western Allies would have no reason to be pleased. It would be much better not to interfere with the national will—which, I told the archbishop in conclusion, was in the process of revealing itself despite every obstacle. I cited as examples the shift of opinion in North Africa, the attitude of the sailors and, above all, the news from France. All things considered, Monsignor Spellman did not seem annoyed by this. Indeed, I must say that later I had evidence that I had won his sympathy during our conversation.

Mr Churchill intervened next. At his request, I went to see him on April 2nd, accompanied by Massigli. The Prime Minister, with the help of Sir Alexander Cadogan, explained that my arrival in Algiers would present serious inconveniences if the *entente* between Giraud and myself were not achieved beforehand. For Mr Churchill the *entente* signified, of course, the acceptance of the conditions that I had been informed of at Anfa. He pointed out the disagreeable consequences that my presence in North Africa would have unless agreement could be reached on this basis, from the point of view of public order and the military situation. The plane I had asked for was ready, the Prime Minister affirmed, but would it not be better to wait until Mr Eden, then on a trip to the United States, had returned and until General Catroux, in Algiers only a week, could exercise his influence? Wanting Mr Churchill to show his hand, I made public upon leaving him that I was still planning to fly to Algiers without accepting any conditions beforehand. The Prime Minister then announced that General Eisenhower asked me to postpone my trip. But I readily established the fact that Eisenhower had requested nothing of the kind, which forced Churchill to acknowledge publicly that the initiative for such behaviour had been entirely his own and that it was indeed he who opposed my departure.

On April 6th I saw first Mr Eden and then Mr Winant, both of whom were just back from Washington. They painted a lurid picture, evidently prepared beforehand, of the anger my obstinacy had aroused in America, and of all that France would fail to gain by it. They then described, in contrast, the advantages which the goodwill of the Allies would assure her if I consented to subordinate Fighting France to General Giraud.

'I should have done so with all my heart,' I told them, 'had Giraud been in command of North Africa on June 18th, 1940, and had he continued the war by repudiating Pétain's and Weygand's injunctions. But today the facts remain. The French nation is aware of them.'

At the very moment I was resisting Allied pressure, I had to endure that of several of my colleagues as well. Some, influenced by the anxiety the London and Washington *parti pris* inspired in them, by the insinuating accusations to which they were subjected and lastly by their tremendous desire to see the union effected at whatever cost, ended by yielding. In the bosom of the National Committee, those who felt this way did not conceal it. Even General Catroux, who in Algiers was inevitably plunged into the milieu of the men in office and of the Murphy and Macmillan parties, proposed in his dispatches that we let Giraud have political preponderance and the military command. Without mistaking these intentions, I did not follow such advice. For behind the trees which these immediate difficulties constituted for us was the forest—that is, the French nation.

And indeed it was the nation's future that was at stake. The entire National Committee recognized the fact when, on April 10th, it received Giraud's answer to the February 23rd memorandum, which Catroux brought from Algiers. This document did make an outward show of attachment to high principles. But its suggested application really consisted in keeping France from having a government until the end of the war and in enabling the authority of the Commander-in-Chief—that is, the power of the Allies—to be exercised without limits.

In fact it was proposed again that we establish at Algiers only a Council of Overseas Territories which would include Giraud, de Gaulle, the Residents-General and Governors-General and a number of Commissioners with certain special tasks. The said council would be denied any political power whatever. It would play a role of administrative co-ordination but not of national leadership. As for the Commander-in-Chief, General Giraud, he would be subordinate to the inter-Allied command and, in his military functions, would be answerable to no French authority. Further, it would depend on him, as the liberation permitted and under cover of the state of siege, to assure public order and to appoint officials throughout the entire territory of metropolitan France. Thus, without a genuine central French authority, the essentials of power would be at the discretion of a military chief dependent on a foreign general. This strange apparatus was to operate as long as the war lasted. After that, far from proceeding at once to a national plebiscite, there were plans to invoke a law dating back to 1872, the so-called Tréveneuc Law, which provided that in the absence of a National Assembly it devolved upon the general councils to provide an administration and appoint a government. All in all, according to the memorandum signed by General Giraud, everything would continue as if France no longer existed as a state, at least until victory. Such was indeed Roosevelt's intention.

The effect of this document was to restore the unanimity of our London committee. Every member saw clearly where the national course lay. At the session of April 15th only one motion was required to determine the text of the note General Catroux was to take to Algiers. The note was simple and firm. Acknowledging what was satisfactory in General Giraud's declaration of principles, the committee reiterated the conditions necessary for their application: the formation of an effective power exercising its authority over all territories that were or would be liberated, particularly that of metropolitan France, and having under its command all French forces without exception; the subordination to this power of all Residents-General and Governors-General, and, above all, of the Commander-in-Chief; the removal of the men who had taken a personal responsibility in the capitulation and in the collaboration with the enemy. In order to constitute a governmental organ, it was, we repeated, indispensable that the president and several members of the National Committee should go to North Africa without any conditions being imposed upon them. Further, in order to cut short the rumours that the press was spreading on the subject of our differences, all the members of the committee issued a formal statement that they were more than ever of one mind with General de Gaulle.

Since Fighting France remained unshakeable, the obstinacy with which the Algiers system had attempted to subordinate us now approached its end. In Africa itself the situation no longer brooked delay. What dominated men's minds, what was written on walls, what echoed in the streets was, 'Let de Gaulle come!' On March 14th, when Giraud left the hall where he had announced his new orientation, the crowd that had gathered outside received him with cries of *'Vive de Gaulle!'* No one doubted that the attitude recently adopted by the local authorities, the changes made in the Vichy legislation, the dissolution of the Légion, the release of political prisoners and the dismissal of prominent persons were so many successes for the National Committee. The Cross of Lorraine appeared everywhere. The Combat movement moved to the front rank. On April 19th the general councils of Algiers, Oran and Constantine sent me their respects at the opening of their sessions. On the 26th M. Peyrouton, paying a visit to General Catroux, informed him that as soon as I arrived and in order to facilitate union, he would resign his position as Governor-General of Algeria and would ask to serve in a purely military capacity. On May 1st the parades organized for the May Day labour holiday marched to the rhythm of 'We want de Gaulle!' The day before Mr Churchill and I had had a satisfying conversation. Having read me Mr Macmillan's latest reports, the Prime Minister admitted that, in his opinion, I had won the first round.

How, moreover, could one justify the distance at which I had been kept, when African troops and Free French forces were engaged on Tunisian soil in the same battle with the same ardour, towards the same objectives? And the Tunisian struggle was a fierce one. By the end of February Rommel had come on stage. Delaying Montgomery's victorious march by rearguard action, then covering himself by the fortified Mareth line to the south, he drove from Sfax towards Tebessa to open an Algerian corridor. An American Army corps and the French Welwert Division—whose valiant general was to be killed shortly afterward—had kept him in check with the greatest difficulty. At the same time General von Arnim, Nehring's successor, attacked both along the northern coast in the region of Tabarca, which was defended by General Montsabert's Volunteer Corps and the Moroccan *tabors*, and towards Medjez-el-Bab, which the British held. Serious reversals were to be feared, but the whole Allied position was maintained despite everything, thanks particularly to the energy of the French troops, badly armed and equipped though they were, and to the leadership of General Juin, who, out of the bits and pieces that he had to deal with, found the means of making an effective fighting instrument. In the middle of March the entry into the line of the Eighth Army, and with it the units of Fighting France, was to be the decisive factor.

Montgomery, with Leclerc constituting his left wing and Larminat one of his reserves, attacked and, turning the Mareth line, reached Gabès. This break-through permitted Patton to retake Gafsa. On April 11th Sfax, on the 12th Sousse and Kairouan were liberated in their turn. Then the Allied general offensive was launched. On May 7th Bradley and Magnan took Bizerta, Anderson entered Tunis, while Koeltz carried Pont-du-Fahs. On May 11th the Larminat Division seized Takrouna. The next day General von Arnim, trapped on Cape Bon, surrendered with 250,000 men.

As our soldiers from Chad and the Middle East made contact in the heat of battle with their brave comrades in Tunisia, Algeria and Morocco and with the populations of those regions, so popular enthusiasm mounted around them. On March 26th Larminat telegraphed to me that the centres of southern Tunisia, Medenine, Djerba, Zarzis and others, were multiplying their requests to be joined again to Fighting France. On April 6th Leclerc informed me that upon seeing him with his men Gabès had looked like an explosion of joy. On April 14th the American press reported that during the entry of the British and the Free French into Sfax, everyone shouted, '*Vive de Gaulle!*' The New York *Herald Tribune*, under the headline 'Where Our Strength Resides', wrote:

> The wildest enthusiasm came as some bit of dusty tricolour, fluttering from a lorry, announced the Fighting French. The correspondents who report these scenes seem to have been a little staggered themselves . . . Faced with the enthusiasm with which men of all former parties have responded to de Gaulle's simple demand, before the tears, the cheers, the flowers in the liberated Tunisian towns, who can doubt any longer where the real strength and glory of our cause is to be found?

On April 30th Colonel Vanecke, former commissioner of Vichy's *Chantiers de Jeunesse*,[1] and now commander of the Seventh African Chasseurs, asked to come under my command with his entire regiment. On May 3rd, at Sfax, the Fourth Spahis, with the exception of a few officers, addressed themselves in a body to General Leclerc asking the same favour. As soon as the battle was over, many soldiers in African units went so far as to leave the ranks in hopes of being included in the forces under the Cross of Lorraine. On May 20th the Free French detachment received its fair share of cheers during the Allied military parade at Tunis in honour of victory.

Thus it was popular judgment that finally meted out justice to all tergiversations. On April 27th General Giraud wrote to tell me that he renounced preponderance, but he still maintained his conception of the 'council' without real powers on which both of us would be seated with the Residents-General and Governors-General. Further, no doubt fearing mob reaction, he proposed that our first meeting take place far away, either at Biskra or at Marrakesh. On May 6th I replied by declaring once again the firm intention of the National Committee as to the character, the composition and the authority of the government organ that was to be formed, rejecting the notion that this could be done in a remote oasis and stressing that I must

[1] Youth Camps—TR.

go to Algiers. Two days before, in a public address, I had quite bluntly declared that the matter must be settled.

Then, on the night of May 15th, Philip and Soustelle triumphantly brought me a telegram just received from Paris. Jean Moulin informed me that the National Council of the Resistance had been formed and in its name addressed the following message to me:

> Every movement, every party of the resistance, from both northern and southern zones, on the eve of General de Gaulle's departure for Algeria, pledges anew its total adherence to the principles he and the National Committee embody and uncompromisingly uphold.
>
> Every movement, every party formally declares that the designated meeting must take place at the seat of the government-general in Algeria, openly and among Frenchmen.
>
> They further declare: (1) that political problems cannot be excluded from these talks; (2) that the French people will never tolerate the subordination of General de Gaulle to General Giraud and demands the immediate installation at Algiers of a provisional government under the presidency of General de Gaulle, with General Giraud as military chief; (3) that General de Gaulle will remain sole leader of the French resistance whatever the result of the negotiations.

On May 27th the National Council of the Resistance, assembling in full and with Jean Moulin presiding, held its first meeting at 48 Rue du Four, Paris, and confirmed its message to me.

Thus everywhere, and in particular on the aching soil of France herself, a well-prepared harvest was ripening against the crucial moment. The telegram from Paris, sent to Algiers and made public by the American, British and Free French broadcasting stations, produced a decisive effect not only because of what it declared, but also because it proved that the French resistance had been able to achieve unity. The voice of this crushed yet reviving France suddenly blotted out the whispers of intrigue and the palavers of compromise. I was immediately the stronger for it, while Washington and London weighed gloomily, but not without lucidity, the significance of the event. On May 17th General Giraud asked me to come to Algiers at once to form the central French power with him. On May 25th I replied, 'I plan to reach Algiers by the end of this week and I shall be delighted to work directly with you in the service of France.'

Before leaving England, I wrote King George VI to tell him how grateful I was to him, to his government and to his people for the reception they had given me during the tragic days of 1940 and for the hospitality they had subsequently accorded to Free France and its leader. Intending to pay a visit to Mr Churchill, I learned that he had just left for an 'unknown destination'. It was therefore Mr Eden to whom I made my adieux. The meeting was a friendly one.

'What do you think of us?' the British minister asked me.

'No one could be more agreeable than the British people,' I observed. 'As for your politics, I cannot always say the same.'

When we were discussing the many occasions on which I had had dealings with the British Government, Mr Eden good-humouredly asked, 'Do you know that you have caused us more difficulties than all our other European allies put together?'

'I don't doubt it,' I replied, smiling in my turn. 'France is a great power.'

IV. ALGIERS

ON MIDNIGHT OF May 30th a Fighting French plane with Marmier as chief officer landed me at Bufarik. Massigli, Philip, Palewski, Billotte, Teyssot and Charles-Roux accompanied me. General Giraud was there to meet us and General Catroux as well, and behind them the representatives of the American and British missions. The *garde mobile* presented arms, a band played the 'Marseillaise', the cars were French. Signs such as these, compared with those marking our reception at Anfa, showed me that Fighting France, and thereby France herself, had been making progress in North Africa.

The public did not know of our arrival. All the censors of Algiers, London and New York had forbidden the news to be announced. Hence the localities our entourage passed through did not, on the whole, give any special demonstration. Only certain vigilant 'Gaullists' cheered when we happened to encounter them. At Bir Kadeim the people, alerted at the last moment, rushed out to meet us shouting, *'Vive de Gaulle!'* But the local authorities had made sure that our entrance into Algiers would take place without a public gathering. From Bufarik, whose remote and isolated airfield had been chosen intentionally in preference to that of Maison-Blanche, we reached the Summer Palace without crossing the city itself.

A great banquet was served. This splendid French habit is current whatever terms the guests are on and whatever their troubles. Giraud and I were seated opposite each other. On my right I was not surprised to find General Georges, who told me how the English had just brought him from France. On my left was M. Jean Monnet, who immediately began to talk to me on economic subjects. Catroux and Massigli sat on either side of Giraud. André Philip and René Mayer, Palewski and Couve de Murville, Linarès and Billotte en-

tered into conversation, as did thirty other guests. Thus were reunited all these Frenchmen, so different and yet so much alike,
whom the tide of events had swept toward such different shores and
who now seemed just as active and self-confident as they had been
before the drama began! Glancing down the table, one might have
thought that nothing tragic had occurred during the past three
years. All the same, two parties were present.

It was easy to establish the apparent relationship of forces between
them. On one side everything, on the other, nothing. In Algiers the
Army, the police, the administration, the treasury, the radio, the
press and communications were under the sole domination of the
'Civil and Military Commander-in-Chief'. The Allied might, thanks
to which he had been put in power, was oriented in his favour alone.
I had no troops in this country, no police, no officials, no funds, no
fitting means of making my voice heard. Yet the attitudes, the remarks and the looks of those I had met during the last two hours
already revealed where the ascendancy lay. Each man knew in his
heart how the contest would end.

The crowd shouted it at the top of its lungs in the Place de la
Poste, where at four o'clock I placed a Cross of Lorraine at the foot
of the monument to the dead. Although this ceremony was un-
planned, ignored by the newspapers, unattended by any troops,
thousands of patriots warned by the Combat movement had
gathered swiftly and welcomed me with great acclamation. After my
tribute to all the Algerians who had given their lives for France, I
struck up the 'Marseillaise', in which innumerable voices joined me.
Then, surrounded by overwhelming enthusiasm, I reached the villa
Les Glycines, where I was to establish my residence.

Already messages had begun to flow in. The first letter I read was
from General Vuillemin, former Chief of the General Staff of the
Air Force, who after the misfortunes of 1940 had retired to his home
with his griefs and his hopes. In the noblest terms this great leader
asked me to give him the command of a Fighting French air
squadron, with corresponding rank. After the cheers of the crowd,
Vuillemin's gesture made the essence of the situation clear to me.
Here, as elsewhere, national feeling had made its choice. In the game
about to be played, the trump card was in my hand. Among the
Frenchmen of Africa my only obstacles would be the narrow-
mindedness of those in office and the mistrust of certain prominent

individuals. I would also have to reckon on the determined opposition of the Allies, who would back the rival clan.

A painful duel! It began the very next morning. At the Lycée Fromentin, where the future government would hold its sessions and install certain of its services, I met General Giraud. He was accompanied by Monnet and Georges, I by Catroux, Philip and Massigli. We were all in agreement as to the procedure to be followed. The seven men present would constitute themselves a government committee and would be joined subsequently by other members to complete the administration. But I intended to take the initiative before anything had been concluded.

'In order to form ourselves into a single team working in co-operation,' I said, 'certain essential points must be established. Until our country is in a position to express its own wishes, the authority we establish here must assume every national responsibility. The military command, even though the man who wields it may be a minister or a president, will therefore be appointed by the government and will remain subordinate to it. If it is thought that this army chief should be placed during operations under the strategic command of a foreign general, this can be done only by order of the French authority. I cannot, for my part, agree to replace the French National Committee by any other if it is not understood from the start that the responsibility and authority of the new organism will be supreme in every area, in particular the last. Further, so as to indicate clearly that France has never left the war and that she repudiates Vichy entirely, it is necessary that we relieve General Noguès, Governor-General Boisson and Governor-General Peyrouton of their duties.'

Giraud lost his temper. He did not agree that the military command should be subordinated to the government. As for the 'proconsuls', he declared with extreme vehemence that he would not give them up. I insisted on my conditions. We agreed to adjourn the session and resume the debate later on the basis of written proposals. During the discussion only General Georges had agreed with Giraud; Monnet sought compromise, while Catroux, Philip and Massigli all approved, though in different ways, the position I had taken. After this unpromising start, the government could scarcely be said to be launched. But I saw myself as a navigator enveloped in a heavy squall, certain that if he kept his course the horizon would clear.

Meanwhile the storm redoubled. A crisis broke that seemed likely to jeopardize everything, had we not felt that the crux of the matter was already decided. On June 1st I assembled as Les Glycines all the newspapermen then in Algiers. This numerous band arrived burning with curiosity, headed by the Allied reporters, who did not conceal their satisfaction at breathing henceforth the keen air which produced big headlines and explosive articles. The French were somewhat withdrawn, divided between sympathy toward me and fear of the censorship wielded by the Director of Information of the 'Civil and Military High Command'. In a short statement, I pointed out that I had come to North Africa with my colleagues in order to create an effective French power there, an authority directing the national war effort, insisting on the sovereignty of France, established in accordance with the resistance and excluding those who symbolized something else. Such language and tone, unheard of in these parts, were immediately reported everywhere.

The evening of the same day, Colonel Jousse brought me a letter from M. Peyrouton. The Governor-General of Algeria, 'realizing that unconditional union among Frenchmen is the only means of obtaining a victory that can restore our greatness, and in hopes of facilitating its achievement', sent in his resignation and asked me to intervene on his behalf with the military authority so that he might have a chance to serve in the Army. Nothing in the letter indicated that a similar message had been sent to Giraud. I replied to M. Peyrouton that I accepted his resignation and that, 'in the terrible ordeal our country is undergoing, I am sure that the French people will appreciate as I do the disinterested courage of your action'. I sent copies of the Governor-General's letter and my reply to General Giraud without delay and issued a statement to the representatives of the press. The next day the news appeared in newspapers throughout the world.

M. Peyrouton's retirement, under such circumstances, immediately produced a considerable stir. It was learned that he had subsequently written to General Giraud in the same terms, but this fact did not change the situation. That the former Vichy ambassador to Brazil, who had come to Algeria to assume the governor-generalship at Roosevelt's request, should hand over his office to me and comply publicly with my demands was a repudiation from within the Algiers system. As a result, the confusion among the men of the system and their Allied advisers reached its peak—all the more so since the city was bubbling over with excitement as from everywhere came signs of the massive exodus of volunteers loading into trucks and pouring down the roads to join Larminat's and Leclerc's troops. Some days earlier Giraud, with Eisenhower's agreement, had forced the Cross of Lorraine units out of the territory. These were now bivouacked around Tripoli, but their distant encampments attracted thousands of young soldiers. Giraud, yielding to anxiety, went so far as to appoint a new prefect of police to maintain order in the city and its environs. He chose Admiral Muselier, who had been brought over by the British and who intended now to make up for his former misfortunes.

I was therefore not surprised to receive, on June 2nd, a letter signed by the 'Civil and Military Commander-in-Chief' but written in a style that betrayed its inspiration. In the familiar tone of the London emigrants who had not joined Free France, it accused me of attempting to drive from their posts men worthy of every confidence, to damage our alliances and to establish a dictatorship composed of myself and the criminals who formed my entourage. While I was digesting the contents of this letter, I was informed that the garrison had been confined to barracks, that armoured units were concentrated in the gardens of the Summer Palace, that all meetings and parades had been forbidden in Algiers, and that the military and the police were manning the exits from the city as well as the adjacent airfields. But at Les Glycines, guarded only by the ten spahis Larminat had sent me, I learned that this to-do was not affecting the response to my call of those I wished to consult. Later that night I informed Giraud that his *Putsch* atmosphere, created under the eyes of foreign powers, was deplorable, that we must either break off relations or reach an agreement and that a new explanation was imperative on the next day.

On June 3rd at ten o'clock in the morning, the 'Seven' met again. This time General Giraud's obstinacy gave way. I had brought drafts of a decree and a declaration instituting the new committee. Both were adopted without change. The declaration announced the creation of the French Committee of National Liberation, with both of us as its presidents and with Catroux, Georges, Massigli, Monnet and Philip as members; others were to be appointed soon. We proclaimed:

> The committee . . . is the central French power . . . [It] directs
> the French war effort in all its forms and in all places . . . It
> exercises French sovereignty . . . It assures the management and
> the defence of French interests the world over . . . It assumes
> authority over the territories and the military forces hitherto
> under the French National Committee and the Civil and
> Military Commander-in-Chief.

We added that the committee would turn over its powers to the future provisional government of the Republic when liberation was achieved, and that until such time it pledged itself 'to re-establish all French liberties, the laws of the Republic, and the republican régime, while destroying entirely the arbitrary régime of personal power today imposed upon the nation'.

At the same time the question of the 'proconsuls' was settled. We decided that since M. Peyrouton's resignation was a *fait accompli*, General Catroux would become Governor-General of Algeria while still remaining a member of the committee, that General Noguès was to leave Morocco and that M. Boisson would be recalled from Dakar as soon as the Ministry of the Colonies had been given a head. General Bergeret was to be retired.

Despite obvious defects, the organism thus created was, in my eyes, a workable starting point. True, we would temporarily have to put up with the absurd duality that existed at its head; and it was to be expected that Allied politics, intervening in the inner working of the committee through the men they had introduced there, would give rise to bitterness before the Commander-in-Chief was subordinated to the central power in reality, as he now was on paper. But the French Committee of National Liberation responded to the principles which Fighting France had not ceased to champion. As for the application to be made of it, that was up to me. In confronting the committee with its responsibilities, I intended that its internal evolution, under the pressure of public opinion, should concentrate it around me and assist me to get rid of whatever was erratic and centrifugal in it. In the immediate future, the close association initially adopted put me in a position, despite all its disadvantages, to act on the military and administrative elements of North Africa which had hitherto been outside my authority. As for all those who, in France and elsewhere, had given me their confidence, I was sure that they would willingly continue to follow no one but myself. When the session had adjourned, I had the feeling that a great step had been taken on the road to unity. Overlooking, in view of such a stake, many painful changes of fortune, I embraced General Giraud with all my heart.

But if my satisfaction was considerable, that of the Allies was not. The establishment in North Africa of a central French authority arrogating to itself the powers of government, laying claim to French sovereignty and excluding the 'proconsuls' was in flagrant contradiction to the position flaunted by Roosevelt and his ministers. For that reason the declaration, released at noon on June 3rd by the French Committee of National Liberation and announcing the birth of the latter, was suppressed by the American censors until nine that night. I indeed hastened to inform the representatives of the press of what had been done, knowing that this would sooner or later cause the barrier to fall. The next day, speaking on the radio— where already 'Gaullists' were officially moving in—I announced to the people of France that their government was now functioning at Algiers pending its return to Paris. On June 6th a Fighting France rally attended by an audience of thousands gave me, with Philip and Capitant, the occasion to make heard publicly the words and the tune that would now be official. It goes without saying that the British and American missions showed little eagerness to allow our speeches to be spread round the world.

The Allies' ill-humour did not, moreover, limit itself to the sphere of propaganda. Thus, when I telephoned London to ask that several of my colleagues be brought immediately to take part in the new government, none of them arrived for ten days; the British, under various pretexts, were delaying their departure. And in Algiers itself the British Government, whether on its own account alone or not, followed the development of our affairs without a sign of good will.

No sooner had I landed at Boufarik on May 30th than I learned that Mr Churchill himself, later joined by Mr Eden, had arrived in great secrecy. He had since stayed in his secluded villa, keeping himself informed meanwhile through General Georges of the progress of our discussions. Once the French Committee of National Liberation was established, the Prime Minister showed himself. On June 6th he invited Giraud and me, as well as several committee members, to a so-called 'country dinner', an invitation which my sense of the respect due to him as a personage prevented me from refusing.

When I remarked how strange his presence at such a time and under these conditions appeared, he protested that he was in no way attempting to meddle in French affairs. 'All the same,' he added, 'the military situation compels His Majesty's Government to keep track of what is happening within this essential zone of communications. We should have had to take steps if too brutal a shock had occurred—if, for example, you had devoured Giraud in one mouthful.'

This was not at all my intention. Resolved that the result of my efforts should be a united French Government, I intended to proceed by stages, not considering foreign apprehensions but the national advantage. I hoped to influence General Giraud to range himself of his own accord, on the side of public opinion. Although he had already delayed too long, I was still inclined to have him play the leading role in military affairs, provided that he confined himself to them and that he held his post by virtue of French authority.

As a matter of fact, his role as a military leader could not be in the capacity of a real Commander-in-Chief. I regretted this fact more than anyone else, but what could be done about it? The strategy of the Allied powers included only two conceivable theatres of war in the west, that of the north and that of the Mediterranean. Unfortunately, it was impossible for us to raise enough land, naval and air forces to enable a French general to exercise anything like a high command, properly speaking. To be sure, there were more than enough men; we could, if need be, recruit them from the brave and loyal populations of the Empire. But the officer strength and the specialists at our disposal narrowly limited the number of our units. Again, it was out of the question for us to provide them with arms and equipment ourselves. In comparison with the resources which the Americans and the British mustered in the battles of Italy and France, the strength we could offer there would not constitute a major force. On land especially, it would not for some time exceed the strength of an army detachment—at the most, an army. There was therefore little likelihood that, either in the north or in the south, Americans and British would agree to entrust the direction of the common battle to a French leader.

The situation would, of course, have been different if in June 1940 the Government of the Republic, invested with the appurtenances of legitimacy, accompanied by the core of the central administration, making use of diplomatic means, had had itself transported to Africa. With it would have gone the five hundred thousand men crowding the depots, whatever campaign units could still be shipped, the entire war fleet, the merchant fleet, all the personnel of the pursuit planes and the entire bombing force—which did indeed go to North Africa and was forced to return and hand over its planes to the invader. What France possessed at that time in the way of money and credit would have permitted the nation to buy an abundant supply of American equipment while waiting for lend-lease. With all these resources added to those of Algeria, Morocco, Tunisia, the Levant and French West Africa, there would have been means of rebuilding a formidable military force protected by the wide sea and by the French and British naval squadrons, in particular by one hundred submarines. Given this situation, the Allies, coming to take up positions at our side in the French North African bases, by our own request and probably a year earlier, would quite naturally have recognized the supreme authority of a French general or admiral in this theatre.

But the terrible panic, and then the disastrous surrender, which had prevented what resources there were from being transported to the Empire, which surrendered or demobilized most of those troops already there, which put the public powers and the military command at the enemy's mercy and which welcomed the Allies by cannon fire, had already deprived France of this opportunity as of many others. Never in my life had I felt such disappointment and grief as at these bitter circumstances.

Meanwhile, if General Giraud's experience and capacity could not be employed at the head of operations, they were none the less capable of rendering great services. Renouncing the direction of the government, he could either exercise the responsibilities of Minister of the Armies or, if little inclined to play this administrative role, he could become Inspector-General of our forces and at the same time military adviser to the committee and its representative to the inter-Allied command. I must say that, although I was not opposed to the first solution, it was the second that I regarded as the more appropriate. On many occasions I proposed both to General Giraud, but he never agreed to espouse either one. His illusions, the appeal of certain circles and certain interests, and the influence of the Allies made him determined to keep complete control of the Army for himself and at the same time, as co-signatory of statutes and decrees, be able to prevent the administration from making a move without his consent.

It was therefore inevitable that Giraud should find himself gradually isolated and rejected, until the day when, imprisoned within limitations he did not accept and deprived of the outside supports which were the source of his soaring ambitions, he determined to resign. It was not without sorrow that I had to deal with this painful affair, wounding to the quick a soldier of high quality for whom I had always felt deference and attachment. Along the road that led to national unity, I encountered many times such personal questions, in which the duties of my trust transcended but yet touched my own feelings. Let me say that in no case did it cost me more to impose the iron law of national interest.

This, however, happened gradually. On June 5th the 'Committee of Seven' met again. This time it was a question of selecting further members and deciding their functions. General Georges was named Commissioner of State while Catroux retained the title he held. Massigli and Philip kept respectively Foreign Affairs and the Interior, with which they had already been entrusted. Monnet received the responsibility for Armament and Supply. At General Giraud's request the following became members of the committee: Couve de Murville for Finance, René Mayer for Transport and Public Works, Abadie for Justice, Education and Health. I myself appointed Pleven for the Colonies, Diethelm for Economy, Tixier for Labour, Bonnet for Information. Further, Ambassadors Puaux and Helleu were appointed to Morocco and the Levant respectively, while General Mast was confirmed in his functions in Tunisia.

These choices were subsequently to make my position secure. At Algiers, Rabat and Tunis, as was already the case at Beirut, Brazzaville, Douala, Antananarivo and Nouméa, authority would be wielded by men who were convinced as to the necessity of the war effort and upon whom I could rely. At Dakar, Boisson would be replaced fifteen days later by Cournarie, transferred from the Cameroons. At Fort-de-France there was every indication that we would soon be in a position to set our affairs in order. As for the government itself, it was composed of men of reason and quality, the majority of whom had always been connected with me while the remainder, with a few exceptions, asked only to be so in their turn. Certain that this group was prepared to support me, I made the next move. But before throwing the dice I shook them hard.

On June 8th the committee, which still consisted of only seven members—pending the arrival of those still in London—approached the crucial problem of the military command. We found ourselves with three proposals before us. One, presented by General Georges, provided for the unification of all French forces under the authority of General Giraud, who would act as both minister and Commander-in-Chief, keeping his post as president but remaining independent of the French Government in the military domain. The second plan, proposed by Catroux, aimed at directly entrusting de Gaulle with the Department of National Defence and Giraud with the command of the troops. The third programme, my own, gave the Commander-in-Chief the mission of training all the French forces and of co-operating with the Allied military leaders on joint plans of operations. As soon as possible, he would take an active field command, thereby ceasing to play a part in the government. According to my plan, the organization and distribution of forces would be controlled by a military committee including de Gaulle and Giraud, the ministers concerned and the Chiefs of Staff, and would be subject, should the occasion arise, to the government's arbitration. The majority of the Committee voted against the first proposal. Giraud, backed by General Georges, would accept neither of the other two. Since most of the members were not yet willing to make the 'Commander-in-Chief' yield or resign, the impossibility of reaching a settlement was obvious.

But then what was the Committee for? That was the question I asked, in writing, of its members. Pointing out that in the space of eight days 'we have not even managed to decide the problem of the respective powers of the government and the military command, of which the logical and national solution stares us in the face', and that 'the slightest question, which should be settled in a few moments, involves us in interminable and disagreeable discussions', I declared that I could no longer associate myself with the Committee under the conditions in which it was operating. Then I shut myself up at Les Glycines, shrouded in sorrow, letting it be known to the ministers, officials and generals who came to see me that I was preparing to leave for Brazzaville.

The impression produced by this calculated outburst actually precipitated the march of events. When General Giraud, with no regard for the consequences, convened the Committee for a session at which I was not present, every member pointed out to him that under such conditions no valid decision could be made. On the other hand, the deficiency of the two-headed system, obvious to the well-informed and provoking an avalanche of gibes abroad, aroused both anxiety and exasperation in all French circles. The Army did not escape it; General Juin came to Algiers to tell me as much and to urge Giraud to reduce his claims. General Bouscat, Chief of the General Staff of the Air Force, spoke in the same vein. The Governor-General's office, the university, the editorial offices all seethed with alarming rumours.

After six days of confusion, I decided that the affair was ripe. The Commissioners whom London had detained had just reached Algiers, and so the government was in a position to hold a plenary session. I counted on finding in the full group a less reserved support than that which the 'Seven' had given me and, taking the initiative, called a meeting of the 'Committee of Fourteen' so that it could try to settle the question choking the central power. The meeting took place, but Giraud, in front of his colleagues, flatly refused to have the question brought up, denying the Committee the very jurisdiction defined in a decree signed by his own hand. Thus, even during the last act of this distressing vaudeville show, while the after-effects of Vichy and the interference of foreign powers dragged out the humiliation of France for seven months, Giraud persisted in playing the role of a prime minister who did not want a government.

Of course the Allies did not want one any more than he did. Seeing where events were tending, they made a new effort to prevent France from achieving its government. But their very intervention was to end by further unsettling General Giraud's position.

On June 16th Murphy and Macmillan asked Massigli to submit to the French Committee of National Liberation a request from General Eisenhower, inviting General de Gaulle and General Giraud to confer with him about the problems of the command and organization of the French armed forces. The conference took place on June 19th. Three of us spoke, with one silent witness, General Bedell Smith. But Murphy and Macmillan, with several British and American officials and military men, stayed in the neighbourhood, listening attentively.

I purposely arrived last and spoke first. 'I am here,' I told Eisenhower, 'in my capacity as President of the French Government. For it is customary that during operations the chiefs of state and of the government should come in person to the headquarters of the officer in command of the armies they have entrusted to him. If you wish to address a request to me concerning your province, be assured that I am disposed beforehand to give you satisfaction, on condition, of course, that it is compatible with the interests in my charge.'

The inter-Allied Commander-in-Chief, making an effort to be pleasant, then declared, in substance, 'I'm preparing, as you know, a most important operation soon to be launched against Italy which concerns directly the liberation of Europe and France. For the security of our rear during this operation, I need an assurance which I ask you to give me. It is essential that the present organization of the French command in North Africa undergoes no change. In particular, General Giraud must remain in office with all his present powers and keep complete control of the disposition of troops, communications, ports and airfields. He must be the only one to deal with me on all military subjects in North Africa. Your interior organization is not my concern, but these points are essential to us. I tell you so on behalf of the British and American Governments, which are furnishing arms to the French forces and which cannot continue shipments if the conditions I lay down are not fulfilled.'

'I am taking note of your course of action,' I replied. 'You are asking a promise of me which I will not give you, for the organization of the French command is the province of the French Government, not of yours. But having heard what you have to say, I should like to ask you several questions.

'All states waging war—America, for example—entrust to generals the command of their troops in the field and to ministers the responsibility of outfitting them. Do you claim to forbid the French Government from doing as much?'

General Eisenhower confined himself to repeating that his request aimed at the integral maintenance of Giraud's powers.

'You have referred,' I said, 'to your responsibilities as Commander-in-Chief in relation to the British and American Governments. Are you aware that I have responsibilities toward France, and that by virtue of those responsibilities I cannot admit the interference of any foreign power in the exercise of French authority?' Eisenhower kept silence.

I continued. 'You are a soldier, do you think that a leader's authority can stand if it rests on the favour of a foreign power?'

After a new and heavy silence, the American Commander-in-Chief said, 'I quite understand, General, that you have long-standing worries as to the fate of your nation. Please understand that on my side I have immediate military preoccupations.'

'So have I,' I answered, 'for my government must immediately combine at once the various kinds of French forces—those of Fighting France, those of North Africa and those forming in metropolitan France, which the present system forces us to keep separate. It must also arm them, thanks to the resources which you are furnishing them in the interest of our alliance and in exchange for the many services with which we provide you. Here too I have a question to ask you.

'Do you recall that during the last war France played a role similar to that which the United States is playing today as regards furnishing arms to several Allied countries? It was France then who armed the Belgians and the Serbs, found resources for the Russians and the Rumanians and lastly outfitted your own army with a large share of its equipment. Yes, during the First World War, you Americans fired our cannon, drove our trucks and flew our planes. Did we, in return, demand of Belgium, Serbia, Russia, Rumania, did we demand of the United States, that they appoint this or that leader or institute this or that political system?' Once again the silence weighed upon us.

General Giraud, who had not yet opened his mouth, now declared, 'I too have my responsibilities, in particular as regards the Army, which is small and cannot exist save in the Allied framework. This is as true for its command and its organization as it is for its operations.'

At this I stood up, left the room and returned to Les Glycines.

The next day, as I had requested, Allied headquarters sent me and Giraud a note specifying the Anglo-American requirements concerning the functions of the French Army. I wanted a written record of these requirements. The note, after having formulated the demands concerning Giraud's powers, concluded with the sentence: 'The Allied Commander-in-Chief wishes to emphasize the assurances given by the British and American Governments guaranteeing that

French sovereignty will be respected and maintained in the French territories in North and West Africa.'

Although this last touch, serving as an ironic conclusion to the demands that contradicted it, was signed by the Allied Commander-in-Chief, I recognized in it the procedure frequently employed by Washington and London—paying lip-service to rights even while infringing them. But I knew that such a course of action, if it corresponded to the policies pursued in regard to France by the British and American Governments, proceeded neither from the initiative nor the character of General Eisenhower.

He was a soldier. To him, by nature and by profession, action seemed natural, immediate and simple. To put into play, according to time-honoured rules, certain forces of a familiar nature—this was how he envisaged warfare and consequently his task. Eisenhower approached the test trained for thirty-five years by a technique and a philosophy beyond which he was in no way inclined to go. Yet now he found himself abruptly invested with an extraordinarily complex role. Removed from the hitherto rigid framework of the American Army, he had become Commander-in-Chief of a colossal coalition. Because he had to lead the forces of several peoples into battles on which the fate of their states depended, he was to see national susceptibilities and ambitions irrupt into the tried and tested system of the units under his orders.

It was a piece of luck for the Allies that Dwight Eisenhower discovered in himself not only the necessary prudence to deal with these thorny problems, but also an attraction towards the wider horizons that history opened before his career. He knew how to be adroit and flexible. But if he used skill, he was also capable of audacity. The latter quality was indeed a prerequisite for hurling upon the beaches of Africa an army transported from one side of the ocean to the other; for invading Italy in the face of an enemy still intact; for landing heavy units on a strip of Normandy coast in the teeth of an adversary well entrenched and skilled in manoeuvring; for launching through the Avranches gap Patton's mechanized army and pushing it as far as Metz. Yet it was chiefly by method and perseverance that he dominated the situation. By choosing reasonable plans, by sticking firmly to them, by respecting logistics, General Eisenhower led to victory the complicated and prejudicial machinery of the armies of the free world.

It will never be forgotten that in this capacity he had the distinction of leading them in the liberation of France. But since a great people's needs are on the scale of its misfortunes, it will doubtless be thought too that the Commander-in-Chief might have been able to serve our country still better. Had he linked his strategy to France's great struggle as he bound it to the schemes of the Anglo-American powers, had he provided our troops, those of the secret army included, with heavy arms, had he even in his disposition of forces entrusted a first-class mission to the reviving French Army, our military recovery might have been more brilliant, the future more profoundly marked.

In my own relations with him, I often had the feeling that this generous hearted man inclined towards these points of view. But I was soon to see him turn away from them, almost regretfully. Actually, the politics of Washington dictated his behaviour and necessitated his reserve. He complied, yielding to Roosevelt's authority, influenced by the advisers the latter sent to him, spied on by his peers—his rivals—and not yet having acquired, in the face of power, that assurance which the military leader eventually derives from rendering great services.

Nevertheless, if occasionally he went so far as to support the schemes to keep us in obscurity, I can affirm that he did so without conviction. I even saw him allow my intervention in his own strategy whenever national interest led me to do so. At heart this great soldier felt, in his turn, that mysterious sympathy which for almost two centuries has brought his country and mine together in the world's great dramas. It was not his doing that this time the United States cared less for our distress than for the appeal of domination.

In any case, the course of action that politics had forced upon Eisenhower on June 19th produced an effect contrary to the one that Washington had reckoned on. The Committee of National Liberation, learning of the Anglo-American demands on the 21st, decided, as I urged it to do, to ignore them and make no reply. But, displeased and humiliated, it notified Giraud that he must either accept subordination to the French Government or else cease to be a member of it and resign his command.

Besides, since Giraud was alleging the disadvantage, from the point of view of secrecy, of examining military questions by an

Areopagus of fourteen ministers, it was decided, on my suggestion, to institute a Military Committee comprising, under my chairmanship, the Commander-in-Chief and the Chiefs of Staff, and having authority from the government to determine measures relating to organization, recruiting and the merging of our forces, besides their distribution among the various theatres and territories. As for operations, two military commands provisionally continued, Giraud remaining responsible for the North African forces and de Gaulle for the rest, including the secret army. The principal decisions were still reserved for the Committee of National Liberation meeting in plenary session.

This compromise gave me no satisfaction whatever. I should have preferred us to go further along the road of common sense, and establish the unity of the government's leadership once and for all. General Giraud's powers should be clearly defined, one or several ministers should undertake the administration of the armies as well as the direct exercise of military authority outside the zone of operations, and that within this framework the merging of the French forces of North Africa with those of Fighting France could at last be realized. But the committee, if it saw the goal to be reached, was still too unsure of itself to reach it swiftly. Besides, General Giraud announced that he had received an invitation from President Roosevelt to go to Washington to discuss the question of arms shipments. The Commander-in-Chief urgently requested that we await his return before discussing the structure of the committee and of the command. The majority of the ministers chose to temporize. I agreed to these provisional arrangements with the firm intention of putting each piece of the service in the place it should have before much longer.

Giraud left on July 2nd. His trip had been organized by agreement between the American Government and himself without consulting the Committee of National Liberation. Independently of his practical goal, the arming of our troops, his visit was considered by the United States Government as the occasion to manifest its policy towards France, to affirm, by discussing military matters with only one of our leaders, its refusal to admit that we had a government, to publicize the support it continued to afford to the French general it had chosen for North Africa, and lastly to boost its candidate in American public opinion. Mr Churchill had decided he must lend

President Roosevelt a hand in this matter by addressing to the British representatives abroad and to the editors of the British newspapers a memorandum in which the Prime Minister's grievances against General de Gaulle were set forth. This memorandum, ungracious as it was, was naturally published by the American newspapers as well.

Yet despite all these efforts, results did not come up to expectations. Since the President and his ministers insisted on receiving Giraud in his military capacity alone and indeed the latter laid claim to no other, American public opinion took only a moderate interest in his visit. The crowds were not stirred by the technical side of the operation, which consisted in arming a few French divisions, and their feelings in no way recognized as the champion of France the docile visitor whom many American newspapers eulogized. As for better informed circles, they were repelled by the subservient attitude Giraud saw fit to adopt and by the White House's insistence on exploiting his presence to advertise a policy of which many did not approve.

The same was true of Giraud's statement to the Washington press, which it was known he had agreed to submit beforehand to the United States Government and had even modified a few moments before the press conference. The remarks made on July 10th by Roosevelt à propos Giraud's visit, which, the President said, was merely that of a French soldier fighting for the Allied cause, since at that time France no longer existed: the White House dinner attended only by military personnel, to which not even Ambassador Henri Hoppenot, the accredited representative of the Committee of National Liberation, had been invited: and the speeches the President and Giraud exchanged that evening, making not the slightest allusion to the Algiers Government nor to the unity, the integrity or the independence of France, all pointed the same way. So also did what occurred on July 14th, the national holiday, when Giraud received neither tribute nor message from the government that was his host and addressed none to it, confining himself, in the morning, to boarding the *Richelieu*, and in the afternoon to attending a reception given by the French colony in a New York hotel.

On the way back, the stop he made in Canada and his journey through England did not modify the effect the general had produced in the United States. To the Ottawa newspapermen Giraud declared that his only purpose was to reconstitute a French Army, for nothing else mattered. To the London press, which for three years had watched the Free French effort to sustain the national cause, he declared, 'No one has the right to speak in the name of France!' On the whole, those among the Allies who, whether in responsible positions or not, had seen and heard General Giraud, received the impression that if his person and his career merited respect, he was not made to lead his country in wartime. Many concluded that his role in France's recovery could be only secondary.

Meanwhile in Algiers the government, extricated from its twoheadedness, began to take shape. The reuniting of the Empire, the moral and material necessities of the war effort, foreign relations, the connections with the resistance movements in metropolitan France and the need to prepare what must be done there at the time of the liberation confronted our committee with many problems. We held two sessions each week. The subjects we discussed bristled with thorns, each minister setting forth on the one hand his difficulties and on the other the inadequacy of his means, but at least we attempted to have the discussions well prepared and to reach positive conclusions. Even if opinions differed my arbitration was delivered without difficulties, for there was no profound divergence on any question within the government itself. It must be added that without Parliament, elections and parties, no politics were played among the members of the committee. My task of leadership was thereby made much easier.

This was doubly so since, technically speaking, I was ably assisted. On June 10th we had provided the government with a secretariat and had placed Louis Joxe at its head with Raymond Offroy and Edgar Faure as his associates. Joxe provided links among the ministers and between them and myself, set up the reports upon which, according to the agenda, the Committee deliberated, took note of the decisions, saw to the publication of statutes and decrees, and saw that they were put into effect. A model of conscientiousness and of discretion, he was to attend, as a silent and active witness, all the Committee's sessions for over three years. The secretariat inaugurated at Algiers was to remain thereafter the instrument of the government's collective work.

In July the Judicial Committee was born. With René Cassin as Director and with the help of François Marion, Chairman Tebahar and others, this Committee played the role which devolved normally upon the Council of State with regard to giving of opinions and formation of texts. Since the Algiers Government had to adapt the application of the laws to the circumstances of war and to prepare the legislative, judicial and administrative measures to be taken in France at the time of liberation, the importance of the Judicial Committee can readily be seen. The Committee on Disputes, presided over by Pierre Tissier and also functioning in the absence of the Council of State, handed down provisional judgments of sanction or of reparation which the abuses committed by Vichy made necessary within the public services. Lastly, the Military Committee was provided with a secretary, Colonel Billotte, who helped me directly.

During the course of the month of July, administrative personnel, military staffs and public alike realized that the men appointed to the different departments into which governmental authority was traditionally distributed had become ministers, endowed with the authority and the responsibility inherent in their functions and that the chronic improvisation practised by the Algiers system since the end of the Vichy régime in North Africa had been replaced by the operation of a competent and controlled body. A central administration was now functioning, instead of the spurious federation of Algeria, Morocco, Tunisia and West Africa, which had been instituted for personal reasons and in default of an authority of a national character; in short, that the central power had a head, followed a line and acted in an orderly fashion. The effect produced was such that the unity around me in influential circles, which hitherto had been hoped for only by individuals, was now admitted by everyone, including the majority of Frenchmen.

All in all, it was the state that we saw reappearing in fact and in influence, all the more prominently since it was not anonymous. As Vichy could no longer deceive anyone, enthusiasm and assent, not to mention ambition, automatically inclined toward de Gaulle. In North Africa the ethnic and political structure of the populations, the attitude of the authorities and the pressure of the Allies had delayed this evolution, but henceforth it was irresistible. A tide of will and feeling consecrated that profound legality which derives from the public welfare and which France has always recognized during her worst ordeals, whatever the so-called 'legal' formulas of the moment. Here was a fundamental requirement of which, as its symbol, I was myself no less than the instrument and the servant. It was especially during public ceremonies, of course, that this was demonstrated to everyone: the passionate acclamation of the crowds, the tribute of the constituted authorities, the official gestures that centred upon me, served as an expression of the popular instinct. The national resolve, more powerful than any formal decree, openly appointed me to incarnate and lead the state.

On June 26th I went to Tunisia where I found the Regency suffering under the hocks which the invasion had inflicted upon it, the Vichy prejudice in favour of the Axis forces and the collusion of certain local nationalist elements with Germany and Italy. The material damage was serious, and so were the political contretemps. Before my arrival in Algiers, the 'Civil and Military High Command' had dismissed Moncef Bey, whose attitude during the occupation had shown itself to be troublesome in view of the obligations that linked him to France. Several of the members of the two nationalist Destour parties were in prison. In the countryside, it had been necessary to mete out punishment for outrages committed with the invader's tolerance and his occasional complicity against the persons and property of many French *colons* by looters or fanatics.

Resident-General Mast was working to repair the situation. He was doing his job with intelligence, limiting the sentences of those punished, making as many conciliatory contacts as possible and moderating those who thirsted for vengeance. I gave him my support. To the authorities, the delegations and the French and Tunisian notables presented to me, I pointed out that there were only too many extenuating circumstances for what had occurred. To judge the faults committed by the native people, I said, one must first take into account the example of surrender set for them by Vichy, for instance, the disgrace of the 'African Phalanx' established on its orders to fight at the side of the enemy. I declared that nothing was of greater importance now than to strengthen the union of France and Tunisia, first by restoring the country's normal activity. After this period, it must be said, my government never met with serious difficulties in Tunisia. On the contrary, this noble kingdom associated itself once more with France by its co-operation in the war effort and the courage of its soldiers who were incorporated in our Army.

I went to see Sidi Lamine Bey, who had ascended the throne in the order of succession, after Moncef had been deposed. He received me at Carthage, surrounded by his ministers, in particular M. Baccouche. Despite the eddies of public opinion which the departure of his popular predecessor had aroused, the new sovereign assumed his task with a worthy simplicity. I was struck at seeing in his person, beneath the wisdom of age and character, a great devotion to the service of his country. He, I have reason to believe, saw me personifying a confident and thereby generous France, a France that Tunisia had often imagined and occasionally encountered. Since then I have felt for Sidi Lamine an esteem and a friendship that have not altered.

On Sunday, June 27th, amid popular acclamation after reviewing the troops and attending the services at the cathedral, I proceeded to the Esplanade Gambetta. Here, addressing the crowd of French with whom many Tunisians were mingled, I spoke of France, warning the enemy that she would strike with every means in her power until she overcame him, saluting her great allies and assuring them of her loyal understanding provided that this was reciprocal. After which I declared that if, until the ordeal of war was over, I asked help of everyone, I renounced in advance any subsequent claims on them; that the end of the task I had undertaken for liberation and victory would be reached by victory and liberation; and that once this was accomplished de Gaulle would not be a candidate for any office.

'To France,' I cried, 'to our lady France we have only one thing to say, that nothing matters to us except to serve her. We must liberate her, conquer her enemy, punish the traitors, preserve her friends, tear the gag from her mouth and the chains from her limbs so that she can make her voice heard and resume her march toward her destiny. We have nothing to ask of her except, perhaps, that on the day of liberty she will open her motherly arms to us so that we may weep for joy within them, and that on the day when death comes to us she will bury us gently in her good and sacred soil.'

On July 14th it was Algiers, capital of the Empire and of Fighting France, that provided a demonstration of the revival of the state and the recovery of national unity. The traditional military parade assumed as it were the character of a resurrection. In saluting the troops that marched past, I saw rising towards me like a wall of flame their tremendous desire to take part in the coming battles.

The air of lighthearted confidence, emanating from the army and the people, revealed that spiritual accord which past disappointments had shaken and recent misfortunes destroyed, but which today's hope revived. I received the same impression from the huge crowd which I addressed in the Forum.

'Thus,' I declared, 'after three years of unspeakable torments, the French people reappear. They reappear *en masse*, gathered together, enthusiastic, beneath the folds of their flag. But this time they reappear united. And the union which the capital of the Empire demonstrates so emphatically today is the same union which tomorrow all our cities and all our villages will demonstrate once they have been torn from the enemy and his henchmen.' Taking this as my point of departure, I stressed for the benefit of the Allies, whom I knew were all ears, the absurdity of plans that intended to make use of the French war effort while leaving France out of account. 'Elsewhere in the world,' I said, 'some people have thought it possible to consider the operations of our armies independently of the feelings and the will of the great body of our people. They have imagined that our soldiers, our sailors and our airmen, differing in this from all the soldiers, sailors and airmen in the world, would go into battle without concerning themselves with the reasons for which they were braving death. In short, these supposedly realistic theoreticians have concluded that for the French and for the French alone the national war effort could exist apart from national policy and national morale. We assure these "realists" that they do not know what reality is. The French citizens who have been fighting the enemy on every front, whether for four years or for eight months, are doing so in the name of France, to attain the goals of France, in agreement with what France desires. Any system established on other foundations than these would lead to jeopardy or impotence. But France, who is staking her life, her greatness and her independence, admits in a matter as grave as this neither impotence nor jeopardy.'

The nation that would be victorious tomorrow must have a goal after its liberation, a goal capable of inspiring and maintaining it in its effort. Therefore, after having lauded the activities and the sacrifices of the resistance movement, I invoked the flame of regeneration that was inspiring it in its fight. 'France is not the sleeping beauty whom the prince of liberation will waken gently. France is a tortured captive who, beneath the blows that strike her in the cell where

E

she lies, has once and for all weighed the causes of her misfortunes with the infamy of her tyrants. France has already chosen a new road.' And I indicated at what objectives the resistance aimed at home and abroad once victory was achieved. I concluded by summoning the people to a sense of pride. 'Frenchmen, for fifteen hundred years our country has remained alive in its griefs and in its glories. The present ordeal is not over. But already the end of the worst drama in all our history is in sight. Let us lift our heads. Let us close ranks fraternally and march together, in the struggle, beyond victory to our new destinies.'

The flood of emotion with which the crowd replied to these words revealed on the spot the concluding failure of the intrigues which certain people had long opposed to me. It was quite obvious that the artificial systems successively set up in Algiers to protect incompetence and satisfy foreign powers were crumbling relentlessly, and that if certain formalities still remained, de Gaulle had won the game.

Mr Murphy, apparently impressed, came over to me on the platform to pay me his compliments. 'What an enormous crowd!' he told me.

'Those,' I answered him, 'are the ten per cent Gaullists that you reckoned on in Algiers.'

Morocco in its turn furnished a similar spectacle. On August 6th I reached Rabat. Here those who showed their sympathy for Free France had long been harshly punished and vilified, while many kept silence in the shadows. Now, beneath the brilliant sun, the population, the authorities and the prominent citizens acclaimed me without reserve. Ambassador Puaux, the Resident-General, gave me his report. His immediate concern was to keep alive a country cut off from all supplies and threatened by famine. As for the future, he saw looming there the problems posed by the political development of the protectorate. Nevertheless, the Resident-General was certain that Morocco would remain attached to France and assume its great share of the effort put forth by the Empire to liberate her.

Beneath the official pomp I made more intimate contact with Sultan Mohammed ben Youssef. This young, proud, personable sovereign did not conceal his ambition to be at the head of his country on its march towards progress and, one day, towards independence. Watching and listening to him as he spoke, sometimes ardent, sometimes prudent, always skilful, one felt that he was ready to come to an agreement with whoever would help him play this role, but that he was capable of bringing a great deal of obstinacy to bear against those who wished to oppose him in this design. Furthermore, he admired France, believed in her recovery and did not dream that Morocco could advance without her. If he had on occasion lent an ear to certain intimations which Germany in her triumphs had whispered to him, and if during the Anfa conference he had listened to Roosevelt's insinuations, he had nevertheless shown himself loyal to our country. It must be admitted that Noguès' influence had been happily exercised, in this context, on the sovereign's mind.

I believed I should take the Sultan Mohammed ben Youssef for precisely what he was, a man resolved to become great, and that I should show myself to him for what I was, the leader of a France that was his suzerain but one disposed to do much for those who stood by her. Making use of the credit which the success and the inspiration of Fighting France had stored up for me in his mind, I created bonds of a personal friendship with him. But we also concluded an alliance on the grounds of understanding and common action which neither of us ever broke as long as I could speak to him in the name of France.

On Sunday, August 8th, I made my entry into Casablanca. The walls had disappeared beneath flags and banners. Six months before I had had to reside in the city's outskirts, constrained to secrecy and surrounded with barbed wire and American sentry posts. Today my presence served as a symbol and a centre of French authority. Once the brilliant review of the troops was past, I addressed the human tide that covered the Place Lyautey. I spoke in tones of calm assurance. France's share in the victory was now certain, thanks to her unity and to that of the Empire, I said, citing as an example Morocco, 'who cries out her fervour, her confidence and her hope with the great voice of Casablanca'. That afternoon I visited Meknès. August 9th was spent at Fez. The Arab city, which I rode through in all directions in a tumult of trumpets and beneath a forest of banners, exploded in acclamations quite exceptional for this traditionally withdrawn place. Finally on the 10th, in the region of Ifrana, I received a magnificent welcome from the Berbers and their leaders.

At the very moment when the last clouds of misunderstanding were disappearing in Tunisia, Algeria and Morocco, the French

Antilles joined us with great enthusiasm. They did so of their own accord, without the Allies having directly intervened.

Since 1940 Admiral Robert, the High Commissioner, had kept these colonies under oath to the Marshal. Having at his disposal the cruisers *Emile-Bertin* and *Jeanne d'Arc*, the aircraft carrier *Béarn*, the auxiliary cruisers *Barfleur*, *Quercy* and *Esterel* and the tankers *Var* and *Mékong*, as well as an important garrison, he applied austerity measures and, by guaranteeing his neutrality, obtained essential supplies from the Americans. But as events moved, the population and many military units indicated their desire to join those who were fighting the enemy.

In the spring of 1941 I had sent Jean Massip, alias Colonel Perrel, to the Martinique and Guadeloupe area; his mission was to spread the influence of Free France and to send on to our fighting forces those volunteers who succeeded in escaping from the islands. Massip, despite many obstacles, had done everything possible. Operating from a base in the British colonies of St Lucia, Dominica and Trinidad, and assisted locally by several loyal Frenchmen such as Joseph Salvatori and Adigard des Gautries, he had managed to establish contact with the resistance units of Fort-de-France and Basse-Terre and to send into the active theatres more than two thousand volunteers. At the beginning of 1943 there was every indication that a great movement would soon sweep the French territories in the New World and the troops serving there into the camp of liberation.

In the month of March, Guiana rid itself of Vichy's authority, as it had wanted to do for some time. As early as October 1940 I had seen a detachment of two hundred men from the banks of the Maroni landing in Free French Africa, under Major Chandon's command. Later, a 'Rally Committee' had been formed, headed by M. Sophia, the mayor of Cayenne. On March 16th, 1943, the population gathered in the Place du Palmiste, loudly demanding the removal of the governor, and paraded through the city beneath Cross of Lorraine banners, cheering General de Gaulle. Faced with this outbreak, the governor had retired. M. Sophia had then telegraphed to inform me of his people's rallying to our cause and to ask that a new governor be sent to Cayenne. But on the urgent advice of the United States consul he had sent a similar telegram to General Giraud. At this period union had not been effected between the

London committee and the Algiers organization, so the Americans, who controlled Guiana's means of communication with the outside world, had arranged that Governor Rapenne, delegated by Giraud, should arrive in Cayenne as soon as possible, while Governor Bertaut, sent by me, could not reach the colony. Then, taking advantage of the fact that the colony's supplies depended entirely on their good offices, our allies had forced Guiana to accept an administrator who, though very creditable, was not the one they wanted. It is true that two months later the formation of the Committee of Liberation at Algiers permitted the regularization of what had strongly resembled a hoax.

In June Martinique took decisive action. For several months Admiral Robert had been receiving innumerable petitions urging him to let this ardently French territory do its duty toward France. In April 1943 I had found occasion to send Surgeon-General Le Dantec to Fort-de-France to offer Robert a satisfactory way out of his predicament, and in May proposed to Giraud to send the High Commissioner a letter signed by both of us, inviting him to re-enter the war at our side. These steps had been taken on the Admiral's behalf, but they remained without a reply. On the contrary, threats and sanctions against the local resistance redoubled on the island.

Meanwhile the island's Liberation Committee, having at its head Victor Sévère, the deputy mayor of Fort-de-France, as well as Emmanuel Rimbaud, Léontel Calvert and others, appeared openly. On June 18th, the anniversary of my 1940 appeal, this committee placed a Cross of Lorraine before the monument to the dead. Then it called upon the population to stage a mass meeting, which took place on June 24th. Five days later Major Tourtet and his battalion joined the movement. The excitement spread to the Navy. Admiral Robert was obliged to yield to it. On June 30th he made it public that he had asked the Government of the United States to send a plenipotentiary to establish the means of effecting a change of French authority and that he would retire after that was done. This announcement restored calm, although there was no evidence whatsoever that the Americans were needed to settle this national affair. Two days later a delegation from Martinique arrived in Dominica, informed Jean Massip of the colony's rallying to the cause of Free France and asked that General de Gaulle send a delegate armed with full powers.

At Guadeloupe events had followed an analogous course. For a long time the population's hopes and desires had been inclined toward Free France. M. Valentino, president of the executive commission of the general council, with M. Melor, M. Gérard and other prominent citizens, had formed a Committee of the Resistance. Valentino, arrested and then transferred to Guiana, managed after that colony's liberation to return to Guadeloupe in secret. On May 2nd, 1943, a demonstration in favour of Fighting France took place at Basse-Terre and ended by a bloody fusillade directed on the crowd by soldiers acting under orders. On June 4th Valentino and his cohorts vainly tried to seize power, but subsequently managed to reach Jean Massip. At the end of the same month, Robert's retirement at Martinique finally decided the matter at Guadeloupe.

On July 3rd the Committee of National Liberation, informed of these events, sent as delegate extraordinary to the Antilles its representative in Washington, Ambassador Henri Hoppenot. The latter, accompanied by high ranking Army, Navy and Air Force officers, reached Fort-de-France on July 14th. Beneath a sea of Cross of Lorraine flags, in a storm of '*Vive de Gaulle!*' he was received by Sévère, his committee and an immense throng. Hoppenot and his mission took affairs in hand immediately. With tact and firmness they put everything and everyone in order. Admiral Robert went to Puerto Rico and from there to Vichy. Governor Ponton, sent from Equatorial Africa, was appointed Governor of Martinique. Secretary-General Poirier, and later Governor Bertaut received the responsibility for Guadeloupe. The Bank of France's gold stored at Fort-de-France passed into the control of the Algiers committee. The naval squadron was ordered to the United States, and after being reconditioned it reached North Africa. The troops were incorporated into the army of liberation. In particular, the Antilles Battalion, under the orders of Lieutenant-Colonel Tourtet, was to take a brilliant part in the battle of Royan, where its leader was killed by the enemy.

The rallying of the Antilles completed the fulfilment of a great national plan which had been glimpsed during the disaster by the last government of the Third Republic, adopted by Free France immediately after the 'armistice' and subsequently pursued at all costs, but to which the Vichy governors, obeying, conscientiously or not, the enemy's intentions, had always been opposed. Except for Indo-

China, which Japan held at her mercy, all the territories of the Empire had now re-entered the war for the liberation of France.

As for the French overseas forces, they too had all joined us. The Alexandria squadron, stranded in neutrality since 1940, had in June 1943 placed itself under the government's orders, by its commander's decision. In August, Admiral Godfroy brought to the ports of North Africa by way of the Red Sea, the Cape and Dakar, the battleship *Lorraine*, the cruisers *Duguay-Trouin, Duquesne, Suffren* and *Tourville*, the destroyers *Basque, Forbin* and *Fortuné* and the submarine *Protée*. These splendid units, like those from the Antilles, re-entered the struggle in their turn. Such reinforcements, along with the ships remaining to the fleet in the African ports and those flying the Cross of Lorraine, were to ensure the reappearance on the seas of an important French naval force by which Europe would see victory approach.

The obscure harmony by which events are arranged made the renewal of French power coincide with the weakening of the enemy's. Italy, once again in Byron's phrase, 'the sad mother of a dead empire' and about to be invaded, was heading towards a breach with the German Reich. For the French Committee of National Liberation, the problems posed by the Italian *volte-face* were to lead it to consolidate itself as a government. At the same time, the Allies were compelled to realize that there could be no valid settlement of the Italian question without French participation. Then, too, the rigorous campaign opening in the peninsula soon necessitated the co-operation of our troops and our ships. The Allies therefore were inclined to accord us a proportionate share in the diplomatic realm as on the field of battle. Having need of France, they had to address themselves willy-nilly to the central French power.

On July 10th a British and an American army under the command of General Alexander landed in Sicily. We had not been asked to take part in this operation, the reason given being the insufficient armament of our units, which had in fact received only a small amount of American equipment. Actually Washington and London, counting on the imminent collapse of Italy, preferred us not to be involved in the decisive battle, nor in the armistice that would follow.

In Sicily our allies ran into stiff resistance from the Germans, who had rushed to defend the island. Nevertheless, after six weeks of hard-fought battles, the Anglo-American forces ended by taking

Sicily. Meanwhile it was learned that the Fascist Grand Council had repudiated Mussolini, that the King of Italy had arrested the Duce, that Marshal Badoglio had been appointed Prime Minister. To be sure, the latter proclaimed his resolve to continue the war on the Axis side, but it was obvious that this attitude masked contrary intentions. The Fuehrer was no more deceived than anyone else. In the speech he made on the radio the next day, the anxiety of the betrayed ally could be discerned beneath the screams of threatening assurance. Also noticeable was a human note rare with the dictator. Hitler hailed Mussolini as the fallen comrade; he did so in the tone of a man who was soon to fall himself but who intended to measure himself against destiny until the end.

The Roman *coup de théâtre* occurred on July 25th. On the 27th I took my stand publicly. Speaking on the radio, I declared that Mussolini's fall, the sign of the certain defeat of the Axis and a proof of the failure of the Fascist system, was for France the first of the revenges of justice. 'Mussolini's example,' I said, 'is now added to the history of all those who outraged the majesty of France and whom destiny has punished.' Having stressed the fact that we must redouble our efforts to achieve victory, I stated: 'The collapse of Italian Fascism may very soon lead to a new settlement of accounts. And it is quite obvious that despite the terrible situation in which our country still finds herself, such a settlement can be neither valid nor lasting without France.' I let it be understood, moreover, that in this participation we would be animated by a desire for reconciliation rather than by the spirit of revenge, 'since the nearness and, to a certain degree, the interdependence of the two great Latin peoples are still, despite present grievances, the elements on which the reason and the hope of Europe do not despair of establishing themselves'. Lastly I reaffirmed 'the duties imposed and the rights conferred in this matter on the Committee of National Liberation by the ardent confidence of the overwhelming French majority and its own character as a body responsible for the sacred interests of the nation'.

But how sustained could such a policy be if we ourselves remained plunged in confusion? On July 31st, Giraud having returned from his trip abroad, I took up the question with the committee in a hand-to-hand struggle. This time the government adopted measures that brought us nearer our goal.

Leadership of the Committee and the chairmanship of the sessions

henceforth devolved upon de Gaulle alone. Although Giraud retained as I did, along with the title of president, the privilege of
signing all ordinances and decrees, this was no longer anything but
a mere formality, since their texts were previously determined in
council under my sole arbitration. In the military domain, a coalition of all forces was decided on; the Military High Committee
became, under my chairmanship, the Committee for National
Defence; General Giraud was decreed Commander-in-Chief of the
French forces, it being understood that he would cease to be a
member of the government if occasion should eventually arise for
him to assume command in a definite theatre of war. General
Legentilhomme, recalled from Madagascar, assumed the functions
of Vice-Commissioner, and, shortly afterward, of Commissioner of
National Defence. General Leyer, Admiral Lemonnier and General
Bouscat became the Chiefs of Staff respectively of the Army, the Navy
and the Air Force, with General Koenig, Admiral Auboyneau and
General Valin to second them as deputy chiefs. As for Juin, he was
confirmed in his mission of preparing and, shortly, of commanding
the expeditionary corps destined for Italy.

These arrangements settled the essential problems in theory; they
would still have to be applied. Despite previous experiences, I
wanted to believe this would be possible. I hoped that General
Giraud, having received the highest title and the most extensive
powers the Committee could give to a military leader without relin-
quishing its own, would renounce his claims to governmental
authority; that he would operate in his own domain only, apart
from the man who bore the burden of directing the government.
Right at the beginning it appeared possible that this might happen.

Through the month of August and the first days of September,
the Committee of National Liberation continued to function as it
had in July and played its governmental role. Thus, for matters concerning mobilization, finance, supply, transportation, housing, the
merchant marine, outfitting of ports and airfields, public health, etc.,
many problems could be settled. These were often made very difficult by the extreme penury of territories which were dependent in
peacetime on goods from abroad now no longer available, deprived
of important military equipment, subject to multiple taxation and
over-populated because of the presence of Allied troops and large
numbers of refugees from metropolitan France.

At the same time the committee defined its position in regard to the resistance movement as well as to Vichy. It convoked the Consultative Assembly for November, while on September 3rd, without objection from a single one of its members, it passed the following resolution which was immediately made public:

> *Resolved.* To assure, as soon as circumstances permit, the operation of justice in regard to Marshal Pétain and to those who have taken or are taking part in the pseudo-governments formed by him, who have capitulated, violated the constitution, collaborated with the enemy, handed over French workers to the Germans and compelled French forces to fight against the Allies or against those of the French who were continuing the struggle.

Abroad the Committee's action was affirmed in the same way. The diplomatic, economic and military missions which Fighting France and the Algiers system had respectively and separately maintained in England and the United States were now unified. Viénot in London and Hoppenot in Washington were now our sole representatives, each having under his authority all officials and military men present in the country to which he was accredited. In August we appointed Jean Monnet, Commissioner of Armament and Supply, to engage in negotiations with the American, British and Canadian Governments that would result in reciprocal lend-lease agreements including equipment, foodstuffs and services provided by one party or the other, and to prepare what must be done at the time of liberation to assure France's basic necessities. During this time Couve de Murville, Commissioner of Finance, and the Chancellor of the Exchequer terminated the financial agreement made in March 1941 between Free France and England. On September 7th we addressed to Washington and London a draft of an agreement specifying the 'methods of co-operation to be established, from the day when the Allied forces should land in France, between these forces and the authorities and population', and requesting the immediate discussion of this matter by the three governments. We suspected, in fact, that our allies were cherishing the plan of assuming, under cover of their military command, the governmental control of our country as they penetrated it, and we were of course resolved to keep them from doing so.

Finally, realizing that the Italian capitulation was imminent and that our allies would associate us with the advantages and honours of the triumph in the least possible degree, we informed them officially that the French Committee of National Liberation intended to take part 'first in the armistice negotiations, then in the deliberations and decisions of those bodies whose task it will be to assure the execution of the conditions imposed upon Italy'. This was how we expressed ourselves in a note René Massigli took to Macmillan and Murphy on August 2nd. The same note specified the points directly concerning France which we felt should be inserted in the future convention.

In the military domain, the collaboration of the head of the government and the commander-in-chief seemed, at present, satisfactory. General Giraud, delighted to see himself confirmed in a capacity dear to him and to take the Free French forces under his command, flaunted his loyalty. The Committee for National Defence had no difficulty in adopting the measures concerning the merging of our forces. Leclerc and his column reached Morocco. The Larminat Group took up positions in Tunisia. Various ships and several air groups originating in North Africa were sent to Great Britain to operate from English bases side by side with Cross of Lorraine units. At the same time the Committee for National Defence determined on the plan for reorganizing the Army, the Navy and the Air Force on the basis of the officers and fighting strength at our disposal in accordance with the armament coming from the United States. As for the use of these forces within the coalition, our intentions were established in the form of a de Gaulle-Giraud memorandum addressed on September 18th to Roosevelt, Churchill and Stalin.

Having reckoned the units we could put into the field, we indicated that, without prejudice to what could be done beforehand in Italy with the co-operation of our troops, the principal French effort on land, on sea and in the air would be dedicated directly to the liberation of France and would be engaged in the south of metropolitan France, embarking from North Africa. All the same, we wrote, certain of our forces must take part in the northern operations. At least one French armoured division must be transported to England in time to assure the liberation of Paris. Also, a regiment of parachute troops, some commandos, several ships and five or six air groups would be engaged from the beginning of the landing.

Lastly, we made known our willingness to send to the Far East, once the battle of Europe was won, an expeditionary corps and the bulk of our naval forces in order to co-operate in the struggle against Japan and to liberate Indo-China. All of this was in fact to be accomplished in that order, point by point.

During the month of August I inspected the troops in Algeria, the warships fitted out in the ports of Algiers and Oran, and the air bases. Everywhere I conferred with the officers. Ever since the disaster of 1940, the defection of the Vichy leaders, the weakening of discipline and chance circumstances had led many of these men of honour and duty into paths other than those they were now following. But none, in his heart of hearts, had ever lost hope of re-entering the battle against the enemies of France. Beneath their attitude of attention and respect they were profoundly impressed by the presence of this de Gaulle whom a certain political group had often commanded them to disapprove and occasionally ordered them to oppose, but whom the national instinct and the logic of events now endowed with supreme power and whose authority not one of them dreamed of questioning. I watched them straining to hear and understand me while I spoke to them with the dignity but also with the frankness due to us both. The speech delivered, the salutes exchanged, the handshakes given, I left their company and went on to some other task, resolved more than ever that the French Army should exact its share of the victory and thereby herald the future of the nation.

The consolidation of French authority obliged the Allies to depart somewhat from the attitude of doubt and distrust they had hitherto adopted. Official recognition was granted the Committee of Liberation by the United States, Great Britain and Soviet Russia on August 26th. Mexico, Cuba, Norway, Greece, Poland, Chile and Belgium had already taken the necessary steps.

As a matter of fact, the formulas chosen by the other three great powers revealed profound differences. Washington employed the most restricted, announcing that the committee was recognized as administering the overseas territories which recognized its authority. London used the same terms, but added that in the eyes of Great Britain the committee was the body qualified to pursue the conduct of the French war effort. Moscow revealed itself as the most generous. For Soviet Russia, the committee represented 'the interests of state of the French Republic'; it was 'the only executive body and the only qualified representative of all French patriots struggling against Hitlerism'. The example of the Big Three was rapidly followed by others. On September 3rd, speaking on the radio on the occasion of the war's fourth anniversary, I was able to say, 'The recognition of the French Committee of National Liberation by twenty-six states furnishes striking proof of our solidarity for victory and for peace.'

However, the organization of the central power, as it had been determined on July 31st, could subsist only if the subordination of the military command to the government were confirmed without argument within the committee and abroad. The Italian affair was to demonstrate that this was not the case.

On September 3rd, Badoglio, who for several weeks had been making secret contact with Anglo-American agents, surrendered to them through the intermediary of a delegation sent to Syracuse. At the same time the Allied forces landed in Calabria. An American army under the command of General Clark prepared to land in the vicinity of Naples to join and, if need be, protect the King of Italy and his government with the troops loyal to them which they had concentrated at Rome. On August 29th Macmillan and Murphy had sent Massigli a memorandum in anticipation of the Italians' surrender, asking the French Committee of Liberation to agree that in its name, as in the name of all the Allied Nations, General Eisenhower was empowered to sign with Marshal Badoglio an armistice convention covering all Allied needs, notably those of France. The memorandum indicated the broad outlines of the instrument envisaged and ended with an assurance that the governments of the United Kingdom and the United States would do what they could to make it possible for the French Committee of National Liberation to send a representative to the signing if it should so desire.

We had answered on September 1st by a note agreeing that Eisenhower should conclude the armistice in our name, as in the name of all the Allies, asking that the text of the document be sent to us immediately, and declaring ourselves ready at a moment's notice to send a representative of the French command to wherever the armistice convention was to be signed.

Now came the moment for Washington and London to show whether or not they intended that France should be their full partner in the successive settlements that were to terminate hostilities. This occasion seemed all the more propitious since it concerned Italy, whom French forces had never ceased to fight, whose territory, it was well known, could not be wrested from the Germans without the co-operation of our army, and who had no other neighbour among the Western countries but France and would not be able to have her territorial, political, economic and colonial future decided without France. Nevertheless, we were to discover that in this crucial affair Americans and British alike would proceed quite unscrupulously towards our committee only a few days after having formally recognized it.

In fact, on the afternoon of September 8th Macmillan and Murphy came to tell Massigli that the Italian surrender was a *fait accompli* and that General Eisenhower would announce it in half an hour. They also sent to the Commissioner of Foreign Affairs—ridiculous formality!—the text of the declaration in which the Allied Commander-in-Chief made public virtually that very moment that he had granted the Italian Government a military armistice whose terms had been approved by the British, American and Soviet Governments.

When Massigli pointed out that there was no mention of France, contrary to what England and the United States had, in writing, given us to believe on August 29th, his interlocutors replied that Eisenhower's declaration was above all a manoeuvre hastily employed to impress the Italian Army and population while the Allies were carrying out a new and difficult operation in the peninsula.

'Manoeuvre or not,' Massigli returned, 'you tell me that an armistice has been signed. When was it signed? What were its terms?'

Macmillan and Murphy confined themselves to saying that General Giraud, president of the French Committee, had been kept *au courant* by Supreme Headquarters and that he had had nothing to add on France's behalf. That night Massigli saw Macmillan again, and questioned him; the British Secretary of State admitted that the negotiations of the London and Washington Governments with the Italian Government had been in progress since August 20th. But he repeated that Giraud had been informed of everything.

On September 9th I convened the Committee of Liberation. The report of the Commissioner of Foreign Affairs naturally aroused emotion and displeasure as to the procedure and the probable intentions of the Anglo-American powers. We issued a communiqué expressing France's satisfaction at Italy's defeat, recalling the contribution of the French armies and the resistance, and acknowledging General Eisenhower's declaration, but stating that 'the vital interests of metropolitan France and the French Empire involve the participation of France in any convention concerning Italy'.

During the session I asked General Giraud his reasons for not informing the government, and in particular its head, of the vital news which had been communicated to him by the Allies, which, had we known about it in time, would have let us make the most of what was due to France. Giraud assured us that he had received no information about the armistice. When, on the evening of that same day, Massigli reported this denial to Macmillan and to Murphy, they maintained their assertions, at the same time suggesting with some embarrassment that the ignorance of French in Eisenhower's headquarters and of English among Giraud's General Staff might be the cause of the misunderstanding. The next day they came to apologize, saying that after an investigation they had discovered it was only that morning that General Eisenhower had informed General Giraud of the terms of the armistice.

There could be no doubt: our Allies were in agreement to keep us at as great a distance as they could from decisions concerning Italy. We could expect that tomorrow they would make still greater efforts to determine the destiny of Europe without France. But they had to be made to realize that France would not tolerate this exclusion, and that they could not count on her in the future if they disregarded her now.

On September 12th, on the occasion of my official visit to Oran, I dotted the i's and crossed the t's. Speaking to an enormous crowd before the City Hall: I declared, 'The country wishes to redouble its efforts in order to hasten the enemy's defeat. It also wishes to take part, in its rightful position, in the settlement of the conflict and the reconstruction of the world.' On this point I appealed to the 'solidarity of the nations of good will', adding, 'There exists among them an interdependence which is such that each has an obligation to consider the vital interests and the dignity of the others.' Referring to the suffering French people and the French soldiers of the Empire and of metropolitan France who were taking and would take part in the great battles, I warned, 'The only true realism is the realism that does not deceive them.'

'In the fifth year of the war,' I acknowledged, 'France unfortunately is not in a position to put into the line many of those divisions, ships and air squadrons by which the contribution of states may be summarily reckoned. As a result of a disaster when France, almost alone, confronted Hitler and Mussolini, the spirit of surrender that possessed certain people partially sabotaged the national war effort. We staggered, it is true. But was this not, more than anything, a result of the blood we shed some twenty years before, as much in others' defence as in our own?' I concluded by declaring, 'France claims, in the interest of all, the place she deserves in the resolution of the drama whose dénouement is now beginning.' All the eloquence in the world was in the popular acclamation that greeted this speech.

It was evident, from the behaviour of Messrs Macmillan and Murphy, that our allies had invoked if not employed the ridiculous dualism of our government as an alibi for breaking their word. Almost immediately afterwards, the same dualism was to show its weakness in regard to an important national and military operation: the liberation of Corsica.

In 1941 Free France had sent Captain Scamaroni to the island with a mission to prepare action there. For two years Scamaroni had done excellent work, managing to unite all resistance groups so that no party or clan could monopolize the general effort for its own advantage. The National Front with Giovoni as its political leader and Vittori as its military chief, both of them Communists, had accepted the delegate of Free France, as had the patriots morally committed to Raimondi and the Giaccobbi brothers, and even the bands led by former soldiers, such as that of Lieutenant Alphonse de Peretti. Unfortunately, our valiant delegate had fallen into the hands of the Italians, who had occupied the island the day after the Allies landed in North Africa. Tortured horribly, Scamaroni had died to keep his secrets.

At this period—March 1943—the Battle of Tunisia was drawing to its close. There was every indication that Corsica would be next among the operations directed toward Italy and the south of France. In this island of maquis,[1] fiercely attached to France, where the in-

[1] The scrubby brushland of Corsica, which is often used as a place of hiding by local outlaws and which gave its name to the French underground fighters resisting the occupation forces during the Second World War.—TR.

vader's presence and pretensions provoked the most intense patriotism, a great tide of rebellion was secretly rising. Thousands of
resolute men, supported by the population's active sympathy,
awaited impatiently the occasion to open fire.

The Algiers system, in its turn, made contact with Corsica. The
'Civil and Military Commander-in-Chief' first sent a few agents,
then, in April 1943, Major Colonna d'Istria. In itself, this was entirely praiseworthy. What was less so was the fact that, once our
Algiers committee was constituted in June, General Giraud did not
breathe a word to me of the action he was taking in Corsica.
Colonna described himself on the island, no doubt in good faith, as
the representative of the entire government. In this capacity he dealt
exclusively with the Communist leaders Giovoni and Vittori, either
because he did not realize the disadvantage of this preference, or
because he wished to simplify his task, or because he had received
orders to do so. It must be added that the Communist Party had
sent on a mission to Giraud, from France, Deputy Pourtalet of the
Alpes-Maritimes, who had been in contact with Giovoni for some
time from Nice. Pourtalet had not failed to provide Giraud with
information about the situation in Corsica and suggestions that were
of advantage to his party. During the months of July and August,
General Giraud's secret services were extremely active, without my
knowledge, in their efforts to arm the Corsican resistance. British
intelligence, which ordinarily did not go out of its way to be
generous without ulterior motives, procured ten thousand machine-
guns. These were shipped from Algiers, some by the submarine
Casabianca, which made several perilous crossings, others by British
planes which parachuted them into areas indicated by Colonna. All
these weapons, received and distributed by the leaders of the
'National Front', decisively conferred on Giovoni and Vittori the
monopoly of authority. The Communist leaders seized control of the
whole resistance movement, in which, however, the members of
their party comprised only a minority. All communication between
Algiers and the island's 'Gaullists' being cut off, the latter, lacking
any other resource, compromised with the organization to the point
where my own cousin, Henri Maillot, agreed to become a member
of the National Front Committee in the belief that he was fulfilling
my intentions.

On September 4th, the day after Badoglio signed the armistice which I was not to hear about until the 8th, Giovoni was brought to Algiers by the *Casabianca*. I did not know he was there. He came to confer with the Commander-in-Chief concerning an operation which the Syracuse surrender was to make possible by rendering neutral or favourable the eight thousand Italians occupying Corsica. Giraud told me nothing of this visit; Giovoni made no contact with me and left Algiers on September 6th. On the evening of the 9th we learned that the resistance party had taken control of Ajaccio, that the prefect himself had proclaimed the department's support of the Committee of National Liberation, and that the Italian garrison had offered no opposition. It was then that General Giraud came to tell me for the first time what he had been doing in Corsica.

When he had told his story I replied. 'Amid all the good news now reaching us, General, I am offended and disturbed by your manner of proceeding towards me and the government, in concealing your activities from us. I do not approve of the monopoly you have given to the Communist leaders. I consider it unacceptable that you have let it be thought that this was done in my name as well as in yours. Lastly, having heard what you have to say concerning Giovoni's recent visit, the operation you worked out with him and the conditions under which it was launched, I cannot understand how you could say this morning to our council of ministers that you did not know of the imminence of the Italian armistice. From all this I shall draw the obvious conclusions once we have extricated ourselves from the difficulties which now surround us. For the moment, we must deal with the military situation. Corsica must be given aid at once. The government will then do what it must to dam, once and for all, the source of our disagreements.' At least Giraud and I agreed that troops should be sent to Corsica immediately. The execution of this operation was in his sphere of activity; in that regard I had no doubt he would decide for the best.

The Committee of Liberation convened the next day and adopted a similar attitude toward the Commander-in-Chief. While they entrusted him with powers to settle the military situation, they reproached him for having taken action alone and deliberately in a sphere which did not properly belong to him. During the same session Charles Luizet was appointed prefect of Corsica. He was to leave without delay with a trustworthy team. General Mollard would accompany him as military governor of the island.

The military action in Corsica was carried out with great ardour, although the intervention of the regular troops and of the ships carrying them was quite improvised. Actually a complete plan had been drawn up several weeks before by General Juin at the Commander-in-Chief's request. On the supposition that the Italians would remain neutral, Juin advised simultaneous landings on the east and the west coasts with the aim of cutting the Germans off from the two coastal roads. He anticipated the engagement of two divisions, one of them mountain troops, a *Tabor* Group, a hundred armoured units and some commandos. In this way the German forces already stationed on the island and those that would come from Sardinia could be liquidated or captured. On September 9th the elements of such an expedition were available and eager to get into action, but their transportation required considerable tonnage, as well as heavy naval and air protection. Since the necessary warships, merchant ships and planes had not been assembled in advance, the Commander-in- Chief was in no position to execute so extensive an operation with our own means. Turning to the Allies for aid, he met with a refusal, for at that moment they were fully engaged in their attempt to land at Salerno.

However, matters were at a point where some immediate action had to be taken. Giraud decided, and I approved his decision, to effect the operation on a reduced scale. The troops he could manage to infiltrate into Corsica in the space of three weeks would, with the help of the resistance, be able to protect the greater part of the island against German points of attack, to harass the German columns during their retreat and to inflict important losses on German personnel and equipment. It was true that despite the vigour of their action they could not prevent the enemy from putting to sea; nevertheless, the liberation of Corsica by French forces and French forces alone would make a profound impression on the French and on the Allies.

On the night of September 12th, the valiant *Casabianca* landed our first units at Ajaccio. Day after day the troops arrived: the 'Shock Battalion', the Moroccan First Rifle Regiment, the Second *Tabor* Group, a mechanized squadron of the First Spahi Regiment, units of artillery, engineers and services, as well as the indispensable equipment, munitions and petrol. Everything was transported by the cruisers *Jeanne d'Arc* and *Montcalm*, the destroyers *Fantasque* and

Terrible, the torpedo boats *Alcyon* and *Tempête,* the submarines *Aréthuse* and *Casabianca.* An air pursuit squadron took the Campo del Oro base. The German goal was to evacuate the SS brigade they had on the island, and also the Ninetieth Panzer Division, which they hastily withdrew from Sardinia. Their manoeuvre was executed on the east on the Bonifacio-Bastia road under protection of heavy air cover and strong reconnaissance forces which they launched toward the island's interior. Many motorized barges took them on at Bastia and headed for the island of Elba and for Leghorn.

General Henry Martin was at the head of the French troops. He handled the operation with great competence: first securing a bridge-head at Ajaccio, then sending commandos to support the resistance, which was grappling fiercely with the enemy at Bastia, Bonifacio, Quenza, Levie, Inzecca and other points, and holding the passes along the island's 'spine'. Then he mopped up Porto Vecchio, Bonifacio, Favone, Ghisonaccia, and finally, approaching Bastia, he drove back the Germans over the wooded, mountainous terrain of St Florent and Cape Corse. General Martin also came to a useful agreement with General Magli, commander of the Italian forces. The latter, despite the confusion of the odd situation in which he found himself, agreed to furnish our men with trucks and mule teams and to support them at certain points with his batteries. General Louchet headed the advance in the north, Major Gambiez the shock troops, Colonel de Latour the Algerian contingents, Colonel de Butler the rifles, Colonel de Lambilly the armoured units; all led their troops brilliantly. General Giraud himself reached Corsica a few days after the first landings, examined the terrain and communicated to everyone the resolution that animated him. On October 4th our men entered Bastia, from which the enemy had been able to pull out his rear guard, but not without leaving a great deal of equipment.

The evening of the same day, I went to the Commander-in-Chief to congratulate him in the name of the government on the splendid results of his military operation. He had prepared and launched it, he had assumed the risk. The credit for it was his. Although the means at his disposal were on a rather small scale, the difficulties were great since without preparation he had to take elements from the Army, the Navy and the Air Force, hurl them more than 500 miles from our bases into the unknown, and combine them in a single action. On September 24th I said over the radio from Algiers 'The nation and the Empire salute the French fighters in Corsica, where the Commander-in-Chief of the French Army has just gone into the field himself to give orders for tomorrow's engagement. To these fighters and to their leaders, to those who have risen from the Corsican soil to liberate themselves and those whom the reviving French Army, Navy and Air Force have so boldly sent to them, the Committee of National Liberation addresses the heart-felt testimony of France's love and pride.'

But, justice having been done to General Giraud's military capabilities, the fact remained that he had behaved in an inadmissible fashion *vis-à-vis* the government. I told him this that evening after having complimented him.

'You're talking politics,' he said.

'Yes,' I answered. 'Because we are fighting a war. And war is one kind of politics.' He heard but did not heed my words.

Fundamentally, Giraud could not resign himself to any form of subordination whatever. What he seemed to accept was never actually established. By nature and habit, but also as a matter of tactics, his mind shut itself within the purely military sphere, refused to consider human or national realities and made him blind to the prerogatives of the government. With his temperament he could not disregard the old hierarchy in relation to me, even though he understood the exceptional character of the mission that had devolved upon me. Moreover, he could give generous and moving evidence of this recognition, in public and in private, but he did not see the practical consequences of his words or actions. It must be added that the circumstances that had recently brought him to supreme power in North Africa, the support which American policy gave him, the bitterness and the ill will felt towards me by certain French elements were not without influence on his ideas and his behaviour.

It was essential to put an end to this unsound situation. From that time on I was determined to induce General Giraud to leave the government, but to continue to make use of his services. Furthermore, the members of the Committee of Liberation also understood that we could delay no longer. Two new members whom I had invited to join us during September reinforced the trend towards categorical solutions. François de Menthon, arriving from France,

had been appointed National Commissioner of Justice. Pierre
Mendès-France, resigning from the 'Lorraine' Air Force group on
my orders, assumed the Finance post, replacing Couve de Murville,
who had asked to be appointed France's representative on the Commission on Italian Affairs. Indeed, what seemed to be happening
now in Corsica in the political sphere was making an impression on
the ministers. André Philip, having visited the island to see how
matters stood, had ascertained that the Communists, making use
of the resistance, were installing town councils of their own choosing
and were seizing control of all mass media. At no price did the
ministers wish to see this precedent followed in metropolitan France.
They therefore urged me to make changes in the government's
structure which would protect it from such surprises.

Their concern was my own. But I intended to proceed with circumspection to the last in regard to the great soldier who, throughout his career, had rendered so many brilliant services and whose
family the enemy had seized and was treating in a disgraceful way
at that very moment.

As for Corsica, everything was to fall into place there. I arrived on
the island on October 8th and spent three magnificent days. My visit
dispelled the remaining shadows. At Ajaccio I addressed the people
in the town hall square. In response to the welcome I was given, my
first words were to acknowledge 'the tide of national enthusiasm
which today bears us all onwards'. I paid tribute in the same breath
to both the Corsican patriots and the African army. I indicated the
complete collapse of the Vichy regime. 'Where then,' I said, 'is the
famous National Revolution today? How has it happened that so
many portraits and insignia have given way in the wink of an eye to
the heroic Cross of Lorraine? It was enough that the first tremor of
liberation should cross the Corsican earth for this part of France
to turn with a single impulse towards the government which is
fighting the war, the government of unity, the government of the
Republic.'

Then, remarking that I was speaking 'from the centre of a Latin
sea', I spoke of Italy. I emphasized how ridiculous had been the
ambitions of our Latin neighbour, 'impelled only yesterday to a
monstrous alliance with German greed and alleging our decadence
as a pretext to attempt to seize Corsica'. But I also declared, 'Once
justice has been done, the France of tomorrow will not congeal in an

attitude of bitterness towards a nation which is closely related to us and which nothing fundamental should divide from us.'

'Victory is approaching,' I said in conclusion. 'It will be the victory of liberty. How could such a victory not be the victory of France as well?'

At Ajaccio I was in a position to see that Luizet, the prefect, Mollard, the military governor, and Eugène Macchini, the mayor, had matters well in hand. Corte was vibrant with acclamation, though losing nothing of its rugged dignity. I went to Sartène and then visited Bastia, its streets filled with rubble where the enemy had burned or exploded great stocks of equipment and munitions before fleeing, and where the miserable cemetery, torn apart by detonations, was the saddest spectacle of all. Surrounded by the first inhabitants to return to their homes, General Martin presented me to the victorious troops. Everywhere the para-military groups showed themselves justly proud of having upheld Corsica's glory by fighting for France. Every village in which I stopped lavished the most moving demonstrations upon us, while the Italian soldiers billeted there did not conceal their sympathy. Both on arriving and on my departure, my face stung by the rice my hosts flung according to the old Corsican custom, I heard the crackling of the liberation's machine-guns.

Four weeks later the transformation of the Algiers committee became a *fait accompli*. In any case, the convening of the Consultative Assembly at the beginning of November made its overhauling necessary. After perilous journeys the resistance delegates arrived amongst us, bringing to North Africa the spirit of their constituents. Suddenly a fierce and salubrious spirit swept through the meetings, the offices and the newspapers of Algiers. The delegates made public the messages of trust in de Gaulle which they had been given. They spoke of the underground, of its heroes and of its needs. They were brimming with ideas for the nation's future. In the task of extricating the government from its state of dual control, I wanted to associate myself with certain of the men coming to us from France.

During October the Committee of Liberation adopted, at my suggestion, a measure by virtue of which it would have only one president. Giraud himself set his signature to this. Furthermore, as the outlook for sending a French expeditionary corps into Italy grew brighter, he began again to hope that the Allies would call upon him to assume the high command in the peninsula. On November 6th, in the presence of General Giraud and with his explicit agreement, the committee asked that 'General de Gaulle proceed with those changes he considers it necessary to make in its composition'.

This was done on November 9th. A year after the bloody landing of the Anglo-American forces in Algeria and Morocco and five months after my own uncertain arrival in Algiers, the national will, oppressed and muffled as it was, had ended by carrying the day. So obvious was the current that the malevolence of its opponents could exist only in obscurity. As for the Allies they had to resign themselves to seeing France at war led by a French Government. No longer invoking 'military necessities' and 'security of communications', their policy came to terms with what it could not prevent. The common effort was to gain much thereby. For myself, I felt strong enough in my cause to be certain that tomorrow the battle and the victory of the others would also be the battle and the victory of France.

V. POLITICS

THERE WAS EVERY indication that the coming winter—1943 to 1944—would be the last before the fate of the war was decided by force of arms. But what government was to be established in Paris on the morrow? And what would such a government do? These were no longer questions affecting some remote time in the future. Decisions were imminent. This was why calculations and estimates were stimulated and brought to light. Political debate could be muffled a little while longer by blood and tears, veiled by the constraints imposed upon public opinion; but in spite of everything it was opened not only in the chancelleries and by men in office but in the thoughts of a tremendous mass of French people and in the discussions of great numbers of men abroad. Everyone knew that France would reappear. Everyone wondered what that France would be.

This was what I had in mind when, at the beginning of November 1943, I changed the form of the Committee of Liberation. The country's only hope, during the decisive period now opening before it, was national unity; I meant the government to bear its seal. Each of the principal parties, or, more accurately, each of the spiritual families among which the French people have traditionally distributed themselves, would be represented by men whose affiliations were well known. But today it was the resistance that furnished the war effort and bore within it France's hope of regeneration. It was therefore essential that some of its leaders who as yet had no label should also sit beside me in the government. Lastly, several eminent authorities must be invited to serve on the committee in order to help its activities and reinforce its credit.

Henri Queuille, Commissioner of State, and Pierre Mendès-France, Commissioner of Finance, were Radical members of Parliament. André Philip, in charge of the committee's relations with the

Consultative Assembly, André Le Troquer, Commissioner of War and the Air Force—both deputies—and Adrien Tixier, Commissioner of Labour and Social Security, belonged to the Socialist Party; Louis Jacquinot, Commissioner of the Navy, was a Moderate deputy. François de Menthon, Keeper of the Seals, sat on the executive committee of the Christian Democratic Party. Such was our share of politicians. René Pleven, Commissioner for the Colonies, Emmanuel d'Astier of the Interior, René Capitant of National Education, André Diethelm of Production and Supply, Henri Frénay of Prisoners, Deportees and Refugees were all resistance members who had previously given no evidence of specific political leanings. General Catroux, Commissioner of State for Moslem affairs, Henri Bonnet, Commissioner of Information, René Massigli of Foreign Affairs, René Mayer of Communications and the Merchant Marine, Jean Monnet, Commissioner on a special mission to the United States for supplies and armament, compelled recognition by their skill and their reputations. Without the formal assent of the religious hierarchy, I could not ask Monsignor Hincky to join the government as I should have liked.

I had recast but not overturned the Committee of Liberation. Of the sixteen members only four had just joined it. It is true that four were also leaving it—General Giraud, whose military functions were henceforth recognized by everyone, including himself, as incompatible with the exercise of governmental power; General Georges, who withdrew with dignity; Dr Abadie, who wished to return to his scientific work; and General Legentilhomme, who had asked for a post in Great Britain.

The part that the Communists were playing in the resistance, as well as my own intention that their forces be incorporated with those of the nation at least for the duration of the war, led me to the decision to include two in the government. Since the end of August, the party, foreseeing this, had willingly promised the co-operation of several members. But, at the last moment, all kinds of setbacks kept those whom I invited to join the Committee of Liberation from giving me a positive answer. On one occasion the party's delegation proposed other possible members, on another it asked for details of my programme, on still others it insisted that its members be given certain specific portfolios. Eventually, antagonized by this prolonged haggling, I broke off the negotiations.

In reality, two viewpoints divided the delegation. The extremists, following André Marty, wanted the party to make no alliances and to prepare, in the midst of the struggle against the enemy, to seize power by direct revolutionary action. The tacticians wanted to infiltrate the state by collaborating with others, first of all with me. The originator of this strategy was Maurice Thorez, still in Moscow and asking to be allowed to return. Finally, in March 1944, the Communists made their decision. They would allow Fernand Grenier and François Billoux to accept the posts I offered them—the Air Ministry to the first and a position as Commissioner of State to the second. On this occasion further changes took place within the government. Le Troquer was appointed National Commissioner for the Liberated Territories and Diethelm replaced him as Commissioner of War, while Mendès-France combined the posts of Economy and Finance.

The committee thus composed devoted itself to its consecrated task of raising and organizing the means of making war, and also to preparing what must be done in order that the country could be fed, administered and set on its feet after the liberation. For a long time a whisper from across the sea had prompted metropolitan France to struggle and to hope. Now it was the nation's call that impelled to action those outside France who wanted to come to her help. Harmony was established amongst the active elements at home and abroad. In order to turn this to the best account, I made the reshaping of the Algiers Government coincide with the meeting of the Consultative Assembly of the resistance during the first days of November.

In accordance with the statute of September 17th, about fifty of the delegates from France represented resistance organizations, about twenty the political parties; the latter chosen from among those members of Parliament who had not voted to give full powers to Pétain in July 1940. The designation of both groups was made by committees necessarily limited and clandestine. Nevertheless, all arrived with the sense of being there in the name of the great mass of those who were struggling in the shadows. To these two categories were added a dozen Communists, in particular the deputies from the Seine department, arrested in 1939, interned since then at Algiers and released by General Giraud; twenty representatives of resistance groups in the Empire; and ten general advisers from

Algeria. Whatever their origin, the delegates had common features that gave the Consultative Assembly its character.

What they had in common, what kept them in harmony, was on the one hand a passionate concern about the assistance to be furnished to the comrades of the resistance in the way of arms, money and propaganda, which, of course, they considered still insufficient; and on the other the rather confused but impassioned ideology that filled the minds of the members of the underground, exposed as they were to betrayals, ignored or denied by the cowardice of many, engaged not only against the German invader but also against the police and judicial apparatus of what, in metropolitan France, still passed for the French state. The burning solidarity of all those who 'belonged', their distrust of and even their aversion for the administrator, the policeman, the official, and lastly a stubborn desire for purification—this was what obsessed them and, when the opportunity presented itself, united them in fervent demonstrations.

There was also the attachment they felt for Charles de Gaulle because he had protested against conformity, because he had been condemned to death, because throughout the nation his words, however remote and blurred, defied discretion and aroused nostalgia. Nevertheless, the effort he was leading for the restoration of national unity, the preservation of French sovereignty, the recovery of the state was less accessible to the majority of the delegates. Not that they were unconcerned about the nation's future. On the contrary, ideas and plans abounded in their councils. But if they were enthusiasts for formulas for reconstructing the universe, they showed themselves more reserved in relation to that authority without which a government can accomplish nothing. If they dreamed of seeing France once again in the first rank of nations, they hesitated to take the arduous action that might put her there and preferred to cherish the illusion of a Roosevelt and a Churchill eager to make room for her beside them. If they did not conceive of any Frenchman but me at the country's head after the liberation, if they had some idea that I could remain there while they, having been elected by the people, were advancing toward some vague and marvellous rebirth, they remained reticent about the powers I would need to direct such an operation. Even while fervently acclaiming de Gaulle, they were already whispering about 'personal power'.

In agreement amongst themselves in their feelings, the delegates were divided into several groups in their minds. Some were simple fighters, absorbed by the struggle itself. Others, poets of action, were inspired by the heroism and brotherhood that the resistance showed. The Communists, comprising a solid bloc, dealt harshly with affairs, eagerly outbid the others and applied themselves, above all, to propaganda. Lastly, the 'politicians', convinced that our cause was the cause of France and serving it to the best of their ability, did not, for all that, refrain from thinking of their careers, from manoeuvring to push themselves forward according to the rules of their profession, and from considering the future from the point of view of elections, offices and the power it might one day offer them.

Among the last, the *anciens*, proud of having done their duty by refusing the late abdication but knowing what an ocean of unpopularity the régime had foundered under, walked on tiptoe, spoke softly and renounced all ambition. Yet deep in their hearts they looked forward to a return to the old ways, on condition that a few reforms were introduced. The *nouveaux* were very severe about the old system. They wanted many changes made in it. Even so, beneath these reservations they exposed themselves in advance to the attractions of political life. On the whole, seeing around me these courageous colleagues of such good will, I felt myself full of esteem for all and of friendship for many. But also, probing their souls, I reached a point where I asked myself if among all those who spoke of revolution I was not, in truth, the only revolutionary.

The inaugural session of the Consultative Assembly took place on November 3rd, 1943. It was a profoundly moving ceremony; those who took part had the impression of being there in the name of an army of sufferers and soldiers, of representing a great French force. After greeting the assembly, 'gathered despite extraordinary obstacles', in the name of the Committee of Liberation, I indicated the reasons that had long since decided me to convoke it as soon as possible and showed why and how I asked for its co-operation. What qualified it, I said, was that it proceeded from the resistance, 'the fundamental reaction of the French people and the elementary expression of the national will'.

To support the government in a war effort 'requiring moral cohesion as much as material means'; to uphold its overseas activity 'enabling France to resume, to the advantage of all, her great international role'; to help guide her in choosing the measures 'to be imposed after the liberation by the need to live when the termination of the struggle has left our soil covered with ruins and barren of all reserves of food and raw materials, by the obligation to re-establish everywhere, in order and in dignity, the authority of the Republic, by the duty to assure the justice of the state, which is the only valid and admissible kind, by the changes to be made in the civil service, by the return of our imprisoned and deported youth'; lastly, to study 'the great reforms that must be accomplished when the war is over'—such, I said, was what the Committee of Liberation expected of the assembly. I declared myself 'certain of the result, for twenty centuries can attest that there has always been justification for having faith in France'.

The Assembly, having elected Félix Gouin as its president and divided itself into groups—metropolitan resistance presided over by Ferrière, overseas resistance under Bissagnet, independent resistance groups under Hauriou, members of Parliament under Auriol, Communists under Marty—did, in fact, discuss the principal questions which I asked it to examine. Between the date of its first session and that of its disbanding, it met more than fifty times and its committees worked very hard. All the ministers worked with it. Philip, in charge of the Committee's relations with the Assembly, Commissioner of the Interior d'Astier, Commissioner of Justice Menthon, Commissioner of Foreign Affairs Massigli and Commissioner of Finance Mendès-France were those who were heard most often.

For my own part, I attended about twenty sessions. I took part on these occasions either to give reports on the general situation or during the course of discussions. I was extremely interested in the ideas and the feelings which this exchange of views brought to the surface: what I wanted to know were the real convictions of the French people. I did my best to animate the discussions, to make the delegates reveal their thoughts, to make them say what they believed. And indeed the assembly gave evidence of consciences and convictions that impressed both the French public and the foreign observers. Nevertheless, the subjects that absorbed it longest were, of course, those which concerned it most deeply: national purification, help for the resistance and the establishment of law and order in France during the liberation.

There were many bitter and prolonged arguments on the action to be taken against the Vichy leaders, the punishments to be inflicted on the officials accused of having added to the severity of their orders, the compensations to be awarded to those who had suffered. On these points the delegates urged the Committee to act vigorously, even to change, as much as possible, the normal rules and procedures. So great was the emotion roused by the problem that several national commissioners were harshly taken to task for their supposed weakness. While understanding only too well that this question of justice should preoccupy the resistance assembly to the highest degree, I did not abandon the line of conduct I had decided on for myself: to limit retribution to those who had played prominent roles in Vichy politics and to the men who had made themselves the enemy's direct accomplices. In the overseas territories this meant very few people. But the state of mind revealed by the debates of the Consultative Assembly allowed me to foresee the difficulties I would have in restraining the spirit of vengeance in metropolitan France and allowing justice alone to pass sentences.

The Assembly brought as much concern and passion to the formulation of its opinion on the assistance sent to the resistance groups in France, the liaison established with them and the advantage our propaganda derived from their actions and their suggestions. It was only natural that the secret army, so badly equipped and so constantly threatened, should often have the impression that London and Algiers were not doing all they could on its behalf. At first many delegates began with reproachs and recriminations in regard to the 'services'. But after verification they realized the extent of the work already accomplished and the obstacles to be overcome. They also had to take into account the disadvantages represented by the activities of the Allied services in France. These produced all kinds of local discord and deprived the French authorities of a share of the hearing which the French war effort was gaining for it abroad. Nevertheless, the fear of offending the Anglo-American powers, which for the 'politicians' was second nature, kept the assembly from adopting, on this point, the categorical motion I should have preferred.

The Assembly's discussions on the manner in which the powers of the Republic were to be reconstituted in France were calmer, but no less searching. No one, of course, imagined that the Marshal and his 'government' could do anything but disappear. On the other hand, everyone felt that the French people must be consulted immediately and that a national assembly would have to settle the constitutional question. But the delegates were not in total agreement as to what kind of assembly this should be.

The Communists, in discreet terms, revealed their scheme of elections to be carried out in the public squares, preferably by acclamation, under the control of the organizations and the troops of the resistance. Obviously they calculated that their own *savoir-faire* would reap results advantageous to their cause from such a procedure. Members of Parliament of long service such as Senators Marcel Astier, Marc Rucart and Paul Giacobbi suggested that the National Assembly of July 1940 be reconvened. That body, under the influence of the liberation, would not fail to abolish the powers it had given Pétain, to accept President Albert Lebrun's resignation as a matter of form, to elect a new President of the Republic and to give my government a vote of confidence. It would then dissolve to make way for a Chamber of Deputies and a Senate elected according to the past method, after which the alterations to be made in the constitution of 1875 would be carried out according to the rules which the latter had established. Such was the plan of those who desired a return, pure and simple, to the institutions of the Third Republic.

There were not many of them. According to the great majority, the *ancien régime* was doomed. But it is important to realize that, according to many of the delegates, what had been wrong about the old system was not so much an excess as a lack of demagogy. The confusion of powers and responsibilities that had deprived it of a strong government, that had denied it any firm and continuous policy and set it adrift at the mercy of events, was not, in the majority's eyes, what must be reformed. Or rather, the reform was supposedly to be made by going still further in the direction of making the chief executive nothing more than a figurehead.

To attribute to a single Assembly all powers without exception, to give it the capacity to invest and provide ministers, to abolish the Senate which might constitute a useful counterbalance, to suppress the Chief of State or, at least, to reduce him to a still more ridiculous condition than the one in which the past system had imprisoned him—such was the idea of a great number of the delegates. They dreamed aloud of a 'single and sovereign' Assembly like the Revolutionary Convention, which, though it did not use the guillotine, would, nevertheless, find no obstacle to its energies. Most of the politicians who emerged from the resistance intended to sit some day in such an Assembly.

I did not share this inclination. On the contrary, what seemed to me essential for the nation's future recovery was a régime of action and responsibility. As I saw it, it was essential that the powers be separated so that there would be, respectively and effectively, a government, a Parliament and a judiciary. It was essential that the Chief of State, by the method of his election, by his rank and by his powers, be in a position to fulfil the function of national arbiter. It was essential that people should be able to associate themselves directly, by means of a referendum, with the crucial decisions that would determine their destiny. I was deeply concerned when I realized the state of mind of those who would control the state tomorrow and who were striving to reconstruct the régime for the sport of politicians rather than for the service of the nation. Were we to learn no other lesson from this confusion, this inconsistency which had brought France to disaster and the Republic to abdication, than to go on to further confusion and more serious inconsistency still?

But this was not the moment to organize a public discussion on this subject. Letting the flood of theories sweep past and taking advantage of the prudence of some individuals—Dumesnil de Gramont, Vincent Auriol, René Cassin, Louis Vallon and others— I led the assembly to a cautious conclusion. It was agreed that during the liberation the Consultative Assembly, transferred to metropolitan France and suitably enlarged, would continue to function on behalf of the government; that once the territory was liberated and the prisoners and deportees returned, the country would successively elect municipal councils, general councils and a national assembly, but that the composition and the functions of the latter would not be determined until later on. Furthermore, the right to vote and to hold office was extended to women. The decree of April 21st, 1944, making this tremendous reform official, put an end to controversies that had lasted for fifty years.

Although the Consultative Assembly had no other right than that of expressing its opinion and although the responsibility for what was done or not done continued to devolve upon me until such time as the people could speak for themselves, the Allies followed carefully what was being said on the rostrum and in the ante-chambers.

F

The members of their missions as well as their journalists were assiduous in their attendance at the sessions and in the corridors. The American and British newspapers gave a large amount of space to the Algiers discussions. Doubtless they regretted that this parliamentary representation was not empowered to overturn the government, that the lion tamer could not be eaten. At the very least they were trying to discover and expose differences of opinion.

All these observers were there the day the assembly broached the subject of France's relations to the rest of the world. On this occasion, the voices of the 'resistants' such as Bissagnet, Father Carrière and Mayoux, the voices of the 'politicians' like Auriol, Hauriou and Rucart, and the voices of the Communists, including Bonte, Grenier and Mercier, strongly approved the position of principle I had adopted toward the Allies in the face of the enemy. The assembly stated explosively that so far as it was concerned General de Gaulle represented France at war and his government was that of the Republic; it was in this capacity that the Committee of Liberation was to co-operate with the Allied Nations and the latter must recognize this state of affairs. The order of the day formulating this unanimous opinion, which was to be spread by information sources the world over, brought a very appreciable support to my policy. For my part, I saw to it that news of the decision resounded far and wide.

But the assembly was content to stop there. It preferred not to deal directly with such burning problems as Italy, the Middle East and Africa, with which the Committee's foreign affairs operations were grappling, nor with others such as Germany, eastern Europe and Indochina, which were to beset France and the world in the near future. The same circumspection kept it from making an issue of the political and administrative power which the Allies planned to wield in France under cover of their military command. As for the conduct of the war and the share which the French Government and General Staff would take in it, the Consultative Assembly listened with scrupulous attention while I explained this crucial question, the policies which I had followed since 1940 and the difficulties which were unceasingly put in our way. It approved statements of principle in regard to France's place in world-wide strategy and the contribution which French forces could make. But it did not move to formulate demands in relation to our Allies.

All in all, on the major subjects the Assembly instinctively kept to generalities expressed from the rostrum in terms broad enough to be approved by all. General de Gaulle was applauded when he came to explain what action had been undertaken or when he lifted spirits by pulling a debate together in order to reach a conclusion. On the other hand, everyone made a point of treating coldly and critically one national commissioner or another who outlined the measures used. But almost no one ventured a concrete opinion or a fixed plan of action.

The fact that the assembly was merely consultative, that it did not have to consider an electoral constituency and that its attitude and its votes could not stimulate a ministerial crisis, contributed, of course, to its reserve about such questions. Also the delegates meant to leave my hands free to deal tactfully with the Allies and to maintain their unity. But above all, the Assembly's reticence was a confession of ineptitude. It felt itself capable of expressing opinions but not of resolving problems, fit to suggest a policy but not to adopt one. Its consequent dejection was to recur later on in intensified form in the representative assemblies possessing plenary powers and incapable of wielding them. As for me, seeing in the remarks of the various groups the parties' future pretensions and, at the same time, their impotence, I discerned the coming French constitutional drama. 'Deliberation is the work of many men. Action, of one alone.' For this very reason, they desired only to deliberate.

Nevertheless, the unity of the Algiers Government, together with the meeting of the Consultative Assembly and the choice made by French public opinion, settled the political question in principle for the period of liberation. But if, to a great majority, the facts seemed determined in advance, the speculations inspired by malevolence did not entirely cease, either in France or elsewhere. On the contrary, the various opposition circles which persisted in regarding my success as abhorrent, multiplied in cunning stratagems against me. The more so as the force of events made it inevitable. Without exception these men regarded the collapse of the Vichy régime as a certainty, but there was not one among them who would not have liked to replace that régime without an accompanying triumph for me.

Meanwhile the enemy's behaviour in regard to Vichy hastened the latter's downfall. The Germans, convinced by what had occurred in North Africa that the Marshal and his government did not wield the authority necessary to keep the French from turning against them at the first opportunity, realizing the imminence of the Allied landing, anxious about what, in that event, a national insurrection would do in their rear and requiring French resources for their own war-torn economy, ascribed only a trifling importance to the so-called French state and squeezed the iron shackles of oppression all the tighter. The fiction of internal autonomy, to which Vichy had clung, disappeared altogether.

In any case, Pétain, having transmitted all his powers to Laval, could no longer pretend to the role of protector on which he had hitherto prided himself. He now stepped aside, renouncing any intervention in the 'government's' work, which, anyway, consisted of little but adopting measures of constraint or repression. In November, Pétain found himself literally forbidden to speak on the radio. In December, Laval, returning from a visit to the Fuehrer and reforming his ministry with a view to more complete collaboration with the invader, invited Brinon and Darnand to join it pending the time when Déat could do the same, without the Marshal's taking a firm stand against him. The man who still called himself 'Chief of State' had at his side a German overseer called Herr Renthe-Fink. He actually came to the point of writing to Hitler on December 18th: 'The modifications of French laws will henceforth be submitted to the occupation authorities.' Although subsequently he was to find an opportunity to show himself publicly in Paris, Rouen, Nancy and St-Étienne, where, until the end, testimonials of pity and sympathy were addressed to him as an unfortunate old man, he did so without once saying a word which suggested that he felt his violated independence.

Thereafter certain appearance still surrounded Vichy's absurd powers. Braggarts or madmen claimed ministerial posts; propagandists—Philippe Henriot and Hérold Paquis—used their misplaced talents to deceive the multitude; the newspapers overflowed with scurrilous attacks on those who were fighting; but the fact was that the whole people now condemned the régime and only hoped to see it collapse when the Germans fled.

The French people had, of course, no doubt as to the kind of government which would then be installed in Paris, for which they were preparing a fervent welcome. But among the politicians who had established Pétain and who feared that their careers would thereby be compromised, many did not resign themselves to such a prospect. Since the end of 1943 many intrigues had been afoot to bring about a solution that would limit General de Gaulle's powers when the time came and, if possible, keep him at a distance. The Marshal himself made secret arrangements providing that his powers, if he himself were barred from wielding them, should be assumed by a body of prominent persons who had taken extremely diverse attitudes in the face of events. A 'constitutional act' installing this directorate of neutrality, if the occasion should arise, was put into safe hands. A little later, by another 'constitutional act', in apparent contradiction to the preceding one and destined, in this case, to be made public, the Marshal specified that if he himself should die before having promulgated the constitution he was supposed to be preparing, the powers which the National Assembly of 1940 had conferred upon him would revert to this same assembly. The Germans, of course, opposed the publication of this document, although to the public at large Pétain's codicil was of virtually no interest.

At the same time, those members of Parliament who had not joined me either in fact or spirit continued their agitation. They invoked their constituencies—as if they had not betrayed them. They declared that the National Assembly of July 1940 was still legitimate —although it had formally abdicated. They asked that this assembly be convened in order to settle officially all questions of state. Anatole de Monzie, champion of this plan, got several hundred of his colleagues to agree and, to the Marshal's increasing distress, ordered him to comply with it. But Hitler, annoyed by this to-do, told Ribbentrop to write Pétain a threatening letter forbidding him ever to consider a disqualified Parliament when the German Wehrmacht was the 'only guarantee of law and order in France'. The impatient legislators relapsed into silence, hoping to resume their projects later on.

The Allies, no longer able to rely on Giraud to counterbalance de Gaulle, were looking for some new expedient. Intelligence from France informed me that they had hoped to find it in President Lebrun. The latter, since the vote of the Vichy assembly which had stripped him of his functions and which he had not contested, had retired to Vizille. Was there no way, asked those in Washington or London who aimed at controlling the political destiny of France, of bringing the President to North Africa? Since he had not formally resigned and since his attitude to the enemy left nothing to be desired, could he not lay claim to an untainted legitimacy on arriving in Algiers? Recognized at once as the President of the French Republic by the Allied powers and also—at least so it was hoped—by a great number of French citizens, how could he be challenged by de Gaulle and his followers? From then on it would be up to Lebrun to appoint the ministers, to preside over their councils, to sign the laws and the decrees. After the anxiety which de Gaulle's intransigent primacy had caused the White House and Downing Street, it would be a change and a relief. I was informed that during the last days of August the American and British conspirators were on the point of seizing their opportunity.

This occurred at the moment when Badoglio, hard pressed, had entered into clandestine negotiations with the Anglo-American powers with a view to arranging Italy's surrender. The negotiations were taking place in Lisbon in the profoundest secrecy. The conquerors were in a position to make semi-official suggestions to the conquered which the latter would be grateful to receive. Now it happened that Vizille, where Lebrun was living, was in the Italian occupation zone. One evening officers from Rome presented themselves to the President. Stressing the critical situation into which the imminent course of the war might throw the region and his own safety, they proposed to Albert Lebrun on behalf of their government that he come to Italy, where he would find security and a suitable residence. He would be guaranteed escorts and safe-conducts in advance. It is known that at the same time that this contact was made, the Allied command, in agreement with Badoglio, was preparing an operation which, as soon as the Italian armistice was announced, was to bring the Anglo-American forces to Naples and, if possible, to Rome and in any case to protect King Victor Emmanuel, his ministers and other well-known individuals. Those who were pulling the strings thought that, once Lebrun was in Italy, he could be transferred to wherever it was convenient to have him.

According to my informants, the President categorically refused this proposition, either because he did not see its true purpose or because, having discerned it, he did not wish to play any part in it. He replied to the Italians, 'Your country is in a state of war with mine. From my point of view, you are the enemy. You can take me by force. I shall not follow you of my own free will.' The mission retired. But shortly afterwards Hitler, alerted and infuriated by the 'French obstructions', sent the Gestapo to arrest President Lebrun. The latter, transferred to Germany, was forced to remain there a year.

I must say that these manipulations, devised by various hands to avoid the inevitable, impressed me as little more than a Chinese shadow play. I marvelled at how lively and tenacious the spirit of intrigue still managed to be in the midst of the terrible realities besetting the world, but actually I paid little attention to it. What disturbed me more was the fate of the resistance in metropolitan France. For during this same period tragedy, striking at its heart, endangered both its framework and its orientation.

On June 9th, a few days after my arrival in Algiers, General Delestraint had been arrested in Paris. The loss of the commander of the secret army threatened the disorganization of the para-military elements at the very moment when their leader was beginning to unify them. Jean Moulin decided to convoke the delegates of the various movements at Caluire on June 21st, in order to work out the necessary measures with them. Yet on that very day, during a Gestapo raid that was, to say the least, strangely apt as to the particulars of time, place and persons involved, my delegate fell into the enemy's hands along with those with him. He was tortured to death some weeks later.

The disappearance of Jean Moulin had grave consequences, for he was one of those men who incarnate their jobs and who, therefore, cannot be replaced. The mere fact that he was no longer there caused serious difficulties in the functioning of those services—liaison, transport, distribution and intelligence—which he directed personally. Yet it was just these services which made a coherent whole of the resistance operation. But, above all, this loss was to have political consequences and throw serious obstacles in the way of unity.

Not, of course, that the feelings of the combatants were influenced by it. To the majority of these the various groups concerned with inspiring them were almost unknown and the men who belonged to them generally anonymous. Morally it was to de Gaulle that they pledged themselves in the underground struggle, while practically, in regard to the conditions of life in the maquis, the raids, the sabotage, the smuggling of arms, the transmitting of information—operations necessarily carried out on a small scale—they merely followed their group leaders. On the level of committees, political influences and slogans, matters were not so simple. Although the political elements agreed to set aside their ambitions to a certain extent in the heat of battle, they did not renounce them altogether, especially when they glimpsed, as the ordeal neared its end, the chance of gaining power. The personality of Moulin, who had been delegated and backed by me directly, enabled him to unite and control these factions. Now that he was dead, certain individuals would be inclined to play their own hands more actively.

This was to be the case first of all with the Communists. The National Council of the Resistance aimed at acquiring a majority and making it a sovereign body, theoretically pledged to my government but qualified to act on its own and for its own advantage. It would then be possible to make use of the council to carry out those activities, to put in office those authorities, to formulate those programmes and, perhaps, to seize those powers thanks to which, in the shake-up of the liberation, the future would be theirs.

If I had been in a position to appoint Jean Moulin's successor immediately and if my new agent had been able to assert himself personally among all the elements representing the resistance, he would have assumed the leadership of my delegation and the presidency of the National Council; thus the duality which some people were trying to create would not have resulted. But circumstances prevented me from finding the man I needed at once.

Not that we lacked men of ability and courage at the head of the various movements, despite the continual decimation the resistance suffered. But each of these men, belonging to a faction, would have been unable to impose his authority upon the rest, so rigorous was the individuality of the leaders and of their groups. Moreover, the day was approaching when France, suddenly emerging from oppression, would find that the life of the nation, law and order, and the judgment of the world would depend on the French administrative structure. To represent me in France and to lead our groups there, and also to prepare, everywhere, the confirmation or the substitution of authorities, I needed someone who was a great administrator, someone who had taken part in our battle and knew its prejudices and tangled roots but was not himself committed to any particular tendency. Furthermore, he must be capable, at the crucial moment, of rallying the kind of administration which the government would soon require. Months were to pass before I chose and established the man who answered all these qualifications.

Meanwhile Claude Bouchinet-Serreulles and Jacques Bingen, whom I had sent from London to work with Jean Moulin, vouched for the delegation. The former, in Paris, found means of maintaining all contacts despite the terrible ravages that devastated the executive committees of the various groups at this time. The latter, in the southern zone, devoted himself chiefly to organizing help for the rebels whose forces were growing in the south-west, the Massif Central and the Alps, until, captured by the enemy, he took his own life. In September I appointed Émile Bollaert as the representative of General de Gaulle and the delegate of the Committee of National Liberation. This great leader had refused, since 1940, to give his allegiance to the Marshal and had gone into retirement. His feelings and his capacities qualified him for the post to which I called him. But shortly after his appointment Bollaert was arrested by the Germans on the Breton coast while preparing to embark for Algiers, where he was to receive the government's instructions. He was subsequently deported to Buchenwald. As the climax of our misfortunes, Pierre Brossolette fell into the enemy's hands at the same time as Bollaert; he was later killed trying to escape from a window in the Gestapo building. This valiant colleague was also endowed by nature to fulfil such a post, by virtue of his courage, his willingness, the prestige he enjoyed among the various elements of the resistance, and because he was independent of all political parties. Like Jean Moulin, he expected nothing to be effective, today in wartime or tomorrow in peace, except 'Gaullism' established as a social, moral and national doctrine. In March 1944 Alexandre Parodi, a member of the Council of State and director-general of the Ministry of Labour, who had also refused to serve under Vichy and whose brother René had been one of the first to die for France in the resistance, received the trust in his turn.

The composition of my delegation favoured the Communists in the National Council of the Resistance. They managed to bring it about that, of its fifteen members, five were openly or secretly party members. The council, on its own authority, decided to give itself a president and elected Georges Bidault. As an eminent resist-

ance leader having in the highest degree the taste and the gift
for political life, well known before the war for his talent as a
journalist and his influence among the Christian Democrats, and
ambitious to see this little group become a great party with himself
at its head, he willingly accepted the position he was offered and
assumed its risks. One of these, and not the least, was to find himself
overpowered at the very heart of this Areopagus by a disciplined
group experienced in revolutionary action and excelling in the use
of conflict as well as of camaraderie. I soon had indications of this
group's encroachments, of the bitterness its pressures involved for
Georges Bidault, of the obstacles of its making which I was soon to
find in my path. The council made known, in fact, that since its
plenary sessions were necessarily exceptional it was delegating its
powers to a board of four members, of whom two were Communists,
and instituting an 'Action Committee', dominated by party members, to deal with military questions.

I was particularly concerned about what was happening to our
movement in metropolitan France at the end of 1943 and the beginning of 1944 because, being in Algiers, I was even less in a position
to make myself heard or understood than when I had been in
London. The personal contact which the wireless had enabled me to
make with the French people had more or less slackened. Indeed,
the Algiers frequencies were less well known in France than those
of the BBC. The efforts of Henri Bonnet, Commissioner of Information, of Jacques Lassaigne, director of Radio France, of Jean
Amrouche, Henri Bénazet, Jean Castet, Georges Gorse, Jean Roire
and others succeeded in giving our broadcasts from Algiers, Tunis
and Rabat a certain interest and character. Furthermore, the major
station at Brazzaville, now in full-time operation under the direction
of Gérard Jouve, was finding an increasingly large audience around
the world. Yet, despite their efforts, I realized that my voice was
reaching the French people in a muffled manner. At the same time
that I was finding it more difficult to speak to the nation, our secret
links with France were also becoming more complicated.

It was from London that these had been organized. It was from
there that our instructions and our missions had been sent. It was
there that reports, agents, visitors and refugees arrived. In the use
of planes, motor-boats, telegrams, wireless messages and couriers, a
kind of rhythm dependent on the English capital had become a habit

to the valiant army of informants, transporters and purveyors. It was unthinkable to tear this web apart. As for weaving another which would operate from North Africa, we could do so only in the most cursory fashion, for want of specialized means and because of the distances involved. A light single-engine plane leaving from an English base could land after two hours' flight on a makeshift field in the centre of France and return immediately. A two-engine plane, a lengthy flight, an orthodox landing strip and the means of refueling was needed to connect metropolitan France with Algiers, Oran or even Ajaccio. We had, therefore, left the principal machinery of our communications set up in Great Britain. But as a result there were many re-transmissions, delays and misunderstandings.

The more so since, outside the specialized networks of Fighting France, there existed another, the former Intelligence Service of the Army General Staff. This service, which remained in Vichy until November 1942 and which, under the direction of Colonels Ronin and Rivet, had opposed the Germans to the limit of its ability, had reached North Africa during the enemy's occupation of the southern zone. The 'Civil and Military Commander-in-Chief' had made it his instrument of contact with metropolitan France. As long as the dual direction of the Committee of Liberation lasted, this state of affairs went on, with all the disadvantages involved in having one intelligence service attached to me and another working for Giraud. As soon as the latter had left the government for a purely military job nothing, it seemed, need prevent the unification of the specialized services.

But several months were to pass before this was accomplished, even though on November 27th, 1943, the Committee of Liberation ordered the merger, appointed Jacques Soustelle Director-General of Special Services and attached the whole unit directly to the head of the government. This organization did not intend to eliminate officers of the former Intelligence Service; on the contrary, their abilities were to be widely used in their own sphere. But the kind of warfare we had to wage meant that our network must be constituted as a whole. It must transcend the framework and the formulas of the past, and by the complex means of the networks, the maquis, the independent groups, the large movements, leaflets and underground newspapers, the raids and the administrative sabotage, include all forms of resistance and penetrate into every branch of national activity. Unfortunately, General Giraud obstinately opposed the decision which the government took on this point.

Arguing from his position as Commander-in-Chief, he claimed the right to keep entirely at his own disposal the service that had hitherto been his. In the course of many interviews I wore myself out explaining to him that unity was necessary and that he himself would have every opportunity of using the combined services. Nothing would convince him: General Giraud continued to bear down with all his authority on the officers involved in order to keep them outside the prescribed jurisdiction.

It was obviously not for reasons of strategy that he behaved in this way. Whatever title had been left to him, he was not to exercise actual command of operations, which our well-provided Allies kept jealously to themselves. But a certain group, espousing a certain policy, had not given up hope of making use of General Giraud. In France, in Africa, and among the prominent French *emigrés* in the United States, various people still offered him the hope that he would be their leader. The Allied missions and general staffs remained secretly faithful to their former scheme and did not discourage Giraud from cherishing ambitions to play the supreme role. This was why, despite my warnings, he persisted in maintaining separate contacts with one or another element in metropolitan France, sending there, thanks to American aid, agents who were his alone and who created great confusion.

The vessel overflowed at last. In April 1944, after an incident more serious than the rest, I was forced to call upon General Giraud to stop his activities. Since he persisted in a dilatory attitude, the government stripped him, by degrees, of his theoretical function as Commander-in-Chief and appointed him Inspector-General. This, once and for all, rid his status of all ambiguity and corresponded to the services he could usefully perform. In order to soften the blow, I wrote him an official letter expressing the government's recognition of his services and another, personal letter urging him, in our country's present tragic circumstances, to set an example of self-abnegation. Simultaneously the Committee of National Liberation decided to award him the Médaille Militaire with an extremely fine citation.

General Giraud preferred to retire. He declined the post to which he was appointed, refused the medal and went to live near Mazagran. 'I want to be Commander-in-Chief or nothing', he said.

His departure provoked no reaction among the troops, nor among the people. At the same time the former advocates of Vichy who had been attached to him, criticized his behaviour during the Pucheu trial. Called to bear witness before the court, he had not, they claimed, categorically defended the accused, although the latter had come to North Africa solely because of the 'Civil and Military Commander-in-Chief's' formal guarantee. As for myself, seeing General Giraud abandon all activity when the war was far from over, I deplored his stubbornness. But my regrets did not matter when the safety of the state was in jeopardy.

France was suffering. We were informed of the fact in the messages reaching us by successive couriers, particularly those which our cell organizations in public administrations provided from Paris, by messages received from the delegates to the Consultative Assembly or else from refugees who had managed to cross the Pyrenees. Reports from our *chargés de mission* who came and went between Algiers and metropolitan France—Guillain de Bénouville, Bourgès-Manoury, François Closon, Louis Mangin, General Brisac, Colonel Zeller, Gaston Defferre, François Mitterand, my nephew Michel Cailliau and others—confirmed the fact.

The material conditions under which the French people lived had never been worse. For almost everyone, marketing was a daily tragedy. From the spring of 1943 to that of 1944, the official ration did not exceed a thousand calories a day. Without fertilizer, a labour force, fuel or the means of transport, agricultural production reached scarcely two-thirds of what it had been before. Furthermore, the invader took a large share of whatever was produced, including half of all meat supplies. By means of the black market the enemy reduced what remained, which should have been turned over to the public. What the Germans ate in this way they paid for with money drawn from the French Treasury—more than 300 billion francs by August 1943, more than 400 billion by March 1944. There were still 1,500,000 French prisoners-of-war in enemy camps. It is true, the Germans had sent back a spectacular 100,000; but in return a total of one million civilians were to be handed over to the Germans by the 'Labour Services'. The Reich employed, directly for its own benefit, a third of our factories, burned half of our coal, took over 65 per cent of our locomotives, 50 per cent of our rolling stock, 60 per cent of our lorries and made use of our contractors, our tools and our materials to construct the Atlantic Wall. To get food, clothing, heat and light, or to move from one place to another, became exhausting and, often insoluble, problems in the miserable existence which the great majority of Frenchmen were leading.

Once more war was wreaking its endless destruction, its irreparable losses upon our soil. The respite which had followed the 'armistices', and which the authors of the capitulation had boasted of so loudly, gave way to bloody alarms. At Dieppe, then at St Nazaire, British forces, aided by French groups, made a number of raids in the midst of the residents. The bombardment of our cities redoubled. In particular, Paris, Nantes, Rouen, Lyon, St Étienne and their suburbs suffered serious damage, a prelude to what was to be inflicted upon us during the coming great battle. Before the Allied landing in France thirty thousand people were killed by air raids. In many places, particularly the Ain, the Massif Central, the Alps, Limousin and the Dordogne, the local maquis fought the Germans, who took their revenge with firing squads, arson, the arrest of hostages and reparations. Here the enemy was helped by the militia, whose courts-martial summarily judged and condemned to death a host of patriots.

German repression had become a proper military operation, carried out with a method as precise as it was frightful. The enemy wanted to 'settle' his rear before the battle which he sensed ahead of him. This was why the action of the Gestapo and the German police, combined with that of the local police and the militia, now under Darnand's control—Darnand, who had just been made 'secretary-general for the maintenance of order'—was turned in all its strength against our underground networks and our organization. Every form of intimidation, torture and persuasion were used to tear from the wretched people whom they had been able to capture confessions that would deliver still others into their hands. The period preceding the landing was marked by the death of a great number of leaders, among them Cavaillès, Marchal, Médéric, Péri, Politzer, Ripoche and Touny, the arrest of twenty thousand members of the resistance and the deportation of fifty thousand others. During the same period the shameful horrors of the persecution of Jews were unleashed. Lastly, this was the period when the Reich made Vichy turn over its political prisoners; Herriot, Reynaud, Daladier, Blum, Mandel, Gamelin and Jacomet; arrested others, including Albert Sarraut,

François-Poncet and Colonel de La Roque; seized high officials, prominent businessmen and senior officers and transferred them to Germany so that they could serve as hostages or eventual mediums of exchange.

Yet resistance continued to spread. While it was striking at the enemy with raids, assassinations and the derailing of trains, in which many Germans died, and by the execution of an increasing number of traitors and informers, it was, at the same time, writing its own story, which was published and disseminated everywhere. A great human and national movement, it aroused ideas and feelings, delineated doctrines, inspired art and literature. By miracles of ingenuity the secret newspapers were regularly supplied with paper, composed, printed and circulated. *Franc-Tireur*, *Combat*, *Résistance* and *Défence de la France* reached a total of 600,000 copies a day. Magazines such as *Les Lettres Françaises*, *Les Cahiers de la Libération*, *Les Cahiers du Témoignage Chrétien*, *L'Université Libre* and *L'Art Libre* passed secretly through many doors. The Éditions de Minuit distributed books secretly, among them Vercors' *Silence de la Mer*, of which innumerable copies were printed and circulated. Through the efforts of the Algiers Government, the work of those fighting by thought and pen was constantly disseminated by the radio. In the name of the free as well as of those imprisoned in silence, I addressed solemn testimonial to them on the occasion of a great meeting on October 30th organized by the Alliance Française and broadcast from Algiers.

The flowering of French thought confirmed our policy. The incessant intrigues, the disguised ambitions, the subversion that certain individuals were contemplating—how could such things prevail against this upsurge of courage and regeneration? Perhaps this was to be merely an episode, after which, tomorrow, the sluggishness and the abasement would resume. But 'tomorrow is another day'. As long as the war lasted I had the means, morally speaking, to muster the French people.

The more so since the national instinct seized upon me, more clearly than ever, as the core of its unity. It was indeed in relation to me that the politicians manoeuvred in seeking guarantees for the near future. It was toward me that the so-called 'ruling class' turned —that is, those in established situations and those with fortunes or reputations. In this category, a fraction—generally that group whom money concerned the least—had long followed me; as for the others, whose troubled consciences hoped I would spare them fearful reversals, they now yielded with deference and postponed their criticism and insults until later on. The masses, for whom the drama included no speculation, hoped for nothing more than my arrival, which would be their liberation. Lastly, by those who were fighting I found myself regarded as the symbol of what they wished to obtain at the price of their sacrifice. How describe what I felt when one evening Sermoy-Simon, arriving from France—where he himself was soon to die—brought me the supreme testimonial from a group of young men condemned to death: photographs of the walls of their prison cells, where they had scratched my name during their last hours, last letters written to their families, invoking me as their leader. There were also witnesses who, before the execution squad could fire the last bullet, heard their cry, '*Vive la France! Vive de Gaulle!*'

It was these men who showed me my duty at the moment when my need for guidance was greatest. I felt only too strongly the wear and tear to which exhaustion and the moral ordeal of my task exposed me. At the beginning of 1944 I fell seriously ill; but the enlightened care of Doctors Lichtwitz and Lacroix enabled me to overcome the crisis just when the rumour of 'the General's' possible disappearance from the scene was at its height. The two years through which Free France had endured had also been filled with reversals and disappointments, but then we had had to stake everything to win everything. We had felt ourselves surrounded by a heroic atmosphere and, sustained by the necessity of gaining our ends at any price. Between myself and those—all volunteers—who placed themselves under my direction there existed a profound understanding that had been a powerful help to me. Now the goal was within sight, but as we neared it I had the feeling of crossing less firm ground, of breathing less pure air. Around me interests imposed their claims, rivalries clashed, men became more human every day.

In my office at Les Glycines I kneaded heavy dough. There were papers to read, though my immediate colleagues, Palewski, Billotte and Soustelle, brought me, on my orders, only the most essential. There were decisions to make, even if it was only a question of determining principles. People had to be seen despite the system which I put into effect to limit the audiences to national commissioners, foreign diplomats, top Allied and French military leaders, a few high civil administrators, messengers from France, those who were to be sent there and certain visitors of note. On principle, I used the telephone only rarely, and no one was ever permitted to ring me up. The confrontation of points of view and the choice of measures to be taken I reserved purposely for the government councils. My own nature warned me and my experience had taught me that, at the summit, one can preserve time and strength only by remaining habitually on the remotest heights.

It was therefore all the more necessary at crucial moments to make contact with people and affairs. I did so, as much as possible, by going to see them on the spot. During the fifteen months of my stay in Algiers, I spent, independently of the meetings and the ceremonies which took place in the capital, one hundred days travelling. In Algeria, I visited the cities and the countryside, inspected troops, ships and air squadrons. I paid four visits to Morocco, three to Tunisia and one to Libya. In Equatorial Africa, a long tour took me through the entire area. I crossed Corsica three times, made three trips to Italy to spend time among the troops in action. During the Allied landing in Normandy I went to England and from there to Bayeux in France; shortly afterwards I made my first trip to the United States and to Canada. Such journeys comforted me. Men, so exhausting when manoeuvring for ambition, are so engaging when acting for a great cause!

By taste and expediency, my private life was very simple. I lived at the villa Les Oliviers, where my wife had joined me, with my daughter Anne, whose health worried us as much as ever, and later Elisabeth, who returned from Oxford to work in the office that monitored the foreign press. Philippe continued to navigate and to fight in the Channel and on the Atlantic. In the evenings at Les Oliviers I tried to keep my time to myself in order to work on speeches which were my constant chore. But often we entertained. Many foreign and French guests did us the honour of sitting at our table; the dinners, however, were extremely simple, for rationing necessarily applied to everyone. Frequently we spent our Sundays in a cottage in Kabylia.

At intervals, news of our family reached us. My brother Xavier had been able to take shelter at Nyons, whence he sent useful information to Algiers; his daughter Geneviève, falling into the enemy's hands with the editors of *Défence de la France*, had been deported to Ravensbrueck; his elder son was fighting in Italy. My sister, Madame Alfred Cailliau, arrested by the Gestapo, had spent a year in prison at Fresnes and from there had been transferred to Germany, while her husband, at the age of sixty-seven, had been sent to Buchenwald; one of their sons, Charles, a young infantry officer, had been killed by the enemy during the Battle of France; three others had crossed the Mediterranean to join our forces. My brother Jacques' three sons had done the same; Jacques himself, a paralytic, had been shielded from the German police by Abbé Pierre and his group, who carried him over the Swiss frontier. My brother Pierre had been continually under close surveillance; in 1943 he was arrested by the Germans and deported to Eisenberg. His wife and their five children, as well as an adopted girl, the daughter of a resistance fighter who had been executed, crossed the Pyrenees on foot and reached Morocco by way of Spain. In the Vendroux family, my wife's brothers and sister were serving our cause. In France and in Africa, all our relatives and connections were risking their lives. With so many other encouragements, I evoked those that came to me from my own family when the burden grew too heavy for me to bear.

My ministers also carried their share of this burden. If, in the past, the reduced dimensions of our organization concentrated everything in my hands, today, in order to encompass a domain that was about to be enlarged, authority had to be distributed. Among the national commissioners, of course, various rivalries and distractions broke out. But on the whole my ministers formed a disciplined team around me, though each of them had his own authority and his own responsibilities.

Each also had his own way of fulfilling it. Henri Queuille brought to the chairmanship of the inter-ministerial commissions all the good sense and prudence he possessed by nature, as well as all the experience he had acquired under the Third Republic as a member of twelve governments. René Massigli, a brilliant man of many resources, wise in the ways of diplomacy, worked to establish the network of foreign relations that had been damaged by events. Pierre Mendès-France, with his clear mind and strong will, solved the apparently insoluble problems overwhelming our finances at Algiers. René Mayer, a man of varied abilities, restored the railways, the ports, the roads of North Africa to maximum efficiency. André Le Troquer, generous and truculent, made himself the servant of the Army which he administered. André Philip grappled with the flood of ideas that gushed from his own brain and with the Assembly's successive *malaises*. Jean Monnet, with a tremendous range of talents at his fingertips, applied himself to convincing our American allies that they must organize in time the help they were willing to give us. Henri Bonnet played his role as conciliator among the groups disputing the means of information. François de Menthon, Emmanuel d'Astier, René Capitant and Henri Frénay, whose ministerial departments were respectively Justice, the Interior, National Education and Prisoners and who were above all engaged in preparations for what was to be done in France tomorrow, vied with each other in their imaginative zeal. Fernand Grenier and François Billoux, the one blunt, the other cunning, but both gifted, divided their attention between their respective posts (the Air Ministry and the State Commission) and their party, which watched them from outside. As for the ministers who had been with me since Free France began—Georges Catroux, experienced in affairs of state, René Pleven, André Diethelm and Adrien Tixier, all of whom had been hard at work for four years under difficult conditions—each brought to his task (Moslem Affairs, Colonies, Production and Labour) a competence which nothing could discourage or surprise.

All these ministers, whatever their origin, their inclinations or their personality, proudly associated themselves with Charles de Gaulle and assumed responsibility with him. Theirs was all the more meritorious a role since their ministries were made up of bits and pieces. Yet in spite of all lacunae these ministries, like their leaders, devoted themselves to their tasks with a commendably constant intelligence and fervour if not without that proliferation of projects inspired by the consideration of national rebirth. If, in the offices of Algiers as in the Assembly or in the committee meetings, every possible scheme was discussed that might help to reconstruct France and the world, everyone none the less did his job conscientiously and reasonably. Officials such as Hubert Guérin, Chauvel, Alphand, Paris, in Foreign Affairs; Chevreux, in the Interior; Gregh, Guindey, Leroy-Beaulieu, in Finance; Laurentie, for the Colonies; Anduze-Frais, in Transport; Postel-Vinay, at the central fund; chiefs of executive committees such as Leyer at the War Ministry, Lemonnier for the Navy, Bouscat for the Air Force, were the pillars and models of our services. Ultimately, however, everything came to rest at my feet, and I could not ignore the narrowness of our limits. But the spring of political life lies in the skilful deployment of the possible.

The government now met in the Summer Palace twice a week. With the assistance of Louis Joxe, I had drawn up the agenda. On each item the committee heard the report of the minister concerned and a debate followed. Each member gave his opinion. If necessary, I called on him to do so. I then offered my own, generally at the end of the discussion. Then I formulated the council's resolutions and, if necessary, settled their disputes. The decisions were subsequently reported to the ministries. Often they were handed down in the form of decrees. In that case, the texts were edited beforehand by René Cassin and his Judicial Committee, deliberated in council and finally published in the *Journal Officiel de la République Française*, which was published in Algiers in its traditional format.

It was thus that the decrees of January 10th, March 14th, April 21st and May 19th, 1944, settled the organization of power and the exercise of authority during the liberation. Seventeen 'Regional Commissioners of the Republic', provided with exceptional powers and posted at Lille, Nancy, Strasbourg, Châlons, Dijon, Clermont-Ferrand, Lyon, Marseilles, Montpelier, Limoges, Toulouse, Bordeaux, Poitiers, Rennes, Angers, Rouen, Orléans and in the Prefecture of the Seine, were appointed 'to take all measures necessary to ensure the security of the French and Allied armies, to provide for the administration of the territory, to re-establish republican legality and to satisfy the population's needs'. In each ministry, a high official, previously appointed secretary-general, was to ensure the continuance of services until the minister arrived. The municipal councils of 1939, which Vichy had often replaced by delegations of its own composition, would be re-established in the *communes*. In order to grant a share in the reconstruction programme to local resistance groups, along with a means of expression and a writ of execution for the inevitable outbursts, the creation of a 'Committee of Liberation' was provided for in each department. This committee, composed of local delegates from the movements and parties represented on the National Council of the Resistance, would give advice to the prefect, as the general council had done previously, pending the time when the latter was re-established by election. Lastly, a

'National Commisisoner Delegated to Liberated Territory' would take those immediate measures which seemed necessary locally.

In April, André le Troquer was appointed to this function. The Commissioners of the Republic and the Prefects of the Liberation proposed to the government by Alexandre Parodi and Michel Debré, were appointed in secret, received the authentic text of the decree instituting them in office and were ready to rise out of the smoke of battle at a moment's notice. Two of them, Verdier and Fourcade, were later killed by the enemy; two, Bouhey and Cassou, were seriously wounded and in all nine of these prefects died for France. To the French people, to the Allies and to the defeated invader, the authority of the state would be apparent: integral, responsible and independent.

Justice must appear at the same time. Because of the ordeals endured, the liberation would doubtless unleash an elementary impulse towards punishment, retribution and revenge. Men and women, defending their country, had been shot by the tens of thousands and deported by the hundreds of thousands to camps of hideous wretchedness whence few were to return. Thousands of fighters in the resistance networks, in the maquis, in the action groups, were considered by the enemy as exempt from the laws of war, and had been killed on the spot. Innumerable murders, arsons, lootings and brutalities had been committed, accompanied by tortures and betrayals and with the direct co-operation of the 'ministers', officials, police, militia and French traitors. For years on end many newspapers, magazines, books and speeches had lavished insults upon those fighting for France and printed tributes to the invader. In the 'government', the administration, in business, industry and the world of society, certain individuals had paraded their collaboration with the enemy amid national humiliation and want. Certainly the German retreat would be a signal for summary and bloody revenge. Yet in spite of everything, no individual had the right to punish the guilty; it was the state's concern. Therefore the state must provide, and without delay, that its courts investigate cases and give verdicts. Not to do so was to risk being swamped by the fury of groups or individuals.

The Committee of Liberation, therefore, by the decree of June 26th, 1944, completed by that of August 26th, was empowered to establish the conditions under which the crimes and misdemeanours of collaboration were to be punished. The legal basis of indictments existed in our codes under the heading 'dealings with the enemy'. But the circumstances would be exceptional, in certain cases extenuating, because of the attitude and the orders of the Vichy 'government'. To take account of this unprecedented political situation and to place the judges in a position where they need not automatically apply the usual punishments invoked for faults that were not usual, we established a new type of punishment, 'National Disgrace', which included the loss of political rights, exclusion from public employment and, at its worst, exile. Thus, enlightened as to the nature of the misdemeanours and crimes they were to reprimand and with a sufficiently elastic scale of punishment at their disposal, the tribunals would pass sentence as they saw fit.

What tribunals? It was obvious that the ordinary criminal courts were not made to apply in such cases, either by their nature or their composition. Many magistrates had been forced to support the Marshal and to pronounce judgments in accordance with Vichy's orders. We should have to introduce changes. This the Committee of Liberation did by prescribing, in advance, the creation of 'Courts of Justice' to sit beside the Courts of Appeal. The president of the court and the public prosecutor would be magistrates chosen by the Chancellery. The four jurors would be chosen by lot from a list drawn up by the president of the Court of Appeal helped by two representatives of the resistance designated by the Commissioner of the Republic. In every respect, it was important to associate the resistance with the official work of the courts of justice. Those who had assumed, either in the 'government' or in key positions elsewhere, an important responsibility for capitulation or collaboration, would be answerable to the High Court.

Nevertheless, the fate of one of these was to be settled in Algiers. Pierre Pucheu, as Minister of the Interior in the Vichy 'government', had distinguished himself by his severity towards the resistance fighters, to the point of seeming to them a champion of repression. Having resigned his 'ministry' in 1942, Pucheu went to Spain. On his request, General Giraud, then 'Civil and Military Commander-in-Chief', authorized him to come to Morocco to serve in the Army, on condition that he did so in secret. Since the former minister showed himself ostentatiously everywhere, Giraud had had him put under house arrest. Subsequently, the Committee of Liberation having decided on measures against members of the Vichy 'government', Pierre Pucheu was imprisoned. Now the question was: should he be judged at once?

The government, by a unanimous decision of its members, decided to try him. On principle, there was no reason for postponement and the state itself needed a swift example. The resistance was to become, in the imminent battle, an essential element of national defence. The Laval ministry, in which Darnand had been appointed 'to maintain order', put forth its greatest effort to crush the resistance with the co-operation of the Germans. It was essential for our combatants, and equally essential for their adversaries, to have immediate proof that the guilty would have to answer for their actions. I confirmed this at the tribunal of the Consultative Assembly, quoting Georges Clemenceau: 'War and only war! Justice is deferred: the nation will know it is defended!'

In order to judge Pucheu, the Committee of Liberation, since it could not convene the High Court, had the accused brought before an 'Army Tribunal'. The president was Monsieur Vérin, president of the Algiers Court of Appeal; the judges were Counsellor Fischer and Generals Chadebec de Lavalade, Cochet and Schmidt; the public prosecutor was General Weiss. The accused defended himself skilfully and energetically, but two facts, among others, led the tribunal to pronounce its severest sentence. Pucheu, as minister, had sent his prefects imperative memoranda ordering that the workers the Reich demanded be handed over. Furthermore, there was every indication that, when the Germans were preparing to execute a certain number of prisoners at Châteaubriand in reprisal for attacks against their soldiers, Pucheu had supplied them with a list of names of men whose execution he requested in the order of his preference. The enemy gave him this disgraceful satisfaction. Formal proof of this was discovered after the liberation.

During the trial, General Giraud, called as a witness, spoke of the accused with great reticence. After Pucheu's condemnation Giraud asked me to suspend the sentence but I could only refuse. To his last hour Pierre Pucheu declared that he had acted in the public interest. In his final statement to his judges, referring to de Gaulle, he cried: 'If my life can serve him in the mission on which he bears the supreme hopes of France, then let him take my life! I give it to him.' He died bravely, he himself giving the order to fire.

During the fearful cataclysm through which France was staggering, men divided into two camps had claimed to lead the nation and the state toward different goals, by contradictory paths. From that moment, the responsibility of both groups was measured on earth not by their intentions but by their acts, for the country's salvation was directly at stake. Whatever they might have thought, whatever they might have wished, judgment on all of them could only be pronounced according to their works. Afterwards let God judge their souls; France would bury their bodies!

The nation must live. The Committee of Liberation made every effort to let it do so when its chains were torn away. I was convinced that, confronted with the ocean of financial, economic and social problems that would be our immediate concern, we could do nothing in the practical sphere which had not been planned and worked out beforehand. For this reason I concentrated a great part of the present government's effort on its future objectives. Three mortal perils lay in wait for us: inflation, the intolerably low level of wages and the cost of services, and the lack of supplies.

As a matter of fact, the bank note circulation, as a result of the payments the invader had required, was three times higher in the spring of 1944 than in the whole of 1940, while the quantity of merchandise was, on an average, lower by half. The result was an enormous rise in real prices, a wild black market and, for the majority of the population, unspeakable privations. At the same time, as a result of enemy pressure to entice French workers to Germany, workers' salaries and employees' wages were kept very low. On the other hand, certain businessmen, financiers and intermediaries made scandalous profits. The country, at the liberation, taking into account the psychological slackening which the latter would involve risked, simultaneously, monetary collapse, and the explosion of social claims for recovery, and famine.

For the government to adopt a policy of *laisser faire et laisser passer* would be to hand the nation over to irremediable disturbances: under the shock of the liberation, inflation would be unleashed and all dykes flooded. Yet an anti-inflationary policy implied crushing restraints, and it was difficult to see how the nation would endure them, after the long years of oppression. Such a policy would also provoke social upheavals incompatible with the need to revitalize production; it would empty the markets without the authorities having the means to provide foodstuffs in any other way, since all reserves had disappeared, the treasury had no means to pay for the tremendous purchases required from foreign powers, and the Allied merchant fleet would be in use transporting supplies into battle. Between the two extremes, the Committee of Liberation adopted a middle course which, nevertheless, satisfied no one.

By exchanging promissory notes, taxing profits and confiscating illicit gains; by allowing holders of bank accounts the use of a sum corresponding only to their immediate needs; by taking advantage of the optimism victory would inspire throughout the nation to float a huge loan and absorb the liquid assets, the bank note circulation would be limited. By readjusting prices paid to producers and subsidizing essential produce in order to keep the price down, it would be possible to keep the markets supplied. By according a 'substantial' increase in salaries and wages—about 30 per cent—social unrest would be avoided. It would also be necessary to get extra reinforcements of supplies from abroad. That is why, in the spring of 1944, the government in the overseas territories piled up stocks of goods worth ten billion francs at the time and arranged a 'six months' plan' with Washington to provide for the first slice of American aid.

These measures would stave off the worst, but nothing would keep the nation, once liberated, from undergoing a long period of penury and rationing. No magic formula and no technical skill would change its ruins into riches. Ingenuity and organization could accomplish something but it would take time, order, work and sacrifice to reconstruct what had been destroyed and to renew demolished or outdated equipment. Co-operation in this effort was to be sought from the working classes, without which everything would collapse in disorder and demagogy. For the nation to acquire ownership of its principal sources of energy—coal, electricity and gas (which, moreover, it was alone in a position to develop properly); to assure it the control of credit in order to keep its activities from being at the mercy of financial monopolies; to make accessible to the working class, by labour commissions, the way to association and union; to free men and women from anxiety in their lives, as in their work, by insuring them against sickness, unemployment and old age; and lastly, thanks to a system of generous government allowances, to raise the French birth rate and thereby increase the vital source of the nation's power: these were the reforms I proclaimed on March

15th, 1944, reforms which my government aimed to accomplish and which, in fact, it did accomplish.

In this part of our policy, we could count on public opinion. There is a concordance between men's misery and their impulse towards progress. Many sensed that the ordeals of war would lead to a vast transformation of the human condition. If nothing was done in this direction, the slow movement of the masses toward Communist totalitarianism would be inevitable. Only by acting immediately could the soul of France be saved. The opposition of the privileged class would make itself felt, since this social category had been severely compromised by the errors of Vichy and frightened by the spectre of revolution. The resistance was entirely favourable to this development: combatants who had run the same risks were inclined towards fraternity.

The same basic reasons that required great and immediate reforms in metropolitan France also required the transformation of the status of the overseas territories and the rights of their inhabitants. I was as convinced of this as anyone while I was fighting the war with the co-operation of the Empire's men and resources. I did not doubt, moreover, that on the morrow of the conflict that inflamed the world, the passion for freedom would rise and swell universally. What was happening, or heralded, in Asia, in Africa, in Australasia, would have its repercussions everywhere. If in our overseas territories our misfortunes had not destroyed the loyalty of the people, the latter had, nevertheless, witnessed events that were cruelly prejudicial to our prestige: the collapse of 1940, the abasement of Vichy beneath the enemy's heel and the arrival of the Americans, speaking as masters, after the ridiculous battles of November 1942. On the other hand, through French Africa the native populations had been aware of the example of Fighting France. They saw, on their own soil, the beginnings of French recovery and they participated in it with high hopes. Indeed this was the point where everything must begin again, but on condition that we did not attempt to maintain these states and territories at their former level. Since, in such matters, it is never too soon to begin, I meant my government to take the initiative without delay.

In December 1943 I therefore approved of General Catroux, National Commissioner for Moslem Affairs, when he proposed an important reform concerning Algeria to the Committee of Liberation. The inhabitants of Algeria had been divided into two electoral colleges. The first, consisting exclusively of Frenchmen, by origin or naturalization, wielded (in relation to the second, which comprised the bulk of the Moslem population), an overwhelming majority in the municipal councils and the general councils. Only the first electoral college was represented in the French parliament. We decreed that some tens of thousands of Moslems, among those 'qualified', should form part of the first college regardless to their 'personal status'. All the rest would have the right to vote in the second college. Finally, the proportion of those elected by the second college in the assemblies, including the French parliament, would be increased to parity. This was a considerable step towards the civic and political equality of all Algerians.

Of course this reform raised muffled protests among the French *colons* and among certain Moslem clans. But many Arabs and Kabyles felt a spurt of hope and gratitude towards France, who, without waiting until she herself had emerged from her miseries, raised their condition and linked their destiny more closely with her own. In every milieu, the authority and rapidity with which the government had adopted measures was in striking contrast to the past régime which had temporized for many, many years. On December 12th, 1943, accompanied by General Catroux and several ministers, I went to Constantine. There, in the Place de la Brèche, to an enormous crowd, I made our decisions public. Near the tribunal, I saw Dr Bendjelloul and many other Moslems weeping with emotion.

We created another occasion to confirm the new policy that was leading to the French Union: the African Conference at Brazzaville. René Pleven, National Commissioner for the Colonies, had proposed and organized it. He convened twenty Governors-General and Governors among them Félix Éboué, Félix Gouin; the president, as well as about ten members of the Consultative Assembly would be there as well as various unofficial authorities. The aim of the conference was to pool ideas and experiences 'in order to determine on what practical foundations a French community comprising the territories of Equatorial Africa could progressively be constructed' to replace the system of direct administration.

With deliberate solemnity, I left for Brazzaville. From Morocco I reached Dakar, where the authorities, the Army, the fleet, the *colons* and the population as a whole displayed an indescribable

enthusiasm. Only three years ago it was here that I had been forbidden access to Senegal by cannon shots. Konakry, Abidjan, Lomé,
Cotonou, Douala and Libreville were visited in turn and burst into
demonstrations that revealed the vibrant certainty of victory. Brazzaville gave me a moving welcome that marked its pride at having
served as a refuge for French sovereignty in its worst years. I took
up quarters in the 'Casa de Gaulle', the official residence which the
territory, in its generous devotion, had built for my use on the
magnificent banks of the Congo river.

On January 30th I opened the conference. After Pleven's speech,
I indicated why the government had decided to convene it: 'Without wishing,' I said, 'to exaggerate the urgency of the reasons im-
pelling us to broach these African questions all at once, we believe
that the events now sweeping the world oblige us not to delay.'
Having hailed France's effort in Africa, I noted that even before the
war 'the necessity of establishing here on new foundations the conditions of Africa's development, those of the progress of its inhabitants and those of the exercise of its sovereignty' had been obvious.
How much more urgent this was today, 'since the war, which will
have been, to a large extent, an African war, is being fought to
determine the nature of man's condition and since, beneath the
action of the psychic forces it has everywhere unleashed, every
population looks ahead and asks questions about its destiny!' France,
I declared, had chosen to lead the way down the road to the future
'the sixty million men associated with her own forty-two million
sons'. Why? 'First of all, because she is France . . . Second, because
it is in her overseas territories and in their loyalty that she has found
her refuge and the starting point for her liberation . . . And lastly,
because, today, France is animated . . . by an ardent will for
renewal.'

The conference began its work which was to result in proposals of
an administrative, social and cultural nature. A meeting of governors
obviously could not decide the constitutional questions posed by the
Empire's transformation into the French Union, but the route was
traced and need only be followed. A spirit had been shown which
might make this reform a national undertaking on a universal scale.
No one was in doubt about this in the rest of the world; attention
was suddenly fixed on Brazzaville. This conference had taken place
by France's own choice at the moment when her reviving power and

her reanimated confidence put her in a position to bestow what no one would yet dare claim to tear from her. Having saluted Éboué, who, exhausted by too many efforts, was to die three months later without having seen the liberation, I left the capital of Equatorial Africa by way of Bangui, Fort-Lamy, Zinder, Niamey and Gao, returning to Algiers, where the legitimacy of the banner floating over my roof was no longer questioned by anyone.

But what is accomplished in action must be recorded in words. It was time that the government assumed the name that was its by right. Despite terrible divisions, procrastinating until the last possible moment, I had hoped that this proclamation could be made in national unanimity, permitting a reorganization of the state before events settled matters once and for all. On behalf of certain men, who had considered themselves invested with the public authority when they assumed responsibility for the national capitulation, I had for four long and terrible years safeguarded the possibility of their one day saying, 'We were wrong. We now see the way of honour, duty and combat. Here we are, with those appearances of qualification that the forms of legality still leave us, accompanied by those who, without having done anything unworthy, followed us out of discipline and loyalty. Whatever the enemy makes us pay for it, we order them to combat him by every means wherever he may be. Later on, if you wish, the verdict of politics, of justice and of history! For the supreme effort, make room for us beside you, in the name of the unity and the salvation of France!'

This cry was not to be heard. 'There are more regrets than avowals in this world.' From one day to the next, the liberation armies were to land on our soil. For the nation and for the world, it was urgently necessary that our power, such as it was, be confirmed in its capacity to hold all the rights which the choice of the people confers.

On May 7th, in Tunis, I declared: 'As for those who suppose that, at the time of the liberation, France can return to her feudal past and divide herself up among several governments, we ask them to meet us soon at Marseilles on the Canebière, at Lyon in the Place Bellecour, at Lille in the Grand-Place, at Bordeaux in Les Quinconces, at Strasbourg in the Cours de Broglie, in Paris somewhere between the Arc de Triomphe and Notre-Dame!' On May 15th, I received a motion unanimously passed by the Consultative Assembly on Albert Gazier's suggestion and which was to be translated into a decree on June 3rd, 1944. As I left for England, where the liberating invasion was to set forth three days later, the Committee of National Liberation became the Provisional Government of the French Republic.

VI. DIPLOMACY

BENEATH ITS FORMAL polite conventions, diplomacy recognizes only realities: destitute, Fighting France could move men to sympathy, but seldom to assistance. Today, dawning French unity began to be of material consequence. Proportionately, France reappeared in the world's diplomatic perspectives. The Allies did not contest the fact that soon they must accord her a place there, any more than Frenchmen henceforth doubted their country's salvation. In anticipation of this occasion, the Allies' foreign policy paid us particular attention.

Our co-operation was more appreciable every day. Without our troops, the Battle of Tunisia would have been marred by an initial failure. Soon, French action in the decisive sector would determine the Italian victory. For the coming struggle in France, the Allied governments and general staffs counted on the part which our resistance forces, the Empire's army and the remains of our fleet could play. Of value to the Allies were our African and Corsican bases, as well as the effective aid they found there. Further, our presence beside them constituted a considerable moral triumph. This is why France—her interests and her reactions—assumed an ever-increasing importance in the Allies' manner of envisaging their relations with the world.

Nevertheless, if they concerned themselves on our account, Washington, London and Moscow limited their official relations to what was indispensable. The United States, fearing European involvements and planning to determine the peace settlement by direct arrangement with Soviet Russia, felt that France's admission to the combine of 'big' powers would thwart her intentions. Already, the presence of the British frequently seemed inopportune, despite London's constant concern never to stand in America's way. How

many more difficulties there would be if France appeared among the
victors, with her principles and her ruins. What was more, she
would take her place there as the spokesman of the small and
medium-sized nations. How, henceforth, obtain that Soviet co-operation the White House had planned on and whose price would be
the independence of the Vistula, Danube and Balkan states? As for
Asia and her frontiers, it was America's intention that the European
empires there be brought to an end. In Australasia, the question was
virtually settled: it was unlikely that Holland would be able to hold
out in Indonesia; but how deal with Indo China if the French were
to resume their place among the Great Powers? While willingly acknowledging our recovery, while coming to terms with us when it
suited them, Washington affected, for as long as possible, to consider
France a fallow field and de Gaulle's government an inconvenient
accident scarcely requiring the attentions one paid to a state.

England did not proceed in quite so summary a fashion, knowing
that the presence, the power and the influence of France would be as
necessary to Europe's equilibrium tomorrow as they had been yesterday. England had never assumed responsibility for Vichy's renuncia-
tions, which had cost her dear. British instinct and policy alike hoped
that France would reappear in her role as yesterday's partner, tractable and familiar. But what was the good of hurrying matters?
Victory was certain, and it was certain too that French forces would
help the Allies with all the means at their disposal. As to the successive settlements, perhaps it would be for the best that France participate in them, but on condition that she do so as a subordinate, an
auxiliary, and that she give way before the American stratagem to
which Great Britain had already acceded. But would General de
Gaulle submit to such plasticity? Nothing was less certain. Everything considered, it was advisable that France's sovereignty remain
somewhat nebulous. All the more so since this vagueness could be
put to good advantage to abolish what remained of the old French
competition in the Middle East.

Soviet Russia observed, calculated and remained on her guard.
Certainly everything led the Kremlin to favour the rebirth of a
France capable of assisting it to subdue the German menace and to
remain independent of the United States. But there was no hurry.
For the moment, it was victory that mattered, the opening of the
second front from the Channel to the Adriatic, and not the assump-

tion of a political position too different from that of the Anglo-American powers. Furthermore, if General de Gaulle's France was to be associated directly with the European settlements, would she agree to the disappearance of the sovereignty of Poland, of Hungary, of the Balkan states, of—who knows?—Austria, of Czechoslovakia? Lastly, what was the France of tomorrow to be? Her domestic status would heavily influence her foreign policy, especially in regard to the Soviet Union. Who could be sure she would not turn against them under the influence of the elements that had created Vichy? On the other hand, wasn't it conceivable that the Communists might gain power in Paris? In the one case as in the other, it would be better not to have made too many advances to the Algiers Government. In short, while giving every evidence of attentive sympathy to our cause, Russia, in all essential matters, chose to wait and see.

On the whole, if in Washington, London and Moscow diplomatic policy differed as to basic motives, it was in agreement that a place should be kept for us without any need for haste in inviting us to take it. As for de Gaulle, everyone acknowledged him as the guide and symbol of France's recovery. But it was essential that his action be checked. Already, the fact that he was on the way to uniting a people as divided as the French and that he had been able to constitute a solid and coherent government seemed *abnormal* to the foreign experts—almost scandalous. Everyone was quite willing that France, with such a leader, should climb out of the abyss; but there must be no question of her scaling the summit. Officially, therefore, de Gaulle was treated with consideration but not with enthusiasm. Less officially, whatever was said, written or plotted against de Gaulle was encouraged. Later, every possible effort would be made to unearth again that 'political' France, so malleable in Europe's chancelleries, which everyone was used to.

I must confess that it was of little concern to me whether the diplomatic status of the Algiers Government was regularized or remained indefinite. Looking back, I sensed that the worst was over and that, if we persevered, the formalities would be solemnized sooner or later. Besides, it was not suitable that what we were, or were to become, should depend on the decisions of others. We were sufficiently well established to make ourselves heard where and when we chose. The future of France would develop of itself, not

G

according to the Allies' convenience. Once the Reich was over-thrown, taking into account the difficulties which would confront even the greatest states, nothing would prevent France from playing the role she chose, on condition that it was France that made the choice. This conviction of mine let me look at the grey faces of the Allies with detachment. Not concealing my regret that they should have adopted, so detrimentally to our common action, the reserva-tions characterizing their co-operation, the position I took was never that of the plaintiff.

Massigli, who was in permanent contact with the diplomatic corps in Algiers and who, on his own admission, suffered cruelly from such ill-defined foreign policies; Viénot, who, throughout his career, had been an apostle of the alliance with Britain and who was disappointed at London's present reticence; Monnet, whose negotia-tions with Washington for 'aid and recovery' could not be brought to a conclusion because the question of Franco-American relations was still in suspense, or Hoppenot, whose intelligence and sensibility deplored the negative prejudice of the United States; Garreau, who compared the fervour of Moscow's declarations on France's behalf with the circumspection of the people's commissars—were less serene than I. I allowed them to express their feelings when the opportunity arose. I sympathized with the impatience of our representatives with the other allies: Dejean, accredited to the governments in exile in Great Britain; Baelen, in charge of our relations with the Greek and Yugoslav Governments in Cairo; Coiffard in Chungking; Bonneau in Ottawa; Pechkoff, and later Grandin de l'Éprevier, in Pretoria; Clarac, later Monmayou, in Canberra; Garreau-Dombasle, Ledoux, Lancial, Arvengas, Roux, Casteran and Lechenet in Latin America; Grousset in Havana; Milon de Peillon in Port-au-Prince. I realized how trying the situation was for our delegates to the neutral countries. Truelle in Spain; du Chayla in Portugal; de Saint-Hardouin in Turkey; de Benoist in Egypt; de Vaux Saint-Cyr in Sweden; de Leusse in Switzerland; de Laforcade in Ireland. All the same, I myself deliberately persisted in the attitude of a Chief of State ready to come to an agreement with the others if they asked me to do so. I solicited nothing today since I was sure of having it tomorrow.

Such were the limitations of the game. They were revealed in the Italian question, where, by virtue of the principle of a makeshift compromise, the Allies kept us at a distance without excluding us altogether. On September 27th, 1943, the representatives of England and the United States brought Massigli the complete text of the armistice which was to be returned the same day for Marshal Badoglio to sign. The Anglo-American diplomats pointed out—quite rightly—that this text took into account our previous requests. But they found nothing to answer to the French minister's question: 'Why did you not associate France with you in the armistice?' Some days later, Badoglio was to declare war on the Reich with the joint approval of Great Britain, America and Russia but with no mention of France. At the same time, we learned that a conference to settle the Italian question among the British, American and Soviet foreign ministers was to take place in Moscow; we were not invited.

When Mr Cordell Hull passed through Algiers on his way to the conference, I refrained from expressing the slightest recrimination, but made it clear that no one would make use of what we were and what we had for nothing. 'We are delighted,' I told him, 'to see you making direct contact, on America's behalf, with Soviet Russia; I intend to go to Moscow myself one of these days on behalf of France.' When the Secretary of State inquired as to our position on the Italian question, I replied: 'We shall not fail to express our own point of view when we are in a position to know that of the other states concerned.'

Mr Cordell Hull then indicated that the Moscow conference would probably result in the creation of an inter-Allied commission for Italian Affairs. 'Perhaps,' he added, 'you will take part in it.' 'We shall see,' I told him. 'In any case, to determine the fate of the peninsula, it is first of all essential to recover its territory from the Germans, which implies the co-operation of French forces and bases. I know that Eisenhower is planning to ask for this co-operation, and we are prepared to accede to his request. But to do so, it is obviously necessary that we determine with you, and in the same capacity as you, what will become of Italy. We can engage our soldiers only on behalf of a goal in which we too have a share.' Mr Cordell Hull understood that he was facing a firmly held position, as did Mr Eden after I spoke to him on October 10th. As for M. Bogomolov, he had outstripped the others by explaining that the Mediterranean Commission had been a Soviet notion and that his government would insist that we be invited to participate in it.

Indeed, on November 16th, Massigli received Macmillan, Murphy and Bogomolov. The last informed him that their three governments intended to set up an 'Advisory Commission for Italian Affairs'. This commission would represent the Allies on the spot, would propose to their governments the measures to be taken in common, and would establish a policy for the military command in all matters relating to politics and administration. We were asked to sit on this commission. The Committee of Liberation accepted the invitation. On November 29th, I received M. Vishinsky, who came to assure me of his government's eagerness to co-operate closely with us on the Advisory Commission. This agreed, the representatives, Macmillan, Massigli, Murphy and Vishinsky, then began work. Soon Couve de Murville replaced Massigli, since the latter was too occupied by his ministry. Thus we were directly informed as to what was happening in the peninsula; we would take part in the measures destined either to punish Italy for her crimes or to allow her to recover from her misfortunes; we would be in a position to pursue our policy on the peninsula, a position essential to her destiny, to ours and to that of the West.

I had explained this policy to Count Sforza, who slipped into my office at Les Oliviers one October evening. The old statesman was returning to Italy after twenty years of exile. On the ruins of the Fascist system he had unceasingly opposed, he was preparing to assume the direction of his unfortunate country's foreign affairs. I was struck by the nobility and courage with which Sforza envisaged his coming task. 'That I am here before you,' he told me, 'is proof of my desire to do everything possible to establish that Franco-Italian co-operation for whose lack you and I are paying dearly and which Europe is going to need more than ever.' I indicated to Count Sforza how closely I saw eye to eye with him on this crucial point, but that after what had happened, a reconciliation with Italy could not be made altogether gratuitously, although it was our intention to bring it about as generously as possible.

To liquidate the privileges which Italian nationals enjoyed in Tunisia; to award France the cantons of Tenda and Brigua (which, although French, had been granted to Italy after the plebiscite of 1860); to rectify the frontier along the passes of Larche, Mount Genèvre, Mont Cenis and Little Saint Bernard (in order to abolish several awkward encroachments on our territory); to grant the Val d'Aosta the right to be what it was—that is to say a region spiritually

French; to demand certain reparations, particularly in regard to warships and commercial vessels: these were the limited but precise advantages which I determined to obtain for France.

Given the fact that Yugoslavia had joined the Allied camp and considering the effort which the troops of General Mikhailovitch and those of Tito had unceasingly furnished, it was evident that Italy could not keep her pre-war possessions on the eastern coast of the Adriatic. Nevertheless, we were ready to support her claim to Trieste. Having informed Count Sforza of all these points concerning the Italian frontiers, I added: 'As for your colonies, if Cyrenaica, where the English wish to remain, is lost to you, and since we ourselves intend to remain in the Fezzan, we hope to see you remain not only in Somalia but also in Eritrea and in Tripolitania. To achieve this, you will doubtless have to find a means of association with the local populations; in Eritrea, in exchange for the rights you will retain, you must recognize the Negus' sovereignty. We consider it justifiable that you should be an African power. If you yourselves claim that power, we shall support you firmly.'

In December, at General Eisenhower's request, the Committee of Liberation sent to Italy the first elements of the French Expeditionary Corps. This was subsequently to be reinforced to the point where it furnished the decisive Allied action during the Battle of Rome. As this military participation increased, we spoke louder in the political sphere. Such amplification was necessary, moreover, for the Anglo-American forces, applying a system of expedient devices and maintaining King Victor Emmanuel and Marshal Badoglio in office, were setting obstacles in the way of France-Italian reconciliation and accumulating motives for revolution in the peninsula.

The King, in 1940, had allowed war to be declared on France at a time when she was succumbing to the German onslaught, though it was France whose costly effort of 1859 had liberated Italy and assured its unity and whose Army in 1917 had helped bring the disaster of Caporetto to a halt at the Piave. He had accepted and submitted to Mussolini until the moment when the Duce succumbed to events. Badoglio, merely by virute of the German victory, had had an 'armistice' signed with the plenipotentiaries of Pétain and Weygand according to the terms of which the Italians were to occupy a part of French territory and control our Empire's forces. Further, it was from the Fascist régime that the Marshal-

Prime Minister held his honours and his command. How could this sovereign and this chief of government organize the co-operation of their country with ours and lead Italy along a new road? This was the substance of the Committee of Liberation's communication, on January 22nd, 1944, to Washington, London and Moscow, declaring that the throne and the government must be swept clean.

During the months of March, May and June, I was in Italy inspecting our troops; I saw many disturbing signs, particularly in Naples. The most obvious spectacle was that of extreme poverty and of the deplorable effects which contact with well-supplied troops produced on public morals. As a Christian, a Latin and a European, I was cruelly sensitive to the misery of this great nation that had been misled but to whom the world owed so much. Perhaps the Italian people instinctively sensed my feelings; perhaps, in their ordeal, the thought of France was closer to them, as to all nations in agony. In any case, I was always surprised to find enthusiastic groups following me whenever I appeared in public. Couve de Murville, our extremely well-informed and self-possessed representative, itemized the state of Italy's politics, torn by contrary currents in which it was already apparent that the future would be played out between the Papacy and the Communist Party. During these trips, I was forced to refuse to meet both Umberto and Badoglio, although with some regret. I was not, however, prepared to admit that the one should continue to wear the crown and that the other should remain at the head of the government.

But while we were beginning to pluck the fruits of long effort in the western Mediterranean, in the Near East we had to endure disappointments. In the Levant States, the agitation of the local politicians, as a result of British provocation, precipitated a spectacular crisis in order to take advantage of France's diminished status while there was still time to do so.

The Lebanon, on this occasion, was the field of operations. The elections had taken place in July 1943. After a period characterized by so many events disastrous to French prestige, it was understandable that the new parliament should manifest an unrestrained nationalism. The English, having strongly contributed to the electoral result, now wished to take advantage of it. With M. Béchara Khoury, the newly elected President of the Republic, and with the government of Mr Riad Solh, Spears assumed the attitude of France's adversary, encouraged his faction to outbid our own and promised the protection of his government no matter what the result.

It must be said that Spears's action in Syria and Lebanon corresponded to the general policy Great Britain tended to pursue in the Middle East during the war's final phase. The victorious conclusion of the operations in North Africa had put a great number of British forces at their disposal. While a portion of the latter were sent into combat in Italy, the rest took up positions on both banks of the Red Sea. Seven hundred thousand British soldiers occupied Egypt, the Sudan, Cyrenaica, Palestine, Transjordan, Iraq and the Levant States. Besides, London had created at Cairo an 'Economic Centre' which, thanks to the manipulation of credit, the shipping monopolies and the needs of the blockade, controlled the entire foreign exchange of the Arab nations and thereby, in fact, the life of their people, the opinion of their leaders and the attitude of their governments. Lastly, the presence of an army of specialists provided with vast financial means and, in the world of society, the action of perfectly organized diplomacy and propaganda completed the elements of power, thanks to which England, rid of her enemies' threats in the Near East, intended to affirm her status as sole suzerain.

We were not in a position to counterbalance such pressure. Three Senegalese battalions, some cannons, some tanks, two gun-boats and about fifteen planes comprised all the forces the French had in the Levant. True, there were also the Syrian and Lebanese troops, some 18,000 good soldiers under our command. But what would be their decision should the Damascus and Beirut governments openly take a hostile position to us? Besides, our extreme poverty did not permit us to offer anything to anyone. As for struggling against the flood of tendentious propaganda which all Anglo-American sources, whenever the occasion arose, unfailingly poured out the world over, it was beyond our means to do so. Above all, now that the liberation of France was on the horizon, I would have no chance of urging the French, even my ministers, to think of any other undertaking. All in all, we were too ill provided and too occupied elsewhere to be able to counteract any interference with our position on the spot.

The situation crystallized during the month of November. The Beirut Government found itself, for reasons of domestic policy, in a difficult parliamentary situation. To create a distraction, Mr Riad Solh, President of the Council, and M. Camille Chamoun, Minister of Foreign Affairs, noisily raised the Lebanese claims against the mandatory power. Our delegate-general to the Levant, Ambassador Jean Helleu, who saw the crisis coming, had come to Algiers to consult the government. On November 5th, he presented his report to me in the presence of Catroux and Massigli and received our instructions; we urged him to take decisive steps to open negotiations at Beirut and Damascus with a view to transferring to the local governments certain services concerning the economy and the police which the French authority had hitherto maintained.

At the same time, we told Helleu our theoretical position on the mandate. Entrusted to France by the League of Nations, it could not be deposed except as a result of future international requests and by French powers which were not provisional. This was the position we had always taken with the Allies, notably Great Britain, without ever having heard any objections to it in principle. Legally, if Syria's and the Lebanon's independence had any international value, it was because we ourselves had accorded it to them by virtue of our mandate. But for the same reason, we found ourselves obliged to preserve certain responsibilities in the Levant as a result of the state of war. Given the world-wide scope of the conflict, we felt that the Damascus and Beirut Governments could wait until it was resolved before settling the final formalities that still limited the sovereignty of their states. There was no doubt that they would have waited, in fact, had London not encouraged their demands and offered the support of the British forces in order to impose them.

While Helleu was in Algiers, the Lebanese parliament revised the constitution by removing from it all mention of the mandate, as if the mandate had been abolished. From Cairo, which he passed through on his way back to his post, the Ambassador had telegraphed the Beirut Government, informing it that he was carrying his government's instructions of the opening of negotiations and requesting that the promulgation of the new constitutional law be postponed. But the Lebanese ignored his message. Back in Beirut, Helleu, outraged by this provocation, opposed the constitution by a formal veto on November 12th, suspended the parliament and had the Lebanese Chief of State, the President of the Council and several other ministers arrested, and made Mr Émile Eddé provisional President of the Republic.

While regarding our delegate's actions as perfectly justifiable, and approving the sentiments that had dictated them, the Committee of Liberation was immediately convinced that they exceeded the measures which the general situation would allow it to maintain. All the more so since, without renouncing the principle of the mandate, we did not intend to question the independence we had already conceded. This is why, on the morning of the 13th, informed of what had occurred at Beirut the day before, we decided to send General Catroux there to re-establish a normal constitutional situation without disavowing Helleu. This meant that Catroux, after consultations on the spot, would have Khoury, Riad Solh and their ministers released and would re-establish the president in his functions. After which the Lebanese Government would be re-formed, including, last of all, the Chamber of Deputies. As for our delegate, his presence in the Levant would not be justified as soon as Catroux was there with full powers; we therefore summoned Helleu to Algiers 'for consultations' after a few days' delay.

In order that there should be no misunderstandings as to Catroux's mission, I myself, on November 16th, made a placating declaration to the Consultative Assembly: 'What has occurred in Beirut,' I declared, 'alters neither France's policy in Lebanon, nor the commitments we have made, nor our desire to fulfil them. Our intention consists in seeing a normal constitutional situation established in the Lebanon, in order that we can deal with its government on questions of common interest, both parties in complete independence.' I concluded by saying: 'The passing cloud will not darken the horizon.' The next day, Catroux, passing through Cairo, saw Mr Casey, the British Minister of State, and indicated to him that he would have Khoury and Riad Solh released without delay. On November 19th, having arrived at Beirut, he had a discussion with M. Béchara Khoury. He received the president's many assurances of loyal friendship and informed him that he was to be released and restored to office. No one henceforth could doubt our desire to 'link up' as soon as possible and to adopt a conciliating policy.

But the British could not reconcile themselves to conciliation. Subsequent events made it appear as if London were determined to throw oil on the fire apparently to make the arrangement we were seeking in the Lebanon appear to have been imposed upon us by British intervention, and perhaps, too, in order to take revenge on de Gaulle for the recent alteration of the Committee of Liberation.

Already on November 13th, Mr Makins, replacing Mr Macmillan, had sent Massigli a 'verbal' but peremptory note demanding an immediate Anglo-Franco-Lebanese conference to settle the incident and insisting, on behalf of the British Government, that we recall Helleu. On the 19th, when it had been obvious for several days that the path we had taken led to complete agreement, England still hurled her thunderbolts. This could only be for the benefit of the gallery, of course, and to create the impression of a French loss of face.

On that day, in fact, Mr Casey came to Beirut and, flanked by General Spears, delivered an ultimatum to General Catroux: Great Britain, ignoring the alliance that united us, her promises of political disinterestedness in the Levant States, the agreements with me which Oliver Lyttelton had signed in her name, ordered the French representative to agree to the tripartite conference and to release the president and the Lebanese ministers within thirty-six hours. Unless this was done, the British, with the excuse of maintaining order—which it was not their responsibility to do—would proclaim what they called 'martial law', seize power by force and send their troops to liberate the prisoners under our soldiers' guard.

'Here we are back in the Fashoda days,' General Catroux remarked to Casey and Spears. With this difference nevertheless: that France, at the time of the Fashoda incident, was in a position to offer England resistance, but that in the present case there was no such risk. The Committee of Liberation ordered General Catroux to refuse to attend the tripartite conference, or to release, as had been agreed, M. Khoury and his ministers and, if England carried out her threat of seizing power in the Lebanon, to collect our officials and our troops at some port and bring them back to Africa. I would then take it upon myself to explain to France and to the world the reasons for their departure.

Ultimately, a kind of *modus vivendi* was re-established in the Levant: the British muted their threats; General Catroux negotiated the transference to the states of the 'common interest' services; those in office continued to wobble and war with each other amid the agitation created by those who desired their place. The 'leaders' of the neighbouring Arab countries, for the same reasons, came forward with protests against France. In Cairo, Nahas Pasha, the president of Farouk's council imposed by the English ambassador; in Baghdad, Nuri Pasha, who had only returned to power thanks to the British troops; at Amman from the Emir Abdullah, whose budget was settled in London and whose army was led by General Peake and Colonel Glubb, known as 'Peake Pasha' and 'Glubb Pasha', all complained.

In February, Catroux having returned to Algiers, the Committee of Liberation appointed General Beynet as delegate-general and minister plenipotentiary of France to the Levant. Helleu was not to return. Casey had left Cairo and Chamoun, Beirut, where Spears was to remain to foment the next crisis. With much skill and steadfastness, the new French representative took the situation in hand. Meanwhile, it was clear that a constantly renewed *tour de force* could not be repeated indefinitely. Particularly since our limited means, the anguished passion of French public opinion and the whole world's attention would, henceforth, be absorbed by the military events that were to decide the destiny of Europe.

Politics preceded events themselves and were oriented everywhere to the situation likely to follow a victory. In the Allied camp, this was particularly the case in regard to the small and medium-sized states. In Algiers, we could scarcely hear even an echo of the discussions centring on these states, since their sovereigns and ministers were in London, their diplomacy operating chiefly in Washington and their propaganda directed primarily towards the Anglo-Saxon countries. Nevertheless, we knew enough to understand their anxieties. Nothing, moreover, demonstrated more clearly and more sadly how the fall of France yesterday and the pressure of the three other great powers to keep her at a distance today seriously mortgaged the peace in preparation for the morrow.

As a matter of fact, Belgium and Luxembourg, completely surrounded by Western powers, did not doubt that their frontiers and their independence would be restored to them by the liberation. The problems then confronting them would be of an economic nature. Ruined France and exhausted England could only help them to solve their difficulties after prolonged delays; in the immediate future, it was America on whom they counted. So we saw Spaak, Gutt and Bech haunting the conferences at Atlantic City, Hot Springs and Dumbarton Oaks, where the United States was laying its plans for the revictualling, the reconstruction and the development of Europe, while Monsieur de Romrée, Belgian ambassador to the French Committee of Liberation, was chiefly interested in schemes for a confederation of western Europe. The Dutch, who had scarcely any political anxiety as to metropolitan Holland, were, however, hugely concerned as to the future of their Australasian possessions. Henceforth, their government was to be subject to American pressure which would eventually force them to renounce their sovereignty over Java, Sumatra and Borneo. The remarks of the Dutch minister plenipotentiary, Mr Van Wijk, as well as the reports Dejean was sending us from London, indicated that Mr Van Kleffens foresaw, with some bitterness, that the Allied victory in the Pacific would involve the liquidation of the Netherlands Empire. The Norwegians felt already, through neutral Sweden and a virtually conquered Finland, the crushing weight of all the Russias. Hence Mr Trygve Lie was already working out plans for an Atlantic alliance which Mr de Hougen, Norwegian minister at Algiers, came to discuss with us. But above all it was the refugee governments of Central and Balkan Europe who betrayed their anxiety. Realizing that the Soviets would follow the Germans over their territories, they were devoured by fears for tomorrow.

The Teheran conference, held in December 1943, merely fanned their fears. Of course the participants—Roosevelt, Stalin and Churchill—had launched a number of lenitive statements declaring that their meeting was of a purely strategic nature. But what leaked out was not at all reassuring for the governments in exile. Despite official secrecy, it was not difficult to discern the essentials of what had happened at Teheran. Stalin had spoken there as the man to whom payment must be made. Without revealing the Russian intentions to the other two, he had obliged them to explain theirs to him and even alter them according to his requirements. Roosevelt had agreed with him in rejecting Churchill's plan for a vast western offensive in Italy, Yugoslavia and Greece, sweeping towards Vienna, Prague and Budapest. The Americans had followed the Soviet lead in refusing, despite British suggestions, to examine all political questions concerning Central Europe, in particular Poland, which the Russian armies were on the verge of entering. We ourselves had been excluded from the proceedings to the point where Roosevelt and Churchill—the former flying over North Africa, the latter sailing along its coast to reach Cairo and Teheran—had taken care not to contact us.

Suddenly the prospects, so alarming to the sovereigns and minis-

ters of the Balkans, the Vistula and the Danube States, began to
crystallize. This was why, in Greece, a notable part of the resistance
elements, developed and directed by Communists, allied itself with
the EAM organization, which was fighting against the invader and
at the same time breaking ground for the revolution. The military
instrument of this movement, the ELAS, incorporated a number of
maquis groups operating in the Greek mountains and profoundly
influenced the army and fleet units stationed in the Middle East. In
order to keep contact with the soldiers and sailors and to communicate more readily with the country's interior, the President of the
Council, Mr Tsouderos, and the majority of the ministers had moved
to Cairo. Soon King George II joined them there, arriving just in
time for a violent ministerial crisis. In April 1944, Mr Tsouderos
was forced to retire. His replacement, Mr Venizelos, left office in
his turn, and it was only with great difficulty that Mr Papandreou
formed a ministry. At the same time, serious rebellions broke out
among the troops and on board the ships. To quell them, nothing
less than the bloody intervention of British forces was required.
Although the representatives of all political tendencies, meeting
later at Beirut, were to proclaim national union, dissension soon
broke out again. There was every indication that, in Greece, the
German retreat would be the signal for civil war.

The United States had prudently withdrawn its finger from this
pie long before, but the Soviets were exerting pressure on the Greeks,
while the British, aiming at hegemony in the eastern Mediterranean,
did not hide the fact that, in their eyes, Greek questions belonged to
their sphere of influence. For this reason the French Government
had never involved itself in them. Nevertheless it would have been
in the interests of a united Europe had the influence and force of
France joined those of England in Greece, as had frequently been
the case in the past. No one was more convinced of this than Mr
Argyropoulo, Greek representative to the National Committee; this
patriot, deeply disturbed by the threats hanging over his country,
this politician, convinced that a Europe without France had every
chance of miscarrying, deplored the fact that a barrier should be
established by foreign powers between his government and that of
the French Republic.

In regard to Yugoslavia, our Allies proceeded in the same fashion.
The Serbo-Croatian-Slovene kingdom, even before the war a prey

to impassioned dissensions among its ethnic groups, now found itself
in a state of total upheaval. The Italians had set up a Croat State
and annexed Dalmatia and the Slovene province of Ljubljana.
Colonel Mikhailovitch had valiantly conducted a guerrilla war
against the Germans in the mountains of Serbia, and later on Joseph
Broz, known as Tito, had begun the struggle on his own account
with Communist encouragement. The invaders had reacted to
these facts by massacres and destructions of an unheard-of brutality,
while Mikhailovitch and Tito had become adversaries. In London,
the very young King Peter II and his unstable government were
victims not only of severe national difficulties, but of British political
pressure as well.

The British, in effect, considered Yugoslavia as one of the principal
fields of action for their Mediterranean policy. Further, Mr Churchill had made it his personal concern. Cherishing the scheme of a
tremendous Balkan operation, he wanted Yugoslavia for its bridgehead. Hence a British military mission had been sent first to Mikhailovitch, whom London was furnishing with arms and advice, and
subsequently to Tito, to whom the Prime Minister sent his son
Randolph. Finally, according Tito preference, the British Government sent him what he needed to equip his troops. As for Mikhailovitch, he found himself without any help whatsoever, vilified by the
wireless from London and even accused of treason in the House of
Commons by the Foreign Office representative. Then, in June 1944,
the hapless Peter II was ordered by Mr Churchill to dismiss Mr
Pouritch's Government, in which Mikhailovitch was serving as
Minister of War, and to entrust its control to Mr Soubachitch, who
had previously received Tito's investiture. This reversal received, of
course, Moscow's approval, while Mr Fotich, the Yugoslav ambassador to Washington, did not succeed in obtaining America's support for his sovereign.

The French Committee of National Liberation was systematically
excluded from these events and their development. I had been able
to make occasional contact with General Mikhailovitch, who on his
side indicated an ardent desire to communicate with me. Various
messages had been exchanged. In February 1944, I awarded him
the Croix de Guerre and made a public statement of the fact in order
to encourage him at the moment when the ground seemed to be
giving way beneath his feet. But the officers I tried to send him

from Tunis or Italy never succeeded in reaching him. As for Tito, we never received the slightest sign of recognition from him. I had been on cordial terms with King Peter II and his ministers during my stay in Great Britain; Maurice Dejean, our representative to them there, and Mr Jodjvanovitch, their delegate to us at Algiers, served as intermediaries for exchanges of opinion and information; but on no occasion did the Yugoslav Government—doubtless not being permitted the latitude to do so—turn to us to request our good offices. England herself did not once decide to consult us even in an advisory capacity. I was therefore confirmed in my resolution to devote what resources we had directly to the liberation of France and not engage them in Balkan operations. Why should we offer our military co-operation in a political undertaking from which we found ourselves deliberately excluded?

If the Soviet advance and the action of their agents tortured some refugee governments with anxiety, President Beneš and his ministers, on the other hand, affected to be relatively undisturbed by it with regard to Czechoslovakia. Not that they were any more confident in their heart of hearts; but they decided that instead of trying to defer the inevitable, it would be better to turn it to good account. Their representative, Mr Cerny, kept us informed, moreover, of the progress of this viewpoint. In December 1943, Beneš had gone to Moscow to sign a 'friendly alliance' with Stalin, stipulating 'mutual co-operation and assistance'. Returning to London, he stopped in Algiers on January 2nd. We respectfully received this head of state who, through the most terrible vicissitudes, had always remained a friend to France.

Beneš informed me of the subjects of his conversations in Moscow; he described Stalin as reserved in his remarks but steadfast in his intentions, his ideas both well concealed and well determined on every European question. Then he explained his own policy. 'Look at the map,' he said. 'The Russians have reached the Carpathians. But the Western powers are not yet ready to land in France. It is the Red Army that will liberate my country from the Germans. Afterwards, in order for me to be able to establish my administration, it is with Stalin that I must come to an agreement. I have just done so and on conditions that will not mortgage Czechoslovakia's future. According to what he and I have agreed upon, the Russian command will not involve itself in our political affairs.'

Turning to the European question as a whole, President Beneš
undertook to prove to me, as he had already done on other occasions,
that the Czech state could revive only with a Russian alliance. He
moved his finger over the map, exclaiming, 'Here is the Sudeten-
land, which must be recovered from the Germans. Here is Teschen,
which the Poles are demanding. Here is Slovakia, which the Hungarians plan to recover and where Monsignor Tiszo has formed a
separatist government. Tomorrow, Eastern Germany, Poland and
Hungary will be in Soviet hands. If Russia espouses their various
claims and dissensions, dismemberment is certain. You can see why
the Russian alliance is categorically imperative for us.'

When I referred to the possibility of a Western counterbalance,
Beneš expressed his doubts. 'Roosevelt,' he said, 'is anxious to come
to an agreement with Stalin and withdraw his troops as soon as he
can after the victory. Churchill is not much concerned with us; for
him, the British line of defence is along the Rhine and the Alps.
Once this is assured, nothing will arouse his interest save the Mediterranean. As for us, he will follow Roosevelt's lead in exchange for
a few advantages in the Middle East. By mutual agreement, Czechoslovakia was not mentioned in Teheran. It is true that there remains
General de Gaulle, artisan of that steadfast, strong France which is
so indispensable to European equilibrium. Had you not appeared
after the fall of your country to urge it on to recovery, there would
no longer be any hope for the freedom of Europe. No one, therefore,
has more zealous hopes for your success than I. But I must point out
that Washington and London are hardly of my opinion. Where and
what will you be tomorrow? I must also remind you of Clemenceau's
dismissal by the French Parliament just after the First World War;
I was working with the great Masaryk when the news reached
Prague; we both had the same thought: "This is France's renuncia-
tion!" '

What Beneš told me of Washington's and London's attitude towards Soviet ambitions was already being verified by the situation in
Poland. The nearer the Red Army came to Warsaw, the more
clearly Moscow's intention to dominate Poland and alter its frontiers
appeared. It was apparent that Stalin wanted, on the one hand, to
add the territories of Lithuania, White Russia and Eastern Galicia
to Russia, and on the other hand to extend Poland as far as the Oder
and the Neisse at the expense of the Germans. It was no less clear

that the master of the Kremlin intended to establish a régime answerable to himself on the Vistula and one which the Anglo-American powers would not oppose.

The Polish Government in exile in London was thus at grips with terrifying problems, materially impotent to oppose Moscow's decisions but morally armed with that sombre assurance which a patriotism tempered by centuries of oppression confers on the Polish spirit. Actually, General Sikorski, President of the Council and Commander-in-Chief, had at first, tried to reach an agreement with the Soviets. When the Wehrmacht was at the gates of Moscow, such an agreement had seemed possible; a number of Polish soldiers imprisoned by the Russians in 1939 had been allowed to reach the Middle East with their leader, General Anders, while Stalin had adopted a moderate tone in speaking of frontiers and future relations. Now the picture had become quite different, as had the map of war. Suddenly the Poles gave way again to the hatred and the panic which the Russians have traditionally inspired in them. In the spring of 1943, they had officially accused the Soviets—not without an appearance of reason—of having massacred 10,000 of their captured officers in the Katyn Forest some three years before. Stalin, irritated, had suspended diplomatic relations. Then in July, General Sikorski, returning from Egypt, where he had gone to inspect Anders' troops, was killed in an aeroplane accident in Gibraltar. This eminent man, who enjoyed enough prestige to dominate the passions of his compatriots and enough international reputation to be treated with respect, was irreplaceable. From the moment of his loss, the Russo-Polish crisis assumed the quality of a bitter conflict.

Nevertheless, the new Polish Government, on the authority of its leader, Mr Mikolajczyk, had promised that after the liberation the authorities in Warsaw would be oriented so as to afford Moscow every guarantee of neighbourly relations. As to the frontiers, Mikolajczyk did not reject any plans *a priori* and merely declared that the question could be settled only by the peace treaty. He gave orders to the resistance forces on national territory to co-operate with the Soviet armies. Lastly, he turned to the United States and to Great Britain 'to resolve differences and bring to a solution all problems as yet undecided'. But these conciliatory moves were not echoed in the Kremlin. Quite the contrary: the Russian grievances increased in proportion to their own advance. In January, on the occasion of the entry of their troops into Polish territory, the Soviets published a declaration according to which the so-called 'Curzon line' was to be adopted as the eastern frontier and the government in exile in London completely re-formed. Simultaneously a Polish army corps formed under Russian inspiration appeared, whose leader, Berling, rejected the legal government's authority, while a 'Polish Committee of National Liberation', formed in Moscow and directed by Mr Osuska-Morawski, entered Galicia on the heels of the Soviet troops.

It was obvious that Poland's independence would find only precarious support from the Anglo-American powers. In January 1944, Mr Cordell Hull made an evasive reply to Mr Mikolajczyk's request for mediation. Although Roosevelt, facing an electoral campaign that year, was ambiguous out of consideration for the voters of Polish origin, it could be foreseen that once his campaign was over he would leave Stalin's hands free. The British showed less resignation, but it was likely that their concern to toe the American line would ultimately lead them to yield the essentials of the matter, so long as there was some formal arrangement to conceal it.

Actually, Churchill and Eden, while speaking in favour of Poland's independence, urged Mr Mikolajczyk to go to Moscow. His visit took place in August, just as the Soviet Army reached Warsaw and the Polish secret army, under General Komorowski, known as 'Bor', was taking action against the Germans in the city. After a heroic struggle, the Poles were overwhelmed and accused the Russians of having done nothing to help them, and even of having kept British planes from landing on Soviet bases when they might have taken action to the defenders' advantage. In Moscow, the Polish ministers had obtained only discouraging replies from Stalin and Molotov, while receiving word of an agreement signed by the Soviet Union and the 'Polish Committee of National Liberation', assigning the administration of the liberated territories to this committee.

Our government was in no position to prevent this gradual subjugation of Poland. Since it was not really associated with its great Allies on a diplomatic level and did not participate as an equal in the elaboration of common strategy, how could it have persuaded the Western powers to adopt the political attitude and the military decisions that doubtless would have saved Polish independence while according Russia the frontier she demanded? As for myself, Stalin's idea of according the Poles new acquisitions in Prussia and Silesia in compensation for the amputations they would suffer in the East was quite acceptable, provided he proceeded with humanity in the necessary shifts of population. But I felt that his intention to establish a dictatorship of his followers in Warsaw must be opposed. I considered that America, England and France, by jointly declaring these matters to the world, by acting in co-operation with regard to the Soviet and Polish Governments, by stipulating future access to the Baltic ports for the combined Western fleets in return for opening the North Sea ports to Russian ships, would be able to effect a restoration of liberty to the noble and valiant nation of Poland.

But confronted by Soviet Russia's demands, America decided to keep silent. Great Britain looked for a formula. France did not have a say in the matter. To Mr Morawski, the active and able ambassador from Poland to the French Committee of Liberation, with whom I continued to confer on many occasions; to General Sosnkowski, who had succeeded Sikorski as Commander-in-Chief and whom I received in Algiers in December; to General Anders, whom I saw in March 1944, with his troops before Monte Cassino; to Mr Rackiewica, President of the Polish Republic, with whom I exchanged visits during my trip to London in June 1944; and to Mr de Romer, his Minister of Foreign Affairs, who was at his side, I could only say what our own position was and promise to make its weight felt when we had the means to do so.

Meanwhile we found an opportunity of bringing some assistance to the Polish Government in the matter of the ultimate destination of an important stock of gold which the State Bank of Poland had entrusted to the Bank of France in September 1939 and which the latter, in June 1940, had stored at Bamako. In March 1944 the Committee of Liberation, having received urgent requests from Mr Mikolajczyk, decided to put the Poles in possession of their gold again. Mr Bogomolov did not fail to make a number of urgent demands that the measure be revoked; having requested an audience with me as a last resort; he said: 'The Soviet Government formally protests against the transfer of the Polish gold to the government in exile in London which will not be the government of Poland tomorrow.' I replied that it was such today, that it was so recognized by all our Allies, including Russia, that on its orders the Polish forces

were now fighting beside our own in Italy, and that lastly I did not
see in what capacity the Soviet Union was interfering in a matter
that concerned only Poland and France. Mr Bogomolov retired
without concealing his displeasure.

Thus despite the counsels of abstention from Washington, London
and Moscow, the small and medium sized European states sought
contact with us. Others, geographically remote, also tended to align
themselves with us on moral issues. General Vanier, the Canadian
delegate, brought us the encouragement of his country, which was
proving so exemplary in the war effort, and negotiated the economic
aid which Canada was already lending us, as well as that which it
would provide after the liberation. Our Latin American allies, by
their plenipotentiaries' remarks, indicated that France's return to
her position in world politics profoundly affected their own feelings
and interests. Such, for example, were the assurances that came from
Mr Vasco da Cunha, from Brazil; from Mr de Aramburu, from
Peru; from Mr Freila Larrea, from Ecuador; and from Mr Suarez
Solar, from Cuba. Lastly, Mr de Sangroniz, the extremely distinguished and adroit Spanish delegate, although the only neutral
among the belligerents and somewhat hampered by a rather vague
status, showed great concern in all questions affecting Morocco, the
fate of Tangiers (the destination of all the Frenchmen crossing the
Pyrenees) and trade between French Africa and the Iberian Peninsula. We had insisted on establishing strong relations with the
Spanish, who wanted as much themselves. All the same, I hoped
that it would soon be possible to restore normal relations between
Paris and Madrid under conditions worthy of two great neighbouring peoples.

In Algiers, it was naturally our relations with the three great
Allied delegations that accounted for our principal diplomatic
activity. Without my having to intervene in this domain as directly
as at the time when we had no ministers, I had to follow affairs
closely. I was, therefore, in constant touch with the representatives
of the United States, of Great Britain and of Soviet Russia. If their
governments were supposed to be in doubt as to who or what was
really France, they none the less did not fail to send us their ambassadors, who in no way concealed from us that they intended,
before long, to accompany us to Paris.

After the Committee of Liberation was altered so that it was under my Presidency alone, Washington and London, making the best of a bad bargain, had taken suitable steps in my regard. Mr Robert Murphy, in the vague capacity of 'President Roosevelt's delegate' was transferred to Italy and replaced by Mr Edwin Wilson, whose title as his government's representative to our committee was quite official. Mr Murphy's departure and his successor's attitude produced an agreeable relaxation in our relations with the American embassy. The first incumbent scarcely appreciated the success of the 'Gaullists', but the second seemed to be greatly pleased by it. Mr Wilson's visits were as agreeable and numerous as my interviews with Mr Murphy had been infrequent and uncomfortable. A gifted diplomat, Wilson was also a man of feeling. Though his loyalty did not allow him to disavow the attitude of the White House and the State Department, he evidently found them painful. By his personal action, he was frequently able to make comprehensible if not acceptable to either party the other's point of view, and on occasion to forestall the explosions that were imminent, either on the American side or on ours.

Mr Duff Cooper did as much for the British. Until December 1943, it was Mr Macmillan who had represented Great Britain at Algiers while assuming other responsibilities as well; now he was leaving for Italy, where his post as Minister of State had been transferred. Originally directed by Churchill to associate himself, although with some reservations, with the political actions of the Americans in North Africa, Macmillan had gradually come to understand that he had better things to do. His independent spirit and lucid intelligence had found themselves in sympathy with the French group that desired a France without fetters. As our relations developed I sensed that the prejudices he had nursed towards us were dissolving. In return, he had all my esteem. But as soon as he left, London determined to give him the best possible successor and, at the same time, normalize the British representation. Mr Duff Cooper was appointed Ambassador to Algiers, pending his occupying that position in Paris. This was one of the most friendly and far-seeing gestures which His Majesty's Government had made in regard to France.

Duff Cooper was a superior man upon whom fate had showered many gifts. There was little he did not understand and nothing that failed to interest him in the realm of politics, history, letters, art or

science. But he brought to everything a kind of moderation, perhaps
of modesty as well, which in conferring its charm upon him kept him
from forcing himself upon others. His convictions, nevertheless, were
strong ones; his principles, unshakeable; his entire career bore witness
to them. In his country and at a period when events demanded the
service of the best, he might well have been the Prime Minister. It
was conceivable that he had been kept from this office by one trait
in his nature—integrity—and by one circumstance: the presence of
Winston Churchill. He was not to be Prime Minister in London but
ambassador to Paris. As a humanist, he loved France; as a politician,
he dealt with affairs with noble serenity; as an Englishman, he
served his king unwaveringly. Placed between Churchill and myself,
he made it his duty to absorb the shocks. Occasionally he succeeded;
had it been possible for a man to do so in every instance, Duff
Cooper would have been that man.

    In regard to the Russians, we dealt, as before, with Mr Bogo-
molov, concerned to grasp all the facts and careful not to give in—
eager, in fact, to take the firmest possible stand at the first instance
in order to formulate what his government had to say in the most
categorical way possible. In certain cases, Mr Vishinsky, temporarily
in charge of Italian affairs but familiar with the broadest domain of
world politics, came to discuss various problems. He revealed in this
task a great breadth of mind but also—and somewhat surprisingly
in the former Soviet prosecutor—an amiable playfulness. Nevertheless, there were things that revealed how implacable were the orders
to which he was bound. When I said to him, in the hearing of others:
'It was a fault on our part not to have negotiated an open alliance
with you against Hitler before 1939. But how wrong it was of Soviet
Russia to have come to an agreement with him and allow us to be
defeated!' Mr Vishinsky, suddenly pale, drew himself up. His hand
seemed to brush away some mysterious threat. 'No! No!' he murmured. 'Never—that must never be spoken of!'

    On the whole, France's relations with her allies were developing
on the practical level despite all the precautions inherent in the
formulas. January 1st, 1944, was the occasion of a significant ceremony. The diplomatic corps came with great pomp to Les Oliviers
to offer me its best wishes for the new year, as it is customary to offer
them to the Chief of State. There was even a heated controversy, in
the waiting room, between the Russian and the English ambas-

sador as to which of the two was the doyen of the corps and should
deliver the traditional address. Mr Duff Cooper emerged victorious.
This formal visit and this rivalry were the signs of our ascent.

The fact nevertheless remained that the intentions of the Allied
leaders, in regard to France, maintained their diplomats in a state of
acute tension. Roosevelt persisted in denying us the capacity to
exercise French authority during the liberation. While permitting it
to be said that she regarded this attitude of America's as excessive,
England, nevertheless, followed suit. If it were merely a question of
terminology, the matter would have concerned us only slightly. But
the refusal to recognize us as the French national authority masked,
in reality, the American President's *idée fixe* of establishing his arbitration in France. I felt in a position to render this claim on our independence vain in practice; should the occasion arise, Roosevelt
would be forced to recognize the fact. All the same, the delay resulting from his stubbornness would keep the military command from
knowing in advance with whom it was dealing in its relations with
the French. Further, there would result from it, until the last minute,
incidents between us and our Allies which might otherwise be
avoided.

The Committee of Liberation had, in September 1943, addressed
to Washington and London a memorandum specifying the conditions under which the co-operation of the French administration
with the Allied forces should function during the battle of France.
The memorandum stipulated that in the combat zone the military
command would address itself to the local authorities for the use of
communications, transport facilities and public services. Subsequently the French Government would do what was required
according to General Eisenhower's requests. In order to ensure contacts, it had been arranged that each major unit would be accompanied by French officers 'for administrative liaison', that we would
assign a general provided with the necessary personnel and powers
to Eisenhower, and that, pending the arrival of the government in
metropolitan France, one of its members would be sent there as its
delegate to make the necessary arrangements. In fact, the administrative liaison corps, created in September 1943, under the direction
of Hettier de Boislambert, had already been recruited, briefed and
sent to England. In March 1944, I had appointed General Koenig
and General Cochet to assist the Allied Commanders-in-Chief in the

northern and Mediterranean theatres respectively. On the same date, André Le Troquer was appointed National Commissioner delegated to the Liberated Territory. These measures were found satisfactory by the Allied general staffs. But in order that they could be put into effect, we required the agreement of the Washington and London Governments. The latter did not reply to our memorandum.

The President, in fact, kept the document on his desk from month to month. During this time, in the United States, an Allied Military Government (AMGOT) was being prepared in order to take the administration of France in hand. Into this organization flowed all kinds of theoreticians, technicians, lawyers, propagandists, and also former Frenchmen, recently naturalized American. The steps which Monnet and Hoppenot felt they must take in Washington, the observations which the British Government addressed to the United States, the urgent requests which Eisenhower sent to the White House produced no change in plan. Since, however, some sort of documentary arrangement had to be made, Roosevelt determined, in April, to give Eisenhower instructions by virtue of which the supreme power in France would belong to the Commander-in-Chief, who was, in this capacity, to choose the French authorities to work with him. We soon learned that Eisenhower urged the President not to burden him with this political responsibility and that the British disapproved of so arbitrary a procedure. But Roosevelt, somewhat revising his letter of instructions, retained its essence.

Actually the President's intentions seemed to me like Alice's adventures in Wonderland. In North Africa, Roosevelt had already ventured, in conditions much more favourable to his plans, on a political enterprise analogous to the one he was now contemplating for France. Of that attempt nothing remained. My own government, in Algeria, in Corsica, in Morocco and in Equatorial Africa, wielded uncontested authority. The individuals Washington had counted on to throw obstacles in our path had disappeared from the scene. No one paid any attention to the Darlan-Clark agreement, considered as null and void by the Committee of National Liberation and about which I had openly declared in the Consultative Assembly that in the eyes of France it did not exist. That the failure of his policy in Africa had not dispelled Roosevelt's illusions was a circumstance I regretted for him and for our relations. But I was certain that his intentions, venturing this time into metropolitan France, would not even begin to be applied in fact. The Allies would encounter no other ministers and officials in France than those I had established there. They would find no other French troops than those of which I was the leader. Without any presumptuousness, I could defy General Eisenhower to deal lawfully with anyone I had not appointed.

He himself, moreover, did not dream of doing so. He had come to tell me as much on December 30th, before going to Washington and from there to London, where he was to prepare for the landing in France. 'You were originally described to me,' he said, 'in an unfavourable sense. Today, I realize that that judgment was in error. For the coming battle, I shall need not only the co-operation of your forces, but still more the assistance of your officials and the moral support of the French people. I must have your help, and I have come to ask you for it.' 'Splendid!' I replied. 'You are a man! For you know how to say, "I was wrong".'

We spoke of the vagueness that still remained in regard to the co-operation to be established in France between our authorities and the military command. Eisenhower did not hide how much he was worried by it. 'But,' he added, 'beyond the principles, there are the facts. I can assure you that, as far as I am concerned and whatever apparent attitudes are imposed upon me, I will recognize no other French power in France than your own in the practical sphere.' I then pointed out that we should probably have an opportunity to manifest our mutual understanding in regard to the way Paris would be liberated. 'It must be French troops,' I told him, 'that take possession of the capital. In view of this operation, a French division must soon be sent to England, as the French have requested.' Eisenhower acquiesced.

As the May-June period which the general staffs had chosen for the Allied landing approached, the British increasingly manifested their desire to free the political situation from the impasse in which it was still wedged. Mr Churchill himself assumed the courtier's role, plying between President Roosevelt's claims and General de Gaulle's refusals. But since the greatest weight of strength and the greatest volume of publicity were on the American side, the Prime Minister's efforts primarily consisted in applying pressure on me to yield to Roosevelt's requirements.

At the beginning of January, Mr Duff Cooper came to tell me

'Churchill, as you know, has fallen ill in Tunis on his way back from Teheran. He has subsequently been taken to Marrakesh. He would very much like to see you, but his state of health makes it impossible for him to move about. Would you agree to visit him there?' On French territory, the British Prime Minister's visit was normally due to the President of the French Government; nevertheless, in consideration of the person and the circumstances involved, I went to take lunch with Mr Churchill on January 12th. I found him well on the road to recovery. We had a long conversation, our first in six months. Mr Duff Cooper and Lord Beaverbrook were also present, as well as Gaston Palewski.

The Prime Minister applied himself in the warmest and most picturesque terms to describing the advantages I would gain for myself by coming around to the President's point of view. It was a matter, in short, of my recognizing Roosevelt's supremacy in French affairs since he had resolutely adopted a public position he could not abandon and that he had made promises to certain French personalities compromised by Vichy which he must keep. Concretely, Mr Churchill suggested that I immediately put a stop to the proceedings opened against Flandin, Peyrouton and Boisson. 'I have studied the Flandin dossier,' the Prime Minister told me. 'There is nothing serious against him. The fact that he was in North Africa proves that he had left Vichy. And if Peyrouton came to Algeria to be its governor, it was because he was appointed to that post by the President of the United States. As for Boisson, the President had guaranteed him his post and I myself told him, "Go in and fight and don't worry about the rest." ' Mr Churchill qualified as regrettable the fact that General Giraud and General Georges had had to leave the French Government. 'Even though,' he said, 'Roosevelt had chosen the first, and I had brought over the second.' According to Mr Churchill, I must realize, if I had not done so already, that for the President of the United States and the British Prime Minister, France was a sphere in which their choice compelled recognition and that their principal grievance against General de Gaulle was that he did not admit this fact.

Quite good-humouredly I replied to Mr Churchill that his and Roosevelt's interest in our internal affairs was, in my eyes, the proof of France's recovery. Therefore, I insisted on not disappointing them by permitting the occurrence, tomorrow, of those revolutionary convulsions which would inevitably be the case if justice were not done. I wished no harm to Flandin and Peyrouton. With regard to the former, I was not unaware of his ability and his intentions; nor was I forgetting the service the latter had done our unity by putting his post at my disposal when I arrived in Algiers. But I believed it was in the national interest that they should both give an account of their actions as ministers of Vichy before the High Court. The post assigned to Governor-General Boisson concerned only his chiefs. The presence or absence of General Giraud and General Georges in my government was my affair. I would therefore continue on my way, that of independence, convinced that it was best not only for the state and the nation whose trust I bore, but also for our alliance, which I dearly prized.

In order to lighten the atmosphere, I invited Mr Churchill to join me in reviewing the garrison the next day, and he gladly accepted. The ceremony took place amid the liveliest popular enthusiasm. For the crowd of Marrakesh, as for those everywhere else who would see the newsreels without knowing what went on behind the scenes, the appearance of Churchill and de Gaulle side by side signified that the Allied armies would soon march together to victory, and that was all that mattered. I said as much to the Prime Minister and we agreed that it was the crowd which was right after all.

Unfortunately the Anglo-American powers, in order to penetrate my defences, employed certain procedures not always of the same quality as my conversation with Winston Churchill. During the winter, a sordid affair that was destined to spatter me with filth was trumped up by certain British interests in evident collusion with the corresponding American services. It had begun by an American launched press campaign to the effect that Fighting France and its leader intended to establish a dictatorship in France and were already employing totalitarian practices. The entirely spurious text of a ridiculous oath was published, purporting to be the enlistment form for Free French volunteers. Our services, above all the Bureau Central de Renseignements et d'Action (BCRA), were accused of maltreating and torturing their men in order to break them into our fierce discipline. After this softening-up process, the 'Affaire Dufour' suddenly emerged.

Under this name an 'intelligence' agent recruited in France without our knowledge had been brought to Great Britain by the

British during 1942, had presented himself to Fighting France and asked to enlist in our forces. He said he was a lieutenant and a Chevalier de la Légion d'Honneur. His chiefs soon realized that he was neither the one nor the other, but a member of the British intelligence service. Punished with imprisonment for having usurped a rank and a title he did not possess, Dufour had begun a new enlistment in his real capacity, that of a man of the ranks. One day, as he was working out his sentence in the camp at Camberley, he escaped with the help of the Intelligence Service and rejoined his employers. From the French point of view, he was, therefore, merely a deserter, improperly employed and protected by a foreign power. Not being able to seize the man on British territory, the French command in England had ceased to concern itself with him for over a year, when in September 1943 Pierre Viénot, summoned to the Foreign Office, received an astonishing communication about him.

'Dufour,' the British Government said by this official means, had 'put into the hands of the British courts a complaint about maltreatment against several French officers and against their leader, General de Gaulle. Because of the separation of powers, which in England is absolute, the British Government cannot prevent justice from taking its course. Furthermore, General de Gaulle does not have diplomatic immunity in our country. Perhaps the General could settle the matter by friendly agreement with Dufour? Otherwise, he will be implicated in the trial. We must urge General de Gaulle to attach serious importance to this matter, for a conviction is likely, and would constitute an occasion for disagreeable publicity, particularly in the United States press, with regard to the methods and procedures of Fighting France.' In fact, malevolent allusions appeared at this time in those American newspapers that habitually made a point of attacking us.

I could not mistake the origin or the motives of this basely inspired action. Obviously Dufour, a British agent and a French deserter, was entering an action against me before the British courts only because he had been urged to do so by his masters. As for the London Government, if it ignored the agreements it had signed with Free France by virtue of which Free French military men in Great Britain were answerable only to French military tribunals; if it denied to General de Gaulle the immunity it accorded to the least important secretary in fifty foreign legations; if it attempted to intimidate me with the threat of scandalous calumnies, it did so because it was involved in a political enterprise intended to extricate the Anglo-American leaders from an untenable position. To the demands of public opinion, which urged them to adopt towards General de Gaulle, his government and towards France an attitude worthy of their alliance, the White House and Downing Street were pleased to reply: 'We must refrain from any action until this question is settled.'

I determined to deal with the affair without the slightest compromise. Since several officers serving in England had permitted themselves to be impressed by the Foreign Office's advice and had, of their own accord, entrusted our case to solicitors, I gave orders that these officers be immediately dismissed. I forbade my subordinates to answer any interrogations and any summons of the British courts. I told Viénot to inform the Foreign Office that I was well aware that the object of this enterprise was to besmirch me in order to justify a political error committed by the Allies; that I took the affair for what it was—an infamy—and that the absurd consequences of this 'New York Mystery' or this 'Washington Mystery' would not affect me, of course, but only those who had devised it. Four months passed before London manifested itself otherwise than by periodical warnings to which we did not reply.

But in March the plot came up for discussion again. It must be added that the decree relative to the re-establishment of public powers in France had been adopted on March 21st. The world's newspapers had carried the story stating—and it was true—that General de Gaulle and his committee regarded themselves as the government of France and claimed to be empowered as such without having obtained the consent of the Allies. Roosevelt, hard pressed by the reporters, said bitterly: 'No one, not even the French Committee of National Liberation, can know what the French people really think. For the United States, the question still exists.' Meanwhile, a week after our decree was signed, the final attack in the 'Affaire Dufour' was launched against us. On March 28th, Mr Duff Cooper, apparently not daring to approach me on a subject which was nevertheless supposed to concern me, asked Massigli for an audience. He requested him to tell me that the British courts could wait no longer, that the British Government must allow them to act and that the trial was about to be opened.

It happened that we had the means to make a suitable reply to this communication. In the beginning of 1943, a Free Frenchman, Stéphane Manier, assigned by us to make broadcasts on the British radio at Accra, had returned to England on our orders, after honourable service. By error or by intention, the Intelligence Service had seized him the moment he arrived and confined him for questioning in the 'Patriotic School'. Here, either as a result of his dazed state or, more likely, of a malarial attack, he had died in confinement. His son, serving in the North African navy, had just written to inform me that he proposed to take action in the matter and asked that the circumstances—at the very least, suspect—of his father's death be made clear. He announced his intention of lodging a complaint with the French courts against the officers of the Intelligence Service present in French territory and against the members of the British Government, including Mr Winston Churchill, whenever they happened to be there. I ordered Massigli to send the British ambassador the text of the plaintiff's letter and to add, on my own behalf, that the French Government saw no means of preventing the courts from doing their duty and that one of the unfortunate consequences of the trial, it was to be feared, was a disagreeable press campaign as to the methods and the procedures of the British Intelligence Service, itself responsible to its government. I never knew why the British courts abandoned their intention to let justice take its course, or how the London cabinet arranged to keep them from doing so, despite the separation of powers. It was not, moreover, my responsibility. But from that day on, I never heard of the 'Affaire Dufour' again.

A warm bath followed the cold shower. On April 17th, Mr Duff Cooper brought me a communication from the Prime Minister. Mr Churchill, according to the ambassador, had been profoundly distressed by the state of my relations with Roosevelt. But he was convinced that if I would deal with the President as man to man, the situation would vastly improve. In particular, the question of the Committee's recognition by the Allies would surely find a solution. Mr Churchill was quite prepared to send Mr Roosevelt a request that I go to Washington and assured me of a favourable reply.

I informed Duff Cooper that this so-called invitation, after several others, equally non-existent, had little attraction for me. If the President of the United States wished to receive the President of the French Government, he had only to ask me himself. But why should

I have to solicit the President, even with Mr Churchill as my intermediary, to agree to my visit? What interpretation would be put on my behaviour, when Mr Roosevelt openly professed that all authority in France must proceed from his own investiture? As for me, I had nothing to ask of the President. Formal recognition no longer interested the French Government; what mattered to that government was to be recognized by the French nation. And that fact was now established. The Allies might have helped us to gain countenance when such accessions were useful; they had not done so. Now the matter was of no importance.

As for the relations between our administration and the military command, I informed the ambassador that they would readily be established as soon as the command agreed not to usurp any powers not its own. Failing this, there would certainly be chaos in France, which would be disastrous for both the operations and the policies of the Allies. I concluded that I would doubtless go to Washington some day, but only when facts had settled the discussion; when, on the first strip of liberated territory in metropolitan France, my government's authority was incontestably established; when the Americans had furnished proof that they had abandoned their intervention in France on any level but that of military operations; and when it was definitely admitted that France was one and indivisible. Meanwhile, I could only express the hope that this condition would be a matter of fact as soon as possible and hope that it would allow me to go to the United States under satisfactory conditions. I was, in any case, grateful to Mr Churchill for his trouble on my behalf and for concerning himself with my trip, and I thanked him in advance for what he might still be willing to do in matters relating to this subject.

Having avoided giving any satisfaction to the Allies' advances, I must now expect, according to the law of the pendulum, some retaliation on their part. And in fact, we were notified on April 21st that the coded telegrams sent between us and our diplomatic and military delegations in London would no longer be transmitted. The necessity of safeguarding the secrecy of the preparations for the landing was advanced as an explanation of this move. But this precaution, taken unilaterally by the Anglo-American powers in regard to the French, whose forces, like their own, were to play an essential role in the operations and whose territory would be the theatre of

the battle, appeared to us to be a calculated insult. The Committee
of Liberation forbade its ambassador, Viénot, and its military
delegate, Koenig, to settle any question as long as the Allies demanded to know the orders that we gave and the reports addressed
to us. This abstention greatly embarrassed Eisenhower and his
general staff, while the diplomatic strain was intensified by it. Of
course, coded dispatches continued to reach us, thanks to the French
officials and military men who came and went between London and
Algiers.

The crisis having reached its height and the landing being imminent, the Allies could no longer postpone the issue. I was, therefore, not surprised when, on May 23rd, Duff Cooper asked to see me
urgently. Since, theoretically, we could no longer communicate in
code with London, I had, to my great regret, abstained from receiving the British ambassador. On this occasion my door was open
to him because he had announced 'a new orientation'. He informed
me that the British Government was inviting me to London to settle
the question of recognition and that of administrative co-operation
in France. But the ambassador also informed me that his government
hoped I would be in Great Britain at the time of the landing.

I replied to Duff Cooper that I was very grateful for this invitation,
I was in fact very anxious to be at the embarkation point when the
armies of the liberation were launched, and I intended, thereafter,
to set foot on the first acres of liberated territory in metropolitan
France. Therefore I gladly agreed to go to London. As for signing
an agreement with political implications, I would have to make
many reservations. I repeated to the ambassador that we were not
interested in formal recognition; I informed him, moreover, that the
Committee of Liberation would at once assume the title of the Government of the Republic, whatever the opinion of the Allies on this
matter might be. As for the conditions of our co-operation with the
military command, we had long since specified them in a memorandum to which we had received no answer. At present the British
Government was perhaps disposed to agree to them, but the
American Government was not. What good would it do for the
French and the English to agree subsequently on measures which
could not be applied without Roosevelt's consent? We were, of
course, prepared to negotiate the practical means of co-operation,
but it must be among all three powers, not between two. Lastly, I

informed Mr Duff Cooper that I would go to London only if I had
his assurance that I could communicate in code with my government.

On May 26th, the Committee of Liberation approved the position
which I had outlined to the British ambassador. It was agreed that
no minister would accompany me on my trip, in order to make clear
that I was to observe the beginning of operations and to visit the
French population in the combat zone, should the occasion arise,
but not to negotiate in any way. Then the Committee passed a
measure by virtue of which it became, in name, the 'Provisional
Government of the French Republic'. The next day I received Mr
Duff Cooper again and confirmed my earlier remarks to him. He
gave me the written assurance about codes that I wanted.

Now Roosevelt, in his turn, decided it was time to indicate the
beginning of a policy of appeasement. But since he insisted that this
evolution be a discreet one, he had chosen a rather circuitous path
by which to apprise me of it. First of all, then, Admiral Fénard, head
of our naval mission in the United States, who maintained good
personal relations with the White House, arrived in great haste from
the United States and presented himself to me on May 27th with
the following speech: 'The President has formally asked me to
transmit to you his invitation to come to Washington. In consideration of the position which he has hitherto adopted he cannot, without
losing face, come to the point of doing so officially. He must therefore proceed unofficially. If, under the same conditions, you accept
his invitation, the embassies will arrange your trip without its being
necessary to make public that either Roosevelt or you has taken the
initiative.' However strange the President's procedure may have
been, I could not ignore the desire which he himself formally expressed, nor disregard the interest that our meeting would doubtless
entail. I therefore agreed that the time for me to go to Washington
was near at hand. But enthusiasm was not called for: I told Admiral
Fénard to make an anticipatory answer, acknowledging Roosevelt's
invitation, observing that no decisive project could be envisaged at
present since I was about to leave for London, and concluding that
it was advisable to resume contact later on.

The President's behaviour completed my enlightenment. It was
apparent that the struggle we had waged so long against the Allies
for French independence was to conclude in the desired way. Doubtless there would be some ultimate crisis to surmount; but the issue

H

was no longer in doubt. On June 2nd, a message from Mr Churchill asked me to come to England at once. He had kindly sent me his personal plane. I left the next day, accompanied by Palewski, Béthouart, Billotte, Geoffroy de Courcel and Teyssot. After stopping at Casablanca and Gibraltar, we landed near London on the morning of June 4th, to be immediately caught up in the mesh of events.

A letter from Mr Churchill met me on my arrival, asking me to join him in the train where—an original idea—he had established himself somewhere near Portsmouth, pending the day and the hour of the landing. We went there with Pierre Viénot. The Prime Minister received us; with him were several ministers, notably Eden and Bevin, and some generals, notably Ismay. Marshal Smuts was also there, somewhat embarrassed by the role he was playing. As a matter of fact, some months earlier, he had said in a meeting that France, now that she was no longer a great power, should join the Commonwealth, and the Anglo-American press had given his remarks great publicity. We sat down to luncheon, and Churchill immediately showed his steel.

First he described with great vividness the enormous military enterprise that was to be deployed from the British ports and indicated with satisfaction that the initial phase would be conducted largely by British means. 'In particular,' he said, 'the Royal Navy is to play the crucial role in the landing's transport and protection.' In all sincerity, I expressed my admiration to the Prime Minister for this result of his endeavours. That Great Britain, after so many ordeals so valiantly endured and thanks to which she had saved Europe, should today be the base for the landing on the Continent and should engage in that operation such tremendous forces was striking justification of the courageous policy which he himself had personified since the war's darkest days. Whatever coming events were still to cost France, she was proud to be in the line of attack, in spite of everything, at the side of the Allies for the liberation of Europe.

At this moment, a similar flood of esteem and friendship carried away everyone present, Frenchmen and Englishmen alike. But afterwards we got down to business. 'Let us make an arrangement,' Churchill said, 'as to our co-operation in France. You can go to America later to propose it to the President. It is possible that he will accept it, and then we can put it into effect. In any case, you can talk to him. And he will grow less adamant and will recognize your administration in one form or another.' I replied: 'Why do you seem to think that I need to submit my candidacy for the authority in France to Roosevelt? The French Government exists. I have nothing to ask, in this respect, of the United States of America nor of Great Britain. Once this is recognized, it is still essential for all the Allies that we organize the relations between the French administration and the military command. Nine months ago we proposed as much. Since the armies are about to land in France, I understand your haste to see the question settled. We ourselves are ready to do so. But where is the American representative? Without him, as you well know, we can decide nothing. Furthermore, I notice that the Washington and London Governments have made arrangements to do without such an agreement. I have just learned, for example, that despite our warnings, the troops and the services being prepared for the landing are provided with so-called French currency, issued by foreign powers, which the Government of the Republic refuses to recognize and which, according to the orders of the inter-Allied command, will have compulsory circulation on French territory. I expect that tomorrow General Eisenhower, acting on the instructions of the President of the United States and in agreement with you, will proclaim that he is taking France under his own authority. How do you expect us to come to terms on this basis?'

'And you!' Churchill cried. 'How do you expect that the British should take a position separate from that of the United States?' Then, with a passion which I sensed was destined more for his British colleagues than for myself he said: 'We are going to liberate Europe, but it is because the Americans are in agreement with us that we do so. This is something you ought to know: each time we have to choose between Europe and the open sea, we shall always choose the open sea. Each time I have to choose between you and Roosevelt, I shall always choose Roosevelt.' After this outburst, Eden, shaking his head, seemed to me quite unconvinced. As for Bevin, the Socialist Minister of Labour, he came up to me and declared loudly enough for everyone to hear: 'The Prime Minister has told you that in every case he would side with the President of the United States. I want you to know that he is speaking on his own initiative and not in the name of the British Cabinet.'

After this, Churchill and I left together for Eisenhower's headquarters, which were nearby. In the middle of a wood, in a hut whose walls were covered with maps, Eisenhower explained to us, with great clarity and self-command, his plan for the landing and the state of preparations to date. The ships were ready to leave port at any moment. The planes could take off at the first signal. The troops had been entrained for several days. The great machinery of the embarkation, the crossing and the landing of eight divisions and the equipment which formed the first echelon was prepared down to the minutest detail. The protection of the operation by the navy, the air forces and the parachute troops left nothing to chance. I realized that in this extremely hazardous and complex question, the Anglo-American gift for 'planning' was deployed to the maximum degree. All the same, the Commander-in-Chief still had to fix the the day and the hour and, in this matter, was subject to the severest perplexity. Everything had been calculated, in fact, for the landing to take place between June 3rd and 7th. Once this date was passed, the tide and the moon would require the operation to be postponed for about a month. The weather was extremely bad at this time. For the barges, the landing stages and the landing craft, the state of the sea made navigation and boarding problematical. Nevertheless, the order for launching or postponement had to be given by the following day at the latest. Eisenhower asked me, 'What do you think I should do?'

I replied to him that the decision at stake was of course entirely his responsibility, that my opinion committed him to nothing, and that I approved in advance and without reservation whatever decision he decided to make. 'I will only tell you,' I added, 'that in your place I should not delay. The atmospheric dangers seem to me less than the disadvantages of a delay of several weeks, which would prolong the moral tension of the executants and compromise secrecy.'

When I prepared to leave, Eisenhower handed me a typewritten document with evident embarrassment. 'Here,' he said, 'is the proclamation which I am preparing to make to the peoples of Western Europe, particularly the French people.' I read through the text and told Eisenhower that I did not find it satisfactory.

'It's only a draft,' he assured me. 'I am ready to alter it at your suggestion.' It was agreed that the next day I would inform him in detail of the changes that seemed to me explicitly necessary. Mr Churchill escorted me to his quarters where we would find our own. I did not conceal my concern from him, for over the clear prospect of battle had fallen once again the shadow of a cunning policy.

In fact, the proclamation drawn up in Washington for Eisenhower's use was unacceptable. According to this text, Eisenhower spoke first to the people of Norway, Holland, Belgium and Luxembourg in his capacity as a soldier in charge of a military operation having nothing to do with their political destiny. But subsequently, in quite another tone, he addressed himself to the French nation. He urged that nation to 'carry out his orders'. He declared that 'in the administration, everyone will continue to fulfil his functions unless contrary instructions are received'; once France was liberated, 'the French themselves would choose their representatives and their government'. In short, he appeared to be taking control of our country even though he was merely an Allied general entitled to command troops but not qualified to intervene in the country's government and, moreover, quite incapable of doing so. In this declaration, not a word was said of the French authority which for years had aroused and directed the war effort of our people and which had done Eisenhower the honour of placing under his command a great part of the French Army. At all events, on the morning of June 5th, I sent back to his headquarters a text which we considered acceptable. As I expected, I was told that it was too late, for the proclamation was already printed (it had been ready for eight days) and was to be rained down on France at any moment. The landing, in fact, would begin the following night.

In London, as on a previous occasion, I established my office at Carlton Gardens and my residence at the Connaught Hotel. With pleasure for myself, and some commiseration for him, I learned that the Foreign Office had again assigned Mr Charles Peake to us for liaison work. And precisely at five in the afternoon, this diplomat, who was a great friend to our cause, came to give an account of the scenario that was to be presented on the radio the following morning. First the Chiefs of State of Western Europe would speak to their peoples: the King of Norway, the Queen of Holland, the Grand Duchess of Luxembourg, the Prime Minister of Belgium. Then Eisenhower would make his proclamation. Lastly, it was planned that I should address France. I informed Mr Charles Peake that, as for my part in it, the script would not 'play'. By speaking immediately after Eisenhower, I should appear to sanction what he said—of which I disapproved—and assume a place in the succession unsuitable to the dignity of France. If I were to make a speech, it could only be at a different hour and outside the series.

At two o'clock in the morning, Pierre Viénot came to see me. He had just left Mr Churchill, who had summoned him to shout his fury in regard to me. Mr Peake arrived in his turn. I assured him that the oratorical chain would be played out, later this morning, without my participation. On the other hand, I hoped to be able to use the BBC facilities during the evening. After several unpleasant clashes behind the scenes, the BBC was in fact put at my disposal under the conditions I had requested. I spoke individually at six o'clock in the evening, a prey to intense emotion, declaring to my countrymen: 'The supreme battle has been joined . . . It is, of course, the Battle of France, and the battle for France! For the sons of France, wherever they are, whatever they are, the simple and sacred duty is to fight the enemy by every means in their power . . . The orders given by the French Government and by the leaders which it has recognized must be followed precisely . . . From behind the cloud, heavy with our blood and our tears, the sun of our greatness is now reappearing!'

During the several days I spent in England, the news of the battle was good. The landing had succeeded. A bridgehead was established in the vicinity of Bayeux. The artificial ports were installed as planned. As for the French forces taking part in the operations—ships, air squadrons, commandos, parachute troops—the reports which d'Argenlieu, Valin and Legentilhomme gave of them were excellent. Leclerc and his division were waiting in good order, although with impatience, for the moment to set foot in Normandy. Our services, especially that of the Commissariat, which since the distant days of Free France had been directed by Senior Commissariat Officer Manguy, were busy supplying by far the highest level of French forces yet seen in England and preparing help for the liberated territories. Lastly, Koenig gave me accounts of the action of our resistance forces, engaged in many regions either on missions he had given them or on their own initiative. Several large German units were already delayed at the rear of the front by this action. Everywhere, moreover, the demolition foreseen by our plans was being put into effect. It is true that for the first time the Germans launched their V-1 over London. But these bombardments, painful as they were, could not alter the course of the battle.

Meanwhile, if the strategic horizon seemed bright, the diplomatic firmament cleared only very slowly. Mr Eden did his best to make the clouds vanish. He accepted personal responsibility, obviously with the agreement of the British Cabinet, for the problem of administrative co-operation in France, hitherto dealt with by Mr Churchill alone. Eden came to dine and discuss the matter with me on June 8th, in company with Duff Cooper and Viénot; he insisted that the French Government reconsider its decision, send Massigli to London and sign a Franco-British agreement. 'If you come to an agreement with us,' he told me, 'the Americans cannot keep to an isolated position. When you go to Washington, I shall go too, and Roosevelt will have to assent to what we have agreed.' Eden confirmed his request in a letter which he addressed to Viénot. But we French remained steadfast. I repeated to the British that I was not in London to make deals. The government, consulted in Algiers, substantiated my statement. Massigli remained where he was. Viénot replied to Eden that if the British Cabinet desired to enter into negotiations on the subject of our 1943 memorandum, he himself, in his capacity as ambassador, was in England to make or receive the necessary communications.

At the same time, we did not miss the opportunity of emphasizing publicly the absurdity of the situation in which the Allied armies would find themselves, lacking an organized liaison service with the French authority and officials, and openly denied all value to the currency being circulated in France by foreign powers. On June 10th, in a brief interview with a news agency, I made the matter quite clear. Further, I had decided that the administrative liaison officers, with the exception of a few informants, would not accompany the American and British general staffs, for we did not intend to contribute to the usurpation. It followed of itself that a hue and cry was raised against me in the habitually hostile sections of the American press. But in other quarters, and in the majority of the British newspapers, Roosevelt's stubbornness was condemned. This was the moment when, with a single voice, those who had never ceased to support us with all their talents, whether in the press or on the radio, spoke out most emphatically. In the United States:

Walter Lippmann, Edgar Mowrer, Dorothy Thompson, Jeff Parsons, Eric Hawkins, Helen Kirkpatrick, Mac Wane, Charles Collingwood, Sonia Tamara, etc. In Great Britain: Harold Nicolson, Harold King, Bourdin, Glarner, Darcy Gillie and others. They all made it clear that the joke had lasted long enough.

This was also the opinion of the governments in exile in Great Britain. As the liberation now seemed imminent, almost everyone shed the psychology of exile. All were disturbed by the off-hand manner with which the great powers were inclined to settle the destiny of Europe in the absence of the interested parties. Speaking to the King of Norway, the Queen of Holland, the Grand Duchess of Luxembourg and their ministers, dining with Pierlot, Spaak, Gutt and their colleagues of the Belgian Government, exchanging visits with President Beneš and President Rackiewicz, I found that they were delighted by France's rejection of the Anglo-American encroachments. Between June 8th and June 20th, the governments of Czechoslovakia, Poland, Belgium, Luxembourg, Yugoslavia and Norway officially recognized the Provisional Government of the French Republic despite the immediate American and British appeals that they abstain. Only the Dutch still recognized us as the Committee of Liberation, hoping that by deferring, in this matter, to Washington's desires they would obtain greater American sympathy over Indonesia. The quasi-unanimous attitude of the European states did not fail to impress America and Great Britain; but it was recognition from the tiny piece of France which the battle had just liberated that finally dissipated all shadows.

On June 13th, in fact, I left to visit the bridgehead. For several days I had been prepared to make this trip; but the Allies showed no eagerness to make it possible for me to do so. Even the day before, while I was dining at the Foreign Office with all the British ministers except Mr Churchill, just as I was being congratulated on being able to set foot on the soil of metropolitan France, a letter from Mr Churchill, sent to Mr Eden during the meal, raised last minute objections to my plan. But Eden, having consulted his colleagues around the table, in particular Clement Attlee, informed me that the majority of the Cabinet decided to stand by the arrangement the British had made. Therefore the courageous destroyer *La Combattante*, under the command of Captain Patou, which had just distinguished itself in the course of operations, was able to stop at Portsmouth and take me on board as planned, accompanied by Viénot, d'Argen-lieu, Béthouart, Palewski, Billotte, Coulet, Chevigné, Courcel, Boislambert and Teyssot. On the morning of June 14th, we cast anchor as near as possible to the French coast and landed, together with a Canadian regiment, on the beach between the *communes* of Courseulles and Saint-Mère-Eglise.

General Montgomery, commander of the Allied forces in the bridgehead, notified of our arrival an hour beforehand, had graciously put cars and guides at our disposal. Major Chandon, French liaison officer, hurried to join us with his troops. I immediately sent François Coulet, whom, then and there, I appointed Commissioner of the Republic for the liberated Normandy territory, to Bayeux, and put Colonel de Chevigné in charge of the military subdivisions. Then I returned to headquarters. Montgomery received me in his trailer where he worked in front of the portrait of Rommel, whom he had beaten at El Alamein but for whom he felt all the more consideration because of that fact. In this great British leader, prudence and rigour went hand in hand with zeal and humour. His operations were proceeding as planned. To the south, the first objective was achieved. It was now a matter, the General said, of the Americans taking Cherbourg to the west and the British taking Caen to the east, operations which involved the engagement of new units and stores reinforcements. Hearing him, I was certain that under his orders matters would proceed vigorously, but with neither haste nor temerity. Having expressed my confidence in him, I left Montgomery to his affairs and went to Bayeux.

Here Coulet had taken over his post. In fact, Bourdeau de Fontenay, Commissioner of the Republic for Normandy, had not been able to leave Rouen or abandon his clandestine status. Pending the time when he could appear, I was eager to indicate without delay that everywhere the enemy had retreated, the authority now proceeded from my government. When I reached the gates of the city, Coulet was there with the Mayor, Dodeman, and his municipal council. We proceeded on foot, from street to street. At the sight of General de Gaulle, the inhabitants stood in a kind of daze, then burst into cheering or else into tears. Rushing out of their houses, they followed me, in the grip of an extraordinary emotion. The children surrounded me. The women smiled and sobbed. The men shook my hands. We walked on together, all overwhelmed by comradeship, feeling national joy, pride and hope rise again from the depths of the abyss. At the sub-prefecture, in the waiting room where the Marshal's portrait was still hanging an hour before, Rochat, the sub-prefect, put himself under my orders pending his relief by Raymond Triboulet. All those who held any office, wielded any power or fulfilled any function rushed up to greet me. The first visit I received was from Monsignor Picaud, Bishop of Bayeux and Lisieux. Since the population was gathered in the Place du Château, I went there to address them. Maurice Schumann announced my address by the usual words: '*Honneur et Patrie! Voici Général de Gaulle!*' Then, for the first time in four terrible years, a French crowd heard a French leader say that the enemy was the enemy, that their duty was to fight him, that France would be victorious. And in truth, was that not the 'national revolution'?

Isigny, cruelly destroyed, where the corpses were still being carried out of the debris, paid me the honours of its ruins. Before the war-torn monument to the war dead, I addressed the inhabitants. With a single heart, we raised our faith and our hope above the smoking debris. My last visit was the fishing village of Grandcamp, also ravaged by bombs. On the road, I greeted the detachments of Allied troops going towards the front or returning from it and several squads of our resistance forces. Some of these had effectively helped the landing. At nightfall we returned to Courseulles, then put out to sea and boarded our ship. Several hours passed before we headed back, for the German planes and torpedo boats attacked one after another the ships anchored offshore which had been ordered to remain where they were. On the morning of June 15th I disembarked at Portsmouth. The day before, as we approached France, I had awarded the Croix de Guerre to the valiant ship, *La Combattante*, which was soon afterwards to be sunk.

The proof was given. In metropolitan France as well as in the Empire, the French people had shown to whom they entrusted the duty of leading them. On the afternoon of June 15th, Mr Eden came to see me at Carlton Gardens. He was quite aware of what had happened at Bayeux. News of it was being broadcast and published around the world. According to Eden, Roosevelt expected no better opportunity than my visit to Washington to revise his position. While regretting that the French Government had not adopted the procedure suggested by London, Eden now proposed to establish a plan with Viénot which he himself would communicate to Washington and which, he was certain, would be signed simultaneously by France, England and America. This was a procedure that seemed acceptable; I said as much to Anthony Eden; then I wrote to Mr Churchill to salve the wounds he had inflicted on himself. He immediately replied, regretting the fact that we had not been able to establish Franco-British co-operation on a better basis, since he had so often proved, in good days and bad, that he was a sincere friend to France. He had hoped that my trip to London might provide the chance for an arrangement: now he could only hope that it was not the last chance. Nevertheless, the Prime Minister ended his letter confident that my imminent meeting with President Roosevelt would enable France to establish with the United States 'those good relations which are a share of her heritage'. He himself would help me in this respect, he declared.

On the evening of June 16th, I took a plane to Algiers, where I arrived the next day. Here I heard details of the fortunate turn of events in Italy. As I was leaving for London, the Allied offensive in the peninsula had achieved a great victory. Our expeditionary corps, in particular, having broken the enemy's fortified lines on the Garigliano, opened the road to Rome. Frenchmen, Americans and British drove towards the city on June 5th. As a result of the military success, King Victor Emmanuel had abdicated his powers to his son; Badoglio had resigned and Bonomi formed a new government at Salerno. Eager to see our victorious troops and to see for myself on the spot the significance of these changes, I went to Italy on June 27th.

First of all, I made a brief visit to Naples, where Couve de Murville introduced me to Mr Prunas, Secretary-General of the Italian Ministry of Foreign Affairs. This high official brought me his government's greetings from Salerno, where it was still established. I asked him to tell Mr Bonomi of my desire to establish direct contact with him by the intermediary of Couve de Murville. The President of the Council replied in writing that he accepted such an arrangement with satisfaction. Then came the inspection of the front and meetings with Juin, Wilson, Alexander and Clark. Lastly I went to Rome and, by staying at the Farnese Palace, proclaimed that France was returning to an Embassy that was hers.

On June 30th, I was granted an audience with the Pope. The

Holy See, with its eternal prudence, had been absolutely reserved in regard to Fighting France and later, the Algiers Government. Monsignor Valerio Valeri, who was the Papal Nuncio in Paris in 1940, had retained his functions in Vichy, accredited to the Marshal, whom M. Léon Bérard represented at the Vatican. Nevertheless, we had been using whatever means were available to keep the Apostolic See informed of our aims and our feelings. We had, moreover, active sympathizers there, notably the eminent Cardinal Tisserant. We knew that the defeat of Hitler and his rule was prayed for by the Holy Father and we wanted to establish relations with him as soon as possible. On June 4th, while fighting was still going on in Rome, Major Panafieu and Lieutenant Voizart had brought Monsignor Tisserant a letter from General de Gaulle addressed to Pius XII. The Pope had answered me on the 15th. Now I was going to the audience he had been so good as to grant me.

At the Vatican I first made contact with Cardinal Maglione, Secretary of State, who though ill and near death insisted on getting up to talk to me. Even as Rome, from the height of her serenity, watches from one century to the next while the tides of men and events flow by beneath her walls, ceaselessly attentive to all, so the Church, impassive but compassionate and well informed into the bargain, observed the war's ebb and flow. Monsignor Maglione, convinced of the Allied victory, was especially concerned as to its consequences. In the case of France, he counted on Vichy's disappearance and declared that, in fact, he saw in me the head of the French Government. He hoped that the change of régime could be effected without serious shocks, particularly with regard to the French Church. I told the Cardinal that the Government of the Republic intended this to be the case, although certain French ecclesiastical circles had adopted an attitude that would not make things easier for the Republic tomorrow. As for the future of Europe after the Reich's defeat and Russia's ascendancy, I declared that France's recovery, at home and abroad, would lead to a new equilibrium. I asked the Vatican to use its immense influence in this task.

The Holy Father received me. I was struck, beneath the kindness of his reception and the apparent simplicity of his remarks, by the sensitivity and power of his thought. Pius XII judged everything from a point of view that transcended men, their enterprises and their factions. But he knew how great was the cost to them and took

compassion on all. The supernatural charge with which he alone
was invested evidently weighed heavily on his soul, but it was equally
evident that he bore it indefatigably, certain of his goal, confident
of his path. His own reflections and his information services kept
him well informed about the drama inflaming the world. His lucid
mind was fixed on the consequences: the unleashing of the mingled
ideologies of communism and nationalism over a great part of the
earth. His inspiration revealed to him that only Christian faith, hope
and charity could surmount them, at the very moment when these
were everywhere (and long since) overwhelmed and submerged.
For him, therefore, everything depended on the Church's policy,
its action, its language, the manner in which it was led. This is why
the Pope had kept that policy in a domain reserved for his personal
attention, displaying there the gifts of authority, brilliance and
eloquence which God had showered upon him. Pious, pitying,
politic, in the highest sense of the words. This, together with the
respect which he inspired, was the impression the Sovereign Pontiff
made on me.

We spoke of the Catholic peoples whose fate was in the balance.
As for France, he felt that she would be threatened, at the start, only
by herself. He saw the opportunities she would have, despite her
ordeals, to play a great role in a world where so many human values
were reduced to the last extremity. He also saw the danger she ran
of falling back into the dissensions which all too often had paralysed
her genius. It was towards Germany, which in many respects was
particularly dear to him, that his chief solicitude tended at this time.
'Those wretched people,' he said several times. 'How they will
suffer!' He foresaw long confusion in Italy without its moving him,
however, to extreme distress. Perhaps he thought that after the
collapse of Fascism and the fall of the monarchy, the Church,
morally very powerful in this country, would remain the only force
for order and unity—a prospect he seemed quite willing to entertain.
While he was speaking to me, I thought of what various witnesses
had recently reported: scarcely was the battle over yesterday when
an enormous crowd rushed to Saint Peter's with a single impulse to
acclaim the Pope, just as if he had been the liberated sovereign of
Rome and the salvation of Italy. But it was the action of the Soviets,
today on Polish territory, tomorrow in all of central Europe, which
filled the Holy Father with anxiety. In our conversation, he described

what was already taking place in Galicia, where, behind the Red
Army, the persecution of the faithful and their priests had begun.
He believed that it was here that Christianity was to endure the
cruellest ordeals and that only the close union of those European
states inspired by Catholicism—Germany, France, Italy, Spain,
Belgium and Portugal—could build a dam against the danger. I
realized that this was Pope Pius XII's grand design. He blessed me
and I withdrew.

On my departure, as on my arrival, a great throng of Romans
had gathered near the Vatican to shout their sympathy and re-
assurance. After a visit to the church of Saint-Louis-des-Français,
where Monsignor Bouquin received me, and to the Villa Médicis,
where the hopes of French art would soon blossom again, I received
the French colony in Rome. Since 1940, the French community—
for obvious reasons—had consisted mainly of members of various
religious orders. All had come. Cardinal Tisserant introduced them
to me. Whatever the eddies and currents of the past had been, all
floated, today, on the same tide of joy and hope. The pride of victory
united souls whom the disaster and its afflictions had been able to
disperse.

The indications of French unity were now too clear for anyone to
ignore. The President of the United States at last acknowledged as
much. In order that his reversal might be announced on the occasion
of a new event, and one appropriate to a change of heart, he redoubled his insistence that I visit him in Washington. Admiral
Fénard had reappeared while I was in London: Roosevelt had instructed him to indicate those dates that were most convenient to
him. Then on June 10th, General Bedell Smith, chief of Eisenhower's general staff, paid me a visit at Carlton Gardens, sent by
Eisenhower who was then in the Normandy bridgehead, and by
General Marshall, who happened to be in London. Bedell Smith
literally beseeched me to agree to a meeting with the President, so
eager was the military command to know where to turn for administrative co-operation in France. In Algiers, Mr Seldon Chapin,
who was acting as interim ambassador in place of Wilson, appeared
to think it equally urgent. I knew that the Allied offensive on French
territory was to be launched in August. If some practical agreement
were to be reached, there was no more time to lose.

After searching conversations with my government, I decided to go to Washington, but indicated that I was doing so on the same terms as my visit to London. I had no favours to ask and I would undertake no negotiations. The conversations between General de Gaulle and President Roosevelt would have no other object than their inquiries into the world-wide problems of interest to both countries. Further, my presence in the United States at this decisive period of the war would symbolize the homage paid by France to the American war effort and a proof of the active friendship that linked the two peoples. If, after the White House conversations, the American Government wanted to open negotiations with the French Government about the relations between the Allied armies and our administration, it could do so, like the British Government, through the normal diplomatic channels. It was on this basis that the State Department and our ambassador, Hoppenot, drew up the programme of my visit. It was understood that in Washington I should be the guest of the President and of the government of the United States; this should suffice to give the lie to those communiqués and articles already suggesting that I was coming to America not as a guest but as a suppliant. Canada also requested my presence, and it was with eagerness that I instructed Gabriel Bonneau, our delegate in Ottawa, to settle with Mr Mackenzie King's Government the details of my stay in his beloved and courageous country.

Taking the plane which the President of the United States had kindly sent for me, and accompanied by Mr Chapin, I landed in Washington on the afternoon of July 6th. Béthouart, Palewski, Rancourt, Paris, Baubé and Teyssot were with me. Franklin Roosevelt greeted me at the door of the White House, all smiles and cordiality. Cordell Hull was beside him. After tea, the President and I conferred alone for a long time. The same was to be the case the next day and the day after that. I was staying in Blair House, a curious old residence which the American Government customarily puts at its guests' disposal. A formal but extremely cordial luncheon at the White House, two dinners given respectively by the Secretary of State and by the Secretary of War, a reception I gave at our embassy, this last in temporary quarters since the premises of the former and future French embassy were still closed to us, offered a number of opportunities for conversations with the political leaders and the military chiefs who advised the President.

Mr Cordell Hull acquitted himself of his crushing task with con-

scientiousness and distinction of spirit, somewhat hampered, as well
he might have been, by his summary understanding of what was not
American and by Roosevelt's interference in his domain. Mr Patter-
son and Mr Forrestal adopted, in their capacity as ministers, the
psychology of big business, for in three years their departments (War
and Air for the former, the Navy for the latter) had assumed dizzying
dimensions and absorbed the greater share of American resources,
capacities and pride. Mr Morgenthau, a great friend of our cause,
was in charge of a Treasury which, though inexhaustible, was no
less subject to his scrupulous care. General Marshall, a bold organizer
but a reserved talker, was the animating spirit of a war effort and a
military strategy of global dimensions. Admiral King, zealous and
imaginative, could not conceal his pride that the sceptre of the seas
should pass into the hands of the American Navy. General Arnold,
by sheer method, had been able to weld a mass of planes hastily
designed, constructed and tested, and personnel quickly recruited,
trained and thrown into battle, into the great military corps which
the American Air Force had become. Admiral Leahy, astonished
by the events that had defied his counsels of conformity, was surprised to see me there, but persisted in his prejudices. Mr Connally
and Mr Sol Bloom, respectively chairmen of the Senate and the
House committees on foreign affairs, were eager to be informed of
everything. This general staff formed a coherent group which,
because of the character of each of its members and of Roosevelt's
own glittering personality, allowed itself only a restricted brilliance
but which was, without any doubt, equal to its tasks.

Meanwhile, I saluted the tomb of the Unknown Soldier in the
solemn cemetery at Arlington and visited General Pershing, who
was ending his days in serene simplicity at the military hospital
there. To pay homage to the memory of George Washington, I made
a pilgrimage to Mount Vernon. At Blair House I received many
prominent personalities, first among them Mr Henry Wallace, Vice-
President of the United States, who in his dream of social justice
wished to gain victory 'for the sake of the common man'. Mr Padilla,
Mexican Minister of Foreign Affairs, was in Washington at the time
and also came to call. At the offices of our mission, I made contact
with the French diplomats serving with Henri Hoppenot; then
General de Saint-Didier, Admiral Fénard and Colonel Luguet introduced our officers to me. Before leaving Washington, I held a

press conference and talked with the greatest possible number of the journalists who had come to hear and to question me. During five days in the capital, I saw with admiration the flood of confidence that sustained the American *élite* and discovered how becoming optimism is to those who can afford it.

President Roosevelt, of course, did not doubt for a moment that he could. During our meetings, he avoided any reference to immediate issues, but allowed me glimpses of the political objectives he hoped to achieve through victory. His conception seemed to me an imposing one, although disquieting for Europe and for France. It was true that the isolationism of the United States was, according to the President, a great error now ended. But passing from one extreme to the other, it was a permanent system of intervention that he intended to institute by international law. In his opinion, a four-power directorate—America, Soviet Russia, China and Great Britain —should settle the world's problems. A parliament of the allied nations would give a democratic appearance to the authority of the 'big four'. Short of handing over nearly all of the earth's surface to the other three, such an organization, according to him, would have to involve the installation of American forces on bases distributed throughout the world, some of which would be located in French territory.

Roosevelt thus intended to lure the Soviets into a group that would contain their ambitions and in which America could unite its dependents. Among the 'four', he knew, in fact, that Chiang Kai-Shek's China needed his co-operation and that the British, in danger of losing their dominions, would yield to his policy. As for the horde of small and medium size states, he would be in a position to impose upon them by virtue of the help he could provide. Lastly, the right of peoples to decide for themselves, the support offered by Washington and the existence of American bases would give rise to new sovereignties in Africa, Asia and Australasia, which would increase the number of states under an obligation to the United States. With such a prospect before him, the questions relating to Europe, the fate of Germany, the destiny of the states along the Vistula and the Danube, the Balkans and Italy, seemed to him quite subordinate. He would certainly not go to the lengths of sacrificing the monumental conception that he dreamed of turning into a reality, in order to find a satisfactory solution to them.

I listened as Roosevelt described his plans to me. As was only human, his will to power cloaked itself in idealism. The President, moreover, did not explain matters as a professor setting down principles, nor as a politician who flatters passions and interests. It was by light touches that he sketched in his notions, and so skilfully that it was difficult to contradict this artist, this seducer, on any particular point. I answered him, nevertheless, that in my opinion his plan risked endangering the western world. By considering western Europe as a secondary matter, he was going to weaken the very cause he meant to serve—that of civilization. In order to obtain Soviet approval, he would have to yield them Danubian and Balkan states, to the detriment of Poland and the Baltic, and certain other advantages that threatened the general equilibrium. How could he be sure that China, emerging from the ordeals in which its nationalism was being forged, would remain what she was now? If it was true, as I was the first to think and say, that the colonial powers must renounce the direct administration of the peoples they ruled and put into practice a régime of association, it was also true that this enfranchisement could not be effected against those powers themselves, at the risk of unleashing, among the unorganized masses, a xenophobia and an anarchy which would be dangerous for the entire world.

'It is the West,' I told President Roosevelt, 'that must be restored. If it regains its balance, the rest of the world, whether it wishes to or not, will take it as an example. If it declines, barbarism will ultimately sweep away everything. Now, western Europe, despite its dissensions and its distress, is essential to the West. Nothing can replace the value, the power, the shining examples of these ancient peoples. This is true of France above all, which of all the great nations of Europe is the only one which was, is and always will be your ally. I know that you are preparing to help France materially and that aid will be invaluable to her. But it is in the political realm that she must recover her vigour, her self-reliance and, consequently, her role in Europe. How can she do this if she is excluded from the organization of the great world powers and their decisions, if she loses her African and Asian territories—in short, if the settlement of the war imposes upon her, once and for all, the psychology of the vanquished?'

Roosevelt's powerful mind was open to these arguments. Furthermore, he felt a genuine affection for France, or at least for the notion of it he had once had. It was precisely because of this former affection of his that he was disappointed and irritated by the disaster which had befallen us and by the reactions which this had provoked among so many Frenchmen, particularly those whom he knew personally. He told me so quite plainly. As for the future, he was anything but convinced of the chances of a rebirth and renewal of our régime. He described bitterly what his feelings were when, before the war, he watched the spectacle of our political impotence unfold before his eyes. 'Even I, the President of the United States,' he told me, 'would sometimes find myself incapable of remembering the name of the current head of the French Government. For the moment, you are there, and you see with what kindness my country welcomes you. But will you still be there at the end of the tragedy?'

It would have been easy, but pointless, to remind Roosevelt how much America's voluntary isolation had counted in our discouragement after the First World War, and in our collapse at the beginning of the Second. It would have been equally futile to point out to what extent his own attitude towards General de Gaulle and Fighting France, having helped a great part of our *élite* to play a waiting game, encouraged in advance the French nation's return to that political inconsistency he so justly condemned. The American President's remarks ultimately proved to me that, in foreign affairs, logic and sentiment do not weigh heavily in comparison with the realities of power. What matters is what one takes and what one can hold on to. To regain her place, France must count only on herself. I told him this. He smiled and concluded: 'We shall do what we can. But it is true that in helping France no one can replace the French people.'

Our conversations ended. They had taken place in Roosevelt's office, near his desk cluttered with an enormous number of astonishing objects: souvenirs, insignia, good-luck charms. When I was leaving, the President, who was being rolled along in his wheelchair, accompanied me along the gallery where a door was open. 'Here's my pool. That's where I swim,' he declared, as if in defiance of his infirmity. Before leaving Washington I sent him a toy submarine, a mechanical marvel made by the workers in the Bizerta arsenal. He thanked me with a charming note and sent me his photograph: 'To General de Gaulle, who is my friend!'

Later, however, an anonymous source sent me a photostatic copy
of a letter Roosevelt had written, eight days after my departure, to
Congressman Joseph Clark Baldwin. In it the President alluded to
some shady American deal with the French *'Compagnie Générale
Transatlantique'* and warned his correspondent to be careful I did
not get wind of it, for once I was informed I would liquidate the
company director. In his letter, Roosevelt formulated his estimate
of myself and of our meetings: 'de Gaulle and I,' he wrote, 'have
examined in outline the subjects of the day. But we talked more
deeply about the future of France, its colonies, world peace, etc. In
relation to future problems he seems quite "tractable", so long as
France is dealt with as a world power. He is very touchy in matters
concerning the honour of France, but I suspect that he is essentially
an egoist.' I was never to know if Franklin Roosevelt thought that,
in matters concerning France, Charles de Gaulle was an egoist for
France or for himself.

On July 10th, I paid a rapid visit to New York. In order not to
give opportunities for popular demonstrations which, three months
before the Presidential election, might seem to be directed against
what had hitherto been the President's policy, it had been agreed
that my public appearances would be very restricted. All the more
so since Dewey, the candidate opposing Roosevelt, was the Governor
of New York State. Nevertheless, Mayor Fiorello La Guardia,
bubbling over with friendship, received me with great ceremony at
the City Hall, where a huge crowd had gathered. Afterwards, he
took me on a tour of the city. I placed a Cross of Lorraine on
Lafayette's statue; I visited our consulate-general in Rockefeller
Centre. Led by Guérin de Beaumont I went to the offices of 'France
Forever', an association uniting many Frenchmen and Americans
who had supported our cause, where Henry Torrès spoke for the
feelings of all. The French colony of New York, joined by various
delegations from other regions, had gathered at the Waldorf Astoria,
and I greeted them all. Among the Frenchmen present, many had
hitherto been reserved in regard to General de Gaulle. Some had
even lavished criticisms, not to mention insults, upon him. But the
extreme warmth of the welcome I was given that evening gave no
sign of it. It was proof that, in the great dissension of which she had
been the object, France was now to carry off the victory.

Such was indeed the opinion in Canada, where everything had

been arranged to give moving testimony to the fact. First of all, visiting the city of Quebec, I felt as if I were being inundated by a tide of French pride mingled with an inconsolable grief, both sentiments flowing from history's backwaters. We next reached Ottawa with the ambassador, General Vanier. Mr Mackenzie King, the Prime Minister, was at the airport. It was pleasant to see this worthy man again, so strong in his simplicity. A head of government who had, from the first, used all his authority and experience in the service of liberty. Canada had followed him with all the more merit considering that the country included two co-existing peoples not at all united, that the conflict was a remote one and that no Canadian national interest was directly at stake.

Under its government's urgings, Canada was now engaged in a powerful war effort. By way of large units, crews incorporated into His Majesty's Navy and squadrons furnished to the Royal Air Force, Canada had put considerable forces into the line, all of a high military value. Her armament factories were producing a significant proportion of the Allies' equipment; even her laboratories and mills were participating in the country's research and operations, which were soon to produce the first atom bombs. I was secretly informed of the imminent results by Pierre Auger, Jules Guéron and Bertrand Goldschmidt, French scientists who with my authorization had joined the Allied teams dedicated to this apocalyptic work. In comparison with what had happened during the First World War, Canada's effort had assumed a national character. The result, for the state and the people, was an increase in national stature which filled ministers, parliamentarians, officials and citizens alike with satisfaction. Mr Mackenzie King explained this to me, and Mr Louis Saint-Laurent, his principal colleague, repeated it, insisting meanwhile on Canada's intention to help France's reconstruction to the limit of its powers.

During my stay I was the guest of the Earl of Athlone, Governor-General of Canada, and his wife, Princess Alice, the aunt of George VI. They received me with unforgettable kindness and invited a number of prominent Canadian guests to meet me. The hours scarcely sufficed for the official discussions, the audiences I had to grant, the official ceremony at the monument to the Ottawa war dead, the inspection of the French airmen training in the vicinity, the dinner given by the Canadian Government, a press conference, the speech—there was always at least one—which I made in answer

to Mr Saint-Laurent's address before Parliament, in the presence
of the Governor-General, his ministers, the high officials and the
diplomatic corps. Speaking of international co-operation for tomorrow's peace, particularly in the west, emphasizing the role my
country wished to take in it, I concluded: 'France is sure of finding
at her side and in agreement with her, the people who know her
well. That is to say, she is sure of finding Canada there first of all.'

On July 12th I reached Montreal, which gave the most moving
demonstration of its enthusiasm. After the reception at the City Hall
and the ceremonies at the two monuments to the memory, respectively, of the Canadian and the French war dead, I spoke to an
enormous crowd gathered in Dominion Square and the adjoining
avenues. Adhémar Raynault, the mayor, shouted to his fellow
citizens: 'You must show General de Gaulle that Montreal is the
second French city in the world!' No words can describe the thunder
of applause which rose from every heart. That evening, our plane
took off and on July 13th we were in Algiers.

Here I was to find the text of a declaration published the day
before by the American Government. 'The United States,' it said,
'recognizes that the French Committee of National Liberation is
qualified to exercise the administration of France.' The State Department immediately opened negotiations with Hoppenot and Alphand
for an agreement on administrative co-operation in liberated territory. Already, Eden and Viénot, for their part, had agreed upon a
satisfactory text. By the beginning of August, Washington, Algiers
and London had agreed on common terms. What was concluded was
astonishingly similar to what we had proposed a year before. The
Provisional Government of the French Republic was designated by
name. It was admitted, without reservation, that it alone wielded
authority; that it alone should delegate the liaison organizations to
the Allied forces; that it alone could put the required services at the
disposal of the military command; that it alone could issue currency
in France and furnish what was necessary, in return for pounds and
dollars, to the American and British troops on its soil.

The great battle for France was about to begin. The Allied armies,
side by side with our own and helped by our resistance forces, drove
from Normandy toward Paris and up the Rhone Valley. Between
the North Sea and the Mediterranean, from the Atlantic to the
Rhine, the nation was to be liberated from the enemy, the nation

that for fifteen hundred years no holocaust, not even this last, had been able to strip of her sovereignty nor strike down as she raised her last weapons. We returned to France bearing independence, Empire and a sword.

VII. BATTLE

BUT HOW SHORT France's sword was found to be, as the Allies launched their attack upon Europe! Never had our country, on so crucial an occasion, been reduced to such relatively limited forces. Those who struggled for her liberation were often embittered to recall the might of her great past. But never before had her army been of better quality—a recovery all the more remarkable in that it had begun in an abyss of submission.

For fourteen centuries, military power had been second nature to France. If our country had, on many occasions, neglected her defence, undervalued her soldiers or lost her battles, she had none the less appeared at all times eminently capable of the greatest military actions. The vicissitudes of the contemporary period had not proved an exception to this rule. Whatever our weakness after the Napoleonic conquests, however cruel the defeat of 1870, we retained the psychology and the means of a strong people. Principal artisans of the victory in 1918, we had led the others towards it. That our army should outstrip every other army in the world, our fleet be one of the best, our air force of the first order, our generals the most able—that, for us, was only natural.

Because of this the collapse of 1940 and the capitulation that followed seemed to many monstrous and irremediable. The image of themselves the French had always had, the world's opinion of them and the testimony of history itself, had suddenly been abolished, annihilated. There was no opportunity for France to recover her dignity in her own eyes and in the eyes of others unless she took up arms again. Nothing helped her recreate her unity and recover her prestige as much as the astonishing fact that she could find in her newly mustered Empire, and in her own persecuted country, enough conviction and military valour to reconstitute an army: an army that fought extremely well. After Sedan and Dunkirk; the capitulation of Rethondes and Turin; Vichy's acceptance of military defeat and the subjection of the state, it was an amazing reversal that enabled our forces to take an important and brilliant share in the victory. The enemy was occupying the whole of France, two million Frenchmen were prisoners in German hands, the 'legal' government persisted in punishing the combatants, but still they fought.

There were enough men who could be mobilized in Africa to reach the strength of a campaign army. But the restrictions were many. It was possible to draw on the native populations of Algeria, Morocco, Tunisia, Equatorial Africa and Madagascar for as many soldiers as we wished, but the number of active military men and of reserves prepared to serve as officers and specialists was very low. As a rule only those of French origin fitted the categories that were so indispensable to the formation of large scale modern units. Yet the population of French origin totalled no more than 1,200,000 in these territories. By calling up all military classes as far back as 1918, we would have a total of 116,000 men. A high figure in view of the fact that the administration, business and law and order, absorbed an important proportion of qualified men and that many of those mobilized had been in German captivity since 1940. Free France contributed 15,000 young Frenchmen; Corsica 13,000 soldiers; 12,000 boys escaped from France through Spain; 6,000 women and girls joined up and recruits were eager to be incorporated into our forces. But in spite of everything, we could not muster enough officers and specialists to form an important military force.

The Americans, who provided us with arms and equipment, did so on condition that we adopt their own methods and organization. Their system, in relation to active forces, called for an extremely high proportion of supply services as well as many reserves to compensate for losses. The life and action of American combat units relied on well supplied support. They were willing to arm French divisions only if they were convinced that the corresponding logistic formations were made up of numerous and qualified personnel. On the other hand, our African troops, accustomed to living under improvised conditions, regarded the accumulation of so many men and supplies in depots, supply centres, convoys and workshops as a waste of manpower. This divergence of view produced frequent and,

occasionally, vehement disputes between the Allied general staff and
our own. Furthermore, among the French, it gave rise to disappointment at having to disband crack regiments and make them into
auxiliary forces.

General Giraud, in particular, had difficulty in resigning himself
to this necessity. Having understood Roosevelt to say, during the
Anfa conference, that the United States would undertake to equip
as many troops as we could muster, Giraud had hoped to form
fourteen French fighting divisions and only a few maintenance and
replacement units. He was, therefore, distressed and indignant at
his foreign masters' insistence that he establish complete supporting
units and, as a result, reduce his active troops before they could be
equipped. In addition to this we had to maintain a small force in
Africa to safeguard our sovereignty and keep two brigades in reserve
to go to Indo China as soon as circumstances allowed. These troops
were equipped with French arms and so did not affect American
supply plans, but they absorbed officers from other groups, which
further diminished the size of our active forces.

While I found it painful that the adoption of American military
procedures was a condition of their loans of arms, I was of the opinion
that the imminent European campaign would, in fact, require
extremely well-supplied and reinforced forces. Furthermore, I was
eager to bring to an end the sudden stoppages of supply that were
delaying our appearance at the front. Having become sole head of
the government, therefore, I settled the question. The decree I issued
on January 7th, 1944, concerning the active troops, the irreducible
framework of the organization and the conditions on which the
Allies were furnishing us arms and equipment, was as follows: the
total of the land forces destined for the Battle of France was to be;
one army command, three army corps commands, six infantry
divisions, four armoured divisions, all with essential services and
replacements. Even so, one of the infantry divisions and one of the
armoured divisions called for in this programme could not be completely established in time. On the other hand, three units of *Tabors*,
two regiments of parachute troops and commandos were added to
our large-scale units. It is difficult to do justice to the efforts made
by the Army's general staff, under the command of General Leyer,
to create, despite deficiencies and delays, the exemplary military
force that France was able to put into the field in Italy, then to

bring to France itself, and finally to launch into Germany and Austria.

Our Navy was no less zealous. Absorbed by the technique which is its life and passion and which kept its recent ordeals from deterring it, it reconstituted itself while taking an active share in operations. Admiral Lemonnier, appointed in July 1943 as the chief of the Navy's general staff, brought to this feat of reorganization remarkable ability and a tenacious will, disguised beneath a misleadingly modest manner. On October 14th, 1943, the armament plan proposed by Lemonnier was adopted by the Committee of National Defence. It provided that, in the course of the following spring, our fleet put into combat: two battleships, the *Richelieu* and the *Lorraine*; nine cruisers, the *Gloire*, the *Georges-Leygues*, the *Montcalm*, the *Emile Bertin*, the *Jeanne d'Arc*, the *Duguay-Trouin*, the *Duquesne*, the *Suffren* and the *Tourville*; four light cruisers, the *Fantasque*, the *Malin*, the *Terrible* and the *Triomphant*; three auxiliary cruisers, the *Cap des Palmes*, the *Quercy* and the *Barfleur*; two aircraft carriers, the *Béarn* and the *Dixmude*; fourteen torpedo boats; eighteen submarines; and eighty smaller craft—escort vessels, tankers, pursuit craft, scout boats and minesweepers.

For the majority of the ships this plan involved modernization of armament and reconditioning. The half-destroyed arsenal at Bizerta, the limited capacity of the one at Casablanca, and the embryonic one at Dakar were not in a position to undertake this by themselves, but the Allied shipyards in Brooklyn and Bermuda generously undertook the work. The programme, therefore, was put in hand. In addition to the ships provided: the torpedo boats *Tigre* and *Trombe*, seized by the Italians but now recovered; an Italian submarine, *Bronzo*, which had been rechristened *Narval*; four frigates transferred to us by the English; six torpedo-escort boats given by the Americans and of which the first, the *Sénégalais*, had been formally presented to the French Navy by President Roosevelt; and six flotillas of flying boats, rearmed with Sunderlands and Wellingtons, caused the reappearance of the French naval air force in the Atlantic skies. Two armoured regiments of naval riflemen, one group of heavy artillery and several commando groups would participate in the battle of Europe, while twenty-two shore batteries and seven anti-aircraft batteries, manned by the Navy, would contribute to the defence of African and Corsican ports.

According to General Bouscat's plan, adopted on December 22nd, 1943, by the Committee of National Defence, our air forces were to form thirty aviation groups by the spring of 1944. These were to be made up as follows: seven units, four for pursuit and three for bombardment, were to be based in Great Britain; twenty-one groups, eight for pursuit, four for bombardment, six for defence of coasts and airfields, one for reconnaissance, two for transport, were to operate in the Mediterranean theatre; two pursuit groups were to operate in Russia. Since there were practically no French planes left in Algeria, Morocco or Tunisia after the landing of the American forces, it was these former adversaries who generously undertook to supply the planes for our squadrons in North Africa, the English and the Russians supplying those groups assigned to their territory. Bouscat commanded the French air forces with method and authority. Hastily equipped with new planes, suddenly integrated into Allied units whose conventions and procedures had to be immediately assimilated, they were, nevertheless, eager to get into battle.

All in all, we would put into the field: a campaign army of 230,000 men; forces to be used in overseas territories amounting to 150,000 soldiers; a fleet of 320,000 tons manned by 50,000 sailors; 1,200,000 tons of cargo vessels and steamships of which two thirds were manned by French crews; an air force of 500 fighting planes manned by 30,000 men. A great part of the equipment would be provided by our Allies in accordance with the lend-lease agreements in return for the services we provided them: ports, transport, communications, transmissions, installations, labour, etc. The *morale* of our armies was good. They found themselves re-established, they had a *raison d'être* and they were rid of the oaths and incantations which had largely paralysed or misled them. It was wonderful to see the fervour with which troops and crews greeted their modern equipment, the enthusiasm aroused by marching orders in the units called into battle. During this period, I inspected each regiment, each ship, each air squadron. In every glance that met my own, I read the pride of arms. The French military spirit is a tough, vivacious plant.

The maquis forces gave every indication of the same regenerative powers. Until the end of 1942, they were few and far between and weak in striking force. Subsequently their *morale* improved and with it the number of men who were willing to fight. Besides, the forced labour service, which mobilized 500,000 young men in a few months (particularly workers to be used in Germany), and the dissolution of the 'armistice army', drove many rebels into the clandestine groups. The maquis multiplied, by more or less important groups, and began guerrilla warfare that was to play an important role in the attrition of the enemy and, later, in the evolution of the Battle of France.

The conditions under which these autonomous factions were formed, lived and fought were obviously very diverse, because of the nature of the terrain over which they were operating and the weapons at their disposal. The natural barriers of France became then, as important as they had been when the Celts, the Gauls and then the Franks defended the country's independence against the invaders—Germans, Romans or Saracens. The Massif Central, the Alps, the Pyrenees, the Jura, the Vosges, the Forest of Ardennes and the interior of Brittany were particularly strong maquis centres. There, too, the Allied planes found the best places to build improvised landing strips or parachute their agents and 'containers'. Remote from the coasts, the big cities and the principal communication centres, the enemy occupation was not so dense, and the police surveillance not so close. The old, pitted and heavily wooded mountains of the Auvergne, Limousin, the Cévennes, Lannemezan; the high plateaux of the alpine *massifs* of Savoy and the Dauphiné; the wooded and precipitous hideouts of the Vosgian-Jurassian-Langrois-Morvandiau group; the steep slopes of the French and Belgian Ardennes region; the moors, thickets, hollows and pools of the Ar-goat served as refuges for the partisans during the long waits, as bases for attacks or as hiding places after skirmishes. No one any longer spoke of '*la douce France!*'

The resistance gathered in bands of about ten men. This was usually the maximum number that could be grouped at a single point, given the extent of the hiding places and the difficulties of supply. The men came together by means of some network, often from far away and with many precautions. Once you were incorporated into the network, it was without thought of return. You were quartered in dugouts, huts or caves, sometimes in a hunting lodge, a ruined farm house or a woodman's hut. You had to endure difficult living conditions, cold, rain and, above all, anxiety. The maquisards were constantly on the alert and ready to make off somewhere else. They were kept informed as well as possible by the spider's web of complicities that started on the spot, spread to police stations and even to administrative offices, giving them warnings in case of danger or indicating opportunities for action. The neighbouring farms and villages supplied food to the little band. Children, girls and old men served as porters or messengers, and were unlikely to be suspected. Fiercely but silently, the French peasantry helped these courageous men. The enemy took its revenge by shooting those civilians they suspected of being accomplices, by deporting prominent citizens, and by setting fire to whole towns.

Ambushes on the roads used by German supply convoys, sabotage of the trains transporting enemy personnel or equipment, attacks on careless patrols or badly guarded posts, the destruction of vehicles in depots, of petrol in tanks, of munitions in store—these were the maquis' objectives until the landing of the Allied armies offered them a larger field of action. When an operation was decided upon, it was essential to plan it carefully and to execute it briskly, for there were few men and fewer weapons, and success depended on surprise. The objective accomplished, those involved had to make their get-away as rapidly as possible because the enemy brought in troops immediately, who blocked the roads and combed the surrounding country. Once in hiding, the panting maquisards drew up their balance sheet. It was a triumph when they saw soldiers of the Wehrmacht fall beneath their bullets, trucks burn, railway carriages leap from the tracks, and routed German troops leave their weapons behind. But often the enemy engaged the maquis. Then the battle was merciless. If it turned against them, French survivors who could not escape were shot on the spot or else, after a mockery of a trial, executed against a wall. Whether they died standing, heads high, or lying on the ground because of their wounds, they shouted '*Vive la France!*' at the German firing squads. Later, an inscription on the spot would remind people that they had fallen. The Cross of Lorraine, engraved on the stone, would say why and how.

But in a large part of the country, the terrain did not lend itself to the existence of the maquis. Here resistance was divided into extremely small teams with each man relying mainly on himself. Provided with false papers obtained by groups who made use of ministries, prefectures, mayors' offices and commissariats, they made contact with woodcutters, quarriers, road-menders, they slept in remote farms or disappeared in big cities. Often factories, building yards or offices gave them cover while waiting for raids, after which they vanished. These scattered partisans conducted operations on a very small scale, but nevertheless they increased their objectives every day. Isolated Germans were struck down, grenades exploded under the invader's feet, vehicles were sabotaged. In Paris and its suburbs in the North, the Lyonnais, etc., small scale sabotage was continuous. Eventually we had to create a service to safeguard installations which the Allied armies would eventually need.

It was impossible accurately to estimate the striking power of these groups since they gave neither statements nor lists to anyone. During the creation of the secret army, in the early part of 1943, we had estimated the total at about 40,000 men, not counting about 30,000 men and women who belonged to our sixty intelligence networks. A year later, at least 100,000 maquisards were in the countryside. At the beginning of the Battle of France, their number exceeded 200,000. But the striking force of the resistance soldiers depended directly on the armament they received. When, by chance, a group received what it needed, volunteers flowed in. On the other hand, the leader of a troop without supplies had to refuse recruits. Naturally the question of arms for the resistance was one of the government's primary concerns.

In France itself, resources were weak. Certain military authorities had hidden equipment in 1940. But almost all the hiding places had been discovered by the enemy or betrayed by Vichy; the combatants had only a few French weapons at their disposal. It was true that we managed to send them some from North Africa, but not many, since there were few to be had and the bases from which our planes took off were too far from France. As for weapons seized from the Germans, the quantity was not appreciable until the major engagements of the summer of 1944.

Our Allies possessed the means of arming the resistance, but however frequent and urgent our requests, they did not intend to send specialized planes over France to drop rifles, machine-guns, pistols, grenades, submachine-guns and mortars unless they had a thorough knowledge of the facts. Besides, despite every precaution, half the parachuted equipment fell into the enemy's hands. Furthermore, if the American and particularly the British secret services had gradually come to appreciate the French resistance, the Allied command was behind hand in measuring the effectiveness of this new form of warfare. The general staffs prepared only for battles conducted according to the rules. Until the last minute, there were to be cruel differences between what the maquis asked for, sometimes desperately, and what was sent to them. Nevertheless, more than a half million individual arms and 4,000 larger weapons were sent to our clandestine forces, four-fifths of them by our Allies, before the end of the fighting.

The maquis, the intelligence networks, the movements that supported them and the propaganda that inspired them, required a considerable amount of money. The government did its best to procure this in terms of usable currency that could not be traced. All the Bank of France notes stored in England, Africa and the Antilles were used for this purpose first of all; then the 'liberation bonds', issued by the Algiers Government and with its guarantee were sent to our Pars delegation and secretly exchanged for local currency by credit houses or by individuals. At the moment of supreme crisis, some local leaders, in desperate need, requisitioned funds for which responsibility would ultimately be assumed and made good by the state. All in all, more than fifteen billion francs—100 billion today—were officially disturibted to the resistance. Although certain abuses inevitably followed, more than three-quarters of the expenses could be regularly accounted for in reports to the Court of Accounts.

The leaders of the resistance groups were nearly always men who established themselves as such on their own initiative and who were recognized in that capacity because of their influence and ability. The majority among them proved worthy of this elemental confidence. Some—exceptions—were to commit blameworthy actions. If the conditions under which they were recruited are taken into consideration (how else obtain leaders, unless the army officers had immediately renounced Vichy *en masse* and taken command of the combat groups?), it must be recognized that these isolated, improvised leaders, in the face of terrible tasks, served their country well. Furthermore, once the former 'free' zone was occupied, the 'armistice army' dissolved and the sentimental and legalistic scruples which the Marshal still inspired were swept away, a number of regular officers and non-commissioned officers joined the maquis under the stimulus of the Army Organization of the Resistance and its leader, General Revers.

As long as the clandestine forces had to act spontaneously, as opportunities occurred and in separate groups, there could be no question of imposing a regular hierarchy on them or of assigning them, from Algiers or London, specific missions as to time or place. But there would be serious disadvantages in leaving them to themselves without some connection with central authority. We would run the risk of seeing them slip into the anarchy of the 'great companies' or hand them over to the Communist ascendancy. The latter, in fact, predominated and frequently presided in the 'Francs-Tireurs et Partisans' group which comprised almost a third of the maquis. If de Gaulle did not maintain everyone's allegiance, this faction would become a separate force at the disposal, not of the government, but of the faction that intended to seize it. Furthermore, other groups, not knowing where to turn, would yield to the attraction of this organization and pass into its orbit. This was the time, moreover, when the Communists made every effort to seize control of the National Council of the Resistance, to turn it into a kind of interior government opposed to that in Algiers, and to monopolize all clandestine forces by an 'Action Committee' on which they themselves played the dominant role.

We had, therefore, created a system which, without thwarting the initiative and the individuality of the maquis, attached all groups to the French command by links that they would recognize. In each of the administrative regions and in certain departments, the government placed a 'military delegate' appointed by me. He maintained contact with the armed groups of his region, integrated their activities, connected them with headquarters by the wireless means at his disposal, transmitted our instructions to them and sent us their requests, made requests to our air operations service which parachuted in their arms. The maquis had inspectors: Michel Brault for the territory as a whole, Georges Rebattet for the southern zone, André Brozen-Favereau for the northern. After the enemy arrested General Delestraint, his second-in-command, General Desmazes, and his adjutant, Colonel Gastaldo, the secret army was sent a general Chief of Staff, Colonel Dejussieu. I also appointed a 'national military delegate'—that is, a general staff officer representing the command with regard to all combat elements, maquis, intelligence networks, sabotage teams, and to the National Council of the Resistance. Louis Mangin, Colonel Ély, Maurice Bourgès-Manoury and Jacques

I

Chaban-Delmas successively carried out this mission which demanded, and to which they brought, flexibility combined with
firmness.

As clandestine forces multiplied in the zones favourable to their
activity, as the signs of collapse appeared among the enemy troops,
as collective resistance action became possible, we saw one or
another leader, whether a regular officer, a reservist or a civilian,
take command of all or part of the maquis in his sector: Major
Valette d'Ozia in Haute-Savoie; Colonel Romans-Petit in Ain;
General Audibert in Brittany; Colonels Gaillaudot in Ile-et-Vilaine;
Morice in Morbihan; Garcie, Guédin and Guingouin in the
Auvergne and Limousin; André Malraux in Corrèze, the Lot and
the Dordogne; Ravanel in the Haute-Garonne; Pommiès in the
Pyrenees; Adeline in the Gironde; Grandval in Lorraine; Chevance-
Bertain in Provence; Rol and De Marguerittes in Paris; Chomel in
Touraine; General Bertrand in Berri; and so forth.

At the moment of the landing, it was essential for the military
command to enable these scattered elements to help Allied operations. In consequence, they must be assigned determined objectives,
and procured the means of carrying out what was expected of them.
For the demolitions that were to paralyse the enemy movements,
general plans were laid beforehand, in consultation with competent
specialists in each sphere. The 'Green Plan' applied to the railways
and had been drawn up by the leaders of 'Resistance-fer', Hardy,
Armand, etc. The 'Violet Plan' was established with the co-operation of Postal and Telegraphic Service workers, like Debeaumarché,
and was aimed at telegraphic and telephonic communications,
notably the undersea cables. The 'Tortoise Plan' provided for road
blocks at strategic points, under Rondenay's leadership. The 'Blue
Plan' would neutralize the electric power stations. Yet it was just as
important that, at the right moment, the local attacks of the
clandestine groups should assume the character of a national effort.
They must function with enough consistency to become an element
of Allied strategy: ultimately they must lead the shadow army to
merge with the regular troops into a single French Army.

Therefore in March 1944 I created the 'French Forces of the
Interior', obligatorily including all clandestine troops. I gave orders
that they be organized, as nearly as possible, into military units
according to regulations—sections, companies, battalions and regi-

ments. I decreed that commanding officers would provisionally assume the ranks corresponding to the number of fighting men under their orders. It seemed likely that these arrangements would lead to stripes sewn on berets and sleeves which represented exaggerations which the re-classification commissions would have to deal with later on. But I held that by referring these troops to the traditional army structure (to which, moreover, they aspired), French unity would ultimately be well served. In April, I appointed General Koenig Commander of the French Forces of the Interior and sent him to serve in Great Britain at Eisenhower's side. Once there, he could further resistance activity by integrating it with Allied strategy, communicate with the groups by every available means and furnish the necessary arms and supplies. Koenig would also take under his orders the heterogeneous elements which, under the names 'Alliance', 'Buckmaster', 'War Office', etc., had hitherto been employed in France directly by the Allies.

How would the forces that France managed to reconstitute be used? In this regard, the dualism at the summit of French authority had, for some time, frustrated any real decision. This had been the case after the Tunisian campaign and before the Italian one—that is, during a period of relative inaction. On the whole Giraud's ideas were analogous with my own. But the autumn of 1943 offered the prospect of a continental offensive and at the same time the sole presidency of the committee was made over to me. At the moment when it was essential to act, I had the means to do so, though within narrow limits, and admittedly, painful restrictions imposed by a coalition in which the forces of France were not the principal elements.

My idea of how to conduct the war had not changed since 1940: our army, reconstituted in Africa, should re-enter metropolitan France, contribute with our clandestine forces to the country's liberation, take part in the invasion of the Reich, and obtain on the way the desired pledges so that a final settlement could not be reached without us. This implied that the Allied effort was to be directed towards our territory, that it would call not only for a landing in the north but another in the south, and that we would participate heavily in this second operation. I agreed, in the interim, that the Western powers should continue their Italian campaign, as much to exhaust the German forces as to clear the maritime routes, and that it was essential for our troops, our fleet and our air forces to be engaged in this enterprise.

Meanwhile the Allies' strategy remained vague. In September 1943 they had been in agreement to invade Italy. But they were not so unified as to what was to be done next. The United States, for their part, now felt able to begin the Battle of Europe in the shortest possible way—through France. To establish a foothold in Normandy and from there drive on to Paris; to land in Provence and drive up the Rhone Valley; to integrate these two operations and then, with the Allied armies united from Switzerland to the North Sea, to cross the Rhine. In such strategy the Italian campaign was a diversion not intended to reduce the importance of the main objective.

The British, and Churchill first of all, saw matters otherwise. In their eyes, the American plan tended to attack the enemy where he was strongest, to take the bull by the horns. It would be better to aim for the weak points, to strike at the creature's belly. Instead of fixing Germany as the direct objective and reaching it through France, the attack should aim toward Danubian Europe, according to the English, through Italy and the Balkans. The coalition's great offensive would thus consist of driving up the Italian peninsula, landing in Greece and Yugoslavia, getting the Turks to intervene, and then taking Austria, Czechoslovakia and Hungary.

This strategy corresponded with London's foreign policy, which aimed at establishing British supremacy in the Mediterranean and particularly feared seeing the Russians debouch there in place of the Germans. During the Teheran and Cairo conferences, in the messages which the Prime Minister addressed to the President, in the course of the work done in Washington by the Anglo-American body called the 'Combined Chiefs of Staff Committee', it was this plan, we knew, which the English were attempting to impose.

However hard our Allies tried to exclude us from their deliberations, we now had important forces and they could not ignore our resolutions. Without disregarding the attractive aspects of Churchill's strategy, I did not agree with it. From the military point of view, an operation conducted from the Mediterranean towards central Europe seemed to me to involve too many risks. Admitting that we might manage to crush the enemy forces occupying Italy with some dispatch—though nothing indicated that a swift decision was to be anticipated—we would then have to cross the enormous barrier of the Alps. If we could conceivably land in Dalmatia, how could we get over the mountains of Yugoslavia? Greece, doubtless, was accessible, but further north what obstacles did the complex Balkan mountain ranges hold in store? The American and British armies were equipped to function chiefly on level country, they were heavily reinforced by machinery and accustomed to living without too many privations, thanks to regular supply convoys. It was difficult to imagine them making their way over the difficult terrain of the Balkan peninsula. There would be no convenient ports to serve as bases, only mediocre roads and slow railways for communications, and the Germans were masters of the art of using the natural advantages of the territory. The decision must be sought in France, that is, on a terrain favourable to rapid operations, in immediate proximity to air and naval bases, and where the resistance, acting on the enemy's rear, could put a trump card in the Allied hand.

It was also in French interests that I felt I must reject the British plan so far as we were concerned. While the invader held France enslaved, should we permit the West to engage its armies in a direction that was, to say the least, eccentric? Was our country to be liberated at a distance and indirectly, without having seen her soldiers and her allies achieve their victory and her rescue on her own soil? Would her army march on Prague, while Paris, Lyon and Strasbourg still remained in the enemy's hands? By not allowing our forces constituted overseas to fight and conquer in metropolitan France, would we lose our chance to cement French unity, after so many divisions and discontinuities? Lastly, amid the confusion that would follow the German retreat and Vichy's collapse, what régime would emerge from the chaos if our army happened to be in Austria or Hungary and could not amalgamate itself with the forces of the interior? For England and the United States, the choice of strategy concerned their foreign policy: for France, this choice concerned her entire destiny.

The American scheme, as it happened, carried the day soon enough in regard to the landing in the north of France. In December 1943, our Anglo-American allies, in response to keen urgings from the Russians, decided to carry out, before the end of the spring, that imposing strategy which they called 'Operation Overlord'. We could only approve this choice. But the landing in the south of

France, although planned in theory, and baptised 'Operation
Anvil' in advance, remained in the discussion stage. Mr Churchill
did not abandon his idea of focusing on Italy and the Balkans the
entire Allied war effort in southern Europe: he got, for General
Maitland Wilson, the high command in the Mediterranean, Alexander being already at the head of the armies in Italy; he made every
effort to keep the largest possible number of American and French
divisions and landing craft at their disposal. Unless there were some
reaction from us, the Prime Minister's insistence would lead to the
application of the British plan in the southern theatre.

But how intervene? Given the stakes of the game and the troops we
could put into the field during this phase of the conflict, it was to be
expected that the French be associated with the principal decisions
of the coalition; that the head of the French Government participate
in the conferences in which the President of the United States and
the British Prime Minister decided on the strategy for the conduct
of the war; that the French command—in the person of General
Giraud, for example—be one of the elements of the 'combined general
staff' where the plans for military action were worked out. We
would, thereby, have been in a position to make our point of view
bear weight and influence the conclusions reached. Then the Allied
strategy would become as much our own as it was that of the two
states who had adopted it. The fact that an American general commanded the northern theatre and a British general the southern
would certainly inspire nostalgia for the past, but no anxiety as to
the present and the future. Yet the Anglo-American powers never
consented to deal with us as genuine allies. They never consulted us,
as government to government, on any of their intentions. By policy
or expediency, they sought to make use of French forces for goals
they themselves had chosen, as if these forces belonged to them. In
justification they cited the fact that they had contributed to their
armament and supply.

This was not my point of view. I considered that in a variety of
ways France brought co-operation worth much more to the Allies
than the equipment they had supplied. Since France was excluded
from their discussions, I felt myself justified, whenever it was necessary, in acting on my own behalf and independently of the others.
Such actions were not taken without disagreeable consequences, but
they succeeded in forcing our Allies to compromise with us and to

come to the ultimate conclusion that what was to the advantage of
France was to the advantage of all.

In December, the opportunity arose to indicate that in our present
situation we set great store by our autonomy. This was at a time
when our troops were beginning to participate in the Italian campaign. Three French divisions were there already. Actually, the
Fourth Moroccan Division, the last of the three to be sent, had not
been received with much enthusiasm by the Allies. The latter would
have preferred us to content ourselves with reinforcing General
Juin's troops with a few battalions. I found myself obliged to intervene to keep the Fourth Moroccan Division from being used piece-
meal, for we intended it to go into battle as a unit. Once this was
agreed, the results, on the field of battle, were such that everyone
was pleased. Meanwhile, elsewhere, the Allied command had
changed its attitude and invited General Giraud to send a fourth
large-scale unit to Italy. The Committee of National Defence agreed
to this request and selected the First Free French Division. Now we
suddenly learned that this unit was not to enter the line and that
the Ninth Colonial Division was to take its place on Eisenhower's
orders. I immediately notified Eisenhower that the Ninth Division
was not at his disposal and would remain in North Africa. Eisenhower then referred, on the one hand, to the arrangments he had
made with General Giraud without consulting us, and on the other
to the agreements signed by Giraud and Roosevelt at Anfa and
according to which French troops equipped by the Americans would
be entirely at the disposal of the American command. These arguments only confirmed me in my opposition. I maintained the decision I had taken, and proposed to Edwin Wilson and Harold
Macmillan that all three governments settle the conditions under
which the French forces could be used by the Allied command in
the same capacity as the American and British forces.

Something like an uproar resulted. The Allied General Staff pro
tested that our behaviour compromised operations. The ambassadors declared that the matter did not concern the Washington and
London Governments and must be settled between General Eisenhower and the Committee of Liberation. But since our troops remained in Africa and were urgently needed in Italy, an agreement
had to be reached. On December 27th, as we had proposed from
the outset, a conference was called under my chairmanship. Wilson,

Macmillan and General Bedell Smith (representing Eisenhower, who was away), René Massigli and General Giraud attended.

I let it be known that the First Division—and no other—having been placed at the disposal of the Allied Commander-in-Chief, would join the divisions already in Italy, as soon as its departure was requested according to regulation procedure. Of course, no French force could be used in any theatre of operations without the orders of the French Government. Then I indicated that the incident forced us to specify how the French Government intended its forces to co-operate with those of her allies.

'We are,' I said, 'naturally disposed to provide this co-operation. But we must do so with full knowledge of the circumstances. Yet we are not included in your conferences. With a view to correcting this awkward state of affairs and in order to organize the co-operation of all three governments in the conduct of the war and of all three commands in the strategy, we have prepared a draft of an agreement. If this agreement is found satisfactory, well and good. If not, the French Government will not place its forces under Allied command except on conditions to be established by itself and with the reservation of rescinding them, entirely or in part, when the national interest appears to require it.'

I added: 'At present, the Allied command is receiving co-operation from the French Army, Fleet and Air Force in the Italian campaign, without our knowing to what point or to what date that campaign is to be conducted. For us, the future landings in France are of primary importance. The moment has come to say that we cannot reinforce our troops in Italy, or even leave them there much longer, unless the American and British Governments give us their guarantee that Operation Anvil will take place, that all the French forces in Italy can be engaged in it as well as all of those in North Africa, that a French division will be transported to Great Britain in time to participate in Operation Overlord and to liberate Paris. Should it happen that these guarantees, once given, are questioned, the French Government will *ipso facto* resume the control of its forces.'

The next day, Massigli notified Wilson and Macmillan of our proposals and conditions by letter. He received replies stating that our agreement was being studied by their governments and provisionally granting the guarantees we had requested on the subject of the campaign in France. The transport of French troops to Italy was resumed.

From this moment on, the Allied command kept us informed of its plans, consulted our opinion and addressed its requests for French reinforcements through the regular channels. Satisfactory co-operation between the general staffs was established in Algiers. I had many meetings with the principal American and British leaders. I saw General Eisenhower, Air Marshal Tedder and General Bedell Smith before their departure for Great Britain, to prepare and launch Operation Overlord; General Maitland Wilson when he assumed his command and on several occasions Admiral Sir Andrew Cunningham; Admiral Hewitt, in charge of the transport, escort, protection and landing operations that Anvil would require; General Doolittle, commander of the strategic air forces in the Mediterranean theatre; General Devers, General Gammel and General Rooks and Air Marshal Slessor. At the time of my inspection of our troops in Italy, General Alexander, commanding the Allied forces, General Clark, commanding the Fifth American Army to which the French Expeditionary Corps was attached, General Leese, commanding the Eighth British Army, General Eaker, commanding the air forces, informed me of their plans and inquired as to the French national point of view.

Their attitude, no doubt, corresponded to the needs of the moment; it was, nevertheless, praiseworthy. These men had to overcome prejudices that were, in fact, quite comprehensible. A Chief of State without a constitution, without electors, without a capital, who spoke in the name of France; an officer wearing so few stars, whose country's ministers, generals, admirals, governors and ambassadors considered his orders to be indisputable; this Frenchman condemned to death by the 'legal' government, vilified by many prominent men, opposed in battle by some of his own troops and before whom the flags dipped. Of course he amazed the conventional British and American military men. It is to their credit that they were capable of overlooking these matters and seeing France in the place she truly occupied. In return, my deep and friendly regard was won by these eminent servants of their countries and our common cause. They were honourable men and good soldiers.

Furthermore, the organization through which they were maintaining contact with us facilitated cohesion. The French Government, since it no longer had more than one head, took care not to divide the right to take decisions and the duty of answering for them. The framework given to the command was as clear and simple as possible. Founding my authority upon the organization of the nation in time of war, I was in my capacity as Chief of State, Chief of the Armies and, as President of the Government, had the duty of directing national defence. Anything that concerned the use of French forces and, thereby, strategic co-operation with the Allies, necessarily devolved upon me. The framework I used to bind everything together, involved the Ministers of War, the Navy and the Air Forces in establishing, administering and supplying the armies, and dealing with the American and British services for their supplies and armament. Lastly, leaders appointed by me exercised command of our forces within the Allied system. These were precisely the powers which, for their part and for the same reasons, Roosevelt, Churchill and Stalin exercised. I was aware, of course, of the relative importance of their means and mine.

To assist me in my task, I created the General Staff of National Defence and put General Béthouart at its head, with Naval Captain Barjot and Air Force Colonel de Rancourt as his adjutants. It was Béthouart who noted the decisions, told those concerned of them and supervised their execution. He was also responsible for military liaison with the Allies on the highest level. He kept in touch with the local Commander-in-Chief (Eisenhower, later Wilson), and had at his disposal, outside France, our military, naval and air missions. Apart from the bitterness engendered by my own past differences with the Allies, these functions were difficult as much as a result of their own complexity as from the fact that they touched the susceptibilities of the Allied governments and general staffs, those of the French ministers and upper echelons, and those of individuals everywhere. Béthouart acquitted himself brilliantly at his task.

In the kind of status which we were trying to obtain within the coalition, the quality of the generals commanding our large-scale units was to count for a great deal. They were, as it happened, remarkable men. To judge the enemy, the terrain and the means on the spot, to combine the different weapons, to manoeuvre the troops, is the job of divisional commanders; Generals Dody, de Monsabert, Sevez, Leclerc de Hauteclocque, du Vigier, de Vernejoul, Guillaume, Brosset and Magnan all distinguished themselves in this field, each in his own way. General Poydenot and General Chaillet excelled in using artillery of every type. Commanding the engineers, General Dromard faultlessly arranged passage for our troops over all obstacles, ultimately including the Rhine itself. In commanding an army corps, a wide and far-reaching view is essential, in order to unify and co-ordinate the various and successive actions of several large scale units. General Henri Martin and General de Larminat, who first had this duty, gave proof of such capacities. Events themselves, moreover, were to carry them forward; their means were destined not to fail. Leaders who feel themselves borne towards victory are fortunate.

At sea, since the enemy was not in a position to engage its fleet, naval battles consisted of contending, over immense areas, with the pursuit of submarines, the destruction of raiding vessels, protection against aircraft, the escort of convoys and the defence of bases. Our navy, therefore, acted in units integrated in the Allied system. French admirals, beside their British and American peers, knew how to contribute to this struggle on the high seas where they were forever being caught out, as in a game in which some pieces are always missing. Lemonnier commanded the whole group, sectors or divisions being commanded by d'Argenlieu, Collinet, Nomy, Auboyneau, Ronar'h, Sol, Barthe, Longaud, Missoffe, Battet and others. These men did honour to the French Navy.

The French Air Force was also obliged to distribute its squadrons among the great pursuit, direct support or bombardment groups into which the West's air power was divided. Its Generals: Bouscat in command; Valin, Gérardot, Montrelay, Lechères and others, in charge of the various units, showed themselves worthy of an air force that was burning to regain its rank. Leaders of a new force still unsure of its doctrines, they knew how to lead men with distinction. Both in questions affecting morale and in the technical sphere, they made the most of their men and their equipment.

The first among the leaders who, at the time of this resurgence, were in command of our forces were two men who had the privilege of commanding alternately the only army which France could put into battle. General Juin and General de Lattre de Tassigny had many characteristics in common. Of the same age and background, having advanced their careers at the same tempo, both having emerged unscathed from the traps which the disaster of 1940 and after it the 'armistice' régime had laid for their honour, they were now ready and able to wield the high command for which they had been trained and of which they had always dreamed. Furthermore, they were generous enough, despite their rivalry, to do each other justice. Yet how different they were!

Juin was reserved and self-confident, isolating himself deep in his duties, deriving his authority less from apparent brilliance than from a profound and secret ability, not disdaining guile to clear his path on occasions but avoiding complications wherever possible. De Lattre was emotional, flexible, far-sighted and a man of wide interests, influencing the minds around him by the ardour of his spirit and winning loyalty by the expenditure of his personality, heading towards his goal by sudden and unexpected leaps, although often well thought out ones.

Despite the contrast, both were masters of their craft. For each operation, Juin drew up the plan of manoeuvres beforehand with a firm line. He based his strategy on the information he received from intelligence or from his own intuition; in every case, the facts confirmed his procedure. He chose as a strategic axis a single idea, but an idea clear enough to enlighten his men, complex enough to survive the pressures of action, strong enough to be imposed, ultimately, on the enemy. His successes, even if they were dearly won, did not seem costly and, meritorious as they were, appeared quite natural.

De Lattre, on each occasion, courted opportunity above all. Until he found it he endured the ordeal of his tentative efforts, devoured by an impatience that often provoked scenes among his contacts. Suddenly seeing where, when and how the issue could be determined, he then set about the task of building it up and exploiting it. All the resources of a rich personality and extraordinary energy were put to work, demanding a limitless effort of those he engaged in it, but certain that he was preparing them for success.

Like Larminat, Leclerc and Koenig during the night's darkest hours and with the poorest means, Juin and de Lattre, when the dawn broke, leading the action on a larger although unfortunately a still limited scale, restored the French military command to honour in the eyes of the nation, the Allies and the enemy.

It was in December 1943 that our Expeditionary Corps was engaged in Italy. Although room was made for it, it was given a difficult task. The Allies, under Alexander's command, were between Naples and Rome, in contact with the Tenth and Fourteenth German armies under Marshal Kesselring, from the mouth of the Garigliano on the Mediterranean to that of the Rapido on the Adriatic, passing through Monte Cassino. The Germans, under their skilful and energetic commander, occupied a solid position all along the front, behind which they had organized two others: the 'Gustav Line' and the 'Hitler Line'. All were supplied with good troops efficiently armed, protected artillery and mines. At the beginning of winter, the French zone of operations on the southern slopes of the Abruzzi around Acquafundata, was a mountainous, snowy, desolate region with rocky peaks and hillsides of mud and clay masked in fog and swept by rain. Here our troops, attached to the Fifth American Army, connected the right wing to the Eighth British Army.

Rome was the Allied objective. To reach it, General Clark, commanding the Fifth Army, wanted to debouch into the plain of the Liri, where his armoured formations could function to full advantage. But access to the plain was blocked by the natural barrier of Monte Cassino. Yet it was straight towards the mountain, where the enemy was most strongly entrenched, that Clark wanted to drive the front. It was true that he counted on his powerful artillery and, still more, on his air force, with which he expected to be able to crush everything. The French Expeditionary Corps' mission was to drive a wedge into the enemy defences north of the famous monastery, enabling the Allies to take it from the front.

The second fortnight of December was marked by the arduous advance of the Second Moroccan Division, which, of our major units, was the first engaged. Across mountains rising about 2,400 metres, in snow or driving rain, at grips with an enemy that fought with desperation, this division, commanded by Dody, took the ranges of Castelnuovo, Pantano and the Mainarde, advancing foot by foot. Further south, our allies had approached Monte Cassino, but still could not take it. In the north, the British Army remained in position. In January, a group effort was decided on by General Clark. The attack was resumed along the entire line. At the same time, an Allied corps landed at Anzio in order to turn the flank of the adversary. Fierce battles were to rage until the middle of March without much result.

This was not for lack of effort and even success on the part of the French Expeditionary Corps. At the beginning of January, General Juin had taken command. The Third North African Division, under General de Monsabert, and General Guillaume's group of *Tabors* were put into the line next to Dody's division. Later the Fourth Moroccan Division under Sevez came to join them. In addition, General Utile's Italian Division was assigned to the French sector. The attacks began on January 12th. Three weeks later, the French had overrun a zone about fifteen miles deep, knocked out the first German position, penetrated the second, and taken 1,200 prisoners, all over extremely difficult terrain in which the enemy engaged more than a third of the forces he was opposing to the entire Fifth Army against our men. This success was crowned, so to speak, by the taking of the Belvedere, an organized strong point which was the key of the 'Gustav Line'. On this position, several times taken, lost and taken again, the Fourth Regiment of Tunisian rifles accomplished one of the most brilliant military exploits of the war at the cost of enormous losses. Colonel Roux, the Commanding Officer, was killed with nine of his twenty-four captains. To the left, Monte Cassino remained in the enemy's hands despite terrible bombings and the valiantly repeated assaults of American, Hindu and New Zealand troops. On the right, the Eighth Army did not advance noticeably. Under these conditions, Juin had to suspend his advance.

However, events had left the French with a sense of victory: the enemy had retreated before them; they had responded to a command both lucid and firm whose strategy had been realized point by point; the co-operation of the various large units and the liaison between the armies left nothing to be desired; lastly, our men had discovered that for fighting in mountainous country, which demands maximum effort and manoeuvrability, they had proved themselves without peer in the Allied camp. The Allies, moreover, said so quite openly. Nothing was more noble and more generous than the acknowledgment made by King George VI, Generals Eisenhower, Wilson, Alexander and Clark to General Juin and his troops.

When, on a tour of inspection in early March, I examined the natural fortresses our troops had taken, I felt, as did everyone present, great pride and a solid confidence in our men. But it seemed obvious to me that a new effort could be asked of them only in the framework of a larger strategy. Juin was convinced of this from the start. He had already, with this intention, made urgent recommendations to the Allied command. Soon he was to suggest an entirely new strategy.

According to Juin, it was essential, in order to take Rome, that the Allied action involve a general manoeuvre and, above all, a principal effort to which everything would be subordinated. This effort was to be made over the terrain that led to the objective—that is, south of the Abruzzi. It would therefore be necessary to concentrate the Fifth Army's front in order for it to operate powerfully from the Garigliano, while the Eighth Army, extending its line southward, would operate on its left toward Cassino and the Liri. Thenceforth, General Clark's zone would be reduced to two sectors: to the north, the Aurunci Mountains; to the south, the plain bordering the sea. The Commander of the French Expeditionary Corps proposed to take the Aurunci Mountains himself, while the Americans advanced on his left over less uneven ground.

Having visited our men, I made contact with Alexander at General Headquarters in Caserta. This great leader, of lucid mind and firm character, seemed to me extremely well qualified to command the Allied forces. It was a complex role, for he had to use, side by side, a British army, an American army, a French army detachment, a Polish corps, Italian contingents and a Brazilian division; to direct and integrate easily offended subordinates; to negotiate with various navies and several air forces; to submit to advice and requests for explanations from Washington and London; all in order to join a frontal battle between two seas, which narrowly limited the possibilities of manoeuvre. General Alexander picked his way among these difficulties without ever ceasing to be clear headed, courteous and optimistic. He described his plans to me. I heard him out, taking care not to interfere in his plan of operations, believing that governments must respect both freedom of mind and the responsibility of the command in battle. But when Alexander informed me that he was inclined to change his strategy in the direction Juin recommended, I indicated my satisfaction on this point.

Clark, too, was disposed to accept this modification. I went to see him in the trailer where he lived and worked. He made an extremely good impression on me, not only because he said what he had to say so clearly, but because, too, he remained simple and direct in the exercise of his command. There was all the more merit in this because among the American generals he was the first to command an army in the Western theatre and his country was therefore eager for his personal success. Like Alexander, Clark professed the highest respect for Juin and praised the French troops with an enthusiasm that was certainly not simulated. General Anders, in his turn, expressed the same opinions. In a sector adjoining our own, he was in command of the Polish corps that was lavishing its bravery in the service of its hopes. The Italian General Utile and his division lent a very considerable support to our soldiers with the best of hearts. In Algiers, General Mascanheras, arriving from Brazil with his division soon to be engaged in Italy, declared it to be his intention to take the French leaders as his models. These words salved many wounds!

Shortly afterwards, Wilson informed me that Alexander's decision had been made. The offensive was to resume, in May, on the basis of Juin's recommendations. We immediately reinforced the Expeditionary Corps. The First Free French Division, a second group of *Tabors*, several artillery and engineer groups, and an armoured detachment were sent to Italy. Further, the services which were hitherto those of an army corps received the necessary complements to become those of an army. After which, the Second Armoured Division having left for England, there remained in North Africa, of our large units, only the First and Fifth Armoured Divisions and the Ninth Colonial Division which were finishing their training. We were, therefore, engaging in the peninsula more than half of all our means, which was quite enough! To General Wilson, who vaunted the advantages of a more extended effort along both shores of the Adriatic and expressed his hope of engaging there not only the French troops already on the spot but even those being held in reserve, I repeated that this was not their final destination and that the French Government intended to devote both its troops and its reserves to Operation Anvil. 'Meanwhile,' I told Wilson, 'our army, which includes 120,000 men in Italy, or more than a quarter of the combatants, will assume a share in the coming offensive which I trust will be decisive.'

This was to be the case. The battle began on the night of May 11th, when the French Expeditionary Corps attacked the Aurunci Mountains. It might have seemed that this tangle of mountains for-

bade a swift advance. But it was for just this reason that the French
command had chosen it for their attack. The enemy, in fact, had
every reason to think that he must protect himself not in the mountains themselves, but to the north and the south where the slopes
were gentle, the site of the two main roads to Rome. The Germans
were, therefore, surprised by our attack in force in the most difficult
sector. In this sector, General Juin's manoeuvre was to catch the
enemy napping, for it was by the highest, least likely peak, where
the Germans did not at all expect our break-through, that the
French undertook an accelerated advance, continually overrunning
the German positions to the right and the left and everywhere penetrating his three successive lines before the enemy found time to
re-establish his positions on any one of the three. Again, to take full
advantage of the surprise, though having to run all the more risks
as well, the Commander of the Expeditionary Corps had decided
to capture—without warning, in the middle of the night and without
artillery preparation—the slopes of Mount Majo, a tremendous
mountain mass including the entire system of German defences.

It was true that the Expeditionary Corps included first-class troops
particularly skilful at mountain warfare. In particular, the Fourth
Division and the Moroccan *Tabors* were capable of advancing over
any terrain, and General Juin knew this better than anyone. He
therefore confided to this division and to these *Tabors*, united under
Sevez's orders, the mission of driving as quickly as possible along the
upper part of the ground, flanking the German positions on the
south, and taking as their final objective the Petrella range, near
Pico, in the enemy's rear. An admirable regiment from the Second
Moroccan Division, the Eighth Rifles, under Colonel Molle, would
open the front by seizing Mount Majo in one thrust. Then the First
Free French Division would flank the group of ranges to the north
and assist the Eighth Army's left to debouch on the Liri. Lastly, the
difficult task of taking the German defences on the heights of the
Aurunci Mountains would fall to the Third North African Division
and the Second Moroccan Division.

Like a living machine whose gears were set in motion by men
with a single goal, the French Army in Italy achieved precisely what
its leader had planned. On May 17th, I was in the peninsula once
more, accompanied by André Diethelm, Minister of War, and
General de Lattre and General Béthouart. On the spot, after years

of humiliation and dissension, I saw what a magnificent spectacle the troops of de Monsabert and Dody offered, driving towards Esperia and San Oliva; those of Brosset were engaged around San Giorgio, those of Sevez and Guillaume were reaching the region around Pico; Poydenot's batteries were following close behind the infantry clinging to the slopes. Dromard's sappers having achieved the *tour de force*, on the eve of the attack, of secretly constructing bridges across the Garigliano, were now using every hour of every day and every night to make the mined and blockaded roads usable. Our convoys moved in exemplary order; our depots and workshops supplied the units without slip-ups and without delays. In our ambulances, amid the stream of French and German wounded, the capacity of our hospital services, as well as the devotion of the nurses and drivers under Madame Catroux and Madame du Luart, was fully equal to their task. Each man in each echelon in each emplacement, despite losses and fatigue, showed that brisk eagerness so characteristic of the French when matters are going well.

On May 20th, all the German positions for some thirty kilometers had been pierced by the French, who were already overrunning Pico. On the left, the Second American Army Corps had seized Fondi and was driving towards the Pontine Marshes. To the right, meanwhile, the British and the Poles had taken, respectively, San Angelo and Monte Cassino, but, since this was the sector where the enemy had his greatest strength, had stopped before the Aquino-Pontecorvo line. The French Expeditionary Corps, before plucking its laurels, counting its 5,000 prisoners and gathering the guns and equipment left in its hands, was to participate in a new battle and attack on the Pontecorvo-Pico front in order to help General Leese's left wing to reach the open ground toward Rome. On June 4th, our first groups penetrated the front. On the 5th, Americans, British and French marched into the capital.

With Marshal Kesselring's approval, the German writer Rudolf Böhmler, himself a veteran from Italy, wrote the history of the German Tenth Army in his book *Monte Cassino*. Describing the brilliant share taken in the winter campaign by the French Expeditionary Corps, notably on the 'Belvedere', the author refers to the confusion of the German high command when it realized that the French had left this sector for an unknown objective elsewhere. A new Allied effort to reach Rome was certainly to be looked for; 'but', writes Böhmler, 'only the adversary's offensive would reveal in which region the chief danger would arise. In this regard, it was the position of the French Expeditionary Corps that would give us a precise indication . . . Where, then, would it be? When Juin appeared anywhere, it meant that Alexander was planning some essential operation there. No one knew this better than Kesselring. "My greatest concern," the Field Marshal declared, "came from my uncertainty as to the direction of the French Expeditionary Corps' attack, its components and its location . . . It was only after I knew this that I could make definitive plans." ' Böhmler adds: 'These apprehensions were well founded. For it was Juin who destroyed the right wing of the Tenth Army and opened the road to Rome to the Allies. After months of battle, his Expeditionary Corps broke down the door that led to the Eternal City.'

Military valour, military virtue, service and suffering of the soldiers—without these no country can stand upright or struggle to its feet. France has always been able to furnish such riches in abundance. But there must be a national soul, a will, an action, that is to say, a policy. Had France, between the wars, possessed a capable Chief of State, had she found herself, before Hitler's ambition, inspired by a genuine government, had her army, facing the enemy, been well equipped and well commanded, destiny might have been ours! Even after the disaster of May 1940, our fleet and the remains of our army still had a great role to play, if only the régime and later the leaders had aspired to it. But since, after so many capitulations, the nation must start upon its own recovery from the bottom of the abyss, nothing could be done save by the efforts of the combatants. After Keren, Bir Hakeim, the Fezzan and Tunisia, the glory of our troops' Italian victories gave France her opportunity. Hearing accounts of their operations on my arrival in London the day before the great landing in Normandy, I telegraphed their commander: 'The French Army has won its generous share in the great victory of Rome. Naturally! You have made it so! General Juin, you and the troops under your orders are worthy of our country!'

While the Second and Fourth Divisions and the Moroccan *Tabors* were regrouping near Rome, Juin launched an army corps commanded by General de Larminat in pursuit of the enemy in his sector. This corps, formed of the Brosset and de Monsabert divisions and reinforced by armoured units and artillery, headed towards the

Lake of Bolsena, Radicofani, the Orcia pass and Sienna. Each of these points was to be the scene of bitter fighting where, in particular, along with many good soldiers, we lost Colonel Laurent-Champrosay and Major Amyot d'Inville, respectively in command of the artillery and the regiment of naval riflemen of the First Free French Division. Meanwhile de Larminat, manoeuvring and attacking, settled accounts among the German rearguard. It must be added that the Allied air forces completely dominated the skies and crushed the enemy columns. Nothing gave our troops the measure of the German defeat better than the mountains of scrap metal that lined the roads.

Meanwhile, the French had seized the island of Elba with the support of the special ships furnished by the British and several American fighter and bomber squadrons. The operation had been proposed by General Giraud the day after the liberation of Corsica. But the Allies, involved with the Anzio landing, had not been able to be convinced. Now they asked us to capture the island. I gave my agreement. Under the command of General Henri Martin, the attack was led by the Ninth Colonial Division, the Shock Battalion and the commando groups, all units from North Africa assigned to de Lattre's army for the imminent offensive in the south of France.

During the night of June 16th, General Martin landed Colonel Gambiez' 'shock' troops in small groups which quickly seized the seven German shore batteries. Next the Magnan Division landed in Campo Bay. On June 18th, after bitter fighting at Marino di Campo, Porto Longone and Porto Ferrajo, our troops occupied the entire island, having destroyed the German garrison under General Gall, taken 2,300 prisoners and seized sixty field guns and a great deal of equipment. General de Lattre, who had gone to the island, telegraphed that evening from the Maison Napoléon, reporting the results and reminding me of the fact that they had been achieved on the anniversary of my call to honour in 1940.

Elba's capture seemed a good omen for the great undertaking I had dreamed of when I sounded that call, covering as it did the coast of Provence. But everything still depended on the Allies' final decisions. Impressed by the extent of the victory in Italy, would they not, *in extremis*, renounce Operation Anvil to adopt a different scheme of exploitation in the peninsula? During the last trip I made there, at the end of June and after my return from London and

Bayeux, I found the command extremely eager, in fact, to pursue the campaign with the means now at its disposal and even to extend it by means of new reinforcements. This was quite natural, but nevertheless, for reasons involving my responsibilities to the French nation, I did not agree with this point of view.

In any case, the Americans, bitterly engaged in Normandy, wanted a landing in Provence. Marshall and Eisenhower urgently requested it for August. In order to make assurance doubly sure, I informed General Wilson and General Alexander, for my part, that the French Government asked them expressly to regroup all the forces which it had put at their disposal in time for them to be transported to France during the month of August at the latest. I agreed that groups pursuing the enemy should continue their operations for several weeks more. But they must in no case be engaged after July 25th, nor drive beyond the Arno Valley. To our army in Italy as well as to our forces being grouped in Africa, I gave direct orders informing them of their imminent destination. As for General Juin, despite his regret at leaving his command and the distress I myself felt at removing him from it, I named him Chief of General Staff of National Defence, an essential post in the period of active operations, profound reorganization and inevitable friction with the Allies which the liberation would entail. Until I left power, Juin would be beside me as one of the best seconds and surest military advisers any French leader ever had.

Finally, the date of the landing in the south of France was fixed for August 15th. As we had stipulated, all French land, sea and air forces available in the Mediterranean would participate in it. Meanwhile, some of our troops would be at grips with the enemy until the last minute in the Italian peninsula. Continuing his advance with the de Monsabert and Dody Divisions and a group of *Tabors*, General de Larminat seized Siena on July 13th, taking every care that nothing be destroyed in that city of marvels. On July 22nd, our troops, under Juin's direct orders (Juin himself insisted on leading the last battles in Italy), took Castelfiorentino in sight of Florence and the Arno Valley, where the enemy was to re-establish his positions for long months. Then, transferring their sector to Allied groups, our men hastened to the ships that would land them in France.

Their transport was to be effected across a sea dominated by the Western navies. In September 1943, the Syracuse armistice had withdrawn from the Axis almost the entire Italian fleet, already damaged by Andrew Cunningham's attacks. Further, in the spring of 1944, the *Scharnhorst* and the *Tirpitz*, the last fast battleships of the German Navy, were destroyed by the British. Nevertheless, the enemy still possessed a great number of submarines, raiding vessels and scout craft, which in co-operation with the German Air Force continued to cause heavy losses to the convoys. We therefore had to continue clearing the seas before risking our armadas.

This was why, in the Atlantic, the North Sea and the Arctic Ocean, French cruisers, torpedo boats, submarines, frigates, corvettes, pursuit boats, scout craft and escort vessels, operating out of British ports under Admiral d'Argenlieu's orders, took part in the vast system of attack and defence organized by the Allies. For Operation Overlord all our ships in English ports—that is, forty small warships and some fifty steamships and cargo vessels—were employed in the bombardment, escort and transport operations which the landing of Eisenhower's forces required. To this action were joined those of a division of two cruisers, the *Georges-Leygues* and the *Montcalm*, commanded by Admiral Jaujard and playing an extremely effective role in the bombardment of the beaches, off Port-en-Bessin, and later in support of the landed troops. The old battleship *Courbet*, which for four years had served as a floating landing stage in Portsmouth harbour, was given, for this important occasion, a reduced crew and a good commander, Wietzel, and was scuttled near the French coast under enemy fire in order to serve as a breakwater for the artificial port of Arromanches. Lastly Naval Lieutenant Kieffer's *Commando-Marine* leaped on to the beach at Ouistreham with the first Allied groups.

In the South Atlantic, the French Navy, waiting for Operation Anvil, contributed actively to Western actions. Seven of our cruisers distributed into two divisions, commanded respectively by Admiral Longaud and Admiral Barthe, and soon reinforced by the two cruisers under Admiral Jaujard, made up part of the force deployed between Dakar and Natal to intercept the German 'blockade forces'. One of these ships, the *Portland*, was sunk by the *Georges-Leygues*. Up and down the entire west coast of Africa, the naval and air forces of Admiral Collinet took up operations against German submarines, raiders and aeroplanes.

In the Mediterranean, a division of French light cruisers under

Captain Sala, succeeded by Captain Lancelot, with many British and American formations, supported the Italian armies. Hence in September 1943 the *Fantasque* and the *Terrible* were engaged off Salerno during the landing of the troops. In January 1944 the *Fantasque* and the *Malin* assisted the Anzio landing by shelling the German reinforcements at close range along the Appian Way. Then, reaching the Adriatic, this division assumed responsibility for attacking the supply ships the enemy sent down the Italian coast at night, since Allied aviation prevented his equipment from travelling overland. On March 1st, in the vicinity of Pola, our light cruisers sent five ships to the bottom, including one torpedo boat. On March 19th, they sank five vessels off the coast of the Morea. In June, in the northern Adriatic, they destroyed four more. During the same period, all the Allied convoys navigating off England and Normandy or else towards Italy, Corsica and North Africa included French vessels in their escort. We lost the torpedo boat *La Combattante*, the submarine *Protée*, the dispatch boat *Ardent*, the minesweeper *Marie-Mad*, the tanker *Nivose*, a pursuit boat and several freighters.

Last of all, in the Pacific, the splendid *Richelieu*, under Commandant Merveilleux du Vigneaux, joined the fleet in the line. In April off Sabang, in May off Surabaya, it powerfully supported the action of Allied aircraft carriers. Everywhere, in fact, the French Navy took full advantage of the means it had reconstructed.

If the mastery of the sea permitted the landing on the Continent, it was because it was combined with domination of the air. In the latter as in the former, the French played an active and effective role, if not a decisive one. Seventeen groups of our air forces accompanied our armies in Italy. Seven groups supported the Battle of France, of which two participated in the long-distance bombardments that crushed German industry. Two pursuit groups figured with honour in the implacable struggle from which Russia was emerging victor. On the North Africa coast, several groups were helping to cover the land bases and the convoys at sea. The records of Clostermann, Maridor, Marin la Meslée, the deliberate sacrifice of Saint-Exupéry, as well as other valorous deeds, were like sparks flying out of the crushing machinery of a 'great circus'.

The battle for France formed a coherent whole. The military energy that increased the role of our regular armies was the same that swelled our interior forces. The resistance, before the landings, no longer risked only skirmishes, but ventured into engagements proper. The reports about troop operations and about ships and air squadrons were now reinforced by daily accounts of the activity of the maquis and the intelligence networks. Quite naturally the fire broke out first in the Massif Central, Limousin and the Alps.

On September 10th, 1943, at Dourch in Aveyron, a regular battle was joined which seemed to be a sort of signal. A German company was put to flight by our own men and left its captain and ten soldiers dead behind it. At La Borie, in return, the victorious maquis was to be decimated and its chief, Lieutenant de Roquemaurel, killed by the enemy; but in other points in Aveyron and Cantel new outbreaks occurred in which our men had the advantage. Corrèze was filled with maquisards. At Saint-Ferréol, at Terrasson, brisk engagements in which the invader lost several hundred men were the prelude to the rising of the entire region which would coincide with the landing. In the Puy-de-Dôme, after several well-led raids, Colonel Garcie gathered 3,000 men on the tactical position of Le Mouchet and on June 2nd began a series of battles in which the Germans were to be worsted. In Limousin, in Quercy, in Périgord, many engagements caused the enemy serious losses.

In Haute-Savoie, increasingly intense battles were the rule. As far back as June 1943, at the Dents de Lanfon, and in the month following at Cluses, the Italians occupying the department had been sorely harassed. The Germans who relieved them during the winter had been attacked at many points. In February 1944, five hundred Frenchmen, with about sixty Spaniards, took up a position on the Plateau des Glières, under Lieutenant Morel. The Germans, after thirteen days of battle, succeeded in taking it; six hundred of their men had fallen, but even at this cost they had not destroyed the troops of the defenders, of whom two-thirds had escaped.

The Ain department was the scene of continual engagements. The forces of the interior, well commanded and organized, dominated the situation. They proved this on November 11th by occupying Oyonnax during the whole day of this glorious anniversary. Here, Colonel Romans-Petit reviewed his men before the cenotaph and had them paraded through the city amid popular acclaim. Early in 1944, in order to reduce the Ain maquis, the Germans began a large engagement which cost them several hundred dead. In April, they made a new effort which cost them still more dearly. In June, it was our men who took the offensive everywhere, taking four hundred prisoners.

In the Drôme, through which the great Lyons-Marseilles railway network passed, as well as those from Grenoble and Briançon, the maquis under Colonel Drouot took particular action against the railways. In December, a train full of German soldiers on leave was blown up at Portes-les-Valence; the carriages when they stopped or overturned were machined-gunned by our men, who killed or wounded two hundred soldiers. Several days later, at Vercheny, a troop train was derailed and thrown into the Drôme. In March, in the Donzère Pass, the maquisards opened fire on an ambushed military convoy from which three hundred dead and wounded were removed. Shortly afterwards a French group, attacked near Séderon, fought to the last man. Meanwhile, the department was prepared to cut off the enemy's communications when the great battle began.

What happened in the Isère also made it possible to foresee some vast operation of our interior forces at the moment this battle was joined. The preliminaries were costly for the enemy. For instance, at Grenoble, on November 14th, the resistance blew up the artillery depot where the Germans had stored munitions, petrol and vehicles. Three hundred hostages were arrested. Ordered to release them, the Germans refused; in retaliation, the barracks at Bonne where several Wehrmacht batteries were quartered were destroyed by an explosion which killed two hundred and twenty Germans and wounded five hundred more. Further, according to the instructions left by General Delestraint and the orders of Colonel Descourt, leader of our forces in the Isère, resolute combatants seized the Massif du Vercors under Major Le Ray, in order to make it a drill ground. Access to the Vercors was forbidden to enemy reconnaissance.

It was here, during this period, that perhaps the most striking of all the resistance actions mentioned in our reports occurred. But many others, smaller in scale or concealed, were accomplished at the same time. Through the messages, where places were indicated by numbers, orders and reports formulated by code phrases, combatants designated by strange pseudonyms, we could see to what extent the resistance had become an effective instrument of war. The enemy confirmed it by cruel reprisals. Before the Allied armies set foot on our land, the Germans lost thousands of men in France. Everywhere they were surrounded by an atmosphere of insecurity that affected the morale of the troops and confused the officers. All the more so since the local authorities and the French police, whether in voluntary complicity with the resistance or fearing the punishments in store for 'collaborators', opposed repression much more than they helped it.

It must be added that the Germans, even when they were not the targets for the bullets or grenades from our secret army, were the continual victims of espionage. Nothing concerning the invader escaped our intelligence networks. General Bedell Smith wrote to the Bureau Central de Renseignements et d'Action: 'During the month of May, 700 telegraph reports and 3,000 documentary reports reached London from France.' In fact, the day the battle began, all the German troop emplacements, bases, depots, landing fields and command posts were precisely known, the striking force and equipment counted, the defence works photographed, the mine fields spotted. The exchanges of questions and information between Koenig's staff and the intelligence networks were immediately transmitted by a well-established secret wireless system. Thanks to all the information furnished by the French resistance, the Allies were in a position to see into the enemy hand and to strike with telling effect.

The news of the landing gave the maquis its cue for a concerted action. I had ordered it in advance, on May 16th, by notifying the interior forces, by means of the 'Cayman Plan', of the goals they must attempt to achieve. However, the Allied command regarded the extension of guerrilla warfare with mistrust. Furthermore, it foresaw a prolonged battle and hoped that the resistance would not precipitate matters except in the bridgehead area. The proclamation General Eisenhower read on the wireless on June 6th warned French patriots to stay on their guard. On the same day, however, I urged them to fight with all the means in their power according to the orders given by the French command. But the delivery of arms depended on Allied headquarters and remained, at the start, limited. It was especially with regard to demolition of railways, roads and essential communications that the 'Combined General Staff' was concerned.

As for the railways, the objectives were distributed between the air forces and the resistance. The latter accounted for the more remote regions: Lyons, Dijon, Doubs, the east, the centre, the south-west.

During June and July six hundred trains were derailed. Our men also took the responsibility, on all lines, for the sabotage that immobilized 1,800 locomotives and more than 6,000 cars. As for the underground telegraph cables which the enemy reserved for their own use, skilful demolitions on June 6th and the days following the landings put those serving Normandy and the area around Paris out of commission. Wires above ground were also cut in countless numbers. The Germans were thrown into great difficulties by such chaos in transport and communications. At the same time a military insurrection was launched in a number of departments, producing noticeable influence on the course of operations. At last the Allied high command recognized the advantages of this kind of warfare and gave the maquis help which was no less effective for remaining circumspect.

As for Brittany, we were to wait no longer. General Eisenhower insisted on seeing the Armorican Peninsula cleared of German troops before pushing his armies towards the Seine. Brittany was swarming with maquisards, especially in the Côtes-du-Nord and Morbihan, where the terrain was favourable to their work. It was therefore decided to furnish arms to the Bretons and to send in our First Regiment of parachute troops, trained in England under Colonel Bourgoin. The day before the landing and during the days following, our underground army received a great number of 'containers' and parachute troops. At once the resistance burst into flames. Thirty thousand men entered the campaign, some organized into regular units, others conducting a sort of individual *Chouannerie*. But the Germans, having spotted at Saint-Marcel, near Malestroit, one of the bases where our men received arms from England, attacked it on June 18th. The position was defended by a battalion from Morbihan and several teams of parachute troops under the orders of Major le Garrec. General de la Morlaye, retired, commanded a company which he himself had formed at Guingamp. After a struggle of several hours, the enemy managed to seize a terrain now covered with German corpses. But the defenders had been able to escape.

The news of the battle of Saint-Marcel roused all Brittany. The invader found himself blockaded in the larger cities and ports. Nevertheless, he fought furiously and gave no quarter. But British troops attacked him everywhere and without respite. Among them, Colonel Bourgoin and his men acted as yeast in the dough. The First

Parachute Regiment lost twenty-three of its forty-five officers. When Patton's armoured units, having crossed the Avranches Gap, debouched into Brittany at the beginning of August, they found the country entirely occupied by our men, who had already buried 1,800 German corpses and taken 3,000 prisoners. In order to help reduce the garrisons, the maquisards served in American tanks as accurately informed guides and as escort infantry. The enemy only gave battle in the ports—Saint-Malo, Brest and Lorient—which had been organized beforehand. All in all, the campaign in Brittany cost the Germans several thousand dead, almost 50,000 prisoners and quantities of equipment. Four German divisions were destroyed.

At the other end of the territory, the battle of the Vercors plateau gave similar proof of the military effectiveness of the French resistance. During the first days of June, 3,000 men had taken up their positions on the range. Since the extremely choppy terrain lent itself to defence by autonomous groups, the alpine groups seemed particularly well established, so that a larger effort could be asked for from the Allied command to arm them; fifteen hundred 'containers' were parachuted in to the Vercors. A mission including British, American and French officers was sent from England and installed itself in the Vercors plateau to connect the garrison with Allied General Headquarters and several instructors and specialists from Algiers joined the maquisards. In agreement with the Allied air forces, a landing strip was constructed in the centre of the plateau to permit the landing of a detachment of regular troops, supplies for the fighters and the evacuation of the wounded.

On July 14th the enemy started their offensive. For ten days they continued the operation with considerable forces. Planes machine-gunned the defenders and bombarded the few hideouts. Since German fighter planes were in the sky every day, the Allied air force refused to take action, alleging that the distance from its bases kept it from protecting its transport and bomber planes by its own fighters. The enemy even made use of the landing strip on which the defenders hoped to see reinforcements land, and brought in several companies of their *élite* troops on gliders. Despite everything the garrison, struggling in its base of operations with exemplary stubbornness, held the assault in check until July 24th. On this date, the Germans managed to occupy the Vercors plateau. They had used in the task the equivalent of a division and had lost several thousand men. In their fury, they killed all the wounded and a good number of the villagers. At Vassieux, the population of the town was entirely massacred. Of the Vercors Alpine Rifles, half gave their lives for France; the others managed to withdraw.

These military exploits had vast repercussions in every other region. Of course the Algiers, London and New York broadcasts gave them wide publicity. By the middle of July, forty departments were in open revolt. Those of the Massif Central, the Limousin, the Alps, as well as the Haute-Garonne, the Dordogne, the Drôme, the Jura, like the Breton departments, belonged to one or other of the maquis organizations, the 'Secret Army', the 'Francs-Tireurs et Partisans', the 'Army Organization of Resistance' or the 'Corps Francs'. Willy-nilly, the prefects made contact with the resistance and the 'prefects of the liberation'—whether or not they were the same—appeared, as such, openly. The municipal councils of 1940 resumed their functions where they had been revoked. The Cross of Lorraine appeared on lapels, on walls, on the flags of public monuments. As for the German garrisons, attacked, overworked, cut off from each other, they lived in incessant anxiety. Their isolated men were killed or taken prisoner. Their columns could not be moved without running into skirmishes at every step. They reacted by massacre and arson, as at Oradour-sur-Glane, Tulle, Asq, Cerdon and in other places. While the battle in Normandy grew harder for them every day, their situation in a great part of France tended to become desperate.

By the end of July, the French forces of the interior had engaged eight enemy divisions, of which none could reinforce those fighting at the front. The First Infantry Division and the Fifth Parachute Division in Brittany, the 175th Division in Anjou and in Touraine, the 116th Panzer Division in the vicinity of Paris, the 'Ostlegion' Division in the Massif Central, the 181st Division at Toulouse, the 172nd Division at Bordeaux and the equivalent of a division drawn from the army defending the Rhone Valley, found themselves nailed to the spot. Besides, three Panzer divisions which the German commander had called to emergency service in Normandy—which meant that they were supposed to be engaged within forty-eight hours—were subjected to enormous delays. The 17th Panzer Division, at grips with our men between Bordeaux and Poitiers, lost ten days before its columns managed to clear a road for itself. The 2nd

Panzer SS Division, known as *Das Reich*, left Montauban on June 6th and could not use the railways, which were all out of commission—and found its groups delayed in Tarn, Lot, Corrèze and Haute-Vienne. Not until June 18th did it arrive at Alençon, exhausted and decimated. The 11th Panzer Division, taking eight days to come from the Russian front by rail to the French border, took twenty-four days to cross France from Strasbourg to Caen. The effect produced on the equipment and morale of German units by the failures of supply and liaison was incalculable.

For the same reason, it was foreseeable that the rear of the enemy forces defending the Mediterranean coast would be unable to hold out as soon as the French and Americans landed in Provence. During the first days of August, the military delegate to the southeast, Colonel Henri Zeller, came from France to tell me as much. He declared that once Toulon and Marseilles were taken, our troops could quickly overcome the successive stands the Germans would try to make in the Rhone Valley, for the Alps and the Massif Central were already in the hands of our clandestine army. Zeller repeated his remarks to General Patch and General de Lattre, to whom I immediately sent him. The latter consequently altered the timing of the plans for their advance. Events proved Zeller right. Lyons, which the Allied command counted on taking after two months of battle, was to be in our hands seventeen days after the landing.

The same movement which in France and in Africa drove the French into battle had repercussions in Indo China. In Saigon and Hanoi, while living under the threat of a sudden show of force by the invader, no one doubted, any more than elsewhere, the ultimate victory of the Allies. Aside from symptoms of imminent German collapse, Japan's recession was also acknowledged. Not only had the offensive of the Nipponese fleets and armies been checked, on the whole, since the summer of 1943, but it was the Allies who were now taking the initiative: Admiral Nimitz advancing from island to island in the central Pacific, General MacArthur moving towards the Philippines and Lord Mountbatten gaining ground in Burma with the co-operation of Chiang Kai-shek's forces.

This is why certain French authorities in Indo China gradually turned toward the Algiers Government. Monsieur François, a bank director, came from Saigon to tell us so; M. de Boisanger, head of the Political Office of the Government General, extended discreet antennae towards General Pechkoff, our ambassador to Chungking; General Mordant, high commander of the troops, made secret contact with Colonel Tutenges, chief of the information service we had installed in Yunnan.

In my eyes, the immediate goal to be achieved in the Far East was the participation of our forces in the military operations. The idea that, by maintaining to the end an attitude of complacent passivity towards the Japanese, we might eventually safeguard France's position seemed to me unworthy and ridiculous. I had no doubt that in a strategic position, taking Indo China as its centre, the Japanese, hard pressed and thrown back on all sides, would necessarily be reduced to suppressing any risk of opposition in the peninsula. How, in case of a reverse on the nearby field of battle, could they tolerate amid their own groups the presence of a French army of 50,000 men? This was even less likely since the fiction of France's neutrality would crumble with Vichy. There was every indication that the Japanese would eventually want to liquidate the French troops and the administration. If, in return for new and dishonourable guarantees, they allowed vestiges of our garrisons to subsist along with some scraps of our authority, it was inconceivable that on the one hand the states and the peoples of the Federation and on the other the Allies would countenance the restoration of French power in territories where we had taken no part in the world-wide struggle. It was, therefore, a question of preparing military resistance on the peninsula, in order that the enemy should not seize our posts, sweep away our representatives and make us lose face altogether, without firing a shot. We must also send to the Far East a force destined to re-enter the territories of Indochina as soon as the opportunity arose. On February 29th, 1944, I wrote to General Mordant to confirm him in the good intentions I knew were his and to stipulate what the government expected of him and his troops in the extraordinarily difficult situation in which he found himself. Shortly afterwards, I appointed General Blaizot to command the forces assigned to the Far East. Since these forces could only act from bases in India, Burma or China, the Allies must approve their departure. Yet Washington, London and Chungking appeared very reluctant to do so. Nevertheless, we persuaded the British Government and Lord Mountbatten, British Commander-in-Chief in the Indian Ocean, to give General Blaizot permission to establish himself at New Delhi

in order to prepare the operation. An advance echelon of our troops
left with the General. This was a first step toward the goal. But,
fundamentally, we knew that the problem of Indo China, like the
entire future of France, could be settled only in Paris.

On August 15th, the first elements of the French First Army and
the American Sixth Corps landed on the coast of Provence. Initially,
General Patch commanded the whole operation. De Lattre was at
the head of our troops. I had approved the plan of their operations:
as soon as the troops landed, the Americans were to march towards
Grenoble along the 'Route Napoléon'; the French were to take
Toulon and Marseilles, then drive up the Rhone Valley. That evening, under the protection of a gigantic naval and air bombardment,
the landing of the first American groups took place between Cava-
laire and Le Trayas; that of the parachute troops at Carnoules, Le
Luc, Le Muy; that of our African commandos at Le Rayol and Le
Lavandou took place at night as planned; and, during the course of
the day, three American divisions began their landing. The 16th saw
the beginning of the battle for the Brosset, De Monsabert and Du
Vigier Divisions, which landed at Le Rayol, Cavalaire, Saint-
Tropez and Sainte-Maxime in order to attack Toulon, while the
Americans reached Draguignan.

In human undertakings, it happens that by virtue of long and
exacting labour a sudden and single *élan* is constituted from many
various and dispersed elements. On August 18th the news, arriving
in great waves, lit up all the areas of combat at once, revealed in
each of them what part the French were taking and showed that the
actions of our men formed a coherent whole.

In Provence, de Lattre, realizing the confusion of the German XIX
Army, drove home his advantage. Under his orders, de Larminat's
and de Monsabert's army corps succeeded in investing Toulon, and
certain of our groups were already rushing towards Marseilles. The
Magnan Division, Guillaume's *Tabor* divisions and the services were
on the sea to join them. The Dody, Sevez and De Vernejoul Divisions
were prepared to embark. Our air force began to cross the sea. Our
fleet, with all its naval guns, rushed to the support of the troops. It
was on the same day that the German front in Normandy collapsed
altogether: Leclerc's Division, engaged since August 11th, distinguished itself in the operation. The road to Paris was open. In the
capital, the police and the partisans fired on the invader. From every

region messages flowed in announcing that the resistance was at grips with the enemy. As we had intended it to be, the Allied battle of France was also the battle of Frenchmen *for* France. The French were fighting 'a united battle for a united country'.

Politics, diplomacy and arms had together prepared unity. Now the nation must be rallied and unified as soon as it emerged from the abyss. I left Algiers for Paris.

VIII. PARIS

FOR OVER FOUR years, Paris had been on the conscience of the free world. Suddenly it became the loadstone as well. So long as the great city seemed to be asleep, captive and stupefied, everyone was agreed upon her formidable absence. But scarcely had the German front been penetrated in Normandy than the French capital suddenly found itself the centre of strategy and the stake of political manoeuvres. The campaigns of military leaders, the calculations of governments, the intrigues of the ambitious, the emotions of the crowd immediately turned towards the City. Paris was about to reappear. How many things could change!

First of all, Paris, left to her own decision, would settle the question of authority in France. No one doubted that if de Gaulle reached the capital without being met by some *fait accompli* there, he would be sanctioned by popular acclaim. Hence those who, in the city and elsewhere, in whatever camp, nursed hopes of frustrating this outcome, or at least of rendering it incomplete and open to dispute, attempted at the last moment to exploit the liberation in order to produce a situation by which I would be hampered and, if possible, paralysed. But since the nation had made its choice, public feeling was to sweep their endeavours into oblivion.

One such attempt was led by Pierre Laval. During the very days of August when I was receiving reports of the progressive and decisive victories of the Normandy campaign, the landing in Provence, the battles of our secret forces and the advance symptoms of the Parisian insurrection, I was informed of the conspiracy hatched by this creature of the policy of collaboration. He intended, in fact, to convene in Paris the 'national' assembly of 1940 and form a so-called 'union' government which, invoking legality, would receive the Allies and de Gaulle in the capital. Hence the rug would be pulled from under the General's feet. Of course, room would have to be made for de Gaulle within the executive body and, if need be, at its head, but after having morally uncrowned him and stripped his position of popular support, it would be easy to get rid of him by means suitable to the régime: the attribution of sterile honours, the increasing obstruction of political parties and, finally, general opposition under the double imputation of impotence to govern and aspirations to dictatorship. As for Laval, having engineered the return of the parliamentarians, for which they would be suitably grateful even if they had to inflict a theoretical condemnation upon him, he would step aside and wait until the people forgot and circumstances changed.

But to consummate such a plan, the co-operation of various mutually antagonistic elements was necessary. In the first place, Laval needed support from a celebrated and eminent person, sufficiently representative of parliament, sufficiently outspoken in his opposition to Pétain's policy and sufficiently esteemed abroad, so that the operation give the appearance of a republican restoration. Monsieur Herriot seemed to fulfil all these conditions; all that remained was to convince him of the fact. Another essential condition was that the Allies, on their arrival in Paris, be likely to recognize the new power. The Germans, too, must be willing to do so, since their troops were still in possession of the capital. Lastly, the Marshal's consent must be obtained, for without it, the invaders would refuse their authorization, the Allies their recognition, the parliamentarians their co-operation, while in any case the indignant refusal of the resistance was certain.

Laval might have thought, at the beginning of August, that he would get the support and co-operation he sought. Through M. Enfière, a friend of Herriot's used by the Americans for their liaison with the President of the Chamber and who was in touch with Mr Allen Dulles' services in Berne, he learned that Washington would favour a scheme that tended to silence or set aside de Gaulle. Having consulted the Germans, the head of the 'government' found them equally sympathetic. As a matter of fact, Abetz, Ribbentrop and others thought that once France was liberated, it would be a considerable advantage to have an executive in Paris who would prolong the after-effects of Vichy rather than a government *sans peur et sans reproche*. With the blessing of the Germans, Laval went to Maréville,

where Herriot was interned, and persuaded the latter to accompany
him to Paris in order to convene the 1940 parliament. Pétain let it be
understood that he too would be ready to accede to the strategem.

I must add that despite the apparent support given to Pierre
Laval, his desperate plot seemed to me to lead nowhere. Its success,
in the last resort, required my own adherence and nothing, not even
the pressure of the Allies, could have brought me to admit that the
1940 Assembly was qualified to speak in the name of France.
Furthermore, given the whirlwind the resistance was raising everywhere and which it was about to unleash in Paris itself, I had no
doubt the enterprise would be nipped in the bud. Already, on
July 14th, significant demonstrations had occurred in the outskirts.
In various places the tricolour had been displayed, the 'Marseillaise'
sung, and parades held to the chant of '*Vive de Gaulle!*' At the prison
of La Santé, that very day, the political prisoners, sending the word
from cell to cell and defying the worst reprisals, had decked all the
windows with flags, driven away their jailers and made the neighbourhood ring with patriotic songs. On August 10th, the railwaymen
stopped working. On the 15th, the police went on strike. On the
18th, it was the post office employees' turn. I expected, from one
moment to the next, to hear that street fighting had started. This
would obviously dispel whatever illusions the parliamentarians had
left.

Far more likely to succeed than Laval's plan was one by which
certain political elements of the resistance had determined to seize
power. I knew that these hoped to take advantage of the exaltation
and perhaps of the anarchy the struggle would arouse in the capital,
to manipulate the levers of command before I myself could grasp
them. Such was, quite naturally, the intention of the Communists.
If they managed to establish themselves as directors of the uprising
and to gain control in Paris, they could easily establish a *de facto*
government there in which they would be preponderant.

Benefiting by the confusion of battle; overpowering the National
Council of the Resistance, many of whose members, aside from those
already committed to the Party, might be accessible to the tempta-
tion of power; taking advantage of the sympathy which the persecu-
tions they had suffered, the losses they had endured and the courage
they had displayed gained them in many circles; exploiting the
anxiety aroused in the people by the absence of all law and order;

employing, finally, an equivocation by publicizing their adherence to General de Gaulle, they intended to appear at the insurrection's head as a kind of Commune which would proclaim the Republic, answer for public order and mete out justice. Furthermore, they meant to be careful to sing only the 'Marseillaise', and to run up no flag but the tricolour. On my arrival, I would find this 'popular' government installed; it would bind my brows with laurel, invite me to take the place it would offer me, and henceforth pull all the strings itself. The rest, for those in control, would be nothing more than the alternation of audacity and prudence, penetration of the state machinery under cover of purges, inhibition of public opinion by means of an effectively used propaganda and militia, gradual elimination of their early associates until the day when the dictatorship of what was called the proletariat would be established.

That these political schemes should be mingled with the energies and efforts of battle seemed to me quite inevitable. That the insurrection in the great city must, for some, lead to the establishment of an authority dominated by the Third International, I had known for a long time. Nevertheless I considered it essential that the troops of France act in Paris before those of the Allies, that the people contribute to the invader's defeat, that the liberation of the capital bear the impress of a military and national operation. Hence I ran the risk of encouraging the revolt without rejecting any of the influences that were capable of provoking it. It must be added that I felt myself in a position to direct the operation so that it would turn out for the best. Having taken the appropriate local measures beforehand, prepared to bring a great French unit into the city in good time, I was planning to appear there myself in order to crystallize the enthusiasm of liberated Paris round myself.

The government had done what was needed to see that the command of the regular forces should be in the hands of leaders dedicated to it. In July, Charles Luizet, Prefect of Corsica, had been appointed Prefect of Police. After two fruitless attempts, he was able to enter Paris on August 17th, just in time to assume his functions when the police captured the prefecture from the Germans. Further, General Hary was to put himself, at a suitable moment, in command of the *Garde Républicaine*—which Vichy had called the *Garde de Paris*—of the regiment of firemen, the *Garde Mobile* and the *Gendarmerie*, all units delighted to receive a chief appointed by de Gaulle.

But events dealt otherwise with the groups of partisans banded together in the various parts of the city. These factions naturally followed the leaders they themselves had chosen and whom the Communists, either directly or under cover of the 'National Front', made every effort to provide from their own ranks. As for the upper echelons, the Party tried to furnish them by relying on the National Council of the Resistance. The Council had referred, in military matters, to 'Comac', the Committee of Action, composed of three members, including Kriegel-Valrimont and Villon. The title of Chief of the General Staff of the Forces of the Interior had been given in the same way to Malleret-Joinville after the Germans had arrested Colonel Dejussieu. Rol-Tanguy had been appointed chief of the Ile-de-France forces. Judging by these nominations, one could guess that the direction of the fighting elements would be in Communist hands.

But these were still only titles, not official attributions. As a matter of fact, those who bore them did not exercise command in the hierarchical sense of the term. Rather than by orders given and followed according to military custom, they proceeded by proclamations or by personal action limited to certain districts. The partisans, in effect, numbering at the most 25,000 armed men, formed autonomous groups each of which functioned less according to orders from above than by local opportunities and scarcely left the neighbourhood where concealment and operations were a matter of experience. Furthermore, Colonel de Margueritttes, an extremely loyal officer, was chief of the secret forces in Paris and the suburbs. General Revers and General Bloch-Dassault advised, respectively, 'Comac' and the 'National Front'. Lastly, Chaban-Delmas, the government's military delegate, returning to Paris on August 16th after a visit to London to receive Koenig's instructions, was at the centre of everything. Perspicacious and skilful, having the only means communicating with the outside world, he supervised the proposals and, by means of long and, often, extremely outspoken palavers, checked the tendencies of the Council and the committees. At the summit, General de Gaulle and his government had their local representative.

This function was fulfilled by Alexandre Parodi. On August 14th, reinforcing his authority, I had appointed him Minister Delegate to the territories as yet unliberated. Since he spoke in my name, what he said weighed heavily. Because his conscience was clear, his disinterest complete, his dignity absolute, he had gained conclusive moral ascendancy over all passions and factions. Familiar with government service, he prevailed, amid the confusion, by the prestige of his experience. He had, moreover, his own policy, in accordance with his character, which willingly made concessions in matters of detail but held to what was essential with gentle firmness. Doing justice to the demands of ideology and the claims of individuals, he applied himself to ordering things so that I might find, in Paris, a situation without problematical commitments. It must be added that Georges Bidault, President of the National Council of the Resistance, was in agreement with Parodi and did everything in his power to avoid excesses by using, for his part, the compromise tactics of audacity in words and prudence in action. As for the administration, no one questioned the authority of my delegate and of those I had appointed to direct the services. It was without a trace of difficulty that Parodi, at the right moment, was established in the Hôtel Matignon; that the Secretaries General installed themselves in the ministries; that Luizet, the Prefect of Police, assumed Bussière's functions; that Fouret, Prefect of the Seine, replaced Bouffet. The official framework which the Algiers Government had established beforehand immediately took over the administration in Paris as in the provinces.

On the afternoon of August 18th, I flew from Algiers in my usual plane under Marmier's command. General Juin and a group of my colleagues followed in a 'Flying Fortress' which the Americans had insisted on lending us, alleging that its crew knew the route and the landing field perfectly. First stop: Casablanca. My intention was to take off again that night in order to land the next day at Maupertuis near Saint-Lô. But the 'Fortress' had had some mechanical difficulties on the way which required repairs. Furthermore, the Allied missions, insisting on the authority of the air lanes, stipulated a landing at Gibraltar before proceeding up the coast of Spain and that of France. We were therefore a day late.

On the 19th I left Casablanca. A considerable crowd lined the roads on the way to the airport. The tension in every face revealed that the goal of my journey had been guessed, though we had kept it secret. Few cheers, but every hat off, arms raised, eyes fixed. This ardent yet silent greeting affected me as the people's acknowledgment of a decisive moment. I was moved by it, as was the President-General beside me. 'What a destiny you have!' said Gabriel Puaux.

At Gibraltar, while we were dining with the governor, some Allied officers came in to tell us that the 'Fortress' was not in condition to leave, that since my own Lockheed had no guns it might be unwise to approach Normandy without an escort and that it would be advisable, all things considered, for me to postpone my departure. Without doubting the sincerity of this advice, I decided not to follow it. Boarding my plane, I took off at the scheduled hour. A little later the 'Fortress' followed us. On Sunday, August 20th, towards eight o'clock, I landed in Maupertuis.

Koenig was waiting for me there, as well as Coulet, Commissioner of the Republic in Normandy, and an officer sent by Eisenhower. I went first to the headquarters of the Allied Commander-in-Chief. On the way, Koenig explained the situation in Paris to me. He had had messages from Parodi, Chaban-Delmas and Luizet and information brought by emissaries. I learned that the police, who had been on strike for three days, had occupied the Prefecture at dawn on the 19th and opened fire on the Germans; that teams of partisans were doing the same thing throughout the city; that the ministries were in the hands of detachments designated by the delegation; that the resistance was being installed in the mayors' offices of the *arrondissements* and in the suburbs (not without an occasional struggle, as in Montreuil and later in Neuilly); that the enemy, busy evacuating his troops, had not hitherto reacted very savagely, but that several of his columns were in the process of crossing Paris, which might lead to reprisals at any minute. As for the political situation, it appeared that Laval had been unsuccessful, while in Vichy the forced departure of the Marshal was expected from one day to the next.

Eisenhower, having received my congratulations on the overwhelming speed of the Allied advance, explained the strategic situation. The Third Army, under Patton, leading the pursuit at the head of Bradley's army group, was prepared to cross the Seine in two columns. The one, north of Paris, was to reach Mantes. The other, to the south, was driving towards Melun. Behind Patton, General Hodges, commanding the First American Army, was regrouping the forces that had just finished mopping-up operations in Orne. To Bradley's left, Montgomery's army group, pushing back stiff German resistance, was advancing slowly towards Rouen. To the right there

was a gap through which Eisenhower intended Patton to drive toward Lorraine, as far as fuel and supply lines would permit. Subsequently, the de Lattre and Patch armies would come from the
south to join the Allied position. The Commander-in-Chief's stratagem seemed quite logical to me, save for one point that concerned
me deeply: no one was marching on Paris.

I told Eisenhower of my surprise and my concern. 'From the
strategic point of view,' I said, 'I don't see why you cross the Seine
at Melun, at Mantes, at Rouen—in short, everywhere—and yet at
Paris, and Paris alone, you do not. All the more so since Paris is a
communications centre which will later be essential and which it
will be to your advantage to re-establish as soon as possible. If any
location except the capital of France were in question, my advice
would not commit you to any action, for normally, of course, the
conduct of operations is your responsibility. But the fate of Paris is
of fundamental concern to the French Government. Which is why
I find myself obliged to intervene and to ask you to send French
troops there. The Second Armoured French Division, of course, is
the obvious choice.'

Eisenhower did not conceal his embarrassment from me; I had
an idea that fundamentally he shared my point of view, that he was
eager to send Leclerc to Paris, but that for reasons not entirely of a
strategic nature he could not yet do so. As a matter of fact, he
explained the delay in making this decision by the fact that a battle
in the capital risked vast destruction and heavy loss of life among
the civilian population. Nevertheless, Eisenhower did not contradict
me when I pointed out that this point of view would be justified if
nothing were happening in Paris, but that it was not acceptable
now that the patriots were at grips with the enemy there and every
sort of upheaval was likely. He declared, all the same, that the resistance had started fighting too soon. 'Why too soon,' I asked, 'since
at this very moment your forces are on the Seine?' Ultimately, he
assured me that, without yet being able to establish a precise date,
he would shortly give orders to march on Paris and that it would be
the Leclerc Division that he would assign to the operation. I acknowledged this promise, adding nevertheless that the matter was of such
national importance in my eyes that I was ready to take action on
my own responsibility and, if the Allied command delayed too long,
would launch the Second Armoured Division toward Paris myself.

Eisenhower's uncertainty suggested to me that the military command found itself somewhat hampered by the political project pursued by Laval, favoured by Roosevelt and requiring that Paris be
protected from all upheavals. The resistance had doubtless put an
end to this scheme by engaging in battle, but it took some time for
Washington to admit as much. This impression was confirmed when
I learned that the Leclerc Division, hitherto quite logically assigned to
Patton's army, had been reattached to Hodges' army for the last
three days, placed under the close supervision of General Gerow and
kept in the area of Argentan, as if someone feared it might make off
toward the Eiffel Tower. Furthermore, I noticed that the celebrated
agreement about relations between the Allied armies and the French
administration, although it had been concluded several weeks ago
between Algiers, Washington and London, had not yet been signed
by Koenig and Eisenhower because the latter was still waiting for
authorization to do so. How account for this delay if not by a
summit-level intrigue which was keeping back the White House's
surrender? Juin, visiting Allied headquarters in his turn, came to the
same conclusions as I had from his contacts with the general staff.

At the moment of the Allied armies' most striking success, and
while the American troops were giving evidence of courage deserving
every praise, I found this apparent stubbornness of Washington's
policy most depressing. But consolation was not far to seek. A great
tide of popular enthusiasm and emotion seized me on my entry into
Cherbourg and bore me onward as far as Rennes, passing through
Coutances, Avranches and Fougères. In the ruins of demolished
cities and burned-out villages, the population gathered along the
roads and burst into jubilant cheering. All the windows that survived were hung with flags and banners. The last bells were all set
ringing. The streets, pitted with shell holes, were festive with
flowers. The mayors delivered martial speeches that ended in sobs.
I spoke a few words, not of pity, which no one wanted, but of hope
and pride, concluding with the 'Marseillaise', which the crowd sang
with me. The contrast between the ardour of their spirit and the
ravages endured by them and their property was remarkable. France
would certainly live, because she was equal to her sufferings.

That evening, accompanied by André Le Troquer, Minister
Delegate to the liberated territories, General Juin, General Koenig
and Gaston Palewski, I arrived at the prefecture of Rennes. Victor

Le Gorgeu, Commissioner of the Republic for Brittany, Bernard Cornut-Gentille, Prefect of Ile-et-Vilaine, and General Allard, in command of the military area, presented their staff to me. Here administrative life was invincibly recovering, as was tradition itself. I went to the town hall, where the mayor, Yves Millon, surrounded by his council, resistance colleagues and prominent citizens asked me to reopen the golden book of the Breton capital, adding another link to the chain of time. Then at nightfall in the rain I addressed the crowd that had gathered in front of the building.

The next day, the 21st, news flowed in from Paris. I learned, in particular, of the end of Laval's attempt to form a Government. Édouard Herriot, having been warned by the resistance, realizing the nature of the storm that was about to break, acknowledging the confusion of the Vichy ministers, the senior officials in Paris and the German ambassador, refused to convene the 'national' assembly. His contacts with the parliamentarians, moreover, particularly with Anatole de Monzie, had convinced him that, deeply impressed by the tragic events that touched them closely (the assassination of Georges Mandel, Jean Zay and Maurice Sarraut by Darnand's militia, the execution of Philippe Henriot by a group of resistance fighters), they were not interested in convening in the threatening atmosphere of Paris. The Marshal, estimating that, all things considered, such a path was no way out and following another plan, had refused to come to the capital. Hitler, finally infuriated by an intrigue predicated on his defeat, had called a halt, ordered Laval's transfer to Nancy with his 'government' and had Pétain taken to join them there, either by choice or by force. As for the President of the Chamber, he was returned to Maréville. On August 18th, Laval, Herriot and Abetz said goodbye at a lunch at the Hôtel Matignon. On August 20th, the Marshal was taken from Vichy by the Germans.

Laval's last scheme came to nothing, but up to the end he had supported a faction which no casuistry could clear from guilt. Inclined by nature, and accustomed by the régime, to intrigue, Laval believed that, no matter what occurred, it was essential to be in power. He thought that a certain degree of cunning could always dominate circumstances, that there was no event that could not be turned to his advantage and no man inaccessible to manipulation. He had, in the cataclysm, sensed the nation's misery but he had also seized the opportunity to take the reins of power and to apply, on a tremendous scale, his infinite capacity for compromise. The victorious Reich was a partner that did not intend to compromise in return. To keep the field open despite everything, Pierre Laval had had to espouse the disaster of France. He accepted this condition; he decided that it was possible to take advantage of the disaster, to make use of servitude, to associate himself with the invader, and to make even the severest repression a trump card in his own hand. In order to effect his policy, he renounced the country's honour, the state's independence and the nation's pride. Now honour, independence and pride were reappearing, and as the enemy retreated before them, the people became energetic and exigent.

Laval had played and lost. He had the courage to admit that he was answerable for the consequences. In his government, deploying the limitless resources of guile and the last resorts of obstinacy in order to support the insupportable, he sought, somehow, to serve his country. Let that be left to his credit! It is a fact that, in the worst of their agony, some Frenchmen chose the muddy road and did not renounce their country. The tribute rendered to France from those of her sons 'who had so lost themselves' was a door half open to forgiveness.

Vichy's liquidation coincided with the development of the battle in the capital. What had been reported to me of it during my brief stay at Rennes intensified my eagerness to see the crisis past. It was true that the German command, for reasons that were still not clear, did not seem to want to bring matters to a head. But this passive attitude might give way at any moment to a sudden and ferocious repression. Furthermore, I found it intolerable that the enemy should occupy Paris even a day longer than was necessary while we had the means to drive him out of it. Lastly, I did not wish the capital to fall victim to anarchy because of the upheavals it would suffer. A report from Pierre Miné, in charge of provisions and supply in Paris, described the situation as critical. Cut off from all communication with the country for several weeks, the capital was virtually reduced to famine. Miné indicated that pilfering of the remaining stocks of supplies and of shops was beginning in certain places and, should the absence of police action be prolonged, serious excesses must be expected. Nevertheless, the day drew to its close without the Allied command having given Leclerc orders to move forward.

I had written to General Eisenhower from Rennes, passing on the information I received from Paris, urging him to hasten the movement of French and Allied troops, emphasizing the unfortunate consequences, even from a military point of view, of the nascent disorder in the capital. On August 22nd, Koenig took him my letter with further recommendations of his own, then returned to his post in London, where his liaison with the resistance was more easily effected than in our field camp. Juin left to contact General Patton, who was conducting the pursuit in a masterly fashion. I myself left Rennes, after ascertaining that by requisition of trucks and mobilization of drivers the Commissioner of the Republic was already setting up supply convoys heading for Paris. I travelled by way of Alençon, astir with enthusiasm and covered with flags, stopping first in Laval.

As soon as I reached the Laval Prefecture, where I was greeted by Michel Debré, Commissioner of the Republic, I met an officer with a letter from General Leclerc. The General described the uncertainty of his next mission and informed me of the initiative he had taken in sending an advance-guard group under Major de Guillebon to make contact with Paris. I immediately approved this action, indicating in my reply that Eisenhower had promised to establish Paris as his direction, that Koenig had been to see Eisenhower for this very reason, that Juin had also done so, and lastly that I myself intended to see Leclerc next day to give him his orders. I soon learned that, as I was writing to Leclerc, General Gerow was criticizing him for having sent a detachment towards Paris and ordering him to recall Major de Guillebon at once.

Finally, a few hours after having read the letter I had sent him, General Eisenhower gave orders to launch the Second Armoured Division toward Paris. It must be added that the information coming in at almost every moment from the capital, especially the news Cocteau and Dr Monod brought to General Bradley, supported my thesis. Furthermore, general headquarters was no longer ignorant of the failure of Laval's attempt. While Leclerc spent the night organizing his advance, the messages I received from the Prefecture at Le Mans showed that the events in Paris were moving at breakneck speed.

I learned that on the morning of the 20th, the Hôtel de Ville had been occupied by a Parisian police detachment led by Roland-Pré and Léo Hamon. The Prefect of the Seine Department, Fouret, went there to assume his functions. But I was also informed that Parodi and Chaban-Delmas on the one hand, and the majority of the Council of the Resistance on the other—warned by the American and British agents that it would be a long time still (weeks, they were told) before Allied troops entered the capital, knowing the weakness of the arms at the partisans' disposal in comparison to the 20,000 men, eighty tanks, sixty cannon and sixty planes of the German garrison, eager to avoid the destruction of the bridges over the Seine (which Hitler had ordered) and to save political and military prisoners—had decided to agree to Mr Nordling, the Swedish Consul-General's suggestion and, by his mediation, conclude a cease-fire with General von Choltitz, in command of enemy forces in Paris and the suburbs.

This news affected me very disagreeably. The more so since, as I learned of the signing of the cease-fire, Leclerc was preparing to advance. Their arrangements took no account of the military situation. On the morning of the 23rd, as I was leaving Le Mans, I was informed that the cease-fire, opposed by the majority of the combatants, had only been partially observed, although it had permitted Parodi and Roland-Pré, arrested by the Germans on the Boulevard Saint-Germain, to be released after an interview with Choltitz. I learned, furthermore, that hostilities had resumed on the evening of the 21st, that the prefectures, the ministries and the mayors' offices in the *arrondissements* were still in our hands, that the Parisians were throwing up barricades and that the German general, while reinforcing his strongholds, was not engaging in any repressive action. Were these tactics inspired by fear of the future, a desire to spare Paris or by an agreement made with the Allies, whose agents had been in contact with his general staff ever since Oberg and the Gestapo had left the capital? I could not determine which was the principal motive, but I was inclined to believe that, in any case, help would arrive in time.

There were no doubts about it on the road I took on August 23rd. Passing between two lines of flapping flags and cheering crowds, I was swept on by a veritable flood of joy. At La Ferté-Bernard, at Nogent-le-Rotrou, at Chartres, as well as in all the towns and villages we passed on the way, I had to stop and be cheered by the people and speak in the name of a reviving France. In the afternoon, overtaking the columns of the Second Armoured Division, I installed

myself in the Château de Rambouillet. Leclerc had told me that he
would be in the town. I immediately summoned him.

His plan of attack was ready. The bulk of his division, which was
advancing from Argentan, would not be in place before nightfall.
The advance groups, on the other hand, on the front from Athis-
Mons to Palaiseau, Toussus-le-Noble and Trappes, were in contact
with an entrenched and resolute enemy. This position must be
penetrated. The chief effort would be led by the Billotte group,
taking the road from Orléans to Paris through Antony as its axis.
The Langlade group would advance through Toussus-le-Noble and
Clamart, while a detachment commanded by Morel-Deville would
cover it towards Versailles. As for the Dio group, temporarily held in
reserve, it would follow Billotte's. The action would begin at dawn
the next day. I approved these arrangements and ordered Leclerc
to establish his command post at the Gare Montparnasse when he
got to Paris. I would join him there in order to decide what to do
next. Seeing this young leader already at grips with the battle, and
whose courage was complemented by an extraordinary series of well-
prepared circumstances, I murmured, 'How lucky you are!' I also
thought that, in war, the luck of generals is the honour of governments.

Dr Favreau, having left Paris that morning, reached Rambouillet
in the afternoon, bringing me a report from Luizet. According to the
Prefect of Police, the resistance had gained supremacy of the streets.
The Germans were now cornered in their strongholds, venturing out
only on occasional raids in armoured vehicles. In fact, London
broadcasts announced that evening that the French Forces of the
Interior had liberated Paris. The next morning King George VI
sent me a telegram of congratulation which was published at once.
The information and the telegram were, of course, premature; no
doubt they were intended to force the Americans to renounce their
ulterior motives which the English did not approve. The contrast
between the warm satisfaction expressed by the BBC with regard to
events in Paris and the reserved, even bitter, tone of the Voice of
America led me to realize that this time London and Washington
were not entirely in agreement about France.

I sent the valiant Favreau back to Paris with my answer to Luizet.
I specified my intention of going, not to the Hôtel de Ville, where the
Council of the Resistance and the Parisian Committee of Liberation

were in session, but 'to the centre'. I meant the Ministry of War, the obvious centre for the government and the French command. It was not that I was not eager to make contact with the leaders of the Parisian insurrection, but I wished to establish that the state, after ordeals which had been unable either to destroy or enslave it, was returning, first of all, quite simply, to where it belonged. Reading the newspapers—*Combat, Défence de la France, Franc-Tireur, Front National, l'Humanité, Libération* and *le Populaire*—which the political elements of the resistance had been publishing in Paris for the last two days instead of the collaborationist press sheets, I felt both pleased by the spirit of struggle that was expressed in them and confirmed in my intention of accepting no investiture for my authority save that which the voice of the people give me directly.

This is what I declared, furthermore, to Alexandre de Saint-Phalle, associated with my delegation and whose influence in legal and commercial circles was well known. He came accompanied by Jean Laurent, Director of the Bank of Indo China; Mr Rolf Nordling, the Swedish Consul-General's brother; and the Austrian Baron Poch-Pastor, an officer in the German army, who was also Choltitz's aide-de-camp and an Allied agent. All four had left Paris on the night of August 22nd in order to get swift intervention by regular troops from the American command. Having learned from Eisenhower that Leclerc was already on the way, they came on to see me. Saint-Phalle suggested that I convene the 'National' Assembly on my entry into Paris in order that a parliamentary vote of confidence might give my government the character of legality. I answered negatively. Nevertheless the composition and destination of this delegation offered a strange glimpse into the state of mind of the local German command. The four 'missionaries' were provided with two safe-conducts, one from Parodi, the other from General von Choltitz. In crossing the enemy sentry posts, they had heard soldiers grumble, 'Treason!'

On the evening of the 24th, the bulk of the Second Armoured Division, after fierce engagements, arrived in the immediate proximity of Paris, Billotte and Dio having taken Fresnes and La Croix de Berny, and Langlade holding the bridge at Sèvres. A detachment commanded by Captain Dronne had reached the Hôtel de Ville. The next day would be spent forcing the enemy's last outer resistance, then incapacitating the German strongholds within the city and ensuring protection from the direction of Le Bourget. Leclerc would push the Billotte group towards the Porte de Gentilly, the Luxembourg, the Hôtel de Ville and the Louvre, as far as the Hôtel Meurice, General von Choltitz's command post. The Dio group would enter by the Porte d'Orléans and would march through the organized blocks of the École Militaire and the Palais-Bourbon in two columns—Noiret's following the outer boulevards to the Auteuil viaduct and along the Seine, Rouvillois' going by Montparnasse and Les Invalides. The Étoile and the Majestic would fall to the Langlade group. Everyone would meet at the Place de la Concorde. At Leclerc's right, the Americans were to send a fraction of their Fourth Division to the Place d'Italie and the Gare d'Austerlitz.

On August 25th, everything followed these plans. I myself had already determined what I must do in the liberated capital: I would mould all minds into a single national impulse, but also cause the figure and the authority of the state to appear at once. Walking up and down the terrace at Rambouillet, I was kept informed from hour to hour of the Second Armoured Division's advance, and I thought of the difficulties which a mechanized army composed of seven such units might have spared us in the past. Then, considering the causes of the impotence which had deprived us of them—that is, the bankruptcy of governmental power—I resolved all the more firmly not to let my own be infringed. The mission with which I was invested seemed as clear as it could be. Getting into the car to drive to Paris, I felt myself simultaneously gripped by emotion and filled with serenity.

How many people, on the way, watched for our passage! How many flags floated before the houses! After Longjumeau, the crowds grew thicker; towards Cour-la-Reine they were jammed still more closely; at the Porte d'Orléans, near which shooting was still to be heard, the mob formed a jubilant tide; the Avenue d'Orléans was black with people. It was apparently believed that I would go to the Hôtel de Ville. But by forking off at the Avenue de Maine, almost deserted by comparison, I reached the Gare Montparnasse towards four in the afternoon.

General Leclerc had just arrived. He informed me of General von Choltitz's surrender. The latter, after a last negotiation arranged through Nordling, had personally come to Major De La Horie, chief of Billotte's general staff. He was then brought by De La Horie to the

Prefecture of Police, and signed an agreement with Leclerc according
to the terms of which the German strongholds in Paris must cease
fire. Moreover, several had been captured during the day. Then the
German general had ordered the defenders to lay down their arms
and give themselves up. Officers of von Choltitz's general staff,
accompanied by French officers, went to notify the German troops
of the order. I saw my son, an ensign in the Second Armoured
Regiment of Naval Rifles, leave for the Palais-Bourbon with a
German major to receive the garrison's surrender. The result of the
battle of Paris was highly satisfactory. Our troops brought off a complete victory without the city suffering the demolitions or the
population the losses that had been feared.

I congratulated Leclerc on this. What a stage on his road to glory!
I also congratulated Rol-Tanguy, whom I saw beside him. It was,
in fact, the action of the clandestine forces which, during the preceding days, had driven the enemy from our streets, decimated and
demoralized his troops and blockaded his units in their fortified
strongholds. Furthermore, since morning, groups of partisans with
only the most meagre weapons had bravely assisted the regular
troops in mopping up the nests of German resistance. By their action,
in fact, they had just taken the Clignancourt barracks. Nevertheless,
reading the copy of the German surrender which Leclerc gave me,
I disapproved of the phrase, inserted later, on Rol-Tanguy's insistence, according to which it was to Rol as well as to Leclerc that the
German command had surrendered. 'First of all,' I told Leclerc,
'it is not exactly true. Secondly, you were the highest-ranking officer
present and, therefore, the only person responsible. But above all,
the insistence which has led you to accept this formula proceeds from
an unacceptable tendency.' I read to Leclerc this proclamation published the same morning by the National Council of the Resistance
on behalf of the 'French nation' and making no reference to the
government or to General de Gaulle. Leclerc understood at once.
With all my heart I embraced this noble colleague.

Leaving the Gare Montparnasse, I headed for the Ministry of
War, where a small advance guard detachment under Colonel de
Chevigné had preceded me. The cortège was a modest one. Four
cars: mine, Le Troquer's, Juin's and a machine-gun car. We wanted
to take the Boulevard des Invalides to the Rue Saint-Dominique,
but at Saint-François-Xavier a burst of fire from the nearby houses

forced us to take the Rue Vaneau and the Rue de Bourgogne. We reached our destination at five o'clock.

I was immediately struck by the impression that nothing had changed inside these venerable halls. Gigantic events had overturned the world. Our army was annihilated. France had virtually collapsed. But at the Ministry of War, the look of things remained immutable. In the courtyard, a unit of the Garde Républicaine presented arms, as in the past. The vestibule, the staircase, the arms hanging on the walls—all were as they had been. Here, in person, were the same stewards and ushers. I entered the 'minister's office', which M. Paul Reynaud and I had left together on the night of June 10th, 1940. Not a piece of furniture, not a rug, not a curtain had been disturbed. On the desk, the telephone was in the same place, and exactly the same names on the call buttons. Soon I was to learn that this was the case in all the other buildings in which the Republic housed itself. Nothing was missing except the state. It was my duty to restore it: I installed my staff at once and got down to work.

Luizet came to present his report. Then it was Parodi's turn. Both were beaming, anxious, exhausted by the week without respite or sleep which they had just lived through. For them, in the immediate future, two problems dominated all others: public order and food supplies. They described the irritation expressed by the Council of the Resistance and the Parisian Committee of Liberation when they learned that I was not proceeding directly to them when I entered Paris. I repeated my reasons to the Minister Delegate and to the Prefect of Police. On leaving my office, I would go to the Hôtel de Ville after stopping first at the Prefecture to greet the Parisian police force. We made a plan for these visits. Then I arranged for the next day's parade, about which Parodi and Luizet showed themselves both enthusiastic and preoccupied. After their departure, I received a message from General Koenig. He would not be able to accompany us on this great day. That very morning, Eisenhower had asked him to sign the agreement settling the relations of our administration and the Allied command. Done at last, and better late than never!

At seven in the evening I inspected the Paris police force in the courtyard of the Prefecture: at the sight of this corps, whose service had kept it on the spot under the occupation, now trembling with joy and pride, it was evident that by giving the signal and the example of battle the men had revenged themselves for a long humiliation. They had also, and rightly, taken the opportunity to increase their prestige and their popularity, as I informed them while cheers rose from the ranks. Then, on foot, accompanied by Parodi, Le Troquer, Juin and Luizet, proceeding with difficulty through the crowds that surrounded me with deafening cheers, I reached the Hôtel de Ville. Before the building a detachment of the French Forces of the Interior, under the orders of Major Le Percq, presented arms impeccably.

At the foot of the staircase, Georges Bidault, André Tollet and Marcel Flouret received General de Gaulle. On the steps, the combatants, tears in their eyes, presented arms. Beneath a salvo of cheers, I was led to the centre of the salon on the first floor. Here the members of the National Council of the Resistance and the Parisian Committee of Liberation were grouped. Around me were many colleagues; a number wore the insignia of the resistance on their sleeves, as prescribed by a governmental decree. All wore the Cross of Lorraine. Glancing round the group, vibrant with enthusiasm, affection and curiosity, I felt that we had immediately recognized one another, that there was among us, combatants of the same battle, an incomparable link, and that if there were divergences of policy and ambition among us, the fact that the majority and I found ourselves together would carry the rest along with us. Furthermore, despite the fatigue evident in every face, the excitement of the dangers risked and the cataclysms survived, I did not see a single gesture or hear a single word which was not perfectly dignified. How admirable the success of a meeting long dreamed of and paid for with so many efforts, disappointments and deaths!

Feeling had spoken. Now it was politics' turn. This, too, was a noble voice. Georges Marrane, substituting for André Follet, greeted me in splendid terms in the name of the new Parisian municipal council. Then Georges Bidault delivered a speech of the highest possible level. In my improvised reply, I expressed 'the sacred emotion that grips all of us, men and women alike, in these moments that transcend each of our poor private lives'. I acknowledged that 'Paris has been liberated by her people, with the help of the army and the support of all of France'. I did not forget to mention 'the French troops which at this moment are driving up the Rhône

Valley' and the armies of our allies. Lastly, I called the nation to its duties in war and, in order that it fulfil them, to national unity.

I entered the office of the Prefect of the Seine. Marcel Flouret presented me to the principal officials of his administration. As I was preparing to leave, Georges Bidault cried out, 'General! Here, around you, are the National Council of the Resistance and the Parisian Committee of Liberation. We ask you formally to proclaim the Republic before the people who have gathered here.' I replied: 'The Republic has never ceased. Free France, Fighting France, the French Committee of National Liberation have successively incorporated it. Vichy always was and still remains null and void. I myself am the President of the Government of the Republic. Why should I proclaim it now?' Stepping to a window, I greeted the crowd that filled the square and proved by its cheers that it asked for nothing more. Then I returned to the Rue Saint-Dominique.

That evening, Leclerc drew up an account of the battles in Paris. The surrender of all the German strongholds was now accomplished. The so-called 'Luxembourg' block which included the Palace, the School of Mines and the Lycée Montaigne, that of the Place de la République, organized in the barracks of Prince Eugène and completed by the central telephone offices of the Rue des Archives, ceased fire last of all. During the day, our troops took 14,800 prisoners. Three thousand two hundred Germans were dead, not counting those—at least a thousand—whom the partisans had killed on the preceding days. The losses of the Second Armoured Division amounted to twenty-eight officers and six hundred soldiers. As for the interior forces, Professor Vallery-Radot, who had taken charge of the hospital services, estimated the cost of the battles which had been raging during the last six days at 2,500 men killed or wounded. Furthermore, more than 1,000 civilians had fallen.

Leclerc informed me that north of Paris the enemy's pressure continued to make itself felt. At Saint-Denis and at La Villette, some units refused to lay down their arms, alleging that they were not under Choltitz's orders. Part of the 47th German Division was entrenching itself at Le Bourget and Montmorency, doubtless to cover the columns in retreat farther north. The enemy was advancing small units as far as the entrances to the capital. General Gerow, commanding the Fifth American Army Corps, to which the Second Armoured Division was still attached for operations, had given it the

mission of making contact with the German positions with a view
to attacking them.

However, I was—more than ever—resolved to follow the Étoile-
Notre Dame itinerary the next day, keeping my rendezvous with the
people, and I intended that the Second Armoured Division should
participate in the ceremony. Doubtless the demonstration would involve a certain amount of risk, but it would be well worth it. It
seemed to me, moreover, highly unlikely that the German rearguard would suddenly transform itself into an advance guard and
march towards the centre of Paris, where the entire German garrison
was now a prisoner. There were certain precautions to be taken, in
any case.

I settled with Leclerc on a tactical group commanded by Rou-
maintzoff to be posted early in the morning as covering troops
towards Le Bourget; we also re-grouped the resistance units skirm-
ishing in this direction. The rest of the division would be formed into
three other units during the parade, and would be on guard respectively at the Arc de Triomphe, the Rond-Point des Champs-
Elysées, and in front of the Cathedral. Should the occasion arise,
they would move toward the desired points. Leclerc himself, marching behind me, would remain in constant communication with his
various units. Since the Allied command had not seen fit to make
contact with me, I ordered Leclerc to inform it of the arrangements
I had made. This command, moreover, had the means to supply the
temporary reserve of a part of the French division if need be. To
the contrary orders which the Allies might send, Leclerc was to
reply that he was maintaining his positions according to General de
Gaulle's orders.

The morning of Saturday, August 26th, brought nothing to light
to modify my plans. Of course I was informed that Gerow had
ordered Leclerc and his troops to remain aloof from demonstrations.
The American general even sent an officer to let me know of his
orders directly. Naturally I ignored this advice, not without observing that on such a day and in such a place, this attitude, which of
course was not adopted without instructions from above, testified to
the most remarkable incomprehension. I must say that apart from
this incident, as futile as it was disagreeable, our Allies did not
attempt to meddle with affairs in the capital. General Koenig, who
had been appointed military governor on August 21st, Fleuret, the

Prefect of the Seine, and Luizet, the Prefect of Police, did not have to reject the slightest effort at encroachment. No American troops were stationed in Paris, and the units that had passed by the Place d'Italie and the Gare de Lyon the day before had immediately withdrawn. Except for the presence of reporters and photographers, the Allies took no part in the next day's parade. For the entire distance it was to cover there would be only Frenchmen.

But there would be many of these. Since the night before, the radio, which Jean Guignebert, Pierre Crenesse and their crews had made every effort to restore to its normal functions, had announced the ceremony. During the morning, I was informed that throughout the entire city and its suburbs, in this Paris that had no *Métro*, no buses and no cars, innumerable pedestrians were on the march. At three in the afternoon I reached the Arc de Triomphe. Parodi and Le Troquer, as members of the government; Bidault and the National Council of the Resistance; Tollet and the Parisian Committee of Liberation; Generals Juin, Koenig, Leclerc, d'Argenlieu, Valin and Bloch-Dassault; Prefects Fleuret and Luizet; the military delegate Chaban-Delmas; many leaders and fighters from the secret forces were ranged round the tomb of the Unknown Soldier. I greeted the Chad Regiment, drawn up in battle formation before the arch and whose officers and soldiers, standing on their cars, watched me pass before them to the Étoile as though I were the materialization of a dream. I re-lit the flame. Since June 1940 no one had been able to do so save in the presence of the invader. Then I left the vault and the platform. The observers made way for me. Ahead stretched the Champs-Élysées!

It looked more like the sea! A tremendous crowd was jammed together on both sides of the road. Perhaps two million people. The roofs too were black with many more. At every window were crowded other groups waving flags. Human clusters were clinging to ladders, flagpoles and lamp posts. As far as the eye could see, there was nothing but this living tide of humanity in the sunshine, beneath the tricolour.

I went on foot. This was not the moment for a review with arms glittering and trumpets sounding. Today we were to revive, by the sight of its joy and the evidence of its liberty, the self-awareness of a people who yesterday were crushed by defeat and scattered in servitude. Since each of those here had chosen Charles de Gaulle in his heart as the refuge against his agony and the symbol of his hopes, I must allow the man to be seen, familiar and fraternal, in order that, at this sight, national unity might shine forth. It was true that the General Staff feared that an outburst of enemy armoured cars or a machine-gunning pursuit plane would decimate this mob and unleash panic. But that afternoon, I believed in the fortune of France. It was true that the services of public order feared they would not be able to restrain the pressure of the crowd. But I was convinced, on the contrary, that the people would discipline themselves. It was true that in the cortège of colleagues entitled to follow me a number of supernumeraries figured improperly. But it was not at them that the people were looking. It was true, finally, that I myself had neither the physique nor the taste for those attitudes and gestures that can charm the public. But I was sure they did not expect them of me.

I went on, then, touched and yet tranquil, amid the inexpressible exultation of the crowd, beneath the storm of voices echoing my name, trying, as I advanced, to look at every person in all that multitude in order that every eye might register my presence, raising and lowering my arms to reply to the cheers. This was one of those miracles of national consciousness, one of those gestures which some-times, in the course of centuries, light up the history of France. In this community, with only a single thought, a single enthusiasm, a single cry, all differences vanished, all individualities disappeared. Innumerable Frenchmen whom I walked past, first at the Étoile, then at the Rond-Point, then at the Place de la Concorde, in front of the Hôtel de Ville, on the steps of the Cathedral—if you knew how much alike you were! The children—so pale but dancing and screaming for joy; the women—bearing so many sorrows but now smiling and cheering; the men—flooded with a long forgotten pride, shouting their gratitude; the old—doing me the honour of their tears: how like one another they were! And at the centre of this out-burst, I felt I was fulfilling a function which far transcended my personality, for I was serving as an instrument of destiny.

But there is no such thing as pure and perfect joy, even during a triumphal march. Anxieties mingled with the happy thoughts rush-ing through my mind. I knew that all of France was eager for liberation. The same ardour for rebirth which had broken out yesterday in Rennes and Marseilles and today transported Paris,

would reveal itself tomorrow at Lyons, Rouen, Lille, Dijon, Strasbourg and Bordeaux. One had only to look and listen in order to be
certain of the nation's will to revive. But the war went on and had
still to be won. At what price, then, must victory be won? What
ruins would be added to our own? What new losses would decimate
our soldiers? What moral and physical agonies would the French
prisoners of war still have to endure? How many of our deported
would return—the hardest fighters, the greatest sufferers, the most
deserving of us all? Lastly, in what condition would our people find
themselves and in what kind of world?

It is true that around me rose extraordinary testimonials of unity.
It seemed likely that the nation would surmount its dissensions until
the conflict's end; that Frenchmen would choose to remain together
with mutual recognition in order to recreate their powers; that
having chosen their goal and found their guide, they would vote
themselves the institutions allowed them to be governed. But I could
no longer ignore the obstinate aims of the Communists, nor the
bitterness of so many prominent individuals who would not forgive
me for their own errors, nor the agitation festering again in the
political parties. Even marching at the head of the cortège, I sensed
that ambition as well as fervent devotion was following behind me.
Beneath the waves of popular confidence, the reefs of politics would
not be slow to surface.

At each step I took along the most illustrious avenue in the world,
it seemed to me that the glories of the past were associated with
today's. Beneath the Arc de Triomphe, the flame burned brightly in
our honour. This avenue, down which a triumphant army marched
twenty-five years ago, opened brilliantly before us. On his pedestal,
Clemenceau, whom I hailed in passing, looked as if he were springing
up to march beside us. The chestnut trees in the Champs-Élysées
that L'Aiglon, in prison, dreamed about and which had seen for so
many, many years the grace and prestige of France displayed
beneath them, offered themselves now as joyous grandstands to
thousands of spectators. The Tuileries, which framed the majesty
of the state under two emperors and two monarchs; the Place de la
Concorde and the Place du Carrousel, which had observed the
frenzies of revolutionary enthusiasm and the reviews of conquering
regiments; the streets and the bridges named after battles won; on
the other bank of the Seine, Les Invalides, its dome still sparkling

with the splendour of Le Roi-Soleil, the tombs of Turenne, of Napoleon, of Foch; and the Institute, honoured by so many illustrious minds—these were the benevolent witnesses of the human stream that flowed between them. Here was the Louvre, where the succession of kings had also succeeded in building France; on their mounts, the statues of Joan of Arc and of Henri IV; the Palace of Saint Louis, whose anniversary had occurred the day before; Notre-Dame, the prayers of Paris, and the Ile de la Cité, her cradle—all shared in the event. History, gathered in these stones and in these squares, seemed to be smiling down on us.

And warning us as well. Paris was once Lutèce, subjugated by Caesar's legions, then Paris, which only Geneviève's prayers had saved from Attila's fire and sword. Saint Louis, his crusade abandoned, died on the sands of Africa. At the Porte Saint-Honoré, Joan of Arc was repulsed by the city which she had just restored to France. Quite near me, Henri IV fell victim to fanatical hatred. The Revolt of the Barricades, Saint Bartholomew's Massacre, the outrages of the Fronde and the furious torrent of August 10th all bloodied the walls of the Louvre. At the Place de la Concorde the heads of the king and queen of France rolled on the ground. The Tuileries were to see the destruction of the old monarchy, the exile of Charles X and of Louis-Philippe, the despair of the Empress, and were finally put to the torch, like the old Hôtel de Ville. How often the Palais-Bourbon was the scene of the most disastrous confusion. Four times within two lifetimes the Champs-Élysées was to submit to the outrage of invaders parading in time to their own odious fanfares. Paris, this afternoon, if it gleamed with all the greatness of France, remembered its terrible days.

Towards four-thirty, I went, as planned, to Notre-Dame. Just before, in the Rue de Rivoli, I had climbed into a car and, after a short stop on the steps of the Hôtel de Ville, reached the cathedral square. The cardinal-archbishop did not receive me at the door of the basilica. Not because he did not want to, but because the new government had asked him to abstain. Monsignor Suhard had found it necessary, four months ago, formally to receive Marshal Pétain on his way through the city when Paris was occupied by the Germans. A month after this he officiated at the funeral service which Vichy had arranged in honour of Philippe Henriot. Because of this, many resistance members were indignant at the idea that the prelate could introduce General de Gaulle into the cathedral. For my part, realizing that the Church regarded itself as obliged to accept the 'established order', aware of the fact that the cardinal's piety and charity were so great that they left little room in his soul for the appreciation of temporal matters, I should willingly have overlooked such things. But the state of tension of a great number of the combatants the day after the battle and my own desire to avoid unpleasant scenes directed against Monsignor Suhard, led me to approve my delegation's request that he remain in the archbishop's palace during the ceremony. What was soon to occur confirmed my conviction that this had been a wise measure.

The moment I stepped out of the car, shots crackled in the square, rapidly becoming a running fire. Everyone who had a weapon began to fire at random, aiming at the roofs. The men of the French Forces of the Interior made their powder speak on all sides. Soon even the seasoned troops of the Second Armoured Division, posted near the portals, began aiming their bullets at the towers of Notre-Dame. It was immediately apparent to me that this was one of those contagious shooting matches which high feeling sometimes sets off in over-excited troops on the occasion of some fortuitous or provoked incident. Nothing could be more important than for me not to yield to the panic of the crowd. I therefore went into the cathedral. Without electricity, the organs were silent, and the shots echoed inside the structure. As I advanced toward the choir, the more or less bowed congregation murmured its acclamations. I took my place, my two ministers, Le Troquer and Parodi, behind me. The canons were in their stalls. The archpriest, Monsignor Brot, came to bring me the greetings, regrets and protests of the cardinal. I asked him to express to His Eminence my respect in all religious matters, my desire for reconciliation from the national point of view and my intention of receiving him shortly.

The *Magnificat* rose around us. Was it ever sung more ardently? Meanwhile, the shooting was still going on. Several gamesters, posted in the upper galleries, kept up the fusillade. No bullets whistled by my ears, but the projectiles directed toward the arches of the roof struck off splinters, ricocheted and fell. Several persons were hurt. The policemen whom the Prefect sent to the highest parts of the building found several armed men who claimed that they had opened fire on antagonists they could not see very clearly. Although the attitude of the clergy, the official personnel and the congregation continued to be exemplary, I abbreviated the ceremony. Around the cathedral, the promiscuous firing had now stopped. But as we left I was informed that at points as remote as the Étoile, the Rond-Point and the Hôtel de Ville, the same thing had happened at exactly the same time. There were several people hurt, almost all as a result of stampeding crowds.

Who had fired the first shot? The investigations never disclosed. The hypothesis of snipers on the roofs, German soldiers or members of the Vichy militia, seemed highly unlikely. Despite all efforts to find out who was responsible, no one was arrested. Furthermore, why would the enemy have taken the chimneys for targets instead of aiming at me, when I was passing by quite openly? It was possible to suppose that coincidence of the firing in several parts of Paris was purely fortuitous. I myself felt that we had to deal with an affair inspired by people who wanted to justify the maintenance of revolutionary power and exceptional force because of mob violence. By shooting a few bullets into the air at the agreed hour, but without perhaps foreseeing the bursts of fire that would be the consequence, an attempt had been made to create the impression that threats still lurked in the shadows, that the resistance organizations must remain armed and vigilant, that 'Comac', the Parisian Committee of Liberation and the neighbourhood committees were still to take the responsibility for police action, justice and the purging of collaborators in order to protect the people against dangerous conspiracies.

Naturally I intended to set up an orderly régime. Moreover, the enemy made it his duty to remind us that war admits of no other law. At midnight his planes came to bomb the capital, destroying five hundred houses, setting fire to the wine market and killing or wounding a thousand persons. Sunday, August 27th, was a day of relative relaxation for the population. I had the time to attend, amid several thousand men of the resistance, a Mass, at which their chaplain, Father Bruckberger officiated. I crossed the city in a car, saw men's behaviour and the aspect of the city itself without being too often recognized. But the Second Armoured Division was bitterly engaged from morning to night. At the cost of considerable losses, the Dio group seized the airfield of Le Bourget, and the Langlade group invested Stains, Pierrefitte and Montmagny.

As a searchlight suddenly reveals a monument. so the liberation of

Paris, assured by the French themselves, and the proof given by the people of its confidence in de Gaulle, dissipated the shadows that still concealed the reality of the national will. Consequently or coincidentally, there occurred a kind of upheaval in which various obstacles that still encumbered the road collapsed. August 28th brought me quantities of satisfying news.

I learned, first of all, that in the northern suburbs, after our troops had taken Gonesse, the Germans were in full retreat, which put the finishing touches to the battle of Paris. Furthermore, Juin presented reports from the First Army, confirming the surrender of the enemy garrisons at Toulon on the 22nd, at Marseilles on the 23rd, and announcing that our forces were rapidly advancing toward Lyons on both sides of the Rhône, while the Americans, following the Route Napoléon cleared by the maquisards, had already taken Grenoble. Further, the reports of our chief delegates south of the Loire—Bénouville for the Massif Central, General Pfister for the south-west—indicated the German withdrawal. Some troops were trying to reach Burgundy in order to avoid being surrounded, the rest shut themselves up in fortified pockets along the Atlantic coast, all were in contact with the French Forces of the Interior who attacked their columns and harried their posts. Bourges-Maunoury, delegate for the south-east, reported that the maquisards were masters of the Alps, Ain, Drôme, Ardèche, Cantal and the Puy de Dôme, which could only accelerate the advance of General Patch and General de Lattre. In the east and the north, lastly, our activity was increasing, while in the Ardennes, Hainaut and Brabant, the Belgian resistance was also conducting fierce guerrilla warfare. It could be foreseen that the enemy, driven back from the Seine, pursued the length of the Rhône, assailed at every point of our soil, would not re-establish himself except in the immediate proximity of the Reich frontier. Thus our country, whatever her wounds, was soon to find the possibility of national recovery, on condition that it had a government which excluded any authority parallel with my own.

The iron was hot: I struck. On the morning of August 28th, I summoned the twenty principal leaders of the Parisian partisans, to meet them, to congratulate them, to inform them of my decision to combine the interior forces with the ranks of the regular army. Then came the secretaries general, who were evidently waiting instructions from me and my ministers. Then I received the Committee of the National Council of the Resistance. In the minds of the colleagues who took their places before me, there existed two simultaneous tendencies which I met in different ways. Their pride in what they had accomplished I welcomed without reservation. But the secret intention of certain individuals as to the direction of the state I could not countenance. If the popular demonstration of August 26th exposed General de Gaulle's primacy to the full light of day, there were still some who clung to the project of constituting by his side but without him an autonomous authority, of turning the council into a permanent organization controlling the government, of entrusting to 'Comac' the military formations of the resistance and deriving from the Council certain 'patriotic' militias which would act on the 'people's' behalf, though naturally in a certain direction. Furthermore, the council had adopted a 'programme of the CNR' consisting of a list of the measures to be taken in every sphere, which it proposed to brandish constantly under the executive's nose.

While acknowledging quite loftily the share my interlocutors had taken in the battle, I left them in no doubt as to my intentions towards them. As soon as Paris was torn from the enemy, the National Council of the Resistance would be part of the glorious history of the liberation, but would have no further *raison d'être* as an instrument of action. The government would assume entire responsibility. I would probably include within it this or that member of the Council. But in that case, members would renounce all allegiances that were not ministerial. On the other hand, I intended to integrate the Council with the Consultative Assembly, which would be arriving from Algiers and which was to be enlarged. As the resistance forces, they would form part of the French Army. The Ministry of War would take direct charge of their personnel and their arms as soon as they emerged from their activity. 'Comac' was to disappear. Public order would be maintained by the police and the *gendarmerie* with, should occasion arise, the assistance of the garrisons. The militias had no further object. The existing ones would be dissolved. I read my visitors a decree I had just signed ordering the regular incorporation of the resistance forces and appointing General Koenig, the military governor, to do what was immediately necessary in Paris.

After having made notes of the satisfied or protesting observations
of members of the bureau, I put an end to the audience. From it, I
had drawn the conclusion that certain individuals would try to
engage in various equivocations or misunderstandings in order to
keep the greatest possible number of armed units under their control, that there would be formalities to complete, frictions to endure,
orders to maintain, but that, in the end, the government's authority
would be imposed. I was eager that the road be cleared in this
direction.

It was soon to be so with regard to the Americans. General Eisenhower paid me a visit. We congratulated each other on the happy
outcome of events in Paris. I did not hide from him, however, how
dissatisfied I was with Gerow's attitude as I was entering my own
capital and grasping the boiling cauldron in my hands. I informed
the Commander-in-Chief that for reasons of popular morale and,
ultimately, law and order, I would keep the Second Armoured
Division at my immediate disposal for a few days. Eisenhower said
that he planned to instal his headquarters at Versailles. I approved
this move, believing it a good idea to have the Allied Commander-
in-Chief lodged out of Paris but useful that he should be near. As he
took his leave, I expressed to this great and good leader the esteem,
confidence and gratitude of the French Government. Soon after, the
Americans, without consulting us, published a communiqué according to which the military command, in accord with its agreements,
transferred to the French administration the powers which it held
in France. Of course, the Allies transferred nothing because they
held nothing: they could hardly give away what they had never
had. But President Roosevelt's self-esteem had its requirements, all
the greater now that the United States elections were approaching
and in six weeks Franklin Roosevelt would confront universal suffrage.

At nightfall, I learned of the last act of the Marshal and 'Chief of
State'. Juin brought me a communication which Admiral Auphan,
former Minister of Vichy, had delivered. It was a letter and a
memorandum which the Admiral addressed to me, informing me
of the instructions he had received from the Marshal and which the
latter had formulated in two secret documents. The first was a so-
called 'constitutional' act dated September 27th, 1943, appointing
a college of seven members to fulfil his functions as 'Chief of State'
if he himself were prevented from doing so. The second, dated

August 11th, 1944, was a delegation of power to Admiral Auphan 'to make eventual contact with General de Gaulle on his behalf, in order to find, with regard to French political problems at the moment of the liberation of French territory, a solution of a kind to prevent civil war and to reconcile all Frenchmen of good will'. The Marshal specified that in case Auphan could not refer the matter back to himself, he trusted he would act for the nation's best interests. But he added, 'Provided that the principle of legitimacy which I embody be preserved.'

Admiral Auphan wrote to me that when he learned on August 20th that the Marshal had been taken away by the Germans, he attempted to convene the 'college'. But two of the appointed members, Weygand and Bouthillier, were being held in Germany; one, Léon Noël, a French ambassador, who had belonged to the resistance for four years, formally refused to enter the coalition; two— Porché, vice-president of the Council of State, and Gidel, rector of the University of Paris—did not attend the meeting. Auphan, finding himself alone with Caous, the *procureur general* of the High Court of Appeal, decided that the 'college' had given up the ghost before being born and that he himself was henceforth the 'principal depository of the Marshal's legal powers'. He asked me to receive him.

This procedure did not surprise me. I knew that since the beginning of August the Marshal, who expected to be ordered to leave for Germany, had made contacts with various resistance leaders. Henry Ingrand, Commissioner of the Republic at Clermont-Ferrand, had informed me on August 14th of a visit from Captain Oliol, the Marshal's envoy. The Marshal had proposed placing himself under the protection of the French Forces of the Interior and indicated, at the same time, that he was retiring from power. Ingrand had replied that if the Marshal surrendered to him, the French Forces of the Interior would answer for his security. But Pétain had not pursued this plan, doubtless prevented from doing so by the surveillance of the Germans before they took him to Belfort and to Sigmaringen. Now his proxy presented me with a formal request for negotiation.

Thus, in the annihilation of Vichy, Philippe Pétain turned to Charles de Gaulle. This, then, was the end of that dreadful series of capitulations in which, under the pretext of 'saving the furniture', servitude had been accepted. What unfathomable wretchedness brought it about that such a policy had been endorsed by a glorious

military leader in his old age! Reading the text he had had referred
to me, I felt simultaneously confirmed in what had always been my
certainty and gripped by an inexpressible sadness. *Monsieur le
Maréchal!* You who had always done such great honour to your
arms, you who were once my leader and my example, how could
you come to this?

What reply could I make to this communication? In such matters,
sentiment could not stand in the way of the rights of a state. The
Marshal referred to civil war. If by that he meant the violent confrontation of two factions of the French people, the hypothesis was
quite out of the question. Among those who had been his partisans,
none, now, rose against my power. There was not, on liberated soil,
one department, one city, one commune, one official, one soldier,
not even one individual who professed to oppose de Gaulle out of
loyalty to Pétain. As for reprisals, if certain factions of the resistance
might commit retaliatory actions against the people who had persecuted them in collaboration with the enemy, it devolved upon the
public authority to oppose itself to such actions, while insuring
justice. In this matter, no compromise was conceivable.

Above all, the condition which put Pétain in agreement with me
was precisely the motive that made this agreement impossible. The
legitimacy which he claimed to embody was denied absolutely by
the Government of the Republic, not so much because he had once
received the abdication of a hysterical parliament as because he had
accepted the enslavement of France, practised official collaboration
with the invader and ordered armed opposition to the French and
Allied soldiers of the liberation. Not for a single day had he allowed
his countrymen to fire on the Germans. Furthermore, in the mission
Pétain gave to Auphan and in the *adieu* which the Marshal had just
addressed to the French, there was not one sentence condemning the
'armistice' or crying 'Rise against the enemy!' Yet no French
Government could be legitimate when it has ceased to be independent. We, the French, had, in the course of time, endured many
disasters, lost provinces and paid indemnities, but the state had
never accepted the domination of a foreign power. Even the King
of Bourges, the Restoration of 1814 and that of 1815, the government
and the assembly of Versailles in 1871, had not yielded themselves
to this. When France acknowledged herself a power that submitted
to the yoke, she was putting an end to her own future.

L

A call to honour from the depths of history, as well as the instinct of the nation itself, had led me to bear responsibility for the treasure in default of heirs: to assume French sovereignty. It was I who held the legitimate power. It was in its name that I could call the nation to war and to unity, impose order, law and justice, demand from the world respect for the rights of France. In this realm, I could not renounce, or even compromise in the slightest degree. Without disregarding the intention which inspired the Marshal's message, without overlooking what significance there was for the moral future of the nation in the fact that it was ultimately towards de Gaulle that Pétain turned, the only reply I could give him was silence.

That night, moreover, after so much uproar, all was still around me. It was the moment to acknowledge what had just been accomplished and to confront what was to come. Today, unity had won a victory. Sheltered at Brazzaville, matured in Algiers, it had been consecrated in Paris. France, which had seemed condemned to disaster, despair and dissension, had now the opportunity of enduring to the end of the present drama without breaking asunder. She would share the victory with her Allies, recover her land, her rank and her dignity. It was conceivable that the French might remain re-grouped as they were now long enough for the categories among which they were normally distributed and which, by reason of their objectives, always struggled to disrupt the national cohesion, might prove powerless to overcome that cohesion before the immediate goal was reached.

Having taken the measure of the task, I must gauge my own capacities. My role consisted in bending to the common interest the various elements of the nation in order to lead it to salvation. My duty, whatever capacities I might lack, was to fulfil that role as long as the crisis continued, and then, if the country willed it so, until the moment when institutions worthy of it, adapted to our times and inspired by their terrible lessons, would receive from my hands the trust of leadership.

Ahead of me, I knew, I would find along the way every group, every school, every party revived and more hostile as the danger faded. There would not be a single habit or hostility, not one weakness or claim, not one attitude of surrender or self-interest that would not, first in secret, later openly, rise up against my enterprise of rallying the French in France and building a state that was just and strong. My lot was, therefore, a solitary one. But in lifting the burden, what a lever I had in the loyalty and adherence of the people! This massive confidence, this elemental friendship which their acknowledgments lavished upon me, this would steel me to my task.

Gradually, the call was heard. Slowly, severely, unity was forged. Now the people and the leader, helping each other, were to begin the journey to salvation.

L*

INDEX

made by, 18, 93–4, 95; objects to British policy in Middle East, 21–3, 25–8, 30, 37–8, 39–40; Czech and Russian support for, 41–2; and rally in Albert Hall, 50–1; refusal to accept Darlan, 55-9; recovers Indian Ocean possessions, 59–63; and discord with Giraud, 75–90, 96–102; question of command in, 82–9; and conditions for unity, 96–8; and formation of Committee of National Liberation, 107–13

French Navy: at Toulon, 17, 54; in North Africa, 49–50; scuttling of, 54–5, 68, 73; Darlan and, 72–4; and Antilles, 132, 133-4

French Resistance movement, 11, 14, 58; Communists in, 8, 55, 154, 168, 169–70, 292–3, 294; unifying of, 18, 43, 94–5, 105, 167; formation of National Council, 43–4, 95; Committee of National Liberation and, 158, 167–72, 256–9, 293–5, 303, 306, 308–9, 317–9; factions in, 168–71, 257; German repressive measures, 174, 182–3; secret newspapers, 175, 304; in Battle of France, 230, 252–9, 279–86; and 'military delegates', 257–8; creation of French Forces of the Interior, 258; in Paris, 292–4, 296, 299, 302, 303, 306, 309–11, 317–8; its Committee of Action, 294, 316, 318; incorporation into French Army, 318

Froger, M., 70

Gabès, 66, 103, 104
Gaboon, 35, 36
Gadàmes, 36, 91
Gafsa, 64, 103
Gaillaudot, Colonel, 258
Galissonnière, La (cruiser), 54
Gall, General, 276
Gambiez, Colonel, 276
Gamelin, General, 42, 174
Gammel, General, 265
Gandhi, Mahatma, 30
Gao, 189
Garcie, Colonel, 258, 280
Garigliano river, 269, 271, 274
Garreau, Roger, 44, 194
Garreau-Dombasle, M., 194

Garrec, Major le, 283
Gastaldo, Colonel, 257
Gat, 36
Gatrún, 67
Gaulle, Mme de, 177
Gaulle, Anne de, 177
Gaulle, Elisabeth de, 177
Gaulle, Geneviève de, 178
Gaulle, Jacques de, 178
Gaulle, Pierre de, 178
Gaulle, Philippe de, 177
Gaulle, Xavier de, 177–8
Gazier, Albert, 189
Gence, Lt-Col., 32
Geoffroy, Captain, 67
George VI, King, 106, 270, 303
George II of Greece, 205
Georges, General, 82, 85, 107, 109, 111, 113, 116, 117, 154, 218, 219
Georges-Leygues (cruiser), 251, 278
Gérard, M., 134
Gérardot, General, 267
Gerlier, Cardinal (Bishop of Lyon), 93
German Army: in France, 13–14, 53–4, 230, 254 et seq,; in North Africa, 19, 36, 44, 46–50, 64–6, 103; in Sicily, 135; in Corsica; 147–8; in Italy, 269–76
Germany, 7; bombing of, 11; and North Africa, 29, 47–8; and occupied France, 42–3, 53, 173–5, 249; Italy declares war on, 195
Gerow, General, 298, 301, 309, 310, 319
Ghisonaccia, 148
Giacobbi, Paul, 160
Gibraltar, 18, 19, 47, 49, 68, 226, 296
Gidel, M., 320
Gillet, Louis, 44
Giovoni (Corsican Communist), 144, 145, 146
Giraud, General Henri, 50, 52, 53, 64, 132, 133, 136, 155, 165, 171–2, 182–3, 250, 259, 262, 263, 264, 276; reluctant to join de Gaulle, 15–18; American support of, 47, 75, 97; tries to assume command of North African forces, 47, 48, 49, 68, 69; relations with de Gaulle, 69, 71, 75–82, 84–91, 96–102, 104–5, 107–25, 137, 139, 151–2; 'Civil and Military C–in–C', 75; dispute over military command,